ON THE FOOT
OF A
MOUNTAIN

All inquirers should be addressed to:

Book Savvy International Inc.
1626 Clear View Drive, Beverly Hills California 90210, United States

Hotline: (213) 855-4299
https://booksavvyinternationalinc.com/

Ordering Information:
Amount Deals. Special rebates are accessible on the amount bought by corporations, associations, and others. For points of interest, contact the distributor at the address above.

Printed in the United States of America.

ISBN-13   Paperback   979-8-89190-130-8
            eBook   979-8-89190-129-2

Library of Congress Control Number: 2024901877

ON THE FOOT
OF A
MOUNTAIN

CARMELA ORSINI HARMON

This one is for you, Tommy…
That I could be blessed with a second good man
in my life is a miracle to me. Yes, 3 years ago, I
met & married my very own "Tom".
God is good…

PROLOGUE

Augusta, Georgia
November, 1829

Many travelers arriving in Augusta by stage were sorry to meet the Bully of Lower Broad Street. But he was selective. If the hour was early enough, or late enough, to assure little interference from the law, only those passengers least able to defend themselves were singled out for his greeting.

On this particular November morning, his sights were set on a frail tinker, waiting by the boot of the coach for the driver to return and hand down his sample cases from the top. What happened then would not be forgotten by either man…

CHAPTER 1

Tom rode steadily on leaving Savannah, his mind absorbed by his troubles; his senses keen to every noise on the dark road behind. Yet, by three in the morning, he knew he would have to stop or he and the horse were going to collapse. So in the next town—one he never did hear the name of—he shared a stall with the horse in a public stable and both bedded down. But he slept very little as his thoughts kept galloping the road ahead....*What was he going to do about Mandria?*

With no solutions found and feeling lousy, at sunrise he rose and spotting a stage office across the street, decided to buy a ticket for Augusta. Maybe he could manage a nap while aboard and still not lose travel time or the chance to put more distance between himself and those who might want to chase him down. The next stage arrived about seven o'clock and tying the horse behind, he climbed into a crowded coach, heavy-eyed and uncommunicative with the other passengers. And though he tried, he still wasn't able to do more than doze, for he felt every bone-jarring pot hole along the winding, zigzagging route.

Finally, in the wee hours of the morning, they reached Augusta and when stepping down to the platform, his stiff, aching body rebelled. Immobility had left his legs and hips numb. A cramp threatened to stab his left shoulder where a slightly built man had alternately slept and awakened every few miles to repeat an apology. Now, he had stomped the entire length of the depot platform, hoping to revive his circulation—as well as his ability to reason sensibly. But was there anything sensible in what he was doing? It wasn't every day that a man escaped jail to go chasing after a wife who apparently hated him and vowed to give away their unborn child. And he still had no notion of a plan once he'd found her. It was no wonder he couldn't sleep— less wonder he couldn't think—because the complexities of the whole situation had numbed his brain as much as the stage ride had numbed his lower extremities. Or so he thought…

----⟨⟩----

The Bully of Lower Broad Street bellied the little tinker into the depot alley demanding a share of the man's funds—a random fee, required from those selected for passing through his realm. The tinker bravely refused though his unsteady voice betrayed knowledge of a futile effort. Again the Bully asked payment, sharply rapping the small man's skull with his knuckles. The tinker hesitated, denied him a second time and suffered a stinging slap that bloodied his nose.

It was at this point that Tom neared the corner of the building, still in a state of self absorption; still trying to work the kinks from body and mind, when something in him heard and responded to the tinker's plight. But what he did and how it affected him was amazing. With no warning whatsoever, he grasped the Bully's shoulder, spun him around and planted a blow squarely in the man's mouth, relieving him of his senses as well as uprooting and shattering several of his teeth. And then it was over. The Bully lay motionless between himself and the wide-eyed tinker and it was over.

"…Well, damn," he said in disappointment. With days—no, weeks—of rampaging emotions bottled within; of intangible obstacles that left him no way of proving his strength to overcome them, Tom had needed to fight against something real. But there lay the deserving candidate offering none of the resistance he'd wanted so much. Then he chuckled, because in spite of that, he did feel better.

"Mr. Scott?" the tinker intruded on these thoughts. "—Mr. Scott, how can I thank you?"

The moment of mirth vanished as Tom met the man's eyes. "We rode the same stage, sir, but I never told you my name."

"Please, don't be alarmed!" he glanced at the Bully, wanting none of what that one had received. "You just saved my life—as well as the company's money—and I've no intention of turning you in!" he dabbed a handkerchief to his bloody nose. "…Besides, I never thought you were guilty," he finished meekly.

"You must be telling the truth," Tom nodded. "You had ample opportunity to call for the law at every coach stop.…But how could you know so much about me—or so little, really—and still assume my innocence?"

"Well, what you've done here—coming to my rescue—just proves it further. But the fact is, we have offices in Savannah and I happened to be in the Police Station, reporting the theft of some merchandise, when they brought you in. A Captain there was telling his men things he found peculiar in your case and what he said made sense to me. So, I've been following the news accounts faithfully and haven't read anything yet to change my mind. Also, sir—and I hope you'll take no offense—but I just don't believe you would ever have to beat a woman to get her in bed with you. …And that comes from a man," the tinker smiled, dabbing his nose again, "who would be sorely tempted to try if he thought it might work."

Tom failed miserably at keeping a stern expression while extending a hand. "And your name, sir?"

"Munzenrider," he said accepting the cordial offer. "Joshua Munzenrider.—A very large name for so small a man, don't you think?"

"No, sir. Small men come in all sizes," Tom turned to leave. "And right now, Mr. Munzenrider, you're standing at close to ten feet in my estimation."

"Wait!—A moment, Mr. Scott!" he hopped nimbly over his felled assailant and hurried forward. "Here is my card. I represent The Star Book Ordering Company in Georgia and could I ever be of service, it would be an honor."

"…The Star Book," Tom tried to remember, while un-tying his horse. "That's a catalogue company, isn't it? You carry household goods and such?"

"The whole works!" he beamed proudly.

"…And would you be travelling through Athens anytime soon?" Tom asked, surprising himself once more. His mind seemed to be functioning again.

"Next month. I surely will," nodded the tinker.

"Then, go get your order sheets, Josh," Tom said. And as the man raced to do so, Tom's thoughts raced even faster. Mandria would not succeed with her plan, because his was a better one. And like it or not, she was going to accept it. "I'll need supplies to last…well, I gave her until spring, so that's what we'll plan for," he began, once they'd settled beneath a streetlamp on the edge of the platform. "So: two sets of bed linens; toweling; three or four heavy quilts; some new novels;—oh, a sketch pad and charcoals, too; a couple of warm lady's nightgowns—and a large size might be best; a sewing kit; a few yards of soft flannel—and bunting, I suppose. And for me," Tom grinned, "bring the best damned box of cigars you have!"

"Yes, sir—yes, I have it all down," said Joshua. "And where should I make delivery?"

"Josh, I doubt you could find the place," Tom laughed, and it felt really good. "Just take my order to Miss Susan Rutledge. She's a schoolmarm and anyone in Athens can direct you to her home. … Now, if our business is done, I'll pay you and say goodbye, my friend. I have one hell of a day ahead of me," he finished while mounting the horse.

"…But sir?—Tom?" Joshua called after him, wanting to share whatever it was that had brightened his mood. "Large nightgowns; bunting;—cigars? …Are we having a baby?"

"We are," Tom answered over his shoulder. "And by damn, my wife better behave herself and do it right."

Joshua was still smiling when the driver handed down his cases. And as he started down the street, he uttered, "Josh," liking the sound. He'd always wanted a nickname and this one made him feel taller—

ON THE FOOT OF A MOUNTAIN

close to ten feet, Tom had said. His smile broadened then, because truthfully, he had never enjoyed a more fascinating experience than meeting Tom Scott. It had been like watching a metamorphosis. From the stony, silent man who had boarded the stage, emerged a vital spirit, brimming with enthusiasm for life—and especially, for the life in his pregnant wife. This was a man he wanted to call friend. "Indeed," he straightened to his tallest, siding with Tom in all things, "the lady had best behave-and-do-it-right!"

———◈———

The village of Aiken lay across the Savannah River, some sixteen miles into South Carolina. The road between went through a valley rich with running streams, fertile soil and pine forests that crisped the air with fresh scent. But it was this very freshness that reminded Tom how long he had been without the luxury of a hot tub and a good razor. So dismounting beside a bubbling stream, he went through the saddlebag Allen had packed. Everything he needed was there, from shaving articles to two changes of clothes. "But what a change it will be!" Tom chuckled. For as if guided by providence, Allen had dug out and packed his buckskins—even his hat was there. And while he stripped and bathed in the cold bracing water, he enjoyed another thought. If the sight of him dressed as a backwoodsman frightened Mandria—well, let it! He wasn't going to shave either, because the edge he would need today, would not be found on a razor...

It was nearly noon before Tom located the farm of Trippe and Margery Jones. He heard the lunch bell clang as he ambled his horse along the road and watched as the field hands dropped their harvest sacks to move toward the rear of the main house. His task, then, would be drawing Mandria to the front while the help was occupied with the midday meal.

The four Jones children scampered about the yard generating enough chatter to cover the approach of an army when Tom dismounted beside a gate nestled into head-high hedges. "Pardon me, young sirs?"

he called, smiling at their startled expressions. "…And young ladies," he added with a courtly bow. "Is this the home of Dr. Trippe Jones?"

"Yes, sir," they chimed timidly, their eyes glued to the tall, strangely clad man.

"And is your cousin Mandria visiting here?"

"Yes, sir," they repeated in unison.

"Good. Is she near-by? I have a message to deliver from her mother."

"I saw her at breakfast.—Mandy sat by me," offered a petite, rosy-cheeked girl.

"I saw her after that, Andrea," said a stocky lad. "She was going to the rose garden."

"Well, I saw her last, Garris," said a slender, freckled-nosed miss. "I was in the garden too, and she gave me her toasted poundcake—see?"

"Emily, that's not fair!" said a boy with china-blue eyes. "I wanted more cake too, and Mama said no!"

"Quiet!" Tom interrupted, using his authoritative teacher's tone. And immediately, the children looked at him in silence. "Thank you," he returned an easy smile. "It's really urgent that I give this message to your cousin—and only to her. But as you can see, I'm not dressed to go calling in your very fine home. Could one of you ask her to come down to the gate without letting anyone else know?"

"I can! I will!" they were chiming again.

"Quiet!" he repeated, and they were. "I'll need only the swiftest runner. The rest of you stay here—and the next job is for the one who tells time the best."

Andrea, who was obviously eldest, because none argued with her answers, said, "Doug is the swiftest," she pointed to the blue eyed boy. "And Garris is the best time teller."

"Yeah, I learned on Papa's pocket watch," he announced. "And now I do mantle clocks and grandfathers too!"

"Then you go," Tom chuckled, giving Doug a nod and he took off at full speed. "And you listen," he said to the time-keeper. "It's most important to your Aunt Evelyn that your mother receives this letter," he put it into the care of the little girls. "You are to deliver it exactly one hour after I've gone. Can you do that?"

They all nodded, but Garris was curious. "Why do we got to wait a hour?"

"I've no idea," Tom tried to look as puzzled as the children. "Perhaps she is planning a surprise visit;—or a surprise party for one of you."

"With cake and punch and candy and presents?" asked Emily.

"Could be," he replied. "—If you all do your parts and don't ruin it."

"Oh, we will!" said Andrea, clutching the letter close. "We'll deliver this to Mama, just like you said. In one hour!"

"Very good," he nodded, stepping back a little, for the front door had closed and Mandria was being pulled along by her fleet-footed cousin. "This is a private message," he said to the children. "Tell cousin Mandria I'll be just on the other side of this hedge,"he added, going to stand half-concealed by the horse. And he waited...

"Sir?" Mandria approached, breathlessly. "You have a message for me?" But the tall buck-skinned man did not turn to greet her. Instead, he kept pulling at his saddle cinch and muttered something beneath his hat brim. "...I beg your pardon?" she asked coming closer. "What message does my mother send?—Is she ill?"

Then before she could even gasp from the surprise of it, Tom drew her between himself and the horse. "One word; one sound out of you, Mandria, could bring harm to those children. Do you understand me?" And his voice was so hard and her shock so great, she could only nod.

"Good," he loomed above, piercing her with cold intolerant eyes. "Now, we're mounting this damn horse and we're leaving here."

"Leaving?" she managed a whisper. "Oh, no, I'm not going anywhere with you!"

"Yes, you are!" his grip on her arms tightened. "Alone or with one of your little cousins along to ensure your good behavior. Now, which will it be?"

"No—not even you would use a child that way!"

"Why not? I'm blamed for worse already.—Now mount the damned horse!" And waiting no longer, he lifted her up and climbed into the saddle behind before she could think to react. "Remember what I said," he murmured close to her ear, as they neared the gate and the waiting children, "*Not-one-word.*"

"Cousin?—Cousin Mandy, where are you going?" Doug called.

"Will you be here for the party?" asked Emily.

"If you're not, can I have your cake this time?" added Andrea.

"One hour," Tom said to his timekeeper, over the din. "Starting now." And with arms caging Mandria in, he sent the horse into a gallop.

"Yes, sir!" Garris called with the pride of one-up-man-ship over his siblings. Then he led the way to a gathering about the grandfather clock;—the only time-piece worthy of so important a task...

———◁◎▷———

...*This has to be a nightmare!* Mandria thought. But the jostling ride was dispelling the notion. It was real. Tom was real.—And pressed so close against her back she could feel the heat of his body. But how could this be happening? He had been jailed for rape and attempted murder. She had seen him there—left him there—hoped he would rot and die right there in that cell! "How did you escape?" she asked suddenly. "I know they must be looking for you."

"Probably," he answered. "But you needn't concern yourself."

"I'm not concerned—not for you!" she retorted. "I feel nothing for you at all! You no longer exist in my eyes!"

"I never would have guessed," he remarked. And turning the horse onto a side road, he skirted the stores on Laurnes Street to work his way back toward the valley road.

"But this is ridiculous!" Mandria said now. "Where do think you're taking me? I won't stay. I hope you're intelligent enough to know that. I want nothing more to do with you, Mr. Scott—nothing!"

"The child you're carrying makes that statement rather asinine, lady," he returned. "Now, kindly keep quiet for a while. You're beginning to sound like a fish-wife."

Fury stiffened Mandria's spine. She had not asked to be dragged along with him, and he had no right to insult her for objecting to it. A fish-wife was she? Well, she'd die before speaking to him again—and that was a solemn vow!

Some time later, they reached the Savannah River where Tom dismounted and led the horse into a copse a little upstream from the landing. "We'll wait here," he said, lifting her down. "The ferry will return about four o'clock."

Mandria moved to a log and sat with her back turned, determined to maintain silence. For a time, she could hear Tom moving about—which was tantamount to sitting with her back to a coiled snake, she decided. Then, his movements ceased and that was worse. She could hear the horse cropping grass, the birds, the chilled afternoon breeze in the pines, but nothing from Tom. …Maybe he'd gone to sleep;—maybe she could escape now! But to accomplish the latter, she had to confirm the former. That meant she had to turn around, which seemed a concession, and she'd make none for him. Not one! So for while longer, she struggled with the problem, until curiosity and deviousness won out. Feigning a crick in her neck, she massaged the area, lolling her head far to the right for a quick backward glance. He wasn't there! Swinging to the left then, she was about to rise, when she saw him and gasped in eerie surprise. Tom was just inches away; stretched out on the ground, arms folded across his chest, hat pulled over his eyes;—and his head was propped on the other side of her log! …*He is part cat*, she shuddered, likening the color of his buckskins to that of a Puma.—*And no one trusts cats!* she added, ignoring the fact that those skins fit him very well.

"Are you cold?" Tom asked without moving.

"What?—Oh, damn it!" she swore, remembering her vow of silence too late. Well, she had already spoken, so she might as well enjoy it. "Fish-wives don't get cold," she sniped. "Their busy tongues keep them warm."

"I'll get a coat for you in Augusta," he answered boredly, though he grinned beneath his hat brim. ...*So she was upset by my comment. I'll have to remember that when I need some quiet time.*

"I'll wear my own coats, thank you;—I have plenty of coats! ... *How dare he ignore her barbs!*

"Not with you and you'll need one. Our journey could be a cold one."

"What journey?" she turned to face him. And when he did not answer—still hadn't even moved—she snatched the hat from his head. "I said, *what journey?*" she repeated.

Tom looked up, into angry green eyes, while his showed no emotion at all. "The nights will be colder from here on," he sat up, taking back his hat. "We'll both need coats, I suppose."

"Damn you!" she rose and stomped a foot. "Are you deaf? I don't want to go anywhere with you! Why won't you believe that?"

Tom rose too. "I believe it, Mandria. You have made your feelings for me and the baby quite clear."

"Then why are you doing this? I have not changed my mind.— Not one bit!"

"How far along are you?" he asked, gazing at the river. "—How many months?"

"I—well; ...it will soon be four," she replied. "...Come the 25th," she added, not wanting to at all.

"Then...our first time?" he concluded, looking her way again.

Mandria nodded, lowering her eyes. She did not want to dwell on that black day in history.

"It would be.—Damn it!" Tom swore, fighting memories of his own.

That brought her around. "Well, I don't like it any better than you! But I don't need your offensive remarks—or you—to get me through it! I don't even know why you'd care—or why you're here!"

"I meant nothing offensive. And I'm here, precisely, to get you through it. I mean to see this baby born safely and cared for."

Mandria's eyes widened. "That is impossible!—You can not hold me prisoner for five months!"

"I can try," he shrugged.

"Well—well, someone will find me first. And likely, Uncle Trippe is out looking now!"

"He isn't. That's been taken care of."

"…How?" she asked skeptically.

"Mandria, if I told you, you'd only get angry—and wouldn't believe me anyway."

"I'm already angry!" she snapped, arms akimbo. "And you may have fooled my Aunt and Uncle, but the law will catch up to you, Mr. Scott.—You can't fool them!"

"They can try," he shrugged again.

"But damn it, you can't do this!" she stomped the other foot now. "I won't let you;—I'll escape the very first chance I get!"

"You can try. But I'll stop you."

"Oh? Is that a threat?" And now her eyes narrowed. "Will they find me somewhere like they found poor little Nico?"

Tom exhaled in exasperation. "Lady, have I ever done you any physical harm?"

"You made me pregnant! I'd call that physical harm—since I can not stand the sight of you!"

"And I'd call it a responsibility. Therefore, you will remain in my care as long as you are with child."

"…But why? Do you just want to see it born? You know I'm not keeping it;—that I'm putting it up for adoption."

"*It*, as you insist on saying, belongs to me. And you are not giving my child away."

"*It* was conceived in deception—and you can not force me to keep *it*! Neither can you make me want *it*," she taunted.

"I'm not asking you to do either. When the baby is born, you're free to go and do whatever pleases you."

"Oh my God," she uttered in realization. "—You can't raise a baby alone!"

"I raised Allen. Caring for motherless children seems to be my fate."

"But you are a wanted man;—running from the law! What kind of life can you offer a child?"

"You aren't on the run. What have you offered?" he countered.

"A home; a chance to be adopted and loved as I never could—especially, if *it* looks like you!"

"Tell me, are you well?" he ignored her barbs yet again, "Have you had any problems with the pregnancy?"

"That is none of your damned business!" she began to pace. "So don't concern yourself with my health, because I am not going along with this madness!"

"Well, the ferry is coming anyway," Tom went for the horse. "Perhaps we can finish this charming conversation later?"

"Not if I can help it!" she started for the landing like an avenging angel. "When I tell the boatman my story, you will be right back in jail!" Something told Mandria it was odd that Tom wasn't trying to stop her; that he seemed in no hurry as he led the horse and followed behind. But the ferry was docked now and she was intent on reaching it first and claiming her freedom. "Sir?" she called, hopping aboard the large flat barge. "Help me, sir—please? That man is a criminal;—wanted for attempted murder!" she pointed at Tom. "Hurry, sir, hold your gun on him or he'll get away!"

But the boatman was not responding. He only looked grimly at Tom, who now stood beside them. "That her?" the man asked. "The one her husband sent you to find?"

"That's her," Tom answered. "Real sad case."

"A real waste too," the man allowed his eyes to roam Mandria freely. "She don't look crazy, neither. Just kind of mad about something."

"Crazy?" Mandria stared at Tom in a new rush of anger. "You told him I was crazy?"

"Watch out!" Tom warned, looking truly alarmed. "She near broke my jaw with a shoe the last time she got violent!"

"Oh!—Oh, you bastard!" Mandria shrieked, trying to slap him with her mightiest swing—which he sidestepped, and that sent her spinning into the boatman's arms.

"God damn, but she's a nice little armful!" the man held her pinned against him. "Now, look here, boy, if she's really crazy, ain't nobody going to listen to her anyways. You and me, we could take her into the woods and get us a little bit. Nobody'd know!—Fact is, you've been to the woods with her already, ain't you? Sure you have. I seen you up there! How was it, boy? Is she good as she looks?"

During that speech, Mandria had been struggling to free herself and looking at Tom in desperation—which he found ironic, since she had just tried to send him back to jail and believed he had already committed rape on Nicole. Why should one more matter if he was the monster she thought him to be? But there she was, expecting his help and he wondered if she even realized it. "Friend, you can do as you like, but I'm not touching her," he said then. "The woman is diseased—and likely, it's advanced enough to cause her insanity."

The boatman released Mandria as if he'd been burned. "Damn!" he exclaimed, briskly wiping his hands on his trouser legs. "God damn, but that's a real shame, ain't it?" And turning away, he hurried about his business.

Mandria's cheeks glowed with mortification; and hatred; and confusion; ...and gratification;—and fresh fury, when Tom dared to stand there grinning at her! Then, her throat closed, her head spun and she fainted dead away, cursing him because she'd never fainted in her life before he made her pregnant...

CHAPTER 2

When Mandria opened her eyes again, her head was resting on Tom's thigh, while he sat looking intently at the Georgia side of the river. Sitting up, a little shakily, she resumed conversation expressing the last thought she could remember having. "It's your fault that I fainted.—I was never subject to any stupid behavior before I met you!"

"We'd best mount up," Tom rose, assisting her up too. And looking at the shore line, again, he nodded slowly, climbed onto the horse and reached down to give her a hand.

Mandria started to refuse, but her knees were still wobbly; he seemed in a strange mood; and she had no wish to be hauled up by the hair of the head. ...*Besides,* she thought, *if he does stop to buy coats, I can still rid myself of him. ...Yes, he might have duped that horrid boatman, but the shopkeepers of Augusta will be more apt to believe a lady than a wild man in buck-skins with an unsightly, unshaven face. ...Though, just in case, I'd best approach a male clerk, because those damn skins fit Tom too well and such could turn some poor foolish female shopkeeper's head.*

But Mandria's scheme went untried because of what Tom had seen on the Georgia coast. The Irish Mist was docked there, totally off schedule, which meant one of two things: Either Mike was trying to make up for his lost weeks of trade, or the Captain had come in search of him. So when the barge pulled into its slip, in the haze of late afternoon light, Tom departed the riverfront, keeping to side streets and heading ever westward...

Mandria was starting to worry. Where were the stores? Tom should have turned a number of times, but now they seemed to be on the outskirts of town and she was truly feeling a chill on the air. Perhaps it was time to remind him of his offer. "I think I would like a coat;—if you don't mind," she shivered and it was real.

"Sorry. We'll have to tend that later," he halted the horse and turned to rummage through a saddlebag. "Meanwhile, you're welcome to wear this." And he helped her into his rumpled suit coat, noting her offense at its stale odor. "Sorry about that too," he added. "Prison valets are scarce this season."

"Very funny," she replied and they rode on in silence, but at least she was warmer.

Light gave way to darkness and still they rode—on and on, until Mandria wondered if he ever intended to stop. She wanted to complain; to tell him how hard the saddle was; how her back was beginning to ache; …how hungry she was. But that hunger was exactly what kept her silent. She was sure he would make some humorless remark about her pregnant appetite—and she was so ashamed of it. Why did her condition have to agree with her so damned well, when she would much prefer wretching in sickly protest—which she could then blame on him too! But another hour passed and still they rode on through a thick, wet fog that had set in. And Mandria was not only cold and starving, but miserably weary. If he didn't stop soon she was going to burst into tears and she bit her lip trying to contain a tired little sob…

Tom nodded. Why did he have to be so in tune with her needs? Once, he had considered it a blessing. Now…well, exasperating was a good enough word. "We'll be staying in Thompson for the night," he commented. "You can see the village lights just up the road there." Mandria said nothing, but how she wished he would hurry the horse along. A village meant food! But as they finally—finally—started down the main street, Tom stopped in shadows, a good distance away from a cheery looking, well-lit inn. … *What now?* she thought, sniffing the aromas of the feast being offered inside; listening to the laughter of sated patrons. It was almost more than she could stand.

"Mandria, we had better settle this right here and now," Tom began. "I don't trust you. Therefore, I do not intend letting you out of my sight: not during supper; not after; and especially, not at bedtime. You will have to share a room with me—platonically, I do assure you— but if you can behave, we'll go in, have a good meal and retire to a soft bed with clean sheets. If not, we'll skip supper and sleep wherever I can find a dry place. The choice is yours, lady. Kindly make it."

"But I don't want to sleep in a room with you!" she straightened defensively. "I won't;—I just will not do it!"

"Damn it, that wasn't the choice you were offered!—Hell, maybe it's best to keep moving," he started to turn the horse away. "Maybe I can find a barn where you can make your damned protests as long and loud as you please."

Mandria could think of nothing worse—except skipping supper. "No!—Wait!" she tugged at his sleeve. "I...I'm very hungry," she admitted, though it killed her to do so.

"But do you promise not to cause a scene?—Do you swear it on your mother's life?"

"Yes!" the answer came out in spite of clinched teeth that tried to hold back the word. How she hated herself for such weakness—and him for everything else! "...Anyway," she spoke truth in defeat, "I'm too tired to cause trouble."

"Very well, we have a bargain," he dismounted, only to pause as he stood looking up at her. "...But perhaps I should warn you about breaking the terms and what it could mean to a number of innocent people. Mandria, if you tell anyone I'm wanted by the law and they try to take me, the blood spilled will be on your hands. I will defend myself, no matter whom or how many are hurt."

"I know," she said, sliding to the ground with his help. "I saw Nicole. I know your bloody handiwork well." And though her body screamed with every step, she turned and went forward, hoping she'd stung him a good one.

Once inside the inn's dining room, it was all Mandria could do to remember her mannerly upbringing. She had visions of ripping that large, succulent roast from its spit in the great hearth and gnawing it right to the bone. As they made their way to a table, she was even tempted to snatch a baked and buttered yam from a plate as they passed. And once seated, she attacked a basket of breads there, eating two thick, warm slices before Tom had finished speaking to the innkeeper. Not much was said after their supper was served, for Mandria's attention hardly left her plate. Though as her hunger became appeased, she did begin to worry anew about those sleeping arrangements. ...*What does Tom expect in the bedroom?* she wondered. He said she'd be safe, but she didn't believe that. Hadn't he also said he loved her and gone right after Nicole? She glanced at him with real suspicion in her eyes, and found that he watched her with amusement in his—which did little to ease her apprehensions.

"Would you care for anything else?" he asked pleasantly.

"No thank you," she straightened in her chair, ready to do battle if need be. He was not getting around *her* with that charming smile of his!

Tom nodded and after a moment continued. "You really don't look pregnant, Mandria—which is truly amazing, considering your new appetite."

"Oh, I *knew* you'd say something awful!" she cringed. "—And you didn't disappoint me!"

"...I'm so glad," he replied, wondering what was awful about his simple observation. "But I wasn't trying to please or displease you. I'm just glad you are eating well. It's good for the baby."

"Would you stop reminding me of that?" she asked sharply, though her tone lost some of its edge in a weary yawn.

"All right, lady," he rose and placing a hand beneath her elbow, brought her up too. "Our room should be ready and it's time I put you to bed."

Mandria felt...what? Some immiscible combination of panic, revulsion and far too many warm memories of things dead and gone? Whatever it was kept her attentive as they climbed the stairs. As did the firm hold he still had on her elbow. But she knew, even if she had vowed on her mother's life, she would forfeit her own before allowing anything intimate between them. And she remembered, again, that Nicole almost had...

Tom opened a door and ushered Mandria into a tiny bedroom, made to feel even smaller by a large four-poster bed. A patch-work coverlet, turned down at the corner, revealed bleached white sheets, plump down pillows—and oh, how she yearned to lay her weary self down. Then she spied a steaming tub between the bed and the fireplace. "A bath," her words escaped on a sigh.

"I thought you might enjoy one," Tom said, quietly securing the door lock. "Would you care to go first? I'll wait my turn."

"You don't expect me to disrobe?" she swung on him.

"I believe that's the usual procedure for bathing," he commented.

"Not with *you* in here, it isn't!" she assured him. "I want a bath, but I want my privacy more—and I will not have it any other way!"

"Mandria," he sighed, "you are not some innocent maiden being stalked by a lecher. Lady, we are married; I've seen you from stem to stern;—and all I'm suggesting is a damn bath!"

"Well, we all make mistakes—and our marriage was a huge one," she retorted. "So, no, I am not bathing while you are in this room!"

"Then step aside," he lost patience, "because I'm having one whether you do or not."

"Oh!—I hope you drown!" she stomped to the bed and sat with her back turned.

"Well, I won't," he said and began to undress. "But we do have a long way to go and I can't promise you such comforts every night," he added, slipping the door key into his empty boot.

Mandria said nothing, but she did wince when his buckskins fell across the bed behind her. Then she heard him invade the water—her bath water—working the soap into lather; scrubbing; soaking; rinsing; enjoying himself, while she felt grubbier by the minute.

"Will you hand me a towel?" he asked against a background of dripping splashes that said he'd risen to his feet.

"I certainly will not!" she folded her arms stubbornly. "Get it yourself!"

"Very well," he answered. And now she heard wet feet padding in her direction. "Enjoy the view, lady" he said from just beside her.

"Go away!" she dashed for the corner, hiding her face against the wall. And hearing him come even closer, she went rigid. "Stop!—If you touch me, I'll scream!"

"I'm only after a towel," he said, taking one from the table right at her hip. "There's another here if you decide to be sensible and have a bath." Then, pulling on his trousers, he stretched out on the bed, laced his fingers behind his head and closed his eyes with a weary sigh of his own.

Mandria felt the utter fool—not only for her assumption, but because she was still crouched in a corner and there didn't seem anywhere else to go. She was not going to bathe, he was on the bed and she couldn't even take advantage of the room's only chair, as getting to it meant rounding the bed and squeezing by the tub, just to sit right beside his pillow. And she couldn't get the chair out of that corner, because of the damned tub!

Stealthily then, harboring one last hope, she reached and tried the door. But of course, it was locked and she couldn't have felt worse had she tried and failed at the gates of heaven. Biting her lip, she smothered a sob, but could not stop the tears. ...*Damn him!* she thought, sinking slowly to the floor. ...*Damn, damn, damn him,* she yawned. And curling her arms about her knees, she lowered her head upon them...

Tom heard her try the door knob and didn't bother to open his eyes. Neither was he disturbed when that was followed by the faint rustle of her skirts and snubbing. If she wished to stand there and cry—or pace the room in anger—as long as she made no more noise about it than this, it was fine by him. He was really very tired...

But it was the absence of noise that awakened him. While he slept, had she managed to escape—as had happened their first time together? "Damn it!" he muttered, the notion bringing him upright, searching all directions at once. "...Oh, damn," he repeated softly, spotting her huddled sleeping posture on the floor. "The stubborn little...goat," he uttered. And going to Mandria, he gently lifted her to the bed, removed her shoes and covered her to the chin. Then he dabbed lightly at a tear that still clung to her lashes and stood looking at her beautiful features. "If only Sam had let us be," he nodded. But there was no use going over that again. The damage was done and for the sake of his child, he'd carry on as best he could. For the present, that meant seeing Mandria get a good night's sleep—without waking to find her in another corner. So, taking his pillow, he lay with his head at the foot of the bed, conceding that much to her ferocious determination and pride...

Mandria gave a leisurely stretch and hugged her pillow close. It was morning, but she wasn't going to open her eyes until she had guessed what Joleen was bringing for breakfast. Umm—*coffee,* she sniffed,—*and sausage and biscuits too!* And she rolled over to the nearby sounds of tinkling glassware.

"Morning," Tom said as he placed a tray on the towel table.

Sitting up quickly, she asked, "How did I get in this bed?—And where did you sleep?"

"I put you there," he answered, while rounding the bed to retrieve the chair—and in spite of the tub, managed it so damn easily. "And I slept here," he patted the pillow against the footboard on the way back. Then, sitting before the tray, he poured them each some coffee and invited her to join him for breakfast.

Mandria did accept a cup, noting that Tom had shaved off those horrid whiskers. She eyed the plate of sausage filled biscuits too, but looked away, making a to-do of propping against her pillow. Maybe if she refused to eat and became ill, he would tire of this silly game and release her. But as she sipped her coffee and considered this further, Tom opened a small earthenware jar. ...*Honey,* she thought, watching him spoon out a golden dollop. ...*Sausage biscuits—and honey,* she sighed, tearing her eyes from both. She would not be able to watch him take a single bite...

And now Tom was offering the coveted thing to her. "Lady? You'd best eat something. We'll be on the road a long while today."

Mandria had every intention of refusing, until honey oozed from the side of the biscuit. Catching the drop on her finger, into her mouth it went and she all but snatched the biscuit from his hand. She also ate another that he had waiting when she'd finished the first. And once again, being well-fed triggered her defenses. She looked at Tom as he finished his coffee, his legs stretched before him and crossed at the ankles. It angered her that he could be so at ease with himself after the things he'd done. Didn't it just prove him void of conscience? Yes, she was dealing with a calculating, methodical devil and maybe her only way of escaping him was to use cleverness of her own; to first learn what he was planning and then finding ways to foil him. "Tom?" she began, striving to appear unbothered as he. "Where are you taking me?"

Without looking up, he said, "So, you haven't forgotten my name. That's the first time you've used it since we were...reunited?" he allowed this to end in a question of absurdity.

It was hard, but Mandria kept her tone neutral. "Maybe I didn't recognize you until now. I see you've shaved."

Tom hid a smile in a sip of coffee and said nothing. He was just glad she'd managed two or three sentences in a row that weren't riddled with angry exclamation marks.

"Well?" she lost patience with his silence. "Where are you taking me? I have a right to know!"

...So much for that lasting, he chuckled as he rose from the chair. "I'll tell you in due time. But we'll be leaving in about thirty minutes, so you'd better get up—and wrap the rest of those biscuits in a napkin. You'll be glad to see them later on." And with that, he went out, locking her in.

Mandria made quick use of the bath water—cold as it was—and at least felt clean, if nothing else. But it had been an hour now, Tom was still gone, and she was not only bored, but irritated. She thought of several scathing remarks—practiced them too—yet, when the door finally opened, his only greeting was silence. Why should she waste breath on him? He never listened anyway.

"Sorry it took so long," he explained, depositing a gunny sack on the bed. "But besides some vital supplies, you needed warmer clothes, so I bought them for you."

Mandria peered into the sack and wrinkled her nose. "Buckskin? You don't really expect me to wear animal skins like an Indian?" Then a look of genuine fear filled her eyes. "We're not going west—not into Indian territory?"

"No, but it is November, Mandria, and it's getting colder by the day. Buckskin is easy to travel in, as well as light weight and warm— Here," he reached into the bag, "feel how soft these boots are. Would you really object to wearing them?"

She looked over the knee-high, moccasin laced boots. They were pretty, in a crude sort of way, but he wasn't going to know she thought so. Then, being curious—and a woman—she went through the rest of the things he'd brought. There was a fringed sleeved blouse that laced up the front; a buckskin riding skirt, she'd call it for lack of a better word; a thigh length, fur-lined coat; …and at the very bottom of the sack, a pair of red long johns. "Not for me?" she held them up. "Surely, you…I mean, ladies don't wear men's red underwear—not the ladies of Savannah!"

"Then, where we're going, they'd likely freeze their fannies off But suit yourself. It's your fanny," he shrugged, starting for the door. "I'm going to finish packing the horse and I'll be back in five minutes. Be ready." So saying, he locked her in again.

"Suit yourself," she mimicked, stepping from her pretty, gray, winter weight dress—winter weight for Savannah, but apparently not for the place being forced on her. "Yes, it is my fanny!" she said to the closed door. Then, comparing the long johns to her lacy white chemise and pantalets, she stuffed the awful garment back to the bottom of the sack. "Men's red underwear, indeed," she uttered, donning the buckskins, and carefully adding her folded dress and crinolines to the sack. "He needn't think I'm leaving these here. No, when I return home—and I *am* returning—it won't be in buckskin!" she began to pace…and grudgingly noted the soft comfort of the boots; that the skirt allowed her as much freedom as the gypsy skirts she so enjoyed at the beach;—and this brought on a wave of homesickness. "Lord, how long ago that seems," she sighed...

———⚬⚬———

Leaving Thompson, Tom turned the horse north, and they travelled the edge of an autumn forest. It was a clear day and the sun felt tepidly comfortable. Yet the air standing in shadow smacked with a coolness that promised winter was near—which had Mandria thinking better of her buckskins. There was, however, one major draw-back. Yesterday, there had been yards and layers of material separating her from Tom. Today, she was acutely aware of his thigh muscles, his broad, hard chest and arms—everything male that surrounded her so snuggly. And by mid-morning, her back ached from trying to maintain a distance between them.

About noon, they came upon a brook and Tom stopped beside a large flat rock on the sun-lit bank, where he helped Mandria dismount. "We'll rest here—and eat if you're hungry," he said, scanning the area closely. "Use that clump of bushes over there if you feel the need."

"...What need?" she gave him a puzzled look.

"To go; ...to piss;—to pee!" he all but snapped. "The ladies of Savannah do pee, don't they?"

"Not in the bushes, I can assure you!" she retorted. And turning away, she settled on the rock to glare at him.

Tom stood there a moment and started to laugh. "Have you really never gone to the bushes?"

"Why would I? The proper facilities were always available."

"Even on picnics—or trips, maybe?"

"Our picnics are held on someone's lawn, or in the squares, or at someone's country place," she patiently explained. "Trips are planned with timely stop-overs. Civilized people do take these things into account—not that *you* would know about being civilized!"

"Lady," he continued to grin at her, "you are going to bust a gut before sundown. Now, if you'll excuse me, I intend to avail myself of the...uh, *facilities* available here."

Mandria hurled mental daggers at his back. No one—not even her damned father—could infuriate her the way Tom did. And that he was right—that she did need to go—only made it worse.

Tom returned, got himself a sausage biscuit and placed the rest beside her, as he too, sat on the flat-surfaced rock. "Sun feels good, doesn't it?" he munched away. She didn't answer, but did select the largest of the biscuits and wished for more honey.

When Tom finished his, he rolled to his belly and drank a handful of water from the brook. "Want some?" he offered. "Those biscuits are kind of dry now."

Again, Mandria didn't answer, but this time because she could hardly swallow. So, crawling up beside him, closing her own hands beneath his, she gladly accepted the water he scooped to her mouth. Tom felt her lips brush his palm; saw the autumn sun glisten through her breeze-ruffled tan hair and deep inside, hurt all over again. "Enough!" he said gruffly. And rising he started for the horse, wishing it would kick him, because now he'd have to explain his bad humor. "Any more to drink and you will be making me stop before we've gone another mile."

Mandria scrambled to her feet, arms akimbo, "First, you want me to go;—then you complain because I might have to? Well, damn it, if I'm such a burden, leave me here! I didn't force my presence on you! This is your doing, start to finish!"

Tom knew he deserved that, but she wasn't going to know he knew it. "Exactly!" he retorted inanely, while swinging into the saddle. And what better complimented inanity than a tired adage? "I always finish what I start.—Now shall we go, lady?"

"No!" she marched passed him. "I'm going to the bushes—but only because *I* want to! I wouldn't think of asking you for anything;—not in one mile or a thousand!"

Tom pressed the heel of his hand hard into his thigh. Mandria had always possessed the power to make him behave like an idiot. The knowledge was not new to him and mentally he thought he had steeled himself against it. But it wasn't his mind that had failed him here. No, what started this whole episode was their damned buckskins, catching and clinging together like glue in every possible tantalizing spot. "Well, no more!" he vowed, and when she returned, he put her up behind him…

CHAPTER 3

It was mid-afternoon when they rode into the town of Washington, well-known by Georgians for its gracious homes and affluent society. And Mandria's hopes for escape rose again. There were ladies here of her own class;—ladies, who would send their gallant men to her rescue. But to see that accomplished, she had to elude Tom, which meant persuading him to stop. "I—I'd like to stretch my legs," she began. "May I walk for a while?"

"I suppose," he pulled up, and sliding to the ground, lifted her down. "We'll both walk. There's a restaurant in the next block. We could stop for an early supper—if you can remember the rules?"

"I'll remember, Tom," she searched the street for inspiration. *If I could only get into one of these stores…*, she thought. "Oh, look, an apothecary," she pointed. "Tom, could I please buy a headache powder? My head hurts frightfully."

There was a certain brightness about her eyes that Tom mistook for strain. He had, after all, kept her on the road for the better part of the day. And as she stood holding out a hand expectantly, he pressed a coin into it and watched her rub at her temples as she entered the shop. He stood there all of three seconds. Then grim-faced, he led the horse into the shaded lane beside the store. Mandria had called him by name again—twice—a clear signal she'd been too engrossed in some plot to remember he *didn't-exist-any-more*. And she'd sworn not to ask him for anything—*not in one mile or a thousand*—yet she'd just asked several favors. "Lady," he muttered, "you'd best tread lightly…"

On entering the apothecary, Mandria saw two fashionably dressed ladies chatting with the pharmacist and breathed a sigh of relief. Surely, her deliverance was at hand. She would approach her peers, tell her story and receive assistance. It would be just as simple as that…

What she received, instead, was a snubbing. Who was this creature in buckskins? How dare she assail them with tales of kidnappers and rapist roaming the streets of their very nice town! Why, couldn't she see no one was out there they hadn't known all their lives as family or friend?—Was she accusing one of them of such crimes? She must be deranged and at all costs, avoided! Then those same ladies turned on the pharmacist, all but insisting he remove the girl from the premises while decent folk were about.—Hadn't they been valued customers for years? Surely, he had no wish to offend them by allowing this person to remain!

But the pharmacist, a kindly man, thought the girl in buckskins must be seeking a hand-out, and as that didn't invoke his scorn, he shooed her gently away from the ladies, feeling pity for her look of dismay. Then, as if turned to stone, she stopped to stare at her reflection in his new counter-pane mirror.

Road dust lay like fine powder on Mandria's shoulders. And raising a hand to the hopeless jumble of her curls, her fingers actually trembled. "Oh," she uttered softly. "I wouldn't have believed me either." Tears glistened in her lashes as she turned to face the man who stood watching her. "…Sir, I've caused you enough trouble. Have you a back door?—Please, may I just leave that way?" The pharmacist hesitated, but hearing a new batch of slurs from his patrons, quickly showed her the door she sought.

The alley was quiet and deserted and she was glad. Solitude was best when a place to cry was needed. "Those horrible, horrible women!" she wept as she stumbled along feeling thoroughly humiliated. "And Tom caused this too, damn him! Dragging me around the countryside—"

Then, like the villain from a stage play, he stepped forward right on cue, flattening Mandria between himself and the building wall. "I take it they were out of headache powders," he glared from steely-blue eyes. And before she could recover from the shock, he had a gag in her mouth.

Outraged, Mandria's hands came up, ready to claw those eyes from his head. But with ridiculous ease, he caught her wrists, binding them securely between and among the rawhide laces of her own blouse. And like a sack of potatoes, she was hoisted over the saddle, physically held down by a forearm and unceremoniously galloped out of the fair town of Washington. She had no notion of the distance they traveled while she dangled there fuming in anger, but she did know—no, she swore—Tom Scott was going to be one sorry man for this!

———— ·◁◦▷· ————

When Tom saw a lake shimmering through the trees, he knew he'd found the right trail. A minute smile touched his lips as he recalled his youth, this lake and a Miss Lollie Chastain. One spring, he had wandered into the village of Lexington for supplies during a hunting trip. He was dressed much as he was today, but then his buckskins had seemed a part of him;—a uniform made for adventure. Lollie understood this and openly admired the young stranger in her father's general store. Her father did not, for he'd already planned her marriage to a gentleman planter from Washington. Lollie had no objection to that, but Lollie rarely objected to anything—including a rendezvous with Tom in her own secret cove beside this lake. It was, indeed, a spring to remember...

But it was late autumn now, years had passed and a very different sort of female accompanied him. Mandria objected, literally, to everything about him and to keeping his child, most of all. Remembering this— and that she'd tried, yet again, to turn him in—strengthened his resolve as he lifted her down from the horse. Green warning fires danced in her eyes, meeting the blue flint in his. Both knew an explosion was eminent and when he removed the gag, sure enough, the first words from her mouth, set it off.

"Bastard!—Oh, you damned bastard! How dare you tie me like a dog!—Damn, damn, damn you! Untie my hands, do you hear? Untie me, damn you!"

"No!" he shouted right back. "Not until you calm down. Twice now, you've tried to have me arrested and twice you've paid a price for it. So sorry if you were a little uncomfortable, but you were warned and got only what you damn-well deserved!"

"Well, I don't deserve amputations!" she spat. "There is no blood left in my hands—now untie me!"

"Oh, don't worry, Mandria," he loosened the laces—and again, with ridiculous ease—"if they recover as quickly as your tongue, you've suffered no damage. Just be grateful we didn't have further to ride."

"Grateful?" she seethed, rubbing her numbed wrists. "I'm supposed to thank you for such treatment? Well, here's a token of my gratitude!" And she kicked wildly at his shin, only to yelp in terrible pain and hobble away. Mandria had forgotten she wore the soft moccasin boots and that his were tall leather ones. "Now look what you've done!" she cried, sinking to the ground. "You broke my foot!"

Uttering a prayer for patience, Tom knelt before her, removed her boot, and felt for bone alignment. "It's not broken. Though you likely jammed your toes, and that's just as painful. ...And disabling," he added with a grin. "Maybe I should thank you now."

"I can not imagine why," she retorted, easing her foot back into the boot.

Tom sat back on his heels and folded his arms. "Because, dear one, you have managed to tie yourself down now, better than I did. You won't be running anywhere on that foot."

"Oh, don't you just wish! I'll run—I'll crawl, if I must! I'd do anything to be rid of you!" And jerking aside, she suffered for it. "Oh-oh-oh, my poor foot!" she winced, blaming him all over again. "—Well, now that you've crippled me, are you going to help me back to the horse, or do you plan to sit there grinning like a jackass until dark?"

"And deny you these luxury accommodations?" he swept an arm. "I wouldn't think of it, Mandria. We are here for the night."

"You…you're not serious?" she glanced about fearfully. "We'll freeze to death, if we're not eaten by wild animals first! And what about that lake?" she pointed. "I guess you're not afraid of alligators?"

"…Alligators?" Tom repeated, trying mightily to keep a serious expression.

"Yes! The lakes and ponds around Savannah are full of them and they're likely here too—watching us right now!"

"Then stay away from the lake—and the woods," he played on her fears. "Bears and mountain lions roam the woods at night—not to mention snakes and bats.—And did you know bats are real fond of blonde hair of any shade?" Then he rose and went to unsaddle the horse, hoping he'd discovered a way of keeping her put for the night. "…Alligators," he chuckled to himself. All the same, he kept an eye on her, as he walked about the cove, gathering dry limbs and twigs for a fire. She jumped at every sound from the dense wall of trees. And later, when she hobbled toward the pile of gunny-sack luggage, she froze listening to the mournful hoot of a woods owl, not moving until even the echoes had died away. Retrieving her coat and still limping badly, she hurried into the circle of firelight and sat facing him across the flames. For a time, nothing was said, but Tom could feel the tension building within her, and braced for the next quake. It began slowly.

"…Bats don't really like blonde hair. You were only trying to frighten me, weren't you?"

"A little. But the woods are dangerous at night. And you'd be easy prey on that lame foot. Scaring you was the best I could do with out lock and key."

"Funny—just so amusing. I suppose you find starvation funny too? We have not had a bite to eat since noon."

"And whose fault is that? I warned you how it would be in Thompson and again in Washington. No, lady, you forfeited your right to a decent meal tonight."

"But I'm hungry—and eating isn't a luxury!"

"You may come to think so," he replied, taking a pouch from their supplies. "Tonight we dine on jerky and mush."

"What is that?" she frowned.

"Trail food. It's dried beef strips and ground corn meal. Not what you're used to, but its filling. I'm just glad I had so little faith in your promises and the forethought to buy some this morning, or we'd be without any food."

Stung, she watched in silence as he went to cut and peel a wide piece of bark from a tree. Thoroughly soaking it in the lake and retaining some water in the curved, make-shift bowl, he then poured in a portion of the course corn meal and stirred it as he placed it near the flames to steam. That done, he brought it and came to sit beside her.

"Mush," he said, placing the tree-bark bowl between them. "Spoon," he held two fingers together and scooped out a bite for himself. "And jerky.—Here, try some," he handed her a shriveled, leathery looking lump as he cut bite size pieces and dropped them into the warm mush.

Mandria eyed the bilious corn-yellow mixture and decided she would try the lump. It was like trying to chew up a shoe—and probably about as tasty. So, turning to the bowl again, she drew a finger through it, hoping mush would taste better than it looked. It didn't. "Yuk!" she shuddered. "How can you eat that? It's just a saltless paste!"

"It's meant to keep you alive, not for serving at dinner parties," he countered. "Besides, Indians don't use salt."

"Indians?" her eyes widened. "In Thompson—and you bought this stuff from them?"

"No. I meant the food is preserved and prepared without salt—a way taught to us by the Indians. I bought it at a general store. They all keep a supply on hand."

"I don't know why," she tasted it again and complained, "Oh, it's just awful!"

But Mandria needed nourishment and Tom hoped she might eat if he kept her attention on the conversation. "…Tell me," he began as he pushed mush-softened bites of jerky to her side of the bowl, "why do you fear Indians? You have panicked every time I've mentioned them."

"I did not panic!" her chin came up. "It's not in my nature to panic."

"All right, word it any way you choose. But you don't like Indians, and I wondered why?"

"You can read," she answered, plucking out two mush-covered meat morsels and reaching for another. "You've seen accounts of their savage attacks on the wagon trains."

"Yes, but don't you find it strange that so little is printed about the Indians' side of things?—Do you know the injustices we have done them?"

"There is no excuse for inhuman brutality. But you wouldn't understand that, would you?—Not after the inhuman thing you did to Nico!"

Their eyes met and held, all small-talk forgotten. And the bark mush bowl slid sideways to the ground where it would remain until discovered by creatures and insects of the forest.

"Ev …every time I close my eyes," she went on, "I'm standing in that room again, watching you move over Nicole's broken, mindless body in a drunken stupor."

"Mandria, stop," he uttered, but she wouldn't.

"And that vision—that blood soaked vision—won't fade," she nodded, as tears spilled freely over her lashes. "It never will!"

"But I wasn't responsible—"

"Oh, my father agrees,—if you can believe it," she injected. "Isn't that ironic, since he took me there to find you? Then, on the way home, he said you were mentally ill; that you would have to be locked away; because what you did was more deep-seated than a crime of passion. And he said how dangerous it was to have you teaching children; how next, we'd be finding their little bodies beaten and bloodied—"

"No!—By God, I say no!" Tom exclaimed, realizing just how thoroughly Sam had ruined his marriage. "Mandria, I'm telling you, I was not responsible for anything that happened—and I am certainly not insane!"

"And I'm telling you, I was there! I know what I saw!"

"Were you *there* when your father asked me to stop by his office to discuss our marriage? Were you *there* when he fed me a drug-laced drink? Were you *there* when he had me bodily delivered to that room? What do you know about drugs—or the Dumb Cane leaf, lady? Do you have any idea what they can do to the human body?"

"Liar!—I won't listen to any more of your lying excuses!" she sobbed, struggling to her feet. "You can't sway me the way you used to! You bedded Nico and then beat her! You know it! I know it!—All of Savannah knows it!" she turned and hobbled toward the woods. "Well, I'd rather be eaten by lions and bears than stay with you! At least that sort of death would be over with quickly!"

Tom watched, certain she would stop at the tree line and when she didn't, he was on her heels in an instant. "Damn it, I've had enough of you for one day!" he jerked her to a stop, ignoring her yelp of pain as she turned on her bad foot. "You may not care about your own safety, but I won't allow you to harm that baby;—and you could stumbling around in the dark!"

"Why do you insist on this pretense?" she pried at his fingers. "Our marriage meant nothing to you!—Why should the baby? You must have dozens of bastards all over the state! Round them up if you want children! Then you can just leave me the hell alone!"

"Mandria, shut up!" he shook her, in deepening anger. And he knew to was too deep—too painful—to risk doing or saying more. So grasping her hand, he marched back toward the fire, letting her hop and hobble the best way she could. "Now sit!" he commanded, but Mandria nearly fell, her foot hurt so badly.

"And what is that for?" she snapped when he rolled out a blanket before her.

"Us!" he snapped back. "We are going to bed!—And if holding you down is the only way of keeping you in place, then by God I'll do it!"

"Oh, no! I'm not going through that again tonight!" she began to crawl away. "I am not going to sleep with you!"

Tom hauled her up by the waist this time and carried her back, though she kicked and screamed and did everything in her power to free herself. Then with an arm locked securely about her from behind, he lowered them onto the blanket, pulled her spoon-fashion against his body and held her until she had fought herself into exhaustion. When he thought she'd finally fallen asleep, he pulled a second blanket over them, but never eased his hold. "Good night, lady," he whispered close to her ear. "You too, little one," he added, allowing a hand to rest on her belly.

For a long while afterwards, Mandria lay staring into the darkness...

———◈———

Dawn, and Mandria shivered when a blast of icy air crept down her spine. Where was the warmth she'd nestled against during the night? Shivering again, she rolled to her back and found Tom sitting up to rub at a kink in his arm.

"Morning," he said sleepily. "I seem to have rusted overnight. Slept too long in one position, I guess."

"It's your own stupid fault. You needn't have held me...all night," she finished, wishing she'd never begun. And sitting up too, she pulled her coat closer around her. "Oh, I've never been so cold in my life!"

"Well, we haven't far to go this morning. Comfort yourself with that."

"Does the place you're taking me have a roof and walls?" she asked hopefully.

"It did the last time I saw it," he nodded."

"And food?" she made a pointed reminder.

Tom looked away to conceal a smile. "We'll get some in Athens."

"Athens," she repeated. "I should have guessed that. ...But then, so might the law."

"Yes, they might," he agreed.

"Well, you don't seem worried about it," she puzzled. "...Is that because you have friends there, and you're relying on them to hide you?"

"I could ask it of some."

"But they wouldn't if they knew exactly what you did," she said with a bit too much calculation.

"Mandria, we're not staying, but while we are there, you'd better not interfere—or would you enjoy sleeping outside, like this, all winter?"

"No," she conceded, miserably. "No, I wouldn't enjoy another night like that."

"Neither would I," he said, trying to forget the feel of her against him. "...Anyway, it's time we got started," he rose. But as he helped Mandria up, her foot gave way and he was holding her against him again. There was no denying the heated emotion within him. A single sigh would have baffled it into flame. And that made him angry. On impulse—or maybe to prove he could conquer this particular weakness—he kissed her, taking his own bitter-sweet time about it. Then, looking into her eyes, certain she wanted to recite a whole litany of curses, he placed fingers over lips that were already forming her favorite insult. "Wait!—No, wait, lady!" he insisted. "I know you want my head on a platter, but that kiss...well, it was merely a thank you from me—for the baby." It was the only thing he could think of, even if it did seem to make her angrier. ...But damn it all, he was angrier too. He hadn't proved anything, except that the fires of yesterday still lived and that she could so easily control his life again. In retaliation, he assumed the superior attitude that would force the poison from her mouth and allow his retreat. "And now," he stepped back to make her a sardonic bow, "You may rain curses upon my head.—But only as long as it takes me to pack the horse." And he walked away.

"You...you can take your *thank you* straight to hell!" she yelled at his back. Yet the rest of her tirade went unsaid, for it took her remaining strength to stay erect. She sent him a glare for that too, daring him to notice that his kiss could affect her. ...Then the vision reappeared in torturous clarity: Tom's groping, blood-smeared hands; the sound of the bed frame groaning each time he moved beside Nicole's battered, deathly-still body. And the horrid smells: blood; vomit; whiskey; rancid lamp oil; charred wood; and... And Mandria shrugged away a feeling of annoyance. Some tiny thing kept pricking at her subconscious then becoming lost in the total macabre picture. But was it any wonder? She glared at Tom again with fully restored resentment. Yes, this time her nightmare had come at an opportune moment. ...*He will never catch me unawares again,* she swore inwardly.—*Never!*

CHAPTER 4

The trip into Athens was a quiet one, and riding behind Tom again, Mandria was able to view a landscape bathed in the pinks of early morning light. It was a place of knobby clay hills, totally opposite from her native low country;—*as Tom and I are opposite,* she thought. Yet her eyes could not deny the beauty here and the artist in her instinctively chose scenes she'd like to paint: a rolling meadow, dotted with wild flowers, sprinkled with glistening dew and crowned with smatterings of fog; over there, a weathered old barn that leaned tiredly into a morning breeze; and there, a young boy carrying a large ripe pumpkin as he hurried along a lane of glorious autumn trees. *A boy,* she thought then, *much like Tom might have been...*

Tom was doing some reminiscing of his own. Susan Rutledge had been his mother's first and truest friend in Athens; one of his secondary school teachers, though only a few years his senior; and later, during his college years... Well, he'd always known where he stood with Susan and they'd parted friends. But then, he knew where he stood with Mandria too. Tom nodded, wondering at the choices life forced people to make—and about his sanity for still preferring the woman riding behind him.

Though many of the houses in town were still dark, he knew a light would shine from Susan's kitchen. She was never one to lie abed anyway, but this was Saturday, her baking day and she'd likely been at it for hours. He sniffed the air appreciatively as they dismounted before her small, neatly kept cottage. Yes, he definitely smelled cinnamon buns. And he smiled as he led Mandria to the door, where his knock was immediately answered.

"Why—Thomas Phillip Scott!" smiled the pretty raven-haired woman who was hugging him now.

And Mandria noted that, in spite of a flour smudge on her cheek and a frilly apron tied at her waist, the woman was simply regal. She certainly did justice to the pristine crispness of her white blouse and the fit of a close A-line skirt too. Mandria considered herself above average height, but this one was taller, for where she had to rise on tiptoe to peek over Tom's shoulder, here was a woman whose head easily rested there standing flat footed. Too easily, in fact…

"Oh, it's so good to see you!" Susan continued, now pressing slender fingers along his face. "Just as handsome as ever, I see."

"And you are even more beautiful," he replied, removing the flour smudge. "As generous too, I hope. Susan, I am purely starving!"

"Hope-to-my-die?" she giggled.

"Hope-to-my-die!" he replied; … hugging her again.

"Now, where are my manners?" she said backing into the kitchen. "Come in, both of you, and sit down here," she indicated the table. "I'm just taking a batch of cinnamon buns from the oven—your favorite, if I remember correctly," she said over her shoulder.

And as Mandria hobbled herself into a chair, she watched Susan hobble toward the stove. …*We make a fine pair*, she thought sarcastically. …*Wonder if he crippled her too?*

"There;—just for you," Susan smiled, and placing the buns before him, she bustled after the coffee pot and extra cups. "Well, Tom, are you going to introduce this young lady or must I keep pretending she isn't here?" Susan asked as she sat down to join them.

"My name is Mandria Lucas," she spoke for herself. "And you can expect no better manners from him!"

"Mandria Lucas *Scott*," Tom corrected. "My wife, Susan, but not very happy about it, as you can see. Mandria, this is Susan Rutledge, the friend Allen stayed with until I could send for him."

"...My lands," Susan looked from one to the other, noting the green and blue sparks fly between them. "A new bride, Tom— and you're spatting already? Shame on you both! Here, have some cinnamon buns. Maybe they'll sweeten your moods."

Mandria said nothing as she hungrily savored the hot, buttery confection. It was just the most delicious thing she could hope for and she readily took two more at Susan's insistence.

"You've come a long way from Savannah—and riding double on horseback?" Susan said glancing from the window at the tethered animal. "That would be enough to put anyone's nerves on edge—even those so newly married."

"Then you did get my letters?" Tom asked and smiled at her in a way Mandria found more than friendly.—And when had been writing letters to another woman?

"Yes, I got them and I would have answered eventually;—hope-to-my-die!" she added, whereupon they shared yet another laugh. "It's just that I stay so busy, I usually save writing duties for a cold winter night. It's cozy sitting before a warm fire, pen in one hand; a hot buttered rum in the other."

"Well, you won't have to answer mine now," he bantered. "And should we be in town some evening, we may stop to share your fire and a toddy."

"You will?" Susan looked at Tom with what Mandria considered too much interest. "You're moving back to Athens?" she finished, placing a hand on his arm.

"I'm hoping it's temporary," he nodded. "But we will be here until the baby is born this spring."

"A baby?" she extolled in delight—and Mandria looked away with a sigh. "—Oh, please, don't be embarrassed, Mandria!" Susan turned to her. "Early announcements may not be in fashion, but that is such nonsense.—Besides," she was patting Tom's arm again, "knowing him as I do, you'll likely stay that way most of your married life!"

"I do not fancy myself his brood-mare!" Mandria retorted, catching another teasing glance that had just passed between them.

"—And neither am I blind! Would you two like to be alone?" she rose, favoring her sore foot while hobbling about the room.

Tom nodded. "Susan, forgive her rudeness. She was not raised that way and I'm sure her mother would be appalled by her behavior."

"My mother was not kidnapped and half crippled by a mad man!" she spat.

"No, but she married one!" Tom returned.

"My sakes," Susan stood, looking from one to the other. "If you're going to do battle in my kitchen, let me clear away the china first— But no, I've a better idea," she said, going for a water pail. "Both of you stay here and settle this, while I tend my morning chores." And she went out the back door.

"I did too!" Mandria began at once.

"You did-too what?" Tom turned to face her.

"I also married a mad-man!"

"Well, if I wasn't then, you are driving me to it now," he came to tower over her. "And I would strongly recommend that you curb your tongue, lady, or—"

"Or what? Will you break more of my bones? Tell me, did you also cripple that—that Miss Susan Hope-to-my-die?"

"Mandria, shut up and lower your voice, damn it!" he grasped her arms. "Susan was born with her deformity and has taken abuse for it most of her life! There was no cause for your snide remarks, either— and I'll stand for no more of them!"

"Oh? Will you beat me if I disobey? You're just so good at that!"

"No, I won't beat you," he drew her hard against him. "You'd enjoy proving me a brute. But I could kiss you again—and if that didn't shut you up...?" he left the rest to her imagination.

"You bastard!" she seethed. "You wouldn't dare!"

"Make love to you?" he smiled tauntingly. "I could and like it or not, you'd respond. I wouldn't stop until you did."

"Never!" she hissed. "Never, damn you!"

Still holding her, Tom laughed. "How soon she forgets! Not long ago, you said responding to my touch was something you couldn't help anymore than breathing."

"Let go of me!" she shouted. "That was before you forgot your marriage vows and nearly killed Nico!"

"And that never happened!" he shouted back. "—Oh, hell, what's the use in arguing about it!" And gruffly scooping her into his arms, he started up a kitchen stairway.

Mandria protested his every step, in every way she could, but nonetheless, found herself dumped, unceremoniously, onto a bed from which she scrambled off the far side, to glare at him.

"Don't worry," he said then, "I haven't the time to spare you.— Now," he added deliberately. "Rest if you can, lady. I'm going for supplies again and we'll leave here about noon." And with that, he locked her in, even as she pounded on the other side of the door.

When that failed to prove useful, Mandria rushed to the window, ready to fill the outside air with her fury. But as she reached for the latch, she spotted Susan in the garden below and paused to watch when Tom joined her. She kissed his cheek as they settled on a low rock wall. And while they talked, their heads stayed bent close together—or rather, while Tom talked, for Susan only listened And her occasional comments were always accompanied by another touch. "Oh, you are a bastard," Mandria uttered. "You must know that woman is in love with you." When Tom rose to leave—when he bent to place a kiss on Susan's cheek—Mandria turned away, in tears, unsure of the feeling tormenting her now. ...*Is it jealousy?* she wondered as she sank on the edge of the bed to smother her sobs in a pillow. *After all Tom has put me through, is it possible to hate a man and be jealous of another woman in his life at the same time?* "No!" she swore adamantly. "Damn him, no!" And yet, the tears continued to fall...

-------◁◈▷-------

Some time later, Susan brought up bath articles and Tom followed on her heels with a tub. Once it was filled, both left her to enjoy her coveted privacy. As much as she could anyway, because this time, he hadn't locked her in and she couldn't lock him out with more than a chair against the door. Nonetheless, she was soon in the tub, where she found new reason for cursing Tom as she washed her hair and pulled out a ton of tangles, bits of grass and those stubborn beggar's lice weeds. But even the pleasure of being clean again was lessened, because as she dressed and brush-dried her hair, she had to listen to he and Susan laughing down in the kitchen. Yes, it would be hard forcing herself to join them again—and she wouldn't have had she not been led by the nose. But the venison stew Susan promised for lunch smelled so delicious. It was, and Mandria enjoyed every bite, in spite of the quieted atmosphere once she entered the room...

———◈———

By one o'clock, they were mounted and on their way, towing a little pack mule behind. But Tom had put Mandria before him again and she wondered why, as she thought they'd both been more comfortable riding the other way. His arms seemed to hem her in; his warm breath, contrasting with the chilly air, caused her skin to prickle; and now, he was repeatedly brushing her wind-swept tresses from his face.

"I would appreciate it if you'd tie up your hair," he said after a time.

Mandria shrugged, gathering her thick curls to the front of a shoulder. "I've nothing to tie it with," she responded, at which point a breeze tossed them right back across his mouth.

"Damn," he sputtered, pulling the horse to a stop.

"Well, I could ride behind you," she reminded him. "I'd rather anyway."

"I'd rather you did too. But it wouldn't be safe, considering the terrain we have to cover," And sliding to the ground, he went to the mule, rummaged through one of the smaller bundles and returned with a length of bright green ribbon. "Here," he handed it up to her. "Will you fix it now?"

Mandria sat looking at the pretty color for a moment and turned matching green eyes on him. "...Why did you buy ribbon?"

"I don't know. I've seen you wear them," he nodded, having no better reason to offer. He sure as hell wasn't going to admit the color had reminded him of her eyes.

"And you hoped to bribe me with gewgaws?" she accused.

"No, damn it! I just thought you'd like some ribbon, that's all," he said in exasperation.

"Did *she* rate a gift from you, too—Miss Hope-to-my-die?

"Susan is a *giver,* lady. Not a *taker,*" he replied.

"So, I'm the taker?"

"I didn't say that," he nodded again.

"Then what did you say?"

"I said tie your hair up—please!" And he swung back into the saddle behind her.

"You've always done that to me!" she furiously caught her hair in a careless bow. "You never answer any question I ask!"

"Knit picker," he remarked. "When did you ever listen to any answer I gave?"

"I did once—before I was so cruelly betrayed," she straightened.

"Lady, we were both betrayed," he started the horse forward again. "And as of now, I still have no proof other than my word."

"And I still have perfect eyesight—which makes your word a lie."

Tom heaved a sigh. "Mandria, I am not going to bicker with you all the way through these hills," he pointed up the trail they were ascending.

And they had been climbing steadily higher for some time, but Mandria was so intent on harassing Tom, she hadn't noticed the earthen walls growing steeper on either side of them. "Hills?" she pointed too. "This is a mountain!"

"No, we're in the hills. But these trails can be hazardous and require my complete attention—which I can not give and argue with you at the same time."

Mandria shaded her eyes looking for the tree-tops. "But why must we go this way? Surely there is a real road somewhere."

There was. A nearly flat road passed close to the valley Tom had chosen, but he wasn't going to make it easy for her to plan an escape and had no qualms about deceiving her sense of direction. "This way leads to your home for the winter, lady and I'd like to reach it before nightfall. Now, would you kindly give me some peace?"

So still craning her neck upward, she kept silent as they moved on.—And, ever, upward. It was truly an alien world to her. A world of steep angles and deep, cold shadows; of oddly balanced boulders and vegetation that seemed to spring from solid rock; of water that leaked from crevices leaving its wet sheen in thousands of places; of trees growing so close and so dense and so tall they blotted out the sky. A strange, alien world, this…

They had rounded an especially perilous bend when Mandria found herself overlooking a deep gorge shrouded in gray clouds. "Oh, my God!" she pressed backwards and against Tom without realizing it. "We're up so high—and you said we weren't in the mountains!"

"We're not," he answered. "These are only foothills. The Blue Ridge and Smokies are further north."

"But how could anything be higher than this?" she still questioned.

"Well, I was born in the Smokies and snow stays on the upper peaks there nearly year round, if that gives you any notion of height. It's really beautiful too, summer and winter."

"I think it sounds frightening.—And so does that," she tried to look away from the hazy gorge and couldn't. "It…it makes me feel so small."

"That's the way I felt seeing your ocean for the first time," he replied. "…But I never felt it here. I guess people tend to take their natural surroundings pretty much for granted."

"Well, I don't," she stiffened, suddenly aware of how she'd been leaning on Tom. "I love the sea—and I miss Savannah. Everything I love is there."

"Including your father," he said pointedly.

"And Nico," she counterpointed. So once again, they rode in silence.

Time passed and Mandria knew she was hopelessly lost. She had tried keeping track of direction at first, but they made so many turns and she was distracted so often, there were no directions for her to remember but up, down and around. And now, it seemed to be all downhill—straight down—into a small protected valley.

Then as they rode over near level ground, across a rolling, wheat-yellow, tree studded meadow, she spotted a cabin and wondered anxiously if Tom planned to stop. She dearly hoped so, for the air was no longer chilly, but cold. And God help her, she was starving again. ...*I'll weigh a ton before this is done,* she sighed aloud.

"Are you getting tired?" Tom asked.

"Yes; ...And hungry," she admitted, hoping he would heed a subtle hint. But he said nothing more. So when they drew close to the cabin, she repeated it. "Well, we could stop over there for something to eat. Wouldn't they ask us in—or let us pay for a meal?"

"You must learn to be more observant, lady. It could save your life out here. Now, look again. Do you see any signs of life around that cabin? Smoke from the chimney? Firewood cut? Pets or livestock? Raked yards or tilled earth in the fields?"

"...No," she said in disappointment. "I guess the place is abandoned."

"Well, not exactly," he stopped before the porch steps, and dismounted. "This is your home until spring," he lifted her down too.

Mandria followed him inside, looked about and shuttered. *Home* was truly a dismal sight. There was an icy feel to the air and dust motes swirled in a shaft of late afternoon sun that had fallen through the door behind them. Thicker coats of dust and grime lay upon the sparse, primitive furniture, which consisted of a table, two ladder-back chairs, an open wall cupboard, a sink well and an overturned milking stool. Animal hide covered the room's only window, and assailing her from the far end, was the smell of spattered and burned cooking grease that saturated the thick pile of ash in fireplace.

"It won't be so bad with some cleaning and repairs," Tom said, seeing her dismay. And the look she sent him was not one of agreement. "I'll bring in the supplies and start a fire," he turned, only to pause. "...I never thought to ask. Do you cook?"

"A little," she nodded, looking about again. But it hadn't improved any.

"Well, jerky and mush are my specialty, so will you cook for me—for us?" he quickly amended.

"If I'm to eat, I suppose I'll have to!" she retorted. This was just the ugliest room she'd ever seen. Why, a slave cabin at Marsh Haven would have seemed more a palace.

"That's a relief," he said heading out front.

As Mandria stood there, she realized she was looking at only half of her new domain, because in the dimness, she could now make out a door in each corner of the rear wall. Crossing to the nearest, on her right, she found a storage room lined with shelving and at the rear, a warped back door. Returning to the main room, she went toward the other door, pausing to upright the little stool and to sniff distainfully at that huge mound of grease-soaked ashes in the raised stone hearth.

Then, all at one time, the door at Mandria's elbow flew open, something darted behind her and scurried for the storage room, causing her to straighten in fright and whack her head beneath the mantle! Her vision blurred; her ears rang; and feeling suddenly faint, she sank to the hearth, holding her head.

"Mandria,—damn it!" Tom yelled, either from the front door or the bottom of a well. But no, he'd dropped a mountainous bundle in the middle of the floor and was racing into the store room. Then, he seemed to be calling her from out back and all around the cabin. "Mandria!" he shouted, coming through the front door again.

"What?—For heaven's sake, what?" she moaned, still holding her head.

He was beside her in an instant. "It's not the baby? You're not—It's not the baby?"

"No; ...no, it's my head," she uttered. "I bumped it when..." Then her eyes widened, and in her fear, she was grasping his arm. "Something furry was in here! It—it ran past me into that store room and I bumped my head! ...But you were in there too," she puzzled. "Didn't you see it?"

"I just saw the back door standing open and thought you had... Well, never mind," he rose to lead her to a chair. "Sit down here. I want to look at your head."

ON THE FOOT OF A MOUNTAIN

"Tom, what could it have been?" she asked while he took down a lantern from the mantle.

He paused as he lit the wick. She had used his name, which usually meant trouble, so if there wasn't a bump on her head, he would sorely be tempted to put one there. "Well, a raccoon maybe, or a fox," he answered. And unloosening her hair ribbon, he tossed it on the table while examining her scalp. But she really had taken a nasty blow and he felt more satisfied with her story. It satisfied him too, when she reached for the ribbon and unconsciously smoothed out the wrinkles. She did like it, after all.

"No. No, it was larger than that—taller," she held up a hand in measurement. "It was waist high at least, and it seemed to stand upright. What creature does that?"

"Bears do," he nodded.

"Bears!" she exclaimed. "Inside, where you expect me to stay? With man-eating bears?"

"Lady, if it only came to your waist, it was just a cub. It won't be back, once we've settled in here—which we need to be doing," he said, retrieving one of the bundles for her. "Now, if you will unpack the foodstuffs, I'll go for wood and build you a cook fire." And with her nod, he left.

Mandria was still frightened that a bear had been in the cabin and she wanted to run after Tom, but knowing that would please him, kept her in place. "Well, I do have a lantern now and nothing will sneak by me again," she muttered as she began to transfer the staples from bundle to cupboard. Yet, she wondered about the incident—and that unexplored room. It had to be a bedroom, so what would a bear want from there?

Curious, she took the lantern, pushed the door all the way back, and stepped inside. Light flickered over the skeletal remains of a rope-bed, whose sad mattress sagged to the floor in the middle. There was nothing else in the room, except the cabin's second and only other window. Mandria thought of her elegant bedroom at home;—tried not to think of the one she'd decorated for Tom in shades of green; and a sad little sigh escaped her. "No one could be happy here," she told the walls. "And no baby should be born in such a hovel;—not even a baby someone wanted!"

"I brought in a pail of water and the firewood," Tom said from the doorway behind her. And his expression of disapproval said he'd overheard her speech. "Bring the lantern back in here, will you?" he finished, turning away.

Mandria followed and held the light while he cleared a spot in the ashes to build a fire. She hated it when he made her feel childish, but he should not have eavesdropped. Just as he should not been an unfaithful husband, a kidnapper—and the devil's own bastard! "So what are we going to do tonight?" she retaliated. "Sleep on the dirty floor?"

"It's no worse than the dirty ground you slept on last night—and it does have the requisite roof and walls," he pulled the lantern down to light a long straw, but ignored her attempted barbs. "There now," he rose as the kindling ignited. "I'll bring in more wood when I've tended the animals." But at the front door, he paused and looked back at her. "There are cook pots under the sick-well. A new frying pan and butcher knives are in this sack over here;—if you'd care to try you hand at *hovel* cookery?" And he left again.

"Damn him!" Mandria banged the lantern to the table. And when she found the frying pan, it received a banging too. "Hovel cookery," she muttered, turning to look over her supplies. "…Well, it won't be a feast, Mr. Scott, but it will be better than your damned jerky and mush!"

Tom could smell ham frying while he was still outdoors. But coming in with an arm load of logs, he didn't want to seem overly curious about her endeavor, so he peeked over her shoulder as he stacked the wood beside the fireplace. She finished spooning fried bits of meat into a pot of rice, covered it with a lid and swung that pot hook back over the fire. Then, she poured a spoon-bread batter into the hot grease left in the frying pan, put a lid on that too, and placed the pan on a grate to the side of the fire. Green beans and ham chunks cooked in a smaller pot on the other hook.

"Are we to eat from the pots?" she asked, not turning around. "I didn't find any table ware."

"Oh, that basket is still on the porch," he went toward the door. "And you can thank Susan for giving it to us."

"While you're waiting for me to do that, don't hold your breath," she uttered under her own. *...Maybe he expects me to thank Susan for being in love with him too,* she added a thought.

"Want me set the table?" Tom asked, coming back with a woven hamper.

"If you're capable," she replied tersely. And while he went about that, she quartered two sweet red apples for their dessert.

"Let's treat ourselves to a cup of tea, shall we?" Tom said from beside her.

"...Tea?" she asked hopefully.

"Tea," he answered, holding up a tin container and a cornflower-blue glazed pot. "If that's water you're heating in the back, I'll fill this and set it to steeping."

"Yes," she nodded, "...please," she blinked away tears, certain nothing so civil as a cup of tea was ever had in this cabin. Then she turned, saw the table and her eyes grew misty again. "Oh," she said. "It...it's lovely."

A white cloth now draped the plain little table. A blue cornflower pattern graced the dinnerware, which included plates, cups and saucers, a platter and serving bowls. Pewter flatware gleamed in the lantern light, and more light twinkled along the rims of two tall water glasses.

"It belonged to Susan's mother. She said to consider it a wedding gift," Tom explained. "And there's more in the basket—the rest of the set and some other things for you. She even lent us a clock for the mantle," he added, winding and placing it up there.

"...Well, maybe I will thank her," Mandria managed. "We'll eat now," she nodded and until they were seated, she continued to fight that ridiculous urge to cry.

When Tom pushed his twice emptied plate aside, he smiled. "Lady, your meal was delicious."

"So was your tea," she refilled her cup. "...If only we'd had some lemon," she said wistfully.

"In November?" he laughed. "In a foot hill cabin in north Georgia, you're wishing for a lemon?"

"Savannah has them in November—and December" she tilted her chin stubbornly refusing to admit a fondness for his laughter.

"But of course," he said sardonically. "I keep forgetting: *everything you love is in Savannah.*"

"Well, it is," she replied. If he wanted to argue, she was more than glad to accommodate him. "And we don't have bears in our houses that turn doorknobs and go in and out as they please."

"...What doorknobs?" And now he looked more puzzled than argumentative. "There is a latch string and bar on the back door."

"But not on the bedroom door," she pointed. "I heard it turn before the bear came out. It clicked."

"Mandria, bear cubs aren't that smart. The door had to be standing open—or ajar, at least—and you must have heard a hinge squeak."

"As I told you—about *another occasion*—I know what I saw. And heard," she insisted. "I heard the knob turn and click and then the hinges squeaked. Check it for yourself."

Which Tom did and found she was right. He also found it took a firm grasp to twist the rusted knob. ...*What in the hell?* he puzzled inwardly. *No bear opened this door. ...So what did?* Still pondering the mystery, he returned to the table and sat down while Mandria stacked the dishes on the sink and began washing them "I knew I was right," she said smugly, not bothering to turn from her chore. "And I was right about that other occasion too. I know exactly what I saw in that hotel room." When the expected denial didn't follow, she swung around, ready to confront him, but he was no longer in the room. "The damn Puma cat!—Where is he now?" she muttered, starting for the front door. But spotting Tom in the storage room, she stopped and watched as he pulled in the latch string and barred the door. "What are you doing?—Locking me in again? Where would I go out here?"

"It's just a precaution," he answered. "Do you need more water before I lock the front door?"

"No. ...Are you trying to frighten me again?" she asked.

"No;—yes. ...Well, we are in the wilds, lady. It's just wise to be careful. So don't throw food scraps in the yard for a while—not even bread crumbs for the birds. But rest easy. I'm sure your bear won't return."

"You are so trying to frighten me!" she said going back to her dishes. "—And you're doing it too!"

"Good. Then you'll remember what I said," Tom replied, and that brought on another round of silence as he went to his stash, retrieved a stack of blankets and made them a pallet before the fire.

Mandria didn't argue about sleeping next to him that night. Of course, her back was turned and one of the blankets was rolled and wedged between them.

Tom was content with that too. He was not content with the riddle of the bear, however, and it plagued him a long while before he could sleep. He did not like riddles—never had—and until this one was solved, he would remain alert to all that went on near the cabin...

CHAPTER 5

For the next few weeks, Tom worked from sun-up until long after dark, winterizing the place. Using a mixture of clay mud and field straw, he re-caulked spaces around the windows and sealed any gaps found between the log walls. He patched the roof with tree bark shingles and laid in a huge supply of firewood and kindling. He emptied an out building, erected a tree branch corral and turned that area into a small stable and work shop—glad to have found and made use of the many tools that had been stored there.

The labor needed inside the cabin seemed to get done at the same time. First, he drug the sad looking mattress outside, emptied it and washed the cover. While that dried in the sun, which took most of two days, he rewove the bed frame with what was salvageable of the original rope and filled in with the new rope he'd used to strap their supplies on the pack mule. He gave the hearth a thorough cleaning and from the surrounding fields, gathered hay for the animals as well as sweet, fresh straw to re-stuff the mattress and several grain sack cushions and pillows. In the evenings, he continued to lug his supply stash into the store room and organized the goods along the shelves.

One morning, in the corner by the fireplace, Mandria discovered a straw broom he'd made. It was so like the ones used to sweep the yard and walks at Marsh Haven, that it made her homesick again—for which Tom received an icy stare when next he passed through the room.

Somehow, he even found time for hunting and haunches of deer meat and rabbit now hung curing in the store room. From the pelts, he fashioned another insulating curtain to replace a missing one on the bedroom window, and from the scraps, he made Mandria a pair of soft slippers. These, she also found beside the hearth.

Mandria was glad he stayed busy, though. It kept him from bothering her. Not that she was the least bit busy. She did cook and sweep, but couldn't seem to stay awake for anything more. And had he been underfoot, she knew he would have made reference to her pregnancy being the cause and the very thought brought tears to her eyes. ...But then, so did everything else, lately. She had just never felt so out of sorts—and, of course, that had to be his fault too...

On this evening, as she was starting supper, Tom came in carrying an oversized barrel he'd commandeered from the eaves and carefully reconstructed. "Where do you want this?" he asked.

Mandria sat by the fire peeling an onion. "What is it?" she sniffed, wiping her smarting eyes with the back of a hand.

"Come and see," he answered, lowering the barrel to the floor.

"Oh!" she grasped the edge as if it might vanish. "Oh!" she rubbed the smooth, newly planed interior. Then she was truly crying and couldn't seem to stop.

"Mandria?" Tom puzzled. "What is it?"

"A bathtub!" she looked at him as if he'd lost his senses. Hadn't he just carried it in?

"Well, I know that," he chuckled. "I meant, why are you crying?"

Mandria couldn't explain it, but he had to be the culprit. He kept her in these sparse surroundings; he forced her into this world of vertical landscapes; he denied her the horizontal simplicity she adored in her marshlands. Didn't it follow, then, that he was responsible if she cried over bathtubs? It was just another of his bribes—like the ribbons, the slippers and even the broom. She knew all that, and yet she cried most because she wanted the tub so badly. And, she decided, if keeping it meant humoring him—just this one time—she would have to do it. "Onions," she seized on the obvious. "Peeling onions makes me cry." And turning, she went back to her meal preparations.

Tom shrugged and pressed it no further, but he did hope she liked his gift. She wouldn't want to be reminded, but if he'd kept track of the date correctly, this was the 25ᵗʰ of November and their fourth month of marriage. Why he had troubled to celebrate it in some way remained a mystery, but he had and he wanted her to accept the damn tub.

As they ate, he noticed the number of wishful glances Mandria sent that way, and a smile touched his lips. Was it possible he had finally done something to please her? ...Dare he try for a second miracle? Logic told him to let it be, but he couldn't seem to hear that plainly enough. So while she cleared the table, he drew the tub close to the fire and after several trips to the well, had it partially filled. Other buckets of water were put on to heat and now he knelt before the fire, adding logs and stoking it for greater warmth within the room too.

Mandria finished her tasks and watched Tom ease back on his heels, hands resting on those buckskinned thighs. At one time, the sight would have sent her flying to him; throwing herself on his back; hugging him from behind to start with... Then, realizing how dangerous her thoughts were, she shakily lowered herself on a chair at the table, wondering if this was her punishment for allowing him a single concession. Did wanting a bath make her a traitor to all that was right and just? She had sworn he wouldn't catch her unawares again and now, from half a room away, he was causing her to feel that he had.

Not that Tom had attempted to breach the walls she'd erected—well, other than the kiss beside the lake and the threat he made at Susan's, he hadn't. And she still kept that blanket roll between them at night, which he hadn't questioned either. No, it was from herself that she needed the most protection and knowing so—admitting it—made her feel awkward. She hated Tom; that was a fact. She wanted him; that was a fact too. And both made it imperative, as never before, that she bathe alone. "...Are you fixing the tub for me?" she finally asked.

"I thought you might want to try it out," he nodded.

"Well...is it very cold outside?"

"Yes, ma'am, it is," he still looked into the fire. "Winter is with us, I'm afraid."

"Then you could go in the bedroom while I bathe—if you'd stay until I call you."

Tom turned, sat on the hearth and looked at Mandria. She never ran out of ways to hurt him. Now she was making it seem his whole purpose in giving her the tub was a chance to ogle her bare flesh. And with that angry notion, his own stubborn streak surfaced. "Now, we have been through this before. I see no reason for standing out in the cold—nor being sent to my room like a bad little boy. Lady, you are expecting my child and damn it, you did not get that way by yourself. So why this attack of modesty when it comes to taking a bath?"

"It's not modesty; it—it's you!" she aimed at her favorite target, because she would never admit the truth to him. "I don't want you watching for the baby to show," she alibied

"Well, I do that anyway and whether you're dressed or not, it won't stop me—though, I will credit you for trying. If you can slip into that tub the way you slip into bed, there will be precious little to see."

"Thank you so much!" she snapped. "I do try never to offend those around me."

"…And what the hell does that mean?" Tom asked in exasperation.

"It was clear enough the night I found you with Nico! Even when you'd half-killed her, you found nothing offensive about her body. And right in front of me, you wanted to—to have her again!"

"Oh, hell, here we go again," Tom rose and removing the buckets from the fire, he filled her tub. "Your bath, my lady," he made her a bow. Then going to the store room, he returned with his coat and a bottle of whiskey. "You know something, Mandria," he paused at the front door. "I sometimes wish I could remember the sin I'm accused of committing. I wonder if I enjoyed myself enough to make it worth all of this."

"Oh!" she fumed. "—Even for you, that was rotten!"

"It was rotten being set up the way I was too," he uttered as he left the cabin.

Needless to say, Mandria did not have a leisurely bath. Anger powered the scrubbing she gave her skin, her hair, her underthings and even her buckskins. Fear that Tom might return got her out of the tub far sooner than she would have liked, whereupon frustration brought forth a curse. "Damn him!" she stood looking at her wet clothes. For now that she was out and dry, what was she to wear? "Damn him!" she repeated, stomping off to the bedroom with a towel draped about her. "He makes me so mad I can't think straight!" she slammed the door, and went to a wall peg, which had become her closet…

A few minutes later, Tom returned, quaking from the cold. Going directly to the fire, he didn't wonder that Mandria wasn't there. He heard the bedroom door slam and figured she'd gone on to bed to avoid speaking with him again. Anyway, he was freezing—and still angry about spending the last hour huddled between the mule and the horse. "At least they didn't yell at me," he grumbled, adding the rest of his bottle to the left-over coffee and swinging the pot over the fire. Then, pulling a chair front and center, he removed his boots and propped his icy feet on the warm hearth, waiting for his brew to heat…

Mandria knew Tom had come in and certainly had planned to go to bed—especially since the only thing she could find that fit were the long-johns. Then she remembered that her clothes were still in the tub and unless they were hung to dry, she'd be forced to wear this ridiculous outfit again tomorrow. However, forcing herself back through the doorway now would not be an easy thing. She had never felt so clownish; nor would she ever be more vulnerable to his remarks. But it had to be done, so raising her chin she went, passing close behind his chair.

A blur of color was all Tom saw of Mandria, until turning the other way. "Lady?" he grinned; and she cringed, swearing to slap him with her wet chemise if he laughed. But humor died when her seat flap came unfastened. First one side fell as she stooped to wring the water from her clothes; the other as she stretched to drape her things along the mantle, which left him staring directly at her exposed and shapely bottom. "Are you…warm enough?" was what he managed—but could not manage to look away. "I mean, you'll catch cold with your bare ... feet," he added, hoping they were bare too, because he certainly didn't know. "Oh, hell," he groaned. "You'd better cover yourself, God damn it." And drawing her backwards a step, he rebuttoned the flap himself.

"Oh!" Mandria blushed, her color rivaling the long-johns. "—Oh, how perfectly awful!" And she flew to the bedroom, slamming the door again. It seemed to be a night made for that.

"...Perfectly shaped, maybe," Tom mused. "But I didn't see anything awful about it." And going for a cup, he enjoyed some of the hot spiked coffee...

After a time, Mandria returned wrapped in a blanket. "It...it's cold in there," she began.

"Leave the door open, as we usually do," he shrugged. "The heat will go in."

"I know," she nodded. "But I'm not sleepy any more."

"Well ...maybe you've finally caught up on your rest," he suggested.

"Maybe so," she huddled sideways on the hearth and turned her feet toward the fire—which, trivially, Tom noted, were slippered. "Is there more of that coffee?" she asked.

"Here; taste mine first," he offered. "Wouldn't want you saying I plied you with drink, unbeknownst."

"What's in it?" she tasted.

"Bourbon. I'm still trying to thaw out."

"Well, I'm cold too. And my hair is still damp, so I think I'll have some while it dries," she went for her own cup and filled it. For a time then, they sat quietly watching the flames. "I do wish I had a brush," she said then, pulling her fingers through her hair.

"My comb is in the bedroom. You're welcome to use it," Tom offered.

"I do use it;—I did tonight, but you can't tell, can you?"

"...What would a brush do differently?" he asked curiously.

Mandria opened her mouth to answer, but closed it again. Nodding then, she got up to rewarm her cup.

"Did I say something wrong?" Tom asked, never sure when he had or hadn't.

"No," she replied. "A dissertation on combs and brushes just seems useless, that all."

"At least we weren't shouting about it," Tom commented. "That was kind of nice."

"True," she agreed, curling up on the hearth again. And after a few more sips, she asked. "Whose cabin is this?"

"Susan's now. Her grandparents settled this valley."

"Well, what is it the two of you kept saying—that Hope-to-my-die?"

"It's the same thing as *cross my heart and hope to die*. Only that's as close as Allen could get as a child. Now, it's just a joke between all of us;—a reminder, I guess, of how long we've been friends."

"...And did you and Susan ever come up here together?"

"Yes. She likes to hunt—and is quite an expert archer."

"She is also in love with you," Mandria said matter of factly.

"Lady, that's absurd." But Tom's denial lacked something and both knew it. He was not really comfortable with where this might be headed, ...and yet, he was definately fascinated by Mandria's strange mood. So hoping to change only the topic, he rose to refill his cup and politely offered her some too.

"Yes, please," she accepted, feeling more relaxed than she had in a long while. "But I'm not stupid, you know."

"...I've never thought so," Tom stood looking at her up-tilted face. Something was different about her, but what exactly, escaped him.

"And I'm curious about you and Kathy—I mean Susan," she shrugged, as if to say, it was difficult keeping track of his harem. "Anyway, as I'm no longer involved, I thought we might talk about it—as adults, of course."

"Of course," he nodded, sitting before her again. He was starting to enjoy this now, and wondered why.

"Yes, and I do have a lot to ask.—But," she took aim behind a finger, "will he answer? That is the question."

Stretching his legs toward the fire again, Tom had to chuckle, for suddenly, he recognized the change. This was the Mandria he'd fallen in love with—at her best. The one he'd brought from Aiken was a hollow shell by comparison. From the first, he'd known she was a passionate creature, but as she loved, so did she hate, denying him even a glimpse of her most alluring asset.—And that was the warmth; the graceful animation; the freedom of her gestures and expressions. Now, thanks to the whiskey, his *pretty lady* was here. Tom nodded in wonder. He didn't know how long her visit would last, but he'd do all he could to prolong it—which included answering her questions. She had already relegated his soul to the deepest pits of hell, so what did he have to lose? "Ask away, lady—whatever you'd like," he nodded again.

"Then admit that you've slept with Susan," her eyes narrowed slightly as she leaned forward, "—and that you know she is in love with you."

"Consider it done," he said simply.

"...Oh," she pulled back in surprise—and the color change in her eyes, delighted him. "Well, is she the reason you came back to Athens?"

"No. It was on her advice that I left. I guess her feelings were growing deeper than she wanted them to;—that, somehow, our roles had become reversed."

"What ...roles?" she asked, suspiciously.

"Susan had been one of my teachers, Mandria—and a family friend. During the years after Mama's death, when Allen and I were moving from farm to farm, her home was always open to us if we needed a place to stay. Then, two years ago, while I was still in college, she offered help with some of my courses and...well, we became involved."

"So the student ended up teaching the teacher a lesson—is that it?"

"Not exactly," he paused to admire the green ice crystals dance in her eyes and the pout on her beautiful mouth. "Susan is very proud of her accomplishments; of the life she has made for herself. I think she was just wise enough to see our paths led in different directions."

"Oh, I see. You didn't love her either."

"I did at first;—oh, I most certainly did. No one takes their first serious romance lightly. I'll wager you haven't forgotten yours."

Mandria resented that. Had he forgotten she was a virgin when she came to him; that *he* was her first serious romance? And that sparked a question. "—Was Susan a virgin before you landed in her life?"

"Well…I don't see what that has to do with anything, but no. When she was very young, she fell in love with a man and believed they would marry. But her deformity was more than he could accept— though it didn't keep him from taking advantage of her faith in him."

"You do the same thing. How is it you can use women so easily and then…just move on to the next one?" she waved a hand airily.

"Mandria, don't make me out a gigolo," he nodded. "I've been asked to move-on a number of times too—and I doubt those who did so, even remember my name."

"Don't bet on it," she said with a tilt of her chin. And because she hadn't meant to say that aloud, she rushed on. "But still, Susan, Kathy, me—even Nico? All of us are so different, yet none could hold you for long. …So what is it you're looking for in a woman? Do you even know?"

"Oh, yes, lady, I know," he answered, wanting to say he had married her for that reason. But she would run like a rabbit if he dared.

"When we were at Susan's house, did you…bed her while I was locked upstairs in that room?" But this was said with lowered eyes and the glimmer of tears in her lashes.

"No, Mandria!" he laughed aloud, trying to lighten the moment. "Just trying to keep up with you has been a full time job, believe me;—please!"

"I saw you with her in the garden. …I just wondered," she ran slender fingers over the design on the cup. Then lifting it to her lips, she drank deeply and sat looking into the dregs as if considering a decision.

Tom said nothing, content with watching her this openly. God, but she still intrigued him!

"Are you going to?" she asked suddenly.

"…Am I going to what?" he brought himself back with difficulty.

"See Susan—take her to bed again."

"No," he answered.

68

"She'd let you—even I could see that," she shrugged free of the confining blanket.

"The answer is still no," he repeated. "It's over and would serve no useful purpose." And again, he could not speak the whole truth; could not say that Mandria was the only woman he seemed to want.

"Like it is with us," she said now. "Time to cut ties and make new beginnings."

This, Tom could not let pass unchallenged. "It will never be over with us," he replied, rising to place another log on the fire. "The baby makes that impossible."

"Oh, yes, the baby!" she gave an ironic laugh and held her cup for more coffee "But tell me, won't raising an infant put a crimp in your romantic adventures? I'll bet you hadn't thought of that."

Tom said nothing as he gave her the last of the coffee or while he knelt to poke the crackling logs into a better alignment.

"Well?" she asked, daring him to meet her eyes. "Had you considered what a burden this baby could be?"

She was so close. Tom could see the fire-glow dance softly on her skin; in the moss green depth s of her eyes; and he wanted very much to kiss her. "…I'll manage," was all he could find to say.

"I wish I was as sure of my future," she uttered. And her abandoned tone drew his eyes to her again. "I can't seem to find any point to it."

"Mandria—damn it, this is so wrong," he reached to cover her hands with his. "You belong with me; to me and our child—"

"No—damn you!" she rose, backing away. "You won't use me again, Tom Scott—never again!" And fleeing to the bedroom, she remained, crying herself to sleep.

Tom felt utterly helpless—useless, too—and having to hear her sobs made it no better. He finished that miserable night bedded down on the floor before the fire…

CHAPTER 6

A s time passed, Mandria grew curious about the life she carried, in spite of swearing she wouldn't. To conceal the unbuttoned waistband of her skirt, she'd taken to wearing her blouse untucked, certain Tom wouldn't notice. He did, but had learned these observations were best kept to himself. She was frightened when she felt the baby's first gentle flutters of movement, but happy too, as it meant half of her time in captivity was now over. When the movements grew steadily stronger—and if Tom was away from the cabin—she'd often raise her blouse to watch in fascination. It was something she wanted to keep secret and wondered at the why of that. ...*Because it would lessen my enjoyment if Tom shares this too? Yes*, she admitted, *that is the truth of it...*

By early December, however, Tom discovered her secret on his own. One very cold morning, she awoke to find him raised on an elbow over her, an open palm pressed to her stomach. "What do you think you're doing?" she demanded, noting his strangely enchanted expression. His head was cocked to one side as if listening for distant sound and the smile he wore caused her to try moving away.

"Be still, Mandria!" he said, holding her in place. And then it happened: a roiling wave of movement beneath his wide-spread fingers—his seed, sprung to life; growing and protected within her. "Damn!" he declared, falling back to his pillow. "I'll just be damned," he said happily. "I was laying here, lady, thinking about getting up, when I saw the cover move over your belly—"

"Well I'm so sorry you were disturbed," she said sarcastically. And because he ignored that and still looked so happy, she rolled toward the wall, fighting tears.

"I wasn't complaining," he turned her face back to his; pausing when he saw her misty eyes. "Was the baby? I didn't press too hard; —Mandria, I didn't hurt you, did I?"

"…No," she answered after a moment, disliking him intensely for making his concern sound genuine.

"Well, how long have you felt movements?" he asked now.

"A few weeks," she uttered, toying with her own fingers. "…And the kicks have grown stronger, so it must be healthy." Then, because she had shared something personal, he had to be censored for causing it. "It will have to be strong to survive a life with you!"

"I plan to love and care for our child. Is that so wrong?"

"It—it's selfish, that's what it is. The poor thing will come to depend on your love—and we both know why that would be a mistake! What will happen to the baby when the law comes and takes you back to prison? No, it would be less cruel, all around, to let it be adopted, as I still want to do."

Tom sat up beside her. "Your advice would make perfect sense—if I were guilty. But I'm not, and I won't agree to giving away the only child I'm ever likely to have, when there is still hope of proving my innocence."

"Well, you can't prove anything from here," she sat up too. "And hiding only proves guilt."

"I know it looks that way, but what else could I do? Saving the baby was just more important than saving my damned reputation. But," he paused, "…when the baby is born and I know you are both well and safe, I do intend to straighten out my life."

"You'll turn yourself in?" she asked in honest surprise.

"Lady, I know you'd like seeing that," he laughed, "but I'm hoping my brother and friends haven't been idle. If they've found a way to clear me, I'm taking the baby to Savannah and raising him in our— *my*—own home," he corrected before she had to. "If not, well, there has to be a place somewhere between here and the Pacific Ocean where I can make a new home for my brother and child."

"But that's crazy.—You'd just disappear forever?"

Because she had listened longer than ever before—and before she grew defensive or angry—Tom had to end the conversation. So rising, he began to dress. "Maybe it is crazy and I hope it doesn't come to pass. No, I'd rather present a solid defense and beat this thing. You wouldn't deny anyone that chance, would you—not even me?" And going to the hearth, he stoked the morning fire to life.

Mandria sat looking at him from the bed. "No, as long as the defense wasn't contrived—and yours would have to be. Why, you can't name one reputable witness and you know it."

Tom paused in the doorway only long enough to smile at her. "What about your mother?" he asked.

"My mother?" she exclaimed. "Come back here! What could my mother have to do with your defense?" But getting no answer and swearing under her breath, she climbed from the bed and stomped into the main room. "Thomas Scott?" she called. "Damn it, where are you?"

"Here," he answered from the store room. "Come and look, lady. It's been snowing."

"…Snowing?" she hurried to join him at the back door. And for a time, all else was forgotten.

"It must have fallen during the night, "Tom said while buttoning on his coat. "I'd better feed the animals and bring in more wood and water. It could start up again, by the look of those clouds to the north."

"It's…so beautiful! Like a painting…," Mandria gazed from the door in wonder. Then, she looked at him with pleading in her eyes. "I want to go too. Please—can I go out with you?"

"Get dressed, then," he agreed, stepping down into the yard. "I'll come back for you in a few minutes. And you'd better wear my extra socks;—the long-johns, too. …But for heaven's sake, button all the flaps?" And surprising Tom, she actually smiled as she closed the door.

When he'd finished stacking logs on the front porch, Tom went in for the water buckets and found Mandria bundled and ready to go.

And surprising him again, she had a hot cup of coffee waiting, lightly sugared, the way he liked it. "…Thank you," he nodded, wise enough to make no more of it.

"Well, hurry up," she paced impatiently from the door to the window. "It won't melt before we go out, will it?"

"No," he smiled, enjoying her excitement. It had been a long while since he'd seen her eyes sparkle so and he vowed to make the adventure a happy one.

As they started toward the well in a foot-deep snow, Tom held her arm while she learned to maneuver. "Got your snow-legs now?" he asked.

"…I think so," she nodded, brushing a curl from her cheek. "Listen how it crunches when you step down!"

And while Tom filled the buckets, he watched her tromp around beside him; smiling to herself while making footprint patterns and stooping now and then to touch the snow with curious fingers. "My mother used to make snow cream for us," he offered. "It was a treat Allen and I looked forward to every winter."

"…But this has no flavor," she said after scooping some to her mouth.

"She added the flavors," he chuckled. "Don't you think it would be asking too much if it came that way?—Can you imagine the confusion?" he added, raising hands and eyes heavenward. "Hey, Lord, how about some strawberry snow? Now Farmer Dan, down the road, wants chocolate, but please send us strawberry!"

Mandria couldn't help laughing—or joining in. "And…and it would be pink! And Farmer Dan's chocolate brown; and somebody else would get lemon yellow or cherry red!"

"Yes, and of course, the flavors would stop and change colors at every property line," he said starting toward the cabin with full buckets.

"Wouldn't that be something to see?" she asked, hopping along in his foot prints now. But at the back door, she came to a standstill. "We're not going in;—not so soon?"

"No, I'll just put the water inside and then we'll feed the animals," he assured her.

"All right;—but do hurry!" she smiled a second time.

Tom returned with two spoons and two cups, each about a third filled with heavily sugared coffee. "Come here," he sat making room for her on the dry, top-step of the small back stoop. "Now, fill the rest of your cup with snow and stir it a bit."

Mandria did and eagerly sampled a taste. "Oh, this is delicious!" she exclaimed, again and again while eating the rest. "Let's change our order to coffee. Can we?

"Maybe," he replied. "But wouldn't that blend too closely with Farmer Dan's chocolate?"

"And he might try to cross the line and take some of ours!" her eyes widened magnificently.

"Then I'd have to duel him," Tom took aim. "Spoons at ten paces"

"Or snowballs!" Mandria jumped to her feet in new excitement. "I'm going to make a snowball!" Whereupon, she scooped up some snow, patted it into a ball and tossed it into the air, only to watch in disappointment as it crumbled before landing. A second attempt did not fare any better.

"No, lady," Tom rose and joined her with a handful of snow. "You have to pack it harder—compress the snow as you shape it. See?"

"Like a meatball?" she asked, watching closely. "Are you mashing the air out?"

"…Damn if I know," he laughed. "I've never made a meatball."

"Only jerky and mush—don't remind me of that!" she laughed too. Then, trying again, she created her first decent snowball. And when Tom's landed against a distant tree, hers followed making a split-splat sound, for which he was granted her most smug expression.

"Very good!" he said, starting for the stable shed. "Your aim is still deadly—so I guess I'd have chosen you to soldier my side in the Great Snow Wars we had as kids."

"What were the Great Snow Wars?" she followed, rubbing her icy hands and hopping in his footprints once more.

"Well, it consisted of two armies, two snow forts and all the snowballs each could stockpile, "he ushered her in. And while he mucked the floor and put down fresh hay, she listened, marveling at the difference climate made in children's games.

"...So it was kind of like dodge-ball," she commented. "If you're hit, you're out?"

"Well, yes, but by our rules, dead soldiers were relegated to making more ammunition so the battle could go on. And when the winners were declared, they got to chase the losers home, pelting them with snowballs all the way," he finished, breaking the ice in the water trough. "Listen, I'm going for more water. Wait here and warm up a bit. Then, we'll build a snowman, if you'd like to."

"Yes!" she agreed. "A giant snowman!"

"All right. There's an old hat behind the door in the tool room," he started away. "And see what else you can find to fancy him up."

"Oh...goodie!" Mandria hurried to begin her treasure hunt. She found the hat with no trouble and turned to look over the small room. She had not been in there before, but it was easy to see Tom had. Everything was so organized: nails in one box; nuts and bolts and screws divided into others; harness and rope hanging on nails in precisely sized loops; hand tools, neatly ranked on a work bench; long-handled tools standing in one corner; and in the other, a crate of wood scraps along with another of his straw brooms.

From the scraps, she chose a bulbed wood-knot for the snowman's nose, then two large nuts for eyes and a row of bolts for his mouth. "And there is the perfect scarf!" she decided, spying a grain sack draped over an oblong box beneath the work bench. Yet as she snatched it up, the box teetered and reaching quickly to steady it, she realized it was not falling, but rocking. "...A cradle," she uttered, running fingers along the wood. And looking at the grain sack again, she saw that it had been cut to size—a mattress cover, ready for stuffing in the spring.

The baby moved at that moment, as if sharing her discovery, and for the first time, Mandria spoke to her child. "I wish things were different, little baby," she said, laying a hand on her belly. "If they were, do you know what I'd do to your cradle? I would paint flowers here, on the head and foot—or birds, maybe, with brilliant feathers. You could look at them and coo at your colorful friends...," she stifled a sob and went on. "Can you feel the ache in my heart? It's there because I...I don't hate you. I can't love you—but I don't hate you!" And covering her face, she wept. All the happy times she'd had with Tom passed in a parade of memories; then the nightmare, in all its bloody glory...

The day was ruined, as Tom was to learn when he opened the stable door and she rushed by him, "Damn you to hell!" she swore, searing him with angry green eyes. "You and that—that cradle too!"

In stunned silence, Tom watched her march to the cabin. Then setting the water pails aside, he uttered, "Mandria, you are running again. ...But from what?" Going to the tool room, he stood looking at the cradle and rocked it with his boot-toe. It was only a piece of furniture—and a needed one, at that. She hadn't objected to the other things he'd made, so why was this different? ...Because it was for the baby instead of her? No, Mandria wasn't shallow and certainly not jealous of an unwanted child. "Maybe, she feels excluded or something," he hoped, remembering his mother's pregnancy and the hours she spent making things for her expected baby. Mandria had made no preparations, but had she wished to, there was precious little to work with around the cabin at present. "Joshua," he said then, "where the hell are you?" A sigh followed for the loss of Mandria's happy mood. He was desperately sorry to see it go...

Mandria brooded for the rest of the day and by supper time she was spoiling for a fight. Eyes glued to her plate, she dug at her food, clanging her fork noisily and banging her tea cup between sips.

"You'll cause an avalanche if keep that up," Tom ventured. "The snow will tumble right off the roof."

"I hope you're standing under it!" she retorted. "—And what did you mean about my mother being a witness for you? Poor little Nico is in her care five days a week—and she sees what you did, up close! Mama would never help you—not ever!"

"She told me where you were."

"She never did! That is a lie! You couldn't force my mother to betray me—not at gunpoint!" And in the same instant, her anger turned to horror. "You didn't—You didn't beat my mother too?"

"Damn it, Mandria—no!" he rose. And trying to calm down, he paced before the fire. "The night I escaped, I went to see her—"

"And Mama was just so glad about that—so anxious to have her daughter reunited with an abuser of women—she told you right where to find me? Tom Scott, I am not a complete fool—now, how did you get her to tell you?"

"I didn't," he faced her then. "Nicole convinced her to do so."

"...Oh, dear Lord," she nodded in disbelief. "Is there no end to the lies you can tell? You spit them without a breath in between!"

Tom banged the heel of his hand against the mantle in frustration. She wasn't listening and he was growing too angry to put up with her ridicule. "Good night, lady," he started for the bedroom. "Do have a pleasant evening," and he closed the door on her scathing reply.

"...Damn him," Mandria swore, still staring at a bedroom door that was evidently going to remain closed. "Damn, damn, damn him!" she looked now at the cluttered table. "I will have a pleasant evening. I'll do just as I please—and it would not please me to wash his damn plate!" So saying, she opened the front door and flung it across the snow. Finding she enjoyed that, she proceeded to clear the rest of the table in exactly the same way. "Let him make of that what he will," she closed the door with great satisfaction. "And now, my pleasant evening begins."

Putting water on to heat, Mandria made her plans. She was going to bathe and wash her hair. Yes, even in a bucket, it would be heavenly to pamper herself without Tom's ever-irritating presence.

Then she thought of another treat. "...Something gooey and sweet," she uttered taking a lantern to the store room to look through the supplies. "Stewed apples with lots of extra sugar?" she debated, taking down a jar of the fruit. "Or pan-fried apple pies with cinnamon sprinkled on top?" But remembering Tom's fondness for anything cinnamon—and knowing in her heart, that was why Susan had sent it—she returned the unopened can to the shelf. "Stewed and sweet—with a dash of brandy!" she brought that bottle with her too. Returning to the hearth, she put the apple concoction on to cook and took the bucket of heated water to the table. "I think I'll just have a glass of brandy too," she decided. "Why the hell not?"

So while stripping to her underthings, she sipped on the brandy, enjoying the strong flavor and heated trail it left from mouth to stomach. It just suited her mood. Her toilette done, she sat on the warm hearth and towel-dried her hair. But the apples were really smelling good now, and going for a bowl, she dipped some out, dashed the top with a bit more brandy and tasted. "Umm," she smacked. "Maybe I'll eat all of it.—He doesn't deserve a single bite anyway." She had finished a third helping, when she wished she'd settled for less. "It's too hot in here," she uttered, rising unsteadily. Her head felt light, her stomach heavy and queasy. "Oh damn," she moved toward the door. "If I don't get some air, I'll be sick—and wouldn't he just enjoy the hell out of that!"

Quietly, then, she stepped out on the porch, breathing deeply in the cold night air. And as the minutes passed, she did begin to feel better …if a bit giddy. What would Tom say when he found the dinnerware in the snow? That had been the most fun of the evening. Laughing, she imitated the way she had sailed plates and bowls in every direction and gazing over the yard, admired her handiwork anew. "Well, I don't care what you think, Thomas Scott," she smiled, "but I wouldn't miss seeing your face in the morning for all the world!" So turning saucily, she went inside, planning a list of nasty retorts to anything he might offer. However, there was one last thing to do before retiring. The front door opened a final time and the rest of the apples went flying across the moonlit snow…

CHAPTER 7

The Mantle clock was striking nine when Mandria opened her eyes. She was alone in the bed—and now, wide awake, she listened for Tom's movements within the cabin, but heard nothing. "Damn!" she uttered. He had already gone out and she wanted to see that. So rushing to the front window, she lifted the pelt curtain and rubbed at the frosty pane, only to meet with a second disappointment. There were a lot of footprints, but no Tom. "Well, where is he?" she demanded, going to the bedroom window now. There she saw more prints—some of theirs from yesterday; some new ones and those of the horse leading toward the woods. ...But wait, could that be the mule's prints too?

"Well, damn him, he has either gone off to sulk or to hunt, but I'll not let him off so easily. He'll be back and then the Great Dish War can begin!" she stomped to the hearth and stoked the fire with a vengeance. Then she put on the coffee, made the bed and dressed. It was after she had poured herself a cup and gone to the table that she found the note:

Mandria,

Stay inside until I return. I've locked the front door and will push the latch string in from the back as I leave. Keep both locked! Visitors during the night. Gone to track them. May have been Indians.

Tom

"Indians?—It was me!" she laughed. "...So he saw the dishes and is off on a silly goose-chase.—Oh, how utterly marvelous!" she approved. And merrily, she tidied up the room, humming as she opened the front door to sweep out the morning dust. "Indians," she giggled, pausing to look over the yard again. Tom's large boot prints were everywhere—like someone who had been on an egg-hunt. "Or a dish hunt," she added pleasurably. ...But where were the dishes, or the food scraps and stewed apples for that matter? He had warned her that animals could be drawn to food left outside, but would they have eaten brandied apples...or taken the dishes? Her skin prickled apprehensively as she noticed now that the foot prints varied in size. "...Indians?" she breathed. "—Oh, my God!" And scampering inside, she bolted and barred both doors, then checked the window latches in a state of near panic. While pacing before the fire, she kept remembering one horrible tale about Indians cutting an unborn baby from a woman's body and crushing its skull before her dying eyes. "No!" she cried with determination. "They won't do that—I won't let them do that!" And recalling Tom's story about the snow fort, she began, at once, constructing one of her own. First, she overturned the table, drug it across the room and wedged it into the corner beside the fireplace. Behind the table, she stockpiled every pot, pan and dish in the cupboard; and all the jars, boxes and tins she could carry from the store room. Finally, with a butcher knife in-hand, she sat on the hearth, ready to leap into her fort and praying, all the while, that her aim was as true as Tom claimed. "...If not," she said bravely, "I'll fall on the knife. I won't watch them crush my baby." And she bit hard on her lip, for in her worry, she had claimed the child she did not want...

The hours passed, each measured by whirring gongs from the mantle clock and each time, it nearly frightened Mandria to death. Never had she been so intensely aware of sound—or more grateful for the lack of one in particular: the crunch of footsteps in the snow. Surely, not even an Indian could sneak across it unheard...surely!

It was noon before Mandria dared to move and she did so then, only because her body had grown stiff from tenseness. Sidling to the window, still clutching the butcher knife, she dared a peek and was greeted by bright winter sunlight glaring off the melting snow. "—Melting?" she all but screamed. "No, God, don't let it melt until…Tom comes back." And wiping frightened tears with fingers that quaked, she admitted she wanted him there. But the why of that boggled her mind, sending her thoughts through that tortuous night again. …Yes, there she stood, held in place by her father, head reeling at each sight; each sound; …each smell? Why couldn't she name the thing that kept pricking at her subconscious?

Shaken, she turned from the window, expecting the dreadful hatred that usually consumed her. Instead, she was wondering how it would all end? Theirs had never been a story-book romance. She had doubted Tom more than once and should have been forewarned. Yes, he deserved to go back to jail—yes he did! …But when he did, of what would her freedom from him consist? A safe life, certainly, but one with no direction, no hopes and never—*ever*—any more to do with love. "Damn him!" she rallied and hurried to peek from the bedroom window again. "Where is he?—Can't he see that the snow is melting?"

By nightfall, Mandria was exhausted from the wait and worry of her vigil. The fire had died to embers and she wouldn't stoke it or light the lanterns, fearing any glow might lead those Indians back to the cabin. So, curled on the hearth in a blanket, she sat in the cold darkness fighting a new foe. Mandria kept falling asleep…

The night was moonless, the only light coming from a sprinkling of stars. A cold wind sank its teeth into the back of Tom's neck as he pulled the horse to a stop before the cabin. Not for the first time during the long ride back, he shuddered, though it was as much over his miserable experience as the cold. He slid to the ground, his arms numb and nearly useless, as he started up the steps. Missing one, he would have fallen had his shoulder not caught against a porch column. "Damn!" he muttered through a swollen lip. Reaching the door, he realized how quiet and dark the place was. Had Mandria gone on to bed, thinking his note just another attempt to frighten her into staying put? Or had she run away again? The thought had crossed his mind more than once that day, and he was relieved to find the door locked—though managing to try it, was no easy task. He seemed to hurt all over. "Mandria?" he called softly. "Open the door—and for God's sakes hurry!"

Mandria woke with a start, unsure of what she'd heard or what to do. Should she keep still, crawl into her fort, or dare to peek from the window?

"Mandria?" he repeated as loudly as he dared, tapping his toe against the door.

"Tom!" she breathed, racing across the dark room, throwing the bolt and swinging the door back. "Where have you been?" she demanded. "—Where?"

But he stumbled past her, quieting her with a "Shush," as he went. "Get some light in here," he still whispered. "I'm afraid you have some patching to do."

"My God, he's been hurt," she now whispered too.—*And maybe they're still out there if he's being so quiet!* she thought. So quickly locking the door again, she searched franticly for the tinder box in the dark and when she finally had the lamps lit, turned to see him hang his coat on a closed bedroom door-knob, while pausing to look over her fort. "It wasn't Indians," he smiled crookedly. "But I'm glad to see you were prepared."

"What then?" she questioned. And as he neared, her anger mounted with each step. "Your idea of a joke?"

"No, lady—no jokes," he towered over her. "There wasn't a damned thing funny about my day."

"...Your mouth," her eyes widened. "And your shirt! Is—is that blood?"

"Mostly his, but blood, nonetheless," he nodded, rubbing at the soreness in his arm and shoulder.

"Well what happened?" she asked. "Who was out there?"

"Mandria," he gave a weary sigh, "I'm cold, my lip hurts like hell, I'm sore all over and I'm starving. Could we tend those things while we talk?"

"Oh, I don't see why not!" she went to poke at the fireplace embers. "I've only waited all day long!" she jabbed harder. "All day! Alone! And in absolute terror of my life!"

"Here," he took the poker from her. "I'll start the fire. And I'll settle for coffee and a piece of your spoon bread, if there was any left from supper."

"…There wasn't," she nodded, remembering how she'd sailed it over the snow. She remembered, too, that neither had she eaten a bite all day. "But I'll make more, and while it cooks, I'll tend your lip—and you will talk, Mr. Scott!"

"Yes, ma'am," he turned his attention and his smile back to the fire. He loved it when she tried to order him about—always had—even if he might want to strangle her once she answered the questions he had to ask.

"There," she said, popping a lid on the spoon bread and swinging the coffee pot over the fire. Then, going to an unlit lamp, she poured kerosene on the edge of a dish cloth and proceeded to cleanse his battered lip.

"Easy, lady," Tom winced after a time. "Please, that's good enough."

"Not quite," she pointed to her fort. "Not until you've helped me straighten this room—since it was all your fault that I wrecked it."

"Not quite all my fault," he said, lifting the table into place. "And I brought what remains of the proof…on a horse I left standing in the cold," he remembered. "Damn, I'll be back before the coffee boils," he added, snagging his coat as he passed it.

Mandria nodded watching him leave. "What proof—and why is he never still? You couldn't pin him down with a stake through his foot!" But unable to sit still herself, by the time Tom returned, she had straightened most of the room and the spoon bread and coffee waited on the table.

"Smells good," he said, rubbing at his arm again. "And I see you're joining me?"

"Yes," she answered, seeing no reason to mention that she, too, was hungry. "Now, will you please sit down and tell me what happened? I think I've been more than patient."

"And more than a little foolish, apparently," he bit into the soft hot bread. "Tell me, Mandria, how is it I found part of this very dinnerware over five miles from here?"

"...Five miles?" her color deepened prettily.

"Five miles," he repeated, reading her guilty expression. "Care to explain that, lady?"

"Well...I didn't want to wash dishes last night," she said, feeling childish—which in turn, brought up her defenses. "And you can't deny telling me to have a pleasant evening, so—so I threw them out the door!"

Tom stared at her for a moment longer and began to laugh. All sorts of reasons had passed through his mind—especially that she'd used the dinnerware to bribe a passer-by into sending the law for him—but her look said she was only challenging him to deny she'd been justified in flinging dishes if she wished. "Lady, couldn't you have chosen something less needed around here?" he asked then.

"Yes, but I can't lift you!" she retorted. "Now stop laughing, and tell me how the dishes got that far away."

"They were stolen by a family of thieves," he replied. "Not a real family, but a man and a woman who sent two children out to steal for them;—and the oldest can't be more than eight or nine."

"In the middle of the night?" she said in disbelief. "—In the snow?"

"Mandria, hunger doesn't disappear at sun-down or because of the weather. Those children were hungry and knew they wouldn't be fed until they brought home something the man could sell. So they took our pack mule and—"

"Our dishes," she concluded, hoping the children had eaten the food scraps first.

"Yes. And when I reached their camp, the man tried to sell everything back to me."

"So you fought him," she rose and refilled their cups.

"No, first I told him I had followed tracks from my door to his wagon and that I'd turn him over to the law if everything stolen wasn't returned. Then he said he was told the dishes were found and had no notion they'd been stolen. The presence of the pack mule he couldn't explain."

"Then you fought him," she nodded.

"No. That's when he hauled the children from beneath the wagon—where they were made to sleep on the ground, by the by. Anyway, he claimed they were orphans he and his woman had taken in—out of *the goodness of their hearts*—but that they were liars and born thieves and had caused him nothing but trouble. Then he put on a grand show of reprimanding them, both verbally and physically, hoping I'd be satisfied to take my stuff and leave."

"So that's when you fought him;—to keep him from hurting the children."

"...Lady?" he grinned. "You sure are anxious to get me into a fight."

"But you did stop him!—Certainly, you didn't stand there and let him abuse them!"

"No," Tom hesitated, "...I offered him a trade instead. I said he could keep the pack mule and I would take the children."

"Tom, you can't trade animals for children!" she exasperated.

"It seems that I did. They're sleeping in the bedroom now," he said. And he watched as Mandria opened her mouth, but closed it again when nothing came out. "It was after he accepted the offer, that we fought," he continued. "I had started for the horse with the kids, when he decided the deal wasn't good enough. And if those children had not yelled out a warning—hadn't known him well enough to be watchful—he would have buried an axe in my spine."

"Dear God," she uttered. "But what if he followed you back here?"

"He was following the back of his horses the last I saw of him. And the way the woman was driving, they must be two counties west by now. Besides, I think his leg was broken and I hope his jaw was too," Tom finished, massaging his arm and shoulder yet again.

"...And your arm? You keep rubbing it," she observed.

"No, but I'm sore as hell. It wasn't easy riding with those two kids. They were freezing cold and tuckered-out. I bundled them beneath my coat as best I could, but when they fell asleep, they were nothing but dead weight."

"And frightened. They had to be," she nodded.

"You'd think so, wouldn't you? Yet they answered my questions calmly enough. They are orphans and had lived with that pair of no-goods for about a year. But why a home would release them to people like that is beyond me."

Mandria was quiet for a time and Tom let her be, knowing she was troubled by more than his story. "…I suppose you'll want to keep them here," she said finally. "How did you put it;—that caring for motherless children seems to be your fate?"

"Have you a better suggestion?" he asked. "Should I have left them there—or do you think we should wake them now and set them free; …out in the snow; …in the dark of night?"

"Don't be absurd! Where would they go? Tom, you make me so angry—"

"I'm sorry!" he laughed. "But that, too, seems to be my fate."

"Anyway," she ignored his idea of humor, "do you know their names?"

"The oldest is John. His sister is Brittany."

"They made a thief of a little girl?" she said in dismay. "…Can I see them?"

"Come on then," Tom rose, but paused as he lifted the lamp. "Mandria, don't expect too much. They're in need of a good scrubbing—and a few days for healing their bumps and bruises."

"Give me that lamp!" she took it from him impatiently. "The way they look wouldn't make me turn my back on children!—But come spring, they will also be yours to deal with, because I'm not leaving here with any attachments. Besides, they've already been bought once today, so stop trying to sell them to me!" And, because Tom had been trying to do just that, he said nothing more as he stood in the doorway watching Mandria gently pull back the blanket for a look at the snuggled sleepers.

Brown, uncropped hair framed the boy's handsome features, which somehow, made Mandria think of Leprechauns. The girl's hair was blonde and fine to the touch, though it lay in a hopeless mesh of dirty tangles. Her nose was pert, sprinkled lightly with freckles and down one cheek, tears had left a trail through a dirt smudge. "She's been crying," Mandria whispered. "And with plenty of reason, I suppose."

"Are you sure?" Tom joined her. "Has she been crying?"

"See?" Mandria pointed, curious about his interest.

"Good," he said. "And John?"

"…Not that I could tell," she was looking at Tom now as if he'd grown horns. "Would you kindly explain what you find *good* in a child's tears?"

"If you will *kindly* follow me out," he answered, leading the way, but this time, leaving the door open so the room would warm. Then, instead of joining Mandria at the table, he headed for the storage room.

"Well?" she called, keeping a low volume. "I'm waiting—again."

"I know," he returned carrying the spare blankets. "And a living example of the point I hope to make."

"Which is?" she watched as he knelt to make them a pallet before the fire. "Why were you glad Brittany had been crying?"

Tom rested on his heels and looked at her. "Because, Mandria, it's natural to cry if you're frightened or hurt. But those two never shed a tear: not when the man slapped them around; not during that bloody fight; not even when a stranger—the same one they'd stolen from—picked them up and rode away on a horse. Don't you see? It's not healthy to bottle emotions so tightly. Good or bad, they have to express their feelings. As you do so well. …And so often," he added with a beleaguered smile. "Now, lady, shall we retire? It has been a very long day for me."

This was a left-handed compliment at best, but still enough to make her rise and turn her blush away from his notice. "In a moment. I want to clear away these dishes first."

"Should I duck?" he asked, rolling to his side with a weary sigh.

"It wouldn't hurt to stay in practice, "she replied.

"…I will," he yawned, already half-asleep. "…Good night, love," he murmured.

Mandria nodded sadly at his slip of the tongue and went about her chores. ...What more could happen to her life? How on earth had she ended up on the foot of a mountain, in north Georgia, in the middle of winter? Why was she, a lady of some social prominence, doing dishes? And not only that, the man she hated most—whose child she carried and did not want—had just talked her into helping him care for two, grubby, little thieves!

"How does he do it?" she uttered, drying her hands on a towel. And kneeling on the pallet behind Tom, she looked at his large frame trying to solve the puzzle. ...*He needs a haircut*, she thought—and without thinking—reached out and smoothed a stray curl at the nape of his neck, while continuing her perusal of shoulder breadth; of muscled arms filling the sleeves of his buckskin shirt. ...But these were physical things that had nothing to do with the power of his even stronger personality. And in all honesty, she feared this in him most. He had never raised a hand to her, yet was still able to control her life. ...*Is it possible he does love me in some strange way; that he could be violent with Nicole but ever-gentle with me?* It was not a sane or sensible thought and she'd do herself a service by not dwelling on it. So, easing downward, she wished for the peaceful release of sleep, knowing she had only become more confused by the mystery of the man beside her...

That man now lay staring into the fire, instantly awakened by the touch of Mandria's fingers. What it had meant, he dared not guess— just as he'd dared not move. But she had touched him; put her hand on his hair. And smiling, he closed his eyes again, happier than he'd been in nearly two months...

CHAPTER 8

The next Morning—and again without moving—Tom was awakened
by a medley of whispers from the bedroom doorway. "Don't tell
him, John!" Brittany pled. "Maybe you're wrong;—maybe this ain't
the same cabin!"

"Yeah, it is! That's the woman I run from;—the one what bashed
her head on the mantle!"

"Please don't tell him.—He'll whip us for sure!"

"But we was cold and I only took the fur off-en the window in
here. They come in afore I could get you the one from the window in
there."

"It's just as well," she comforted. "Mr. Short would've sold it
too—like the other."

"Yeah," John paused. "...Do you think we ought to be staying?
Maybe we should sneak out afore they wake up."

"What if Mr. Short finds us? He could, you know. Remember
what he done the last time we run off?"

"But we didn't run last night. That man took us off—and whipped
Mr. Short right good, too!"

"I was glad," Brittany vowed. "Wasn't you?"

"Yeah, I was," John paused again. "...He talked to us kind of nice
too—and put his coat round us and all."

"And look at the lady, John. She's beautiful—like a princess!"
Brittany decided. "Do you think maybe she is?"

John was skeptical. "This ain't no castle, Brit, and a princess wouldn't have no lump on her belly like Mrs. Short—and she's a witch!"

"…You mean this lady could be too?" the girl's voice grew fearful again. "You mean she could turn ugly and pinch us and switch us like Mrs. Short done?"

"I don't want to know!" John led the way. "Come on, Brit, let's get out of here!"

Joining the hushed conversation, Tom rose on an elbow to face them. "Hold it, *Bear*," he chuckled. And two pair of startled, round eyes stared back at him. "Front and center," he pointed to a spot on the other side of his sleeping wife. "Now, sit," he ordered, and they sat. "To put your minds at ease," he began softly, "I am not going to whip you and the beautiful lady, here, is not a witch."

"She has that lump on her," John uttered.

"So does Mrs. Short!" Brittany added.

"Mrs. Short is just a lardy-fat woman—and probably as mean as a witch," Tom explained. "But this lady isn't."

"Then why does she have that lump?" John asked suspiciously.

"Because it's not a lump, but a baby," Tom explained. "And it will stay in her belly until it grows strong enough to be born."

"A real baby?" Brittany smiled excitedly. But it faded when Mandria began to stir.

"Watch out, Brit!" John cautioned, and instinctively, the pair drew close together.

Mandria looked at the fearful, huddled children and then at Tom in confusion.

"Good morning," he smiled. "Would you like to meet our guests? They think you're a witch."

Mandria glanced at the frightened youngsters again and quickly sat up to blame Tom for that. "Are you mad—totally mad? Why did you tell them such a dreadful thing? You've scared them half to death!"

"It was their notion, lady," he defended. "I've been trying to assure them of your kind and gentle nature—which I doubt they'll ever believe now."

"...Oh," Mandria realized he was right. Her outburst had frightened them more, and she now had to do something about it. "...John; Brittany, I'm sorry if I sounded like a witch. And I'm sorry if you think I look like one. Honestly, I'm not. Why, I'd run as fast as you if a witch came to my door."

"Which witch?" Tom smiled, remembering a rhyme his mother taught him. "The trick witch or the stick witch; the thick witch or thin? Pick which—and hurry—or all will come in!"

Brittany giggled and when Mandria did too, John allowed himself a smile.

"Where on earth did you learn that?" Mandria asked, grateful for the injection of laughter.

"Oh, I have learned a lot of things! And today, I solved a big mystery. It's about a lady and a bear. Want to hear my story?" he asked all of them.

"I do!" Brittany clasped her hands. "Don't you, John?"

"Yeah," he said dryly. "Did the bear eat her?"

"No," Tom nodded. "This was a magic bear that could turn rusty door-knobs and run like the wind standing on his hind legs," he now looked Mandria's way. And seeing she had not yet caught on, he continued. "You see, a while back, a man and his wife made a long tiring journey to find a new home. When they had, the man started to unload their belongings, while the lady went inside to snoop around— because beautiful ladies sometimes do things like that. Anyway," he went on, sensing rather than seeing green sparks ignite in Mandria's eyes, "the lady saw one big room with two doors in it. She opened one and found nothing. That room was empty.—But!" he raised a finger and made a dramatic pause, "There was one more door: a door with squeaky hinges and a rusty old knob. This was a brave lady too, so she started toward that second door, when suddenly, it flew open! A magic bear ran out and then...it just disappeared. Well, the man looked everywhere, but couldn't find anything—not a single clue to tell him where the bear could have gone. And for a long while, he stayed close to home, because the mystery bothered him so much. Then, one morning—on a day much like this—the man woke up and heard the magic bear talking. It was back in that same room again and just as frightened of the man and the lady as they had been of him. And when the bear tried to run away and disappear a second time, the man looked him right in the eye and guess what he said?" Tom gazed directly at John. "He said, *Hold it, Bear!*"

John's mouth dropped open and then closed on a loud gulp. But Brittany swallowed the bait. "B...but that's what you said to us!" she exclaimed.

"I know," Tom said.

"But we ain't no magic bears," she assured him.

"He knows, Brit," John nudged her. "He knows everthing."

"...Well, I don't understand any of this," Mandria shrugged prettily.

"Beautiful lady," Tom chuckled, pointing at John, "meet your bear."

"Now, just a minute," she straightened. "I would certainly know the difference between a child and a wild, furry bear!"

"Not if the room was dim; you'd just whacked your head; and the child was wrapped in an animal pelt.—Like the one we found missing from the bedroom window, for instance?"

Brittany slid an arm about John's dejected shoulders and her small mouth quivered as she spoke. "Don't whip him, Mister. John might of scared you, but he didn't mean to."

"Oh, you poor little things," Mandria gathered them both to her. "He's not going to whip you.—Tom, for goodness sake, tell them you're not!" And her eyes glistened with tears and a look that said his life would be in peril should he refuse.

Fighting a stubborn mist from his own eyes, Tom rose and went to the table. ...*If only Mandria would show such caring for our child*, he wished "I have a few things to say first," he said sitting down. "Would you three kindly get off the floor and join me?"

Mandria steered the children into her chair and stood behind them as Tom leaned back, folded his arms and looked at each. It was so quiet, she could hear the clock tick. ...*Is it so hard for him to utter a few words of assurance?* she wondered. Then, it occurred to her that he might have changed his mind about keeping them. It was possible, if she'd undermined his motive. *Stop trying to sell them to me,* she'd said. *No attachments.* And she still meant it…so why was she holding her breath?

"John; Brittany," Tom began. "The number one rule in this house will be respect for my wife. She is a lady—and for now, a pregnant lady—who will need all the help we can give her. Is that understood?"

"Yeah," John uttered and Brittany nodded.

"Yes, *sir,*" Tom corrected. "And it will be yes *ma'am* and no *ma'am* to Mandria. That, too, is a point of respect for your elders."

"Yes, sir," they chimed softly.

"Now the second rule will be honesty. There will be no lying and no more stealing. Is that understood?"

The children looked at each other and then at Tom. "…So how we going to eat?" John asked.

"Providing food is my responsibility," Tom explained. "Yours will be helping with the chores around here."

"Like we done at the Home, Brit," the boy gave her a knowing look. "We got to earn our supper."

"That's all right, John," she assured him. "I'm bigger now. You won't have to share yours with me no more. It's better than being with Mr. Short! …Ain't it?"

"Maybe we'd better discuss punishment right here," Tom said. "First of all, food will not be used as a reward—nor withheld as punishment. You will be welcome to join us whenever there is a meal on this table. However, I do believe in discipline. If I feel you deserve a spanking, you will get one—and I said a spanking, not a beating. I'll deal with you as fairly as I can, trying never to judge without listening to your side of things first." He said this looking at Mandria, who lowered her eyes. "So, are there any questions?

"Naw," said John.

"No, *sir!*" Brittany elbowed him sharply.

"Sir," John added, rubbing his side. "—I would of remembered, Brit. You didn't have to punch a hole in my gizzard!"

"Never mind," Tom chuckled, rising before them. "Brittany, you help Mandria start breakfast. And John, you come with me. We have some work to do."

But John paused in the doorway and turned with a word of encouragement for his sister. "I won't be long, so don't you worry none. She ain't no witch;—just *pregernant*, like the man said." Then, he hurried after Tom.

"Will you help me, Brittany?" Mandria smiled at the little girl, who looked back with beautiful blue-green eyes. "This *pregernant* lady would appreciate it.—And please call me Mandy. It's much friendlier, do you think?"

When Tom and John returned, they brought a bench for extra seating at the table. It was one that had seen many years of yard duty and had to be sturdied, but as John was allowed to drive some of the nails, he was proud of the results; anxious to show his sister...until he took note of what she was doing. Then he grew quiet again.

"John, look—come look what I done!" she chattered, tugging at his sleeve. "Mandy, she showed me how to set the table! See? I done this all by myself, glasses and all!"

"Don't break none, Brit," he murmured confidentially, as he sidled onto the bench. "It's the same what we took and he come looking for. And he ain't settled with us about that yet."

"No, it's settled," Tom nodded, taking his place at the table too. "Of course, some of the plates were lost—broken in that fight, as I remember it. But you know what, John? For another swing at Mr. Short, I'd give up a few more. I really liked the sound of him landing on broken glass."

"Me too," John smirked as admiration flickered in the depths of his wide brown eyes.

"Well, I'd help," Mandria added, placing a large bowl of oatmeal on the table. "I'd sail teacups at that witch—and I wouldn't miss, either. Tom says my aim is very good."

Brittany giggled as she sat next to her brother. "I would too, Mandy—me and John. Wouldn't we, John?"

"Yeah," he answered, distracted by the smell of the oatmeal; and more by a plate of hot spoon-bread and fried side-meat Mandria brought as she took her chair. "...Ma'am, I'm sorry I called you a witch," he grinned. "Ain't no witch can cook this good."

"Thank you, John," she said filling their bowls with oatmeal. "And as a special treat this morning, you will each get an extra spoon of sugar—and a dash of cinnamon."

"Me too?" Tom asked hopefully. "I love cinnamon."

"...All right," she agreed, her eyes adding emerald green splinters to his serving. "It was kind of Susan to remember your preferences so well, wasn't it?"

"Whoa, lady," he chuckled. "I might think you cared, one way or the other."

Mandria had a ready reply, but the children didn't need to hear that language, so for a time she ate in silence, watching as the hungry pair wolfed down their portions and reached for more. She wasn't surprised at their lack of manners, and again noted their unkempt appearances. *No attachments*, she had vowed. ...Still—until spring—the least she could do was to teach them proper behavior and grooming. It wasn't much, but might make them want to better their lives. ...And Tom was a teacher, wasn't he? Surely their grammar could be improved—along with teaching them to read and write. Yes, she would have to speak with him about this...

Tom saw Mandria's pensive expression and figured he hadn't heard the last about his fondness for cinnamon. But that would have to wait. "May I ask a favor?" he began, while finishing his coffee. And the children looked his way.

"What is it?" she questioned, and two pair of eyes swung toward her.

"If I bring in the water, would you give Brittany a bath—and do something about her clothes? John needs it too, but I'll tend to him tonight." With that both children examined their clothing, looked at each other and shrugged.

"All right," Mandria nodded. "...And when you can spare a moment, I'd like a word with you."

"I thought you might," he grinned, motioning to John. "Let's go, Bear. We have something else to build—something really important."

⸺⸺◈⸺⸺

Come nightfall, all were tired, but much pleased with the day's labor. By removing the wall between the stable and the tool room, Tom and John had commandeered enough plank to build a set of bunk beds, which were permanently anchored to the wall between the two interior cabin doors. Mandria padded the bottoms with the spare cushions and pillows Tom had made and covered each bed with spare blankets. That she had to use the one usually kept rolled between Tom and herself bothered her, but it couldn't be helped. And now that both children had been bathed and fed, they were anxious to try their new beds. So, Tom tucked them in and before Mandria had finished the dishes, they were fast asleep.

Tom now sat at the table, enjoying a second cup of coffee. He smiled as he looked at John and remembered the authority the boy used in claiming the top bunk. "Brit," he said, "it ain't right that a girl in a dress goes climbing up things, showing her petticoats." Then Tom looked at Brittany and his smile broadened. Mandria had taken the ragged little moppet and created an enchantress. Her clean hair was shades lighter and combed to a silkiness that complimented her small, soft features. He recalled coming in for lunch to find her prancing about in his white dress shirt, the sleeves in big rolls, her waist cinched with his tie to keep the hem from dragging the floor. Seeing him, she'd skidded to a stop. "Mandy, she said I could wear this while my clothes dry. You ain't going to whip her, are you?"

His smile faded when he turned to find Mandria studying him with a serious expression. "May we talk now?" she sat with her own cup of coffee. And when her chin rose and her posture became very erect, Tom was certain the matter of Susan and cinnamon was at hand.

"Have at it, lady," he sighed, leaning to the back of his chair.

"*Have at it*," she repeated. "Very poor grammar—and not the example we should set. Now, those children need more than regular

96

baths and meals. They need to learn manners; their grammar is atrocious; and I think we should do something about it."

"We?" he uttered, caught off-guard by her topic. "I mean, the help would be appreciated, but I thought you said—"

"What I said was no attachments, but neither will I neglect them!" she snapped, but immediately lowered her voice when John stirred. "You are the teacher, so you will see to their schooling—and we'll set aside part of each day for that. I will teach them manners and deportment on my own time. Now is this acceptable?"

"Yes, Ma'am," he nodded, and would have said more, had she not risen and headed for the bedroom.

"Oh, and by the way," she paused to look back. "I don't care if you like cinnamon or not. The children do—and that the only reason I opened that damned can." So saying she turned and for once, closed the door quietly.

Tom sat there for a minute and then grinned. He knew she'd have the last word on that…

CHAPTER 9

Nearly three Weeks had passed and late one afternoon, John raced through the door with some news. "Visitors a-coming! A man and a woman! I seen—I mean, I *saw* their wagon a-topping the hill!"

"A wagon?" Mandria looked at Tom. "Could it be the Shorts—coming after the children?"

"No—oh, no!" Brittany ran into Tom's arms. "Make them go away! Please, don't let them have us!"

"Land sakes!" John threw up his hands. "It ain't the Shorts, Brit! Don't you think I'd know them a hundred miles off?"

"Then who could it be?" Mandria asked, following the others to the porch. "It's nearly dark. They'll surely stop here. ...Won't they?"

Tom turned to face her. "It has been a while, but need I remind you of a promise to defend myself—and what will result from testing this warning?"

"...No," she nodded, unable to look away from the serious expression framing those still captivating cobalt eyes. "How can I forget?" And even to her that sounded more a plea from another time and place.

"Hello!" called the man in the wagon. "Hello, Tom—and a Merry Christmas to all!"

"...Christmas?" Mandria uttered, recognizing the woman, if not the man, as both climbed to the ground. It was Susan Rutledge and for some reason, Mandria's knees felt watery. ...*Miss Hope-to-my-die herself,* she thought forlornly. *...And as regal as ever in her starched white blouse and well fitted skirt.—But, damn it, did the skirt have to be green, when that's Tom's favorite color? ...Or is that the point?*

"Josh; Susan!" Tom hurried out to greet them, with hugs for both. "Damn, if I can believe my eyes! And Christmas, you say?—Is it really Christmas?"

"Nearly so," Susan laughed, hugging him—a second time. "Tomorrow is Christmas Eve and as Joshua arrived with your order just this morning, we decided to play Saint Nick!"

"Josh," Tom placed a hand on the small man's shoulder—but did not, Mandria noted, remove the other one from Susan's waist. "Friend, I have never seen a more welcomed sight than the pair of you. Come on, now. Come inside.—Mandria, heat up some coffee!"

"Let's go, children," Mandria shooed them before her, through clinched teeth, "Or we'll likely be trampled underfoot." And wide-eyed, John and Brittany scurried to the hearth, where they sat to watch as a parade of boxes and bundles were carried in by the exuberant men.

"Mandria, Merry Christmas, my dear," Susan smiled, placing a huge wicker hamper on the table.

"And to you," Mandria straightened and forced a cordial reply. She wouldn't let Susan know how much she resented her presence. No, it was these times in life that proved a lady's breeding—and too, the children were watching their every move. "I'm afraid we lose track of time up here. Is Christmas truly so near?"

"It is—and you had to know, because I see two of Santa's helpers right there on the hearth!" she smiled on—and on. "Mandria, who are these adorable youngsters?"

"It's a long story, but now they belong to Tom.—And me," she added impulsively. Then, wondering why it seemed important to do that, she turned to the hearth. "Children, stand up, please—and remembering your manners—say hello to Miss Rutledge."

"I-am-very-glad-to-meet-you,-Miss-Rutledge," John made her a bow that was nearly as stilted as his speech. "My-name-is-John," he finished.

"Me too!" the little girl bobbed a crooked curtsy. "I-am-glad-to-meet-you-too,-ma'am....And-my-name-is-Brittany-Ann!" she remembered to add, flashing a beguiling smile.

"Oh, that was nice!" Susan reached into her basket. "So nice, you both deserve a surprise. Who wants a ginger-bread man?"

"I do!" they chimed. And each taking one, they skipped through the door for a look at the wagon the men seemed determined to empty.

Mandria raised grateful eyes heavenward. At least Susan hadn't given them a damned cinnamon bun. But her thanks were premature.

"I know you weren't expecting us," Susan said as she began to unpack the hamper, "so I brought all my Christmas goodies—and enough food for an army. We will not have to cook until the day after Christmas!"

"...We won't?" Mandria cringed, when two trays of cinnamon buns went onto the table. But she was more disturbed by what Susan had just said. "...So you're planning to stay over?"

"Yes! I convinced Joshua that this is a terrible time of year to be alone. He has no family either, you see, so here we are: a ready-made Mr. and Mrs. Claus—gifts and all!"

"...Gifts," Mandria realized. "Oh, Susan, we have nothing to give the children. It won't be Christmas without presents to open."

"Then they'll have some—even if we must take them from Joshua's orders."

"What orders?" Mandria asked. "—Who is Joshua, anyway?"

"A tinker. I only met the man today, myself, but we're already fast friends. He is just full of juicy tid-bits from all over Georgia—and as loyal to Tom as you and I."

"I see," Mandria hid a grimace by going to fetch cups. "Would you call them in, please? The coffee is coming to a boil." So was she, but a lady would not reveal that. She would, however, stomp a foot in protest of said *loyalty* and whisper a string of damns as soon as Susan cleared the door. She felt much better for it too, and able to greet them with a smile, as all filed into the room.—That is, until Tom made his show of boldness.

"Josh, I'm afraid I've neglected something important," he said, sliding an arm about her shoulders. "This is my very beautiful wife, Mandria. And this, Mandria, is Joshua Munzenrider, the Star Book Agent in Georgia—and a friend who has restored my belief in the spirit of Christmas."

"Joshua, I'm pleased to meet you," Mandria extended a hand; hoping this would dislodge Tom's hold as well. When it didn't, she tried another ploy. "Tom, would you get the children? They shouldn't play too long in the cold."

"Yes, my love," he drew her closer and before she realized his intent, he'd planted a kiss on her mouth. "I never could refuse you much of anything," he added as he left.

Mandria was blushing furiously—and furiously angry with him at the very same time. "I—I must apologize for that display," she began, as she poured their coffee. ...And yet, something in Susan's eyes gave her pause. What had she seen reflected there; envy...or was it regret? "But Tom is Tom and none of us can explain him," she finished lightly, surprising even herself.

"True," Joshua nodded. "There is a charm about the man. And it works for him even when he isn't around. Otherwise, Savannah wouldn't be so divided over his case."

"Divided?" Mandria said incredulously. "When I left, everyone wanted him hanged!"

"Oh, that faction is still there, but another—including one of the papers—has risen to his defense. And the strangest thing is the position taken by the Police. They know the most, but are saying the least. It's whispered now—by Tom's friends—that new evidence has come to light, but must be kept secret or lives could be endangered."

"That sounds very mysterious," Susan looked Mandria's way. "What do you suppose it's about?"

"I...I don't know," she shrugged, totally at odds with the revelation.

"Well, Joshua, did you tell Tom this news?" Susan asked.

"Of course—first thing. But he is not an easy man to read, so I don't know what he made of it."

Tom returned at this point, with two laughing children, who seemed to set the tone for the rest of the evening. After a quick supper, Susan brought out a rum cake, Tom spiked the coffee and Joshua played many tunes on a penny flute, while the children danced about and laughed all the more. At first, Mandria was quiet, her mind a battle zone over Joshua's news, but like everyone else, she soon warmed to the merriment. Questions could come later...

It was late when she and Susan tucked the children into a pallet before the hearth, using the new quilts Tom had ordered. And Mandria was thinking how much better one of them could be rolled between Tom and her at night. Then she had to watch as Susan gave each child a kiss. It made her uneasy, for though Tom hugged and kissed them often, she had not. Her uneasiness grew when John tried to play the gallant.

"Miss Rutledge," he smiled, "you smell mighty like a flower bed."

"Why, thank you, John," she ruffled his hair. "I'm glad you like my perfume."

"I sure do," he nodded sleepily, "and one day, I'm going to buy Brit and Mandy some just like it.

"I'm sure you will," Susan answered.

"Mandy?" Brittany asked. "I been wondering something all night. Who is St. Nick? Everbody keeps saying he's coming...but where will he sleep?"

Mandria was so touched—so saddened—she couldn't reply.

"My dear child," Susan laid a hand along the girl's small face. "Listen, you two go on to sleep now, and tomorrow I'll tell you a brand new story I found about Santa. It's called A Visit From St. Nicolas and it's full of wonderful, magical things."

"Magic bears?" John asked, without opening his eyes.

"No, but will flying reindeer do?"

"Suppose so," he nodded, rolling over. "Yes, ma'am, that'll do."

"Promise?" Brittany yawned. "You won't forget, Miss. Rutledge?"

"Hope-to-my-die," Susan crossed her heart, as the women returned to the table, where the men had observed that little scene too. "Well you heard them," she whispered now. "It seems we have a job to do."

"Indeed," Joshua sniffed suspiciously. "Those little tykes will know Father Christmas if I have to empty my whole wagon."

"They will have to select gifts to give as well," Susan added. "Giving is the most important lesson of Christmas."

"…And a tree?" Mandria asked. "We should have a Christmas tree and let them make things to decorate the branches."

Tom smiled, looking at each of his fellow conspirators. "…You know, I sometimes wonder that man dares to question fate. Just consider all of us: a pregnant lady; a traveling tinker; a lame teacher; and a man accused of heinous crimes. But we were chosen to be here for them," he pointed to the children. "And you know what? It will be the best damned Christmas I've ever had."

"And me," Joshua agreed. "In truth, it will be."

"Well, won't we be busy tomorrow!" Susan stood, working a sleeve into place. "So Joshua, if you'd kindly fetch my valise, I'm going to retire.—Mandria, I assume we're to share the bedroom?"

Glancing at Tom, Mandria readily agreed. "Yes, of course, that would be the best arrangement—and I'll bring in soap and warm water, if you'd care to bathe."

"Thank you, dear thing," Susan hugged her. "Oh, Mandria, tomorrow will be such fun. I can hardly wait!"

During this, Tom had moved to his mountainous order bundles piled beside the door. "Josh, I need your assistance," he said as the tinker returned to hand Susan her bag.

And as that one went on the bedroom, Mandria poured the promised bowl of water and carried it in, along with the soap and a towel. When she came out again, closing the door behind her, Tom was standing at the table—eating a damn cinnamon bun—and obviously waiting to speak with her. "Where is Joshua?" she asked first.

"Bedding his horses," Tom answered. "Mandria, come here. I want to give you something while he's gone."

"What is it?" she noted the unwrapped package on the table.

"It…it's a nightgown. I thought you might want one as you're sharing a room with Susan."

"Well, I appreciate the thought. ...I just wish I understood it," she raised puzzled eyes to his. "Why would Susan care if I sleep in a chemise or a night gown?"

"She probably wouldn't," he hesitated. "...But you might feel less—well, deprived once you go in there."

"Tom, I was just in there—and you're making no sense. Why would I feel deprived?"

Tom started to speak, but stopped feeling really awkward. "Mandria, it—well, it's her...lingerie," he finally got it out. "It's her one extravagance. Susan has a whole wardrobe of beautiful...well, night clothes and things."

"Oh, and of course, you'd just know all about that!" Mandria hissed at him. "She is likely wearing the best of the lot too—and we both know why! Too bad Joshua had to tag along. Otherwise, I could sleep out here and you two—"

"I told you that was over!" he whispered harshly and stepped closer.

"Not for her!" she met him nose to nose. "You've felt it—I know you have!"

"Yes, damn it, I have!" he grasped her shoulders. "That's why I kissed you earlier. Our visit to Susan's home left doubt about us and I wanted to change that!"

Mandria knew then it had been regret she'd seen in Susan's eyes—sadness and regret. And, somehow, she felt better. "All right, Tom," she said calmly. "You can let go of me. I'll wear the damn gown."

But for several moments longer, he held her arms, studying the same features that had just been so angry. Why weren't they now? She was the most puzzling creature God ever created...

"Oh!—So sorry," Joshua said coming in. "I didn't mean to barge in on you."

"You didn't," Tom grinned, drawing Mandria even closer. "I was just saying good night to my wife." And as the clock struck midnight, he lifted her chin and pecked her a kiss this time. "Sleep well, my love—and be happy. It's Christmas Eve!"

Mandria refused to look at him as she reached for the gown and bid them both good night. Then pausing before the bedroom door, she straightened. …Susan would be waiting for this door to open; fantasizing…what? And grasping the knob, an unbidden smile touched her lips…

Christmas Eve day started early, with Tom, Joshua and the children going in search of a tree, while Mandria and Susan prepared a huge breakfast. Susan had brought eggs, butter and milk in her bottomless hamper—foods Mandria had not tasted in over a month. And when she mentioned this, Susan expressed concern.

"Men!" she declared. "They've no sense most of the time anyway, but a pregnant woman and children need these things. Well, never mind, I'll see that you get them. I'm sending a cow and some chickens up here this week."

Mandria was touched, and for some reason, wanted Susan to know she was grateful. "…It seems Tom has eaten over half the cinnamon buns you brought. You may have to make him some more before you leave." To which Susan nodded and returned a warm smile…

After breakfast, Tom gave Mandria another gift: the sewing kit, which included the scissors needed for cutting tree decorations and the needles and threads for stringing them. The children were anxious to begin, so the ladies gathered pieces of paper that had been wrapped about some of Tom's orders; bits of cloth from wherever they could find any; then sat the children on the floor by the hearth, and put them to work. While they did this, Susan recited the story she had promised, which drew excited giggles from the youngsters, with requests that she repeat it.

Outside, the men did some Christmas shopping in Joshua's wagon. "Josh, I intend to pay you for anything we take from here," Tom nodded. "But if your deliveries are short, won't the company hold you responsible?"

"I'm an honest man, Tom. I'll see that my customers are satisfied. And the company too. It's all in the way you handle the paperwork—which I will adjust as we go along here. Now, please, let's begin with this doll for Brittany—please? It was meant for a real little hell-cat, who bit me right on the hand while her doting mama was placing the order!"

Later, the ladies went shopping. Then the children, which excited them even more than decorating the tree. And Joshua allowed them to browse to their heart's content, while tactfully keeping their selections sensible.

"I know you liked Susan's perfume," he said once to John, "but you must understand that your Mandy might not want the very same scent. Ladies are kind of like the flowers in that bed you spoke of. Each likes to think that she's the sweetest in the garden." Then he whispered, "However, Brittany might love some! What do you think?"

So, by mid-afternoon, after much scurrying about in secret corners, wrapped gifts began to pile up beneath the tree. Some remained in their shipping boxes; some were covered in old newspaper packing sheets or the thick white sort taken from a roll ordered by a butcher along Joshua's route—and they were bound, in all manner of ways, from string, to colorful yarns or hair ribbons. But to John and Brittany, who awaited their first festive Christmas ever, it was the most beautiful sight on earth.

When supper was done, Joshua excused himself for a final visit to his wagon and returned with a box and a bible. Calling the children to the hearth, he took out a small Nativity set and said they should place the colorful little statues into and around the crèche while he read them the real Christmas story. They were much impressed, for this, too, was a first in their young lives.

"Thank you, Josh," Tom said watching them still at play there. "That was needed—and most appropriate tonight."

"Well, there is something else needed here too," Mandria came to stand behind Tom's chair, her hands resting on the tall wooden knobs. "And as you provided the means and Susan has the know-how, both you are John are getting haircuts."

"Now?" John complained, without looking up from the camel statue he held. "Aw, Mandy, not now!"

"Now," she insisted, "because Susan has kindly offered to show me how it's done, so no more arguments."

"Give it up, Bear," Tom leaned his head back to smile up at her. "This lady always has her way." And that was followed by the most pitiful sigh she'd ever heard.

"Well…almost always," Mandria hurried toward the store room, fighting off the urge to smile. "I'll just get some towels, Susan, then we can begin," she added.

"And I'll fetch us a bottle," Tom followed. "Josh, it's time for a round of Christmas cheer! Susan, get some glasses, will you?"

Towels in hand, Mandria turned and collided with Tom, who not only caught her to him, but lifted her feet from the floor and didn't let them down again until she stood against the back door. And, he still had his arms around her. "The last time this happened, you broke a jar of pepper sauce, I believe," he said softly.

"This time it will be your head!" she whispered back. "Now let go of me!"

"In a moment," he nodded. "I just wanted to say that you're an exceptional lady."

"Look, you—you cad! You are taking unfair advantage. If they weren't out there, you know I'd object to this loud and long—just as I would have slapped you for taking that kiss yesterday!"

"Whoa, now," Tom chuckled. "You have made this a wonderful day and I only wanted you to know I'm grateful."

"…Well, everyone has done their share. The children deserve no less."

"But you went the furthest, lady. Susan told me you asked her to bake more cinnamon buns. That was a real gesture of friendship on your part."

"Tom, I like them too," she said uncomfortably. "I ate three, myself!"

"All right," he smiled, brushing the tip of her nose with his finger. "I won't argue the point. Now shall we join the others?—Or would you prefer to stay until I do steal another kiss?" he leaned as if to try. "Oh!" she rushed around him. And when she rushed back into the main room as well, it only drew attention to her flushed cheeks.

"He is—Tom is… He is not to be trusted!" she stammered.

Joshua looked at Mandria's rounding belly, once at Susan, who seemed to share his thought, and both burst into rollicking laughter. "Obviously!" he declared. "Most obviously!"

From that point, the evening seemed to pass too quickly. They sang Yule carols, ate Christmas goodies, toasted the bottle to it's dregs, and Susan told her Santa story yet a final time—the best time, as the sleepy youngsters were tucked in for the night.

"He is such a handsome little fellow," Susan murmured, admiring John's new haircut while she and Mandria sat on the hearth next to the sleepers. "And Brittany is purely an angel. You have a beautiful family, Mandy. You must feel very lucky. How could you not?"

Mandria couldn't reply—nor could she look Tom's way, knowing he must have overheard. But to agree would only encourage him and to disagree would encourage Susan again. There just wasn't an answer she could give and it left her deeply disturbed. "It…it's been a long, tiring day," she rubbed at her temples. "Would you all forgive me if I left you and went to bed?"

"Well, of course," Susan helped her up. "You must have your rest. Come along now. And as I'm sleepy myself, good night, gentlemen." Without glancing back, Mandria allowed herself to be led away; allowed Susan to put her to bed; allowed the tears as she lay in the silent darkness, yearning for things that could never, ever be…

Meanwhile, Tom went to his Star Book order bundles again and brought back cigars for Joshua and himself. "Will you be returning to Savannah anytime soon, Josh?" he asked, as they lit them up.

"In about three weeks. Yes."

"Well, would you hand-deliver a letter to my brother for me?"

"I'm glad you asked. I wanted to meet him the last time I was there;—to tell him I'd seen you? But then, I wondered if he would believe a total stranger. He could have thought me an agent from the other side trying to get information about you from him. So yes, I'll deliver your letter—if you'll include a word or two on my behalf."

"Josh, I could write a volume on you," Tom nodded. "You are a true friend."

The tinker straightened proudly. Tom still had a knack for making him feel taller. "So, anything else I can do for you in Savannah?"

"Yes, would you also call on Mandria's mother? I know she wants news about her daughter. Have Allen to take you, as I want him to give her directions to Susan's."

"But Tom...is that wise? I heard the lady was caring for the O'Rourke girl.—What if she sends the law instead?"

"She won't, Josh. She has asked to be here when the baby comes. ...But I am worried about her. It's possible she's the one who gave the police this new information and if it puts her in danger, I want her to come earlier than planned."

"I've a feeling you know more about this than you're saying."

"No, friend, what I know is only one of many possibilities. Now one thing more: Mandria's birthday is in April and she has a favorite scent. It's a honeysuckle made especially for her by a perfumer. I don't think you can buy it, but her mother can, so ask her to bring some. I know Mandria would like that—and frankly, I miss it too"

"Surely," Joshua nodded, rising to warm his backside by the fire. "...Tom, who is the real culprit? If I knew, I might be of more help. At least I'd know whom to avoid—or when to pay attention, should the name be mentioned."

"You're right, though you may find it hard to believe," he said. "I was framed by Sam Lucas—Mandria's own father, and Evelyn Lucas' husband."

"Holy God," swore the tinker. "I've heard about him. In the business world, he's reported to be a ruthless." Then he paused. "...But if it was Mrs. Lucas who aided your case, she must leave the city.—Her husband would have every chance of doing her harm!"

"Yes, even though her testimony would not incriminate him, it could help to clear me—and that he wouldn't allow."

"Well, what's to be done?—Something must be done!"

"Josh, welcome to my world," Tom rose too. "Listen, you go on to bed now, while I put out a few more Santa gifts and write that letter to Allen.—And Merry Christmas, my friend."

"Merry Christmas," Joshua replied. But like Mandria, it took a while before he could sleep...

CHAPTER 10

"Tom?" Brittany whispered, with both hands cupped about his ear. "Tom, wake up and look over there. He came—Santa really came!"

Tom opened his eyes to find Brittany's so filled with wonder and excitement he laughed. "I do believe you're right!" he whispered back. It was six-thirty according to the mantle clock and still dark outside, but no one was going to sleep later today. "Well, what are we waiting for, Brit? Wake the Bear—and the ladies!" he exclaimed. Then whacking the top bunk, he called to Joshua. "Wake up, man! It's Christmas—and Santa has been here!"

When Mandria and Susan came in, Tom greeted them with a cup of coffee and a smile. Joshua was more vocal. "Ho-Ho-Ho, Merry Christmas!" he said in his best and deepest Santa voice. The children giggled from where they sat before the tree, looking but not daring to touch anything.

"Santa first?" Tom asked his wife.

"Always," she nodded. "Come on, everyone, bring the chairs and the bench, and let's see what is here from Santa!"

"Yes," Susan agreed. "John and Brittany, go ahead. I know those unwrapped toys must be for you!"

They were timid at first and when Brittany lifted the doll, she looked to Mandria for approval. "Yes!" she squealed, then hugged it to her. "Oh, Mandy, it's the prettiest doll in the world!"

"Wow!" John exclaimed, holding a box for all to see. "Tin soldiers!—Must be two dozen or more!"

"And look over here, Bear," Tom pointed. "Marbles! Did you ever shoot marbles—or play Marble War with tin soldiers?"

"No, sir—but you're going to teach me, ain't you? ...I mean, aren't you?"

"Sure I will. We'll have a real battle after while."

"Brittany, what have you found?" asked Susan. "Why, that looks like a tea set."

"It is—oh, it is!" she squealed. "Look: it has four little cups and plates and a real little tea pot!"

"A knife!" John whooped. "A jack knife—just like Tom's!"

"Now there is something every man needs," Joshua said. "Next time I come, John, I'll teach you to whittle."

"And meanwhile," added Tom, "you can learn to play Mumbly-Peg, Bear. In fact, we'll have tournament and winner gets to challenge Josh.—You do play, don't you, friend?"

"Play?" he laughed. "That's a game where size doesn't count—and I was the champ on my block."

"Look!" Brittany went to Mandria. "I got a sewing kit too! Just like you did!"

"Why, you surely did," Mandria looked into the small box. "It has scissors, a thimble, needles and thread—and a pin cushion shaped like a little strawberry!"

"Now you can make your doll some clothes," Susan looked too. "—Or maybe, Mandy will let you help make something for the new baby."

"Can I?" asked the starry eyed little girl. "Oh, Mandy, can I?" she hopped about from foot to foot, in a way that reminded Mandria of Lucy. It was most disconcerting...

"We'll talk about it," she nodded, making no commitments. "Anyway, you have more presents to open. See the one tied with yellow yarn? That's from me, Brittany.—And John, yours is next to it. Yes, the flat one there."

"And here are mine," Joshua fetched his for the children, as did Tom and Susan.

John received a new shirt from Mandria; a buckskin coat from Tom; a story book from Susan; and from Joshua, a checker board set. Brittany's gift from Mandria was a dress of rust colored home-spun; from Tom, a green wool coat; from Susan, another story book; and from Joshua, hair ribbons tucked into a music box.

With all their gifts around them, John heaved a great sigh. "You know what, Brit? I hope I ain't dreaming. Don't you?"

"*Aren't*, John!" she corrected. "You got to remember what Tom teached us."

"Well, you...*aren't* remembering so good yourself. Mandy said we was to thank people for presents and we...haven't done it onest."

"Oh!" she scrambled to her feet. "Oh, John, you're right—and we got presents for them too—remember?"

So when the thank-yous were done, the children delivered their gifts. From Brittany, Mandria and Susan each received a box of buttons—and that not more than a few matched in color and size brought smiles to the ladies as they ooed and aahed over the hand picked selections. She gave Tom and Joshua pouches of tobacco, and from John, the men received corn cob pipes—both of which, Joshua did a wonderful job of pretending surprise about. A lacy shawl was John's gift to Mandria and for Susan, he chose a box of handkerchiefs with flowers tatted along the edge.

"So you'll look as good as you smell, Miss Rutledge," he explained. "—And Brit, I got something for you too!" he went back to the tree.

"Me too!" she followed.

The pair stood facing each other, presents in hand, and for a moment, neither moved. "Here," John pushed his forward with a smile. "Open mine first, Brit. If you like it, I'll get you some ever Christmas forever."

Brittany tore through the paper in a hurry. "Oh, what a pretty, swirly bottle—and you can see rainbow colors in it too. Oh, I do like it, John—I do!"

"Yeah, the bottle is kind of nice, but that's perfume inside, you know. Real growed-up lady perfume—same as Miss Rutledge has."

"Is it?" Brittany's eyes widened. "Thank you, John—thank you so much!"

The boy was very pleased and turned to give Joshua a wink as he opened his gift from Brittany. "…Well, look a here," he held up a stick in one hand and a notched, propellered one in the other. "It's nice, Brit," he turned them first one way, then the other. "But what is it?"

"Mister Josh said it's a Whirly-gig!" she laughed over the name. "Want me to show you how it works?"

It didn't take long for John to master the toy and now, as with all children at Christmas, both were soon involved at play in the midst of their gifts.

"Our turn!" Tom smiled at the others. And gathering closer to the tree, they, too, exchanged gifts.

Susan gave Mandria several large remnants of cloth in varied colors and patterns. She gave Joshua a tin of home made cookies, which he assured her he would enjoy as he drove to his next stop. Tom received a small slate board and chalk to make teaching the children easier.

Joshua presented Mandria with a baby quilt. For Susan, the tinker had selected a book of poems, and for Tom, a small bible and a calendar for the coming New Year.

Mandria gave Susan a beaded change purse and together, she and Tom gave Joshua a bottle of their brandy. Her gift for Tom was chosen under duress, but she would have been shamed by the entire group had she not given him one. So cleverly, she thought, Mandria asked Susan's assistance, and then allowed her to select a shirt nearly matching John's.

"Twins, Bear—we'll be twins!" Tom called, showing his gift, which gained only a moment's notice from the busy youngster. "Anyway," he smiled warmly at his wife, "thank you, I'll enjoy wearing this."

"Thank Susan too," she deferred credit. "She helped me pick it out."

"No, Tom—let *me* thank you!" Susan hugged his gift for her. "Yarn—and such beautiful colors! How nice that you remembered my knitting."

"How could I forget? I still wear some of the boot socks you made me," he said with a more appreciation than Mandria thought needed. But glancing his way, she found him looking back. "…Well, lady?" his tone softened. "Are you going to open my gifts or hold them all day?"

Mandria peeked now at the assortment on her lap and at her feet. There were so many and she felt embarrassed as everyone else had received one gift from each person. Then, as if reading her thoughts, Tom explained that they were part of his larger order from Joshua, and that Christmas just seemed a fun way of opening them—which didn't help her in the least. For what she dreaded most was the number of times she would have to make some silly statement of gratitude. But there was no avoiding the situation…

A second nightgown came in the first package, then the bunting, flannel, bed linens and toweling, which she managed with a minimal loss of grace, as most were for use in the household. Next were the novels and she felt a twinge of exasperation, knowing she would enjoy reading them. The sketch pad and charcoals were harder to ignore, until she announced they would be used—*only*—for teaching the children art. And that was added after Tom mentioned the 25th was also their 5th month's wedding anniversary and the art supplies were his gift for the occasion. Damn him…

"Open the last one," he urged now. "And Merry Christmas, pretty lady."

Sighing hopelessly, she lifted the lid of a flat box, then inhaled that sigh in surprise on seeing the mellow gleam of a scrolled, pewter-handled vanity set. And on their own, her fingers moved to caress the hair brush. As it had been with the bathtub, she really wanted this. … Why was Tom always able to use her weaknesses against her? *My own worst enemy,* she remembered saying not long ago...

"Oh, Mandria!" Susan expounded. "How very beautiful—and I know you'll enjoy using this for years to come."

"It…it is beautiful," she stammered. "Truly, I do…appreciate this, Tom," she said without looking at him. Then, because she was close to tears, she rose and hurried toward the hearth. "Would anyone care for more coffee—or one of Susan's delicious cinnamon buns?"

"I would!" chimed the children.

"Me too!" added Tom. "Come on, Joshua; Susan—Christmas Day has just begun!"

After a light breakfast, the men took the children outdoors and proceeded to teach them Mumbly-Peg, but Susan had another project in mind.

"Get your sewing basket, Mandy," she began, "and the remnants I gave you."

"Why?" Mandria asked. "I was going to straighten the room a bit now."

"Let the room be. I think you need more attention—which is another thing a man wouldn't notice!" she laughed. "But your buckskins are entirely too snug now, and Mandy, it will only get worse. So, we are going to make you some smock tops and I have two extra blouses in my bag I'll leave for you to wear beneath them. We'll make skirts too, with extra waist buttons you can loosen as you need to."

"Oh, Susan," Mandria swiped at genuine tears. "I'm sorry. I don't mean to stand here crying, but I do need clothes. Not that anything would fit, but I miss all of my pretty dresses!—And you are right; these buckskins are truly becoming uncomfortable. I …I'm just such a mess!"

"Come on, then," Susan hugged her. "And dry those tears, Mandria Lucas Scott. You will have your pretty things again—and they'll fit you too. Meanwhile, we'll start with that piece of wine colored cloth. Don't you think it would make a festive skirt?" With that, they gathered everything needed, shut themselves in the bedroom—and Mandria did not forget to take her vanity set…

It was a while later, when the others came inside to warm-up and were told—through a closed door—that the ladies were busy and not to be disturbed.

"Well...is Mandria all right?" Tom addressed the wooden door panels. "—She isn't ill...or anything?"

"Your wife is fine!" Susan insisted. "Just go play with the children and leave us be!"

Tom wasn't entirely convinced of that and after he had explained the rules of Marble War and teams were chosen, he elected to stand his soldiers close to the bedroom, ready to leap at the first sound of distress. After a time, however, he heard Mandria laugh and feeling more at ease, settled back on his knees and into the game. Rolling a marble across the floor, he scored a direct hit, which brought a squeal of delight from his partner, Brittany, and a moan from Joshua and John, leaders of the opposing army...

It was late afternoon and Mandria stood looking at her new clothes with a happy smile. Her wardrobe now consisted of one wine and one navy blue skirt; one powder blue smock and one of navy and wine pin-stripes. It was a far cry from the bulging closets she'd left in Savannah and yet she felt an odd excitement while deciding what to wear. It was wonderful just having a choice...

A cease fire was called in the Marble War when the combatants came to the peace table at lunch time—and still Tom kept a watch on that bedroom door. For a while afterwards, the youngsters played with other toys, but now, tied at ten battles each, the Marble War raged anew for the championship. However, when the ladies stepped out of the bedroom, the odds swung decidedly in favor of Joshua and John, for on seeing Mandria, Tom's marble went way-wide of the mark.

"Whoa, lady," he uttered, gazing up at her from the flat of his back "You look...beautiful."

"Doesn't she?" Susan agreed, along with everyone else. She was glad Mandria had chosen the wine skirt and pin-striped top. It was Christmas, after all—a time for rich warm colors, and she patted a shiny brushed curl on Mandria's shoulder in approval.

"Hope-to-my-die, she does," Tom said of his pretty wife with a look that said much about his feelings.

...And yet, Susan had to wonder again about the relationship between these two. Tom loved the girl—deeply, entirely—but Mandria never seemed to return his affection. At that moment, for example, when she should have been basking in her husband's approval, Mandria was avoiding his eyes. And her smile—when she finally did smile—came after a compliment from Brittany. "…Well, Mandy," she tried to put the puzzle from her mind, "shall we start supper?"

"Yes!" Mandria laughed, leading the way. "Yes, Susan, now I feel like celebrating!"

Susan shrugged and followed. Perhaps she was wrong. Some women were just shy about openly showing fondness for a man…

Christmas supper was indeed a feast. Susan had brought a cured ham, which they sliced thinly and covered with hot red-eye gravy, thickened with sugar. Potatoes boiled in their skins, peas flavored with crisply fried ham chunks, a bowl of stewed fruits and freshly baked spoon bread completed the fare. And once again, from the bottom of Susan's hamper, came a cherry pie for dessert.

Unusually quiet during the meal, Tom contented himself with watching Mandria. Magically, she was once more the enchanting, animated creature with whom he'd fallen in love. And again, he remembered the supper they had shared at The Market; how she had captivated him with this same charming manner. Then, he had vied for her attention. Now, he didn't dare—and it hurt. For as much as he longed to share her happy mood, not one time did those laughing eyes turn to him…

———◦◦———

Susan and Joshua left early the next morning and Mandria's spirit departed with them. She admitted she would miss Susan's enthusiasm and companionship—almost as much as she already missed her mother and friends in Savannah. Tom, of course, was to receive the blame and had the children not been there, she would have told him so. Instead, she spent most of the day cleaning the cabin and squashing all attempts at conversation. Soon after supper, she excused herself and went to bed.

"Tom," John began hesitantly, "…is Mandy mad at us?"

"No, Bear," he answered. "She is just tired. Maybe a little homesick, too—and we did have a lot of company…so she probably over-worked herself a bit."

"Because she's pregernant," Brittany added, climbing on Tom's lap. "I guess we got to help her more, John.—Like Tom said?"

"But we picked up our presents and put them where she said in the store room," John countered. "And I seen…I mean, I still saw her crying some.—Maybe she didn't like the presents we gave her."

"She liked mine!" Brittany insisted. "She used my buttons on her new clothes, didn't she?"

"Now, hold on," Tom intervened. "She liked both of your presents just fine. I think she only needs rest—as do we all—so under the covers with you. But tomorrow, let's surprise her with breakfast in bed. That should make her feel better. …Don't you think?"

"Yes, sir!" they chimed scampering into their beds. And Tom sighed, hoping it would too…

"Mandy?" Brittany called softly. "Mandy—surprise!"

Mandria opened her eyes. There stood John with a plate of warmed over spoon bread and Brittany with a spoon and a jar of Susan's honey. Tom stood behind them with a cup of hot tea.

"Breakfast, my lady?" he smiled, as did the children.

"We fixed it just for you," John explained. "All by our selves!"

"Well, almost," Brittany corrected. "Tom, he fixed the tea."

"Why, thank you," Mandria smiled back, though the warmth of it didn't quite reach Tom. "How very sweet of you," she added, sitting up.

The youngsters were elated and placing their offering on her lap, climbed up to sit beside her. Tom handed her the tea cup, but remained standing near the foot of the bed, waiting for more proof of a better mood.

"Umm, the tea is so hot!" Mandria sipped and then set the cup on the window sill. "While it cools, would you two care to join me for some of this delicious bread and honey?"

It seemed that they would and soon, the trio was chatting and laughing together.

...*Almost like a real family*, Tom thought as he quietly left the room. ...*But you are dreaming again*, he reminded himself. ...*You weren't included in her invitation to share; ...and God knows if the baby ever will be*... He thought about it more while tending the horse and bringing in fresh water for the day. In spite of her wish to remain detached, Mandria seemed to be growing fond of John and Brittany. Wouldn't she learn to care for the baby too? Once it was born—once she held it—wouldn't natural instinct guide her? Mandria might never love him again, but their tiny creation was as much hers as his. Somehow, someway, he had to make her realize that. It was the lone key to his future direction. If she accepted and loved their baby, he could face whatever waited in Savannah. If not, he would not chance a life in prison, plus the loss of his child. He would see her safely back to the city she loved, then he and Allen would return for the three children and quietly disappear. "Lady," he uttered, "please open your beautiful eyes." But he didn't hold much hope for it...

⁂

On Friday of the same week, Tom had to make room in the stable for a milk cow, five laying hens and a rooster sent by Susan. She also sent extra feed grain and a small churn, which Mandria, of course, didn't know how to use. Neither had anyone but Tom ever milked a cow; and Brittany was terrified of the rooster. It took patience and most of the following week, but after numerous spills, failures and frustrations, John learned to milk and the ladies to churn butter. Brittany remained afraid of the rooster, however, and rather than risk more breakage, Tom and John also gathered the eggs. Still, they all enjoyed the healthful additions to their diet; complaints were few; and life returned to as near normal as circumstances allowed...

CHAPTER 11

It snowed in January. And snowed. And snowed, until Mandria thought she would never see the sun again. She was dreadfully bored with confinement, though there was precious little to be done about it. She read the novels twice over, but that soon became boring too. And it bothered her that Tom and the children didn't seem to share her feelings. They spent much of their time playing games or at study. And reluctantly, Mandria admitted that if Tom was good for nothing else, he was an excellent teacher, for before the end of that month, both youngsters could print the alphabet, count and write numbers to one hundred, were even doing simple math problems and reading a little from their story books…

February brought more snow and out of desperation, Mandria took up sewing. When they gathered about the fire, where they seemed to stay most of time, she mended and patched their clothes and even managed to fashion a simple pinafore for Brittany. On clear days, when Tom and John made their too-rare excursions to hunt or catch up on chores, she made baby clothes, reasoning that this was as good a way of passing time as any.

But while searching for a length of yarn one day, Brittany discovered the little gowns folded in the bottom of Mandria's sewing basket. "Mandy!" she said. "Are these for my doll?"

Thankful they were alone in the cabin, Mandria sat beside her on the hearth, trying to think of an explanation as she re-folded and re-hid the garments. "…No, Brittany, they're for the baby. But you can't tell Tom about them—or John, because he'd just tell Tom, I'm afraid."

"Why don't you want them to know?" she turned innocent eyes to Mandria. "Would Tom get mad?"

"Quite the opposite, I'm sure." And Mandria was. She was also sure she would explode in anger if he dared to assume it meant anything. Cabin fever was the name he'd given her testy moods and she truly believed she had it. "…I just want to surprise Tom with these things, that's all," she lied. "Will you help keep my secret?"

"Yes, ma'am," Brittany nodded slowly. "But Miss Rutledge said I could make something for the baby too, so can I?"

"All right," Mandria agreed, though it twinged her conscience to bribe the child. "Tomorrow, we'll start on a crib blanket."

"Oh, thank you, Mandy!" Brittany declared and before Mandria knew it, she was on the receiving end of a hug. "You are the prettiest, nicest lady in the world—and I love you!" Then, she was gone, skipping off to play with her doll in a favorite corner of the store room.

It was a moment Mandria would not soon forget. The little girl had expected no response…but would that day be long in coming? The thought was terrifying! To love was to hurt, and yet, even as she repeated that steadfast rule, she wondered how she could explain that to a child who had suffered as greatly from a total absence of love. "Damn you, Tom Scott!" she murmured, placing blame on his head again. "I won't be caught in the middle of this—I just won't!"

Then, because she was already angry, she remembered the day a few weeks ago when that cradle appeared in the bedroom. Tom had deliberately chosen the 25th of January, their 6th month's anniversary, to present his finished project. And though she didn't want to be, with Joshua's calendar now gracing the wall, even she was aware of dates.

"But why does he insist remembering that one?" she paced about. "The man is ill—truly insane!" Then with a despairing nod, she sat at the table. Next week, she would enter her seventh month of marriage and pregnancy, and there would be another gift from him. It seemed, her only hope of surviving the next two months, was acceptance. Yes, at least there was the sure knowledge that soon she could—and would—free herself from all of this...

But on Saturday, February 25th, Mandria awoke to find she was alone in the cabin. A note of partial explanation, printed in bold letters, lay on the table:

Hello Mandy,

I am gone. Tom took me.

John

P.S. Me too.
Brittany Ann

"Now what?" Mandria sighed. And then to keep busy, she went about her morning chores. When they hadn't returned by lunch, she began to imagine Tom had taken the children hunting and that some accident had befallen them. By mid-afternoon, she had added self pity to the emotional mix. "Well, it is the 25th," she muttered. "I've no wish to celebrate it, but I don't like being ignored either!" Then, knowing how ridiculous she sounded, she began to laugh. "Oh, dear Lord, I'm as crazy as he is!" And she laughed until she had to sit down... where suddenly, she was in tears; sobbing miserably, not knowing why, and not hearing Tom and the children enter the cabin from the back carrying new bundles of supplies.

"Lady?" he rushed forward to kneel beside her chair. "What is it?—Are you ill?"

"Oh, no!" chimed the children, joining him in an instant.

122

Mandria tried to compose herself, but the concern on their faces wasn't helping. And gathering the youngsters to her, she conceded to them her deep need to hold or be held—and still she didn't know why. "No, I'm not ill," she snubbed badly. "Just...*pregernant*," she attempted a laugh.

"Well, we brung you a present," John smiled timidly. "Want to see it?"

"Me and John can go get it, if you do," added Brittany.

"Why don't you then," she nodded, dabbing her eyes. "That would be very nice." And with that, the pair scampered for the back door.

But Tom had not moved an inch. Lifting her chin on his hand, he studied her features closely—and from too close—because she could feel her pulse beat starting to react. "Mandria," he still held her under his direct gaze, "why were you crying?—Are you sure you're all right?"

She started to lie;—to say she had suffered another of those awful nightmares. But she realized, only at that moment, she hadn't had one since...when? The night he brought the children home, wasn't it? "I...I don't know," she nodded in confusion. "Just leave me be, please."

"Lady, if only I could," he expelled a breath. Rising to his feet, he stood there, and after a moment, added, "Your time is getting short now. ...I suppose you're still planning to return to Savannah alone?"

"Of course," she answered, with determination. "And thanks to you, I'll always be alone. Love is not worth the pain.—You taught me that lesson well enough."

Then the children were back, giggling excitedly as they carried in the fattest, fur-ball of a puppy Mandria had ever seen. When they eagerly deposited it on her lap, the pup proceeded to give her hands and face a thorough licking, and Mandria was left giggling too. "Well, who are you?" she finally managed to settle it down.

"Me and John call him Critter," Brittany offered, "because when Tom saw him he said, 'Damn, what a cute little critter!'"

"He said *what*? Brittany, you're not to use that language—and *you*, Tom Scott..." But her reproach found no target. "Now where did he go?" she uttered.

"Out back, I think," John answered, lifting the pup to the floor so he and Brittany could play with him more. "I seen him get a bottle and head out there."

"A bottle…of whiskey?" she asked.

"Yes ma'am. Guess he was thirsty, huh?"

"I guess so," she rose and went to look from the back door. The rest of the supplies lay on the stoop, but fresh horse tracks in the snow led away from the cabin. Glancing along them, she saw Tom on a distant hill, where he had stopped and was taking a long slow pull from the bottle. For what seemed an eternity, he sat there with his head lowered, and then, he slowly turned the horse and ambled back toward the cabin, while Mandria released a breath she wasn't aware she'd been holding. "—Children, go bring in those bundles from the back and unpack them," she hurried to the hearth, unwilling to deal with her feeling of relief. "And I know you must be hungry, so I'll just start an early supper."

"Yes, ma'am, but we ain't too hungry," John said as they went. "Miss Rutledge fed us lunch—and fresh cinnamon buns too!"

"So you went to Athens for supplies," Mandria chatted as she worked. "And you stopped to see Susan. How is she?"

"Fine.—And she's using my handkerchiefs too," said John.

"She gave us a whole stack of books to look at," added Brittany, "And we got to look at every one while her and Tom done their talking."

Curiosity—and another emotion Mandria did not want to deal with—led her to the storage room door, where she watched the youngsters shelve supplies. "Well, what did they talk about?" she tried to keep her tone light.

"Don't know," John shrugged. "They went upstairs for that."

Mandria turned away. There were only bedrooms upstairs at Susan's. "…So how long were they gone?" she had to ask.

"Exactly forty-five minutes!" Brittany announced proudly. "I know, cause I practiced time telling on Miss Rutledge's clock."

Mandria somehow managed to go through the mechanics of preparing the rest of the meal. Why, she didn't know. Eating was the furthest thing from her mind. *Upstairs …forty-five damn minutes?*

With Susan? In a bedroom, damn him? Well, this was some anniversary gift—and one she had no intention of letting go unmentioned!

When Tom came in he suspected something was brewing when she refused to join them for supper and began cleaning the pots with a noisy, banging vengeance. He was certain of it when she insisted the children go to bed early and made no fuss about the puppy going with them. Then, and only then, did she look at him—and with eyes that dared him to refuse—invited *him* to join *her* in the stable. And without waiting, she wrapped a shawl about her and stomped out the back door. Tom tried to guess what had happened as he followed. Surely she wasn't upset about the puppy, for she seemed to like it as far as he could tell. No, considering the length of her strides in the snow, it was more than that…

"Well?" she spun to face him with folded arms as soon as he came through the door. "Get some light in here. I want to see your face clearly for this!"

"Yes, ma'am," he obediently lit a near-by lantern. "…Will one do?" he asked, before extinguishing the match.

"Evidently not!" she spat and began to pace. "*One* is never enough for you, is it? Not one wife, or one child, or one lover—and likely, you'll bring in another dog, so one of those won't be enough either!"

"Then…it is the puppy you're upset about?"

"No, damn you—and I'm not upset for myself! I don't care, but what you did to John and Brittany today was thoroughly indecent!"

"Mandria…what in the hell are you talking about? What was indecent in taking them to buy supplies?"

"You stopped by Susan's didn't you?" she came toward him arms akimbo. "You fed them; gave them books to keep them occupied," she stressed each point with jab to his chest. "Then—oh, and then, you and Susan went up to her bedroom! But not to *talk* as you told those innocent children—not for *forty-five damn minutes!*" And then she came at him, flailing her fists with all the fury of a windmill in a full gale.

"Lady, will you stop?" he backed away. "You're wrong in what you're thinking, but that's not the point!" Yet, she kept coming and

swinging at him. "Mandria, please stop! You're liable to fall and—"
And so saying, he tripped over a water bucket and fell backwards into
the hay.

It didn't deter her. Going to her knees, she continued her attack.
"How? How could you do that in front of those children?" she yelled.
"I know you're a bastard, but did you have to act the part while they
watched?"

"Mandria, God damn it—that's enough!" And moving so quickly
she only had time for a gasp of surprise, their positions were reversed.
She now lay on her back in the hay and he half upon her, a leg holding
her legs down, and both her arms pinned and useless. More infuriating
than all of this, however, was the smile creeping over his mouth. "You
know something, lady?" he asked. "I have the devil's own luck."

"You are the devil!" she turned her head away. "Now, get off of
me!"

"No, I don't think I will," he chuckled. Mandria might believe she
was defending the morals of the children, but she was behaving like a
jealous wife. Tom meant to show her the difference and enjoy it. "As I
was saying, I do have the worst luck with women. My wife won't allow
me to touch her and my...*friend*, Susan? Well, yes, we were alone; in
her bedroom; ...on a bed, we once shared as lovers."

"So you did make love to her!" Mandria's eyes narrowed.

"Did I?" he taunted. "If you don't care, why are you asking?"

"Because of the children!" she repeated. "You had no right to make
them witness to your immoral behavior!"

"They witnessed no such thing," he assured her. "Susan insisted
that I close the door."

"Oh, you bastard!" she tried to squirm away and couldn't. "How
can you make light of this?"

"But I'm not, lady. What went on between Susan and me was
entirely serious and I gave her my very...*closest*...attention."

"Stop—just shut up, Tom! I don't want to hear this!"

"Don't you?" he questioned. "Then you don't want the truth of
it?"

"No!—Yes! …Oh, damn you, I don't know if you can even tell the truth—or if I'm capable of recognizing it any more!"

"Then I will show you truth," he leaned closer. And when Mandria jerked her head away again, he kept coming, placing a kiss on her cheek instead. "There will always be a horrible kind of truth in the attraction between us." And his next kiss, teased at her ear, which brought her head arching backwards, still trying to escape. But as that left her throat bare and inviting, he tasted her there too. "Mandria, you can fight this as long and as hard as you wish," he nuzzled her breasts too, "but we do share this one truth, if none other."

"You must stop!" she pled. "Tom, please—for the love of God, stop this!"

"It seems that I must," he laid his head on her, listening to the pounding response of her heart. "And more for the love of you than anything else." Then, sighing raggedly, he released her hands and rose on an elbow above her. "Lady, I did not make love to Susan." he finished.

Mandria knew his leg still held her in place, but he had freed her hands, which gave her the courage to meet his eyes. "Then…then why did you shut yourself in her bedroom?" And the sharpness of her tone was understandably lacking.

"Because we didn't think the children needed to hear the topic we had to discuss," Tom answered. "I had asked Susan to go by Doc Lewis' office for some literature on pregnancy and birth. She delivered it—along with a very pointed lecture on the care and handling of my wife."

"And you brought this literature back for me to read, I suppose," Mandria took her turn with a sigh.

"Yes, ma'am, I did."

"Well, why did Susan lecture you?—Was it because you didn't think to provide us with milk and eggs before she did?" she asked accusingly.

"That did come up," he nodded. "But she was bound and determined to caution me about something else—and unnecessarily, though I couldn't tell her so. I just had to listen and when I made no comments, she took it for disagreement and called me a pig-headed male. Then she proceeded to show me in print—page after page of print—proving her warnings were valid. And lady, I've never been through anything quite as nerve-wracking in my life."

"Why?" Mandria asked, her hand moving subconsciously to her belly. "W…what did she say?"

Tom dropped down beside her, with a laugh of irony. "Well, it seems the time approaches when we must forego the pleasures of copulation."

"What?" she snapped forward like a spring.

"Oh, yes, lady," he said to her arrow straight spine. "Never mind that I've been without for four months already, but how do you think I enjoyed a lecture on the subject—complete with opposing medical views suggesting longer than a six week abstinence? Of course, modifications were acceptable and substituting manual play was stressed—for the continued closeness of the relationship, it said. And I just enjoyed the hell out of that too."

Mandria groaned. "Well, it's been no picnic for me either. I have to carry this heavy baby everywhere I go," she rolled to her knees. "—Or can't go," she added. "Would you please help me up from here?" she extended a hand to him.

But when Tom had her up on her feet, she stood looking at him, with a smile devoid of warmth. "…Listen, I saw you ride away with a bottle this afternoon, but you didn't bring it back to the cabin. If it's out here somewhere, I would enjoy a drink now—and I think you'd better have one too."

"…And to what do I owe the honor of sharing a drink with you?" he asked, untrusting of that smile; and the glint in her cat-green eyes.

"Call it what you wish," she shrugged. "—A toast to our seventh month of wedded bliss, if you'd like."

"What are you up to?" he questioned. "—Anyway, Susan said you shouldn't be having alcohol either."

"Well, I'm going to have one—and whether it's here or in the cabin, is up to you."

"...Come on, then," he took down the lantern, "The bottle is back here in the tool corner," he conceded, thinking he could at least regulate the amount she had.

"Thank you so much," she followed and perched on a tall stool by the workbench, waiting for him to find something in which to serve them.

Finally, handing her a tin cup, and taking his in a broken-handled water dipper, he stood leaning against the bench facing her. "...To our wedded bliss?" he repeated her suggested toast.

"Oh, forevermore," she touched her cup to his and drank deeply. Then that unfriendly smile returned, along with an equally unfriendly laugh. "So: I'm to be safe from your unwanted mauling for the duration of this pregnancy, is that it?"

"No safer than you already are," he nodded, in uneasy confusion. "I've yet to force myself on you;—well, not for more than a kiss or two."

"You did threaten more, however. But I'm truly safe now, because you wouldn't dare risk harming this baby. Am I right?"

"Yes, but what damn point are trying to make?"

"Only that if the puppy was meant as an Anniversary gift, it wasn't the best one. No, the best—and most appreciated—gift you've ever given me is the knowledge that you are no longer a threat. So, for all the torment you have put me through, its time for paybacks." And setting her cup aside, she began to unbutton her blouse.

"Mandria...," Tom uttered a low warning.

"But you've always liked my breasts. Shall I bare them for you?" she taunted. And as if frozen in place, Tom watched the full, lush mounds appear as far down as her smock would allow. Then sliding from the stool she stepped up to him and pressed herself to his chest. "How does that feel, Tom? And isn't it just awful that you can't do a damn thing about it?"

"The hell I can't!" he spun her before closing her tightly in his arms. "Have you forgotten manual play, lady?" he said against her ear. "I can still make you enjoy it—and then we'll talk paybacks!" With that, one hand went into her blouse and the other between her thighs while his tongue invaded her ear.

"Stop!—You will stop now!" she quivered. But he did not—would not—until she was backing into him instead of pulling away; clinging to his arms, rather than prying at them; and until she climaxed for him...

He had to support her as he turned her to him again. And cupping her face, he enjoyed the sweet, yielding softness of her mouth in a kiss he wished would never end. But it had to, and he had to be certain she understood the point she had forced him to make. "Mandria," he set her at arm's length, "I don't believe that went as you intended, did it?"

"No," she uttered, too ashamed to live, much less meet his eyes. "I never wanted you to touch me. It was a stupid idea and...and I guess I deserved the lesson."

"But it was a tender one—and with no recriminations, if you'll promise never to do that again," he said. "If you will, somehow, we'll make it through the next two months."

"I do promise it," she swore, her eyes on her fidgeting hands.

"All right, then, here: Take the lantern and go on to bed," he suggested. "Who knows? Maybe you'll wake up tomorrow and find this was only a bad dream anyway."

Mandria nodded, looked back at him once from the doorway, and left.

The breath Tom expelled left his entire body feeling totally deflated.—Well, all but one stubborn part. So buttoning on his coat and muttering more death wishes on Sam Lucas than ever before, he spent the next half hour tromping up and down the snowy hills around the cabin...

CHAPTER 12

"The ides of March," Mandria sighed, glancing at the calendar. "A month to go, the snow is finally melting—and yesterday, I saw a robin!" Going to the window, she hoped to see the bird again, but instead, saw Tom talking to the man who had delivered Susan's cow and chickens. This time, he was delivering a letter, which Tom seemed most anxious to read, as he'd torn through the seal, before returning to the cabin, where he sat now on the front steps. Then a kettle began to bubble over and Mandria hurried to the hearth to tend it...

Tom was, indeed, anxious to read this letter. It was from Allen and considering its thickness, there was much news to relate. Plus, he'd sent some needed cash...

March 1st, 1830 Savannah, Georgia

Dear Tom,

I hope this finds you and your "family" well. I'm sorry to have missed such a Christmas! As you can tell, Joshua Munzenrider not only delivered your letter, but news of your growing household too. Do tell John and Brittany their Uncle Allen can't wait to meet them.

Like you asked, we went to see Mamalyn too. She hung on every word Josh could tell her about Mandy and still wants to be there for the birth. But Tom, because of a situation here, she will have to come earlier than planned.

Before I get too far ahead of myself now, let me start this back in January. It was New Year's Day, in fact, and Mamalyn, Hassie and Nicole were in the parlor at Marsh Haven, when Nico became agitated and would not calm down. That is when they discovered Sam had arrived. He was standing in the entry, and as Mamalyn described it, "pale as a ghost and staring at Nico while she and her rhymes became ever more frantic." Mamalyn said it took both she and Hassie to get her upstairs and settled enough for bed, but when they came down again, Sam had left without saying one word. And Tom, two days later, a second attempt was made on Nico's life. Had Hassie not discovered her missing from her room and called for a search that night, Nico would now be dead. They found her in a marsh pool, where the culprit had apparently been trying to drown her, but fled to save himself. Nico was badly frightened and did take ague, but was otherwise unharmed. The very next day, it was rumored you had been seen in Savannah and then, for about a week, the house was watched by an unruly mob again—but this time, at least, Mike wasn't with them. Anyway, on Captain Pat's advice, Mister O'Rourke moved Nico back home where she now lives under hired guard.

Oh, and as you requested, Mamalyn had been recording what Nico says, and because it was different on the night of Sam's visit, she asked that I send it on to you, as she has passed a copy to Captain Pat. It went as follows:

> *Father, mothers, sister, brothers.*
> *Two: one, two; one, two.*
> *Won't die! Bad! Blue Mama, bad!*
> *Bad, bad, bad, bad, bad man!*
> *Two brothers! Two Mamas!*
> *Bad, bad, bad Daddy!*

Two: one two; one two!
(over and over again)

My only thought is the part saying "Two brothers" as we are two brothers and were in her circle of friends. Mamalyn and Captain Pat placed significance on "Blue Mama" because Nico's mother was known as the Blue Lady. I despair that we'll ever really know and would prefer better evidence in your favor.

Evidently, though, Sam gave it importance. You see, when Nico moved home, so did Mamalyn, where several grueling arguments occurred over your case. She told Sam how strange she found it that the murder attempt happened so soon after his visit. He said she imagined his reaction to Nico's "babbling" and when she showed him a copy of the words, he tore it to shreds and forbade her to repeat "her lunacy." (He does not know Captain Pat already had a copy.) Then, unfortunately, Mamalyn mentioned your last visit to Marsh Haven and how differently Nico behaved toward you. In turn, he accused her of engineering your escape and voiced suspicions about Mandy's disappearance around the same time. It worsened when Sam found a letter from Mamalyn's sister asking about Mandy's "condition"; teasing Mamalyn about "becoming a grandmother;" and wondering why Mandy's "husband" had not come in to meet the family before they left. Needless to say, Sam felt his suspicions confirmed and accused Mamalyn of trying to have him blamed for your crimes so she could rid herself of him and you and Mandy could then return with her grandchild. Mamalyn said she stood her ground, claiming no knowledge of where you might be, even under threat of bodily harm. But Tom, it happened. Sam wrenched her arm so badly, she wore it in a sling for some weeks. He will pay for this dearly, however, because Mamalyn filed separation papers that very day and now, she too has left Savannah to *stay with her sister. Joshua is to pick her up there around the middle of this month and escort her on to you.*

Captain Pat continues his investigation with the determination of a bulldog. In November, the Rizza's returned from Pace (or Peace, as Iano now calls his place) and he took them to the Lloyd Hotel, where Kathy recognized the room in which she was held—and it was just next door to the one where you were found. Captain Pat says testimony about her abduction after the ladies' luncheon; along with that of the hotel clerk saying a red haired woman registered as your wife just before that lunch; plus your being carried into the scene, does prove a conspiracy was afoot, but doesn't yet prove Sam's involvement. He does think Mamalyn's testimony about your meeting with Nico might also be of value, and therefore agreed she should leave for her own safety, because he suspects Sam as strongly as we do. But he must be able to prove all of this without question.

As to the other Captain Herb, two or three weeks after your escape, when he had finally sobered up again, he came by the house and wanted to pay for the Grandfather clock he took such pleasure in toppling to the floor. But I had already had it repaired and saw no reason to ease his conscience— especially, after admitting he still hadn't bothered to listen to his Uncle's view of the case.

I told Mike instead of counting out money, he should count the number of times you had proven yourself his friend. Then I read him something I clipped from the paper, after which he seemed a bit ashamed, had little more to say, and left. It's from the 6th chapter of Sirach:

A faithful friend is a sturdy shelter;
He who finds one finds a treasure.
A faithful friend is beyond price;
No sum can balance his worth.
A faithful friend is a life-saving remedy;

Such as he who fears God finds.
For he who fears God acts accordingly;
And his friend will be like himself.

My efforts on your behalf go further. As you advised, I
have remained in Sam's good graces and on February 1st, he
promoted me. My office is now just down the hall from his,
and already it is proving informative. Last week, Sam had
a shouting match with a seedy looking man who came to see
him. I couldn't hear what was said, but as the man left, he
paused in the hallway to put a wad of cash in his wallet.
He mumbled something like "make the old bastard pay"
and that he'd "return to Delilah's in style." Being curious
as to why Sam would give him a large sum of money—
and if he spoke of Delilah's in Augusta—I left work and
followed him. He went straight to the stage depot and sure
enough, bought a ticket for Augusta. Then I followed him to
a tavern, where he went to await departure time, struck up
a friendly conversation and bought him several drinks. His
name was Jack and he said he'd once lived in Savannah and
had come back to collect on a debt—payment for a favor he
and his partner had done for a prominent man.

I laughed and asked, "Who did you have to kill: his girl
friend; his wife; or his wife's lover?"

Jack answered, "No, it wasn't like that, but I was nearly
killed myself. The bitch smashed my head with a vase—and
what she did to my partner, Harry, was worse. He got a
fucking hernia from the kick she gave him in the groin."

Jokingly, I said, "With a temper like that, the bitch had
to be a red-head." And Jack said that she was! Then, I said I
had been in the depot when he bought his ticket for Augusta,
and if he was interested in women of a gentler nature, he
should try the selection at Delilah's. Jack said he was going
to do just that and could now afford the best whores in the
house. He also said, "Poor Harry can't enjoy them none,

because his nuts are still swollen to the size of goose eggs." I sympathized and asked if Harry had seen a doctor. He said, "No, he just keeps lying around the boarding house hoping to get better."

Tom, I reported this to Captain Pat as soon as I left Jack and he said it was our first real lead on the pair who abducted Kathy. We rushed back to the depot, but the stage had left with Jack on it.

For days now, Captain Pat has been requesting permission to go after those two and have them returned for questioning, but has had no luck so far. His immediate superior says he is already spending too much time on this one case; that he is grasping at straws in trying to connect Kathy's abduction with Nico's beating; and that he should stop and "consider the source" of this newest lead. He said, because I'm your brother, I could "not be counted on for reliable information." Captain Pat is furious with the man, but continues to try and persuade him. If he can't, I plan to go to Augusta and find those bastards myself. So take heart, big brother, and don't give up on us yet!

I didn't mean to write a whole book when I started this letter, but there was much to tell and I knew you'd want to hear it. The house is running smoothly, so don't worry about that. Joleen and Willie are fine too, and expect to become parents at any moment. Oh, and so do the Rizza's come September!

I enclosed a draft made out to Susan—as will be my outside envelope, for your continued protection. I'm sure she'll get the money to you, as yours must be running low by now.

Take care of yourself, Brer, and give my love to Mandy and the children. (Did you know Josh has taken a shine to Susan?)

As Always, Allen

---◈---

"Does it never end?" Mandria muttered, picking up toys from the floor. First, the soup had boiled over and while she was tending that, a bright shaft of sunlight revealed dust balls beneath the bunk bed, so she'd taken the time to sweep. Now, here were the toys left where someone might trip and fall. She put them away with a restless sigh and that led her back to the window again, still hoping for a peek at the robin; for a sign of change;—for anything different!

But there was Tom, still sitting on the steps and evidently, finished with his letter, because he now gazed toward the far meadow where the children were playing. ...Or was he? No, he was more engrossed in thought than watching the youngsters. ...So, what had been in that letter—and why had it put him in such a pensive mood? Getting her shawl, she allowed curiosity to lead her onto the porch. "Well, who was the letter from?" she managed a vaguely interested tone.

"Allen," he replied, putting the folded sheets in his shirt pocket. Then, leaning his elbows on the step behind, he stretched out those long legs, crossing them at the ankles, and said no more.

This was not going to be easy. But he hadn't fooled her with the casual way he'd performed all those maneuvers. That in itself proved the letter contained news of some importance—and it angered her that he assumed the right to keep things from her. Yes, there he sat sprawled on the steps in his buckskins, like a lean muscular Puma, and like all cats, perfectly content to ignore anyone's wishes but his own. Well, not this time. "So, what did Allen have to say?" she asked, determined to ferret him out.

"Nothing much," he nodded. "...Joleen is expecting any day now. And Kathy and Iano will have a baby in September."

"I see," she nodded too. "And that has kept you sitting out here in a black sulk for so long?"

Tom glanced up at her and flashed a smile of pure devilment. "Why, Mandria, it just gladdens my heart that you have enjoyed watching me out here."

"Damn you, I don't care…" she stopped as she met his gaze, for there was no merriment or teasing in Tom's eyes. "You are trying to make me mad, so I won't ask about that letter."

He laughed a bit then, but still without glee. "Lady, you know me too well."

"Unfortunately," she agreed, wishing he weren't quite so handsome. "Now, what was in the letter you don't want me to know?"

"Mostly news about my case;—nothing you'd want to hear, certainly."

"Would you stop?" she stomped an impatient foot. "There had to be mention of my parents or friends. Don't you realize how much I want to hear that? …Please?" she added unwillingly.

"Lady, your moods are volatile at best," he ventured. "And as I'm the one who catches hell when you're upset, you're asking a lot."

Mandria paled and Tom knew he had just said too much. "Oh…I knew it! I knew when you stayed out here so long! What happened?— Has something horrible happened in Savannah?"

Tom studied her for a moment and sighed. "Sit down here, will you?" he moved over to make room, "Maybe I should tell you some of it."

"No—nobody died, did they?" she asked with dread, lowering herself beside him.

Tom still wasn't pleased with her coloring and decided to let her reactions guide the depth of his revelations. "No one died, Mandria," he began, "but a second attempt was made on Nicole's life."

"Oh, dear God!" her eyes widened. "…But how? Was she hurt?— Who would do such a thing to her now?"

"Easy," he tried to calm her. "Nico wasn't hurt and they don't know who it was—though rumor had it I was seen lurking about the city," irony flickered through his eyes. "Anyway, she is living at home again and for now, under guard."

"But how could this happen? Mama was with her night and…" And she paled again. "No—Tom, Mama wasn't hurt, was she?"

"…Not in the murder attempt, she wasn't," he answered.

"Well, thank heavens for that," she breathed, so relieved she fell to babbling. "Then Mama is back home too and can still go across the square to check on Nico. It's better this way—much safer. And Uncle Ran must be glad to have Nico at home. Yes, maybe it's all for the best. Maybe—"

"Your mother is not living at home," Tom interrupted. "She and your father have separated."

And this time, Tom truly thought she might faint, but slowly, dramatically, he watched her shock turn to suspicion. "Did Allen say why?" her eyes narrowed. "—Was another woman involved?"

Tom hesitated. Better anger than pain. He had told her enough. "Allen didn't mention another woman," he nodded.

"Then it had to be your fault!" she snapped in the next breath.

"...My fault?" he said in surprise. And resentment. "Why, yes, now that makes perfect sense, when considered so logically. If I could manage an attempt on Nico's life from half a state away, what effort would a mere marital separation take?"

"Well, it was your fault!" she insisted. "Mama is totally blind where you're concerned. She probably defended you just once too often and—and poor Father couldn't take any more!"

Tom could not believe what he was hearing. "You know, it amazes me that in one minute, you can ask if another woman was involved, but when *I'm* found more suitable for blame in the next minute, Sam becomes *poor Father*—and this, after you saw, with your own eyes, what sort of husband he is."

"I saw the kind you are too—with my own eyes," she countered. "Did you forget?"

"Not with you around," he nodded. "Still, it's very strange. Sam *did* hit Kathy—he *did* slap you too—and I am *accused* of hitting Nico. He *was* unfaithful and I'm *accused* of the same. So naturally, you've forgiven poor Father and damned me. ...And you can call your mother blind?"

"Oh, all right! So Father is not a saint. So both of you are bastards. So what?"

"So…forget it," Tom gave a giant sigh. "Your reasoning is only making me crazy and I'm not up to a battle just now. Mamalyn can tell you why they separated. Maybe you'll believe it from her."

"Well, thank you, Tom. I'll only have to wait a month for that. Or do you think I might hear Mama if she yells it all the way from Savannah?"

"She isn't in Savannah."

"…Where then?—Where did she go?"

"For a while, she stayed with her sister in Aiken, just as you did."

"And she isn't there now? Is that what you're saying?

"Well, Josh was to pick her up this week, I think."

Mandria turned on the step to face him, and Tom could almost feel icy green splinters pierce his flesh. "And you still deny a part in their separation? If Joshua is involved, then you are! What trick did you pull on my mother? How did you force her to leave Father—and Savannah, as well?"

Tom's patience snapped. "Damn it, I did not force her to do anything! Your father did—in his usual, heavy-handed…" And he stopped abruptly. "Oh, hell," he muttered. Now he would have to tell her the rest.

"He—Father…he hit her?" Mandria stammered softly.

"He wrenched her arm;—badly enough that she was in a sling for a time."

"I don't believe it," she uttered numbly.

"I knew you wouldn't;—not from me. That's why I wanted you to hear it from her."

"If only I could," Mandria lowered her forehead on clinched fists, "I'd do anything to see Mama."

"Careful, lady," Tom said with a crooked smile. "I might take you up on that offer."

"Please—I don't need any of your unamusing humor," she remarked.

"No, but you do need your mother and I promised she could be with you when the baby comes."

"Here?" Mandria grasped his arm. "Joshua is bringing Mama here?"

"Yes, and—"

"When?—When will they get here?" her grip tightened.

"In a few days, I hope and then I—"

Before Mandria thought, she was hugging him "Oh, Tom—oh, thank you! My mother! My..." And realizing her grievous error, she pushed away and rose in shaky indignation. "I know what you're trying to do!" she started up the steps. "It's merely a matter of bath tubs and hair brushes!" And going in, she slammed the door.

Tom looked after her in puzzlement. "Bath tubs and hair brushes?" he muttered. Then another smile crept over his mouth. The important thing here wasn't her meaning—nor her involuntary hug, regretfully. Rather, it was that beautiful blush, proving her fully aware of their physical contact. So was he. "...A pity men don't just blush," he acknowledged a deeper stirring. And rising only a little more steadily than had Mandria, he headed out to get the children, forcing himself to concentrate on the plan he'd been considering before she came out to join him.

"Thomas Scott!" Mandria called and he turned to see she was on the porch again. "I've just thought of something. Mama is not much of a horsewoman. She will never make it through those hills like we..." And there she halted, her hands flying to her hips. "In fact, how did Susan and Joshua do it? Those ledges were not wide enough for a wagon!"

For a second time in their association, Tom was eternally grateful for the distance separating them. "There is another way in," he replied, stuffing his hands in his pockets. "I didn't want you running away, so I brought you through the hills; ...to confuse your sense of direction."

"Oh!—Oh, damn you!" she stomped one foot and then the other. "Another deliberate deception!" And going inside, the door received its mightiest slam ever.

Tom shrugged and started for the meadow again. "So much for the problem impeding my stride," he said with a chuckle. It was astonishing how easily she controlled that. A look, a gesture, just the sight of her—even nearly eight month's pregnant—and he was fully aroused. On the flip side of that coin, a single disparaging remark and his body reacted accordingly. It occurred to Tom then, that he wasn't only comparing her effect on his physical person, but on his life as a whole. "Well, you can't separate the sides of a coin," he nodded, scuffing the toe of his boot in the earth. "I'll just have to be patient until this one lands.—Or, instead," his thoughts returned to Allen's letter, "I could do something to change the weight of the damned thing…"

CHAPTER 13

It Was Better than a week later that Evelyn arrived, escorted by Joshua and Susan. By then, both Tom and Mandria's moods had grown increasingly anxious. Tom felt each second of lost time, because he worried constantly that alone, Allen would attempt that trip to Augusta and the capture of two men. Mandria's way of hurrying time was to clean—and re-clean—the cabin, though Tom did wonder when. Every time he saw her, she was staring from the window or impatiently pacing the porch.

Impatient, yes, that's how Mandria felt—and if Tom's damnable luck held, her mother would arrive on the 25th, just in time for him to claim he'd arranged it for their damn eighth month's anniversary! Adding to her chagrin, when they did arrive—on the 25th—he met them first and she had to watch her own mother hug him effusively. Yet, when Evelyn turned Mandria's way, all resentment faded, for she had so longed for the sight of that dear, loving face. "…Mama," she rushed into her arms. Then both were crying, talking, and laughing—all at once, as they went arm in arm into the cabin.

Tom smiled as he greeted Joshua and Susan. "Thank you, my friends. You've made my wife very happy, wouldn't you say?"

"Hope-to-my-die," Susan agreed.

"Josh, the trip went smoothly?" Tom asked. "It took so long, I worried that the roads were bad. They usually are this time of year."

"If we'd had more rain, they would have been, but other than a few mud holes, we had no problems. And Evelyn was quite a good sport about everything. She insisted that I take my usual route and make my deliveries along the way.—Said the one she was expecting wasn't due for another month anyway," he chuckled.

"…Which brings up a problem," Tom said. "There's so little time before the baby comes, but I have to do something, and I'm going to need help from both of you yet another time."

"Anything," Joshua straightened, as if girding for battle.

"Indeed," echoed Susan.

"Well, let's go in, shall we—as this involves Mamalyn too?"

On entering the cabin, they saw Evelyn with an arm about each of the children, while Critter sat at her feet and from their expressions, both children and pup felt about her as everyone else did.

"Look, Tom!" Brittany came running. "Mamalyn brought us presents! See my pretty locket?" And when he stooped to inspect it, she whispered confidentially. "She's Mandy's mama. Ain't …I mean, isn't she nice? And she wants us to call her Mamalyn, if that's all right."

"Of course it is," Tom sent Evelyn a warm smile. "In fact, did you know Mamalyn chose me, from all Mandria's beaus, to be her husband?" At that, Mandria, who was about to place the tea pot on the table, lowered it with a bang that rattled the lid.

"Mercy! I do prefer my tea without glass splinters, Mandy," Evelyn laughed, while smoothly insinuating a change of subject. "And Susan, where are those delicious cinnamon buns you baked? I don't think I'll ever enjoy tea without one again."

"Here they are," she dug into the basket she carried. "And along with our buns and tea, Tom has something to tell us."

All eyes turned his way, including the children's. "…Bear; Brit, since Mamalyn brought you gifts—and that's a fine looking slingshot, son—wouldn't it be nice to give her a gift in return?"

"Yes, sir," they chimed, between gobbling bites of cinnamon bun.

"Well, she likes flowers and I saw some early blooms down by that hollow tree behind the stable. You'd like that, wouldn't you, Mamalyn?"

"Yes, I would," Evelyn lent helpful assistance. "Please, pick me a whole armful."

"John," Brittany asked as they started for the door, Critter at their heels, "if Mamalyn is Mandy's mama, don't that make her our Grandma?"

"Almost," he answered sagely, practicing an imaginary strike with his slingshot. "Yeah, she's close as we're likely to get, anyway."

All but Mandria shared a moment of laughter. ...*So Tom wants to speak to the adults—and that means they'll be fawning over him again*, she frowned. *But I don't want to share Mama's attention so soon—damn him!*

"Well, we're listening," Joshua was saying. And Mandria uttered an audible sigh.

At the same moment, Tom took in a breath and watched for her next reaction. "I have to leave here and go to Augusta," he began. And instantly, her eyes pierced him with a mixture of relief, disbelief and suspicion—as if mind, heart and body could not agree on how to accept the news. "I've had saddlebags packed since the day I received Allen's letter and if possible, I'd like to leave now."

Susan nodded as she looked at the calendar. "It's the 25th of March, so it must be important to take you away from Mandy at this late date."

"It is important," he continued, unable to meet the green eyes that still held such confusion. "There are two men there who could help decide my case. I have to find them before Allen goes looking alone, because...well, because I just don't know if he can handle the confrontation this promises to be."

"So who are these dangerous men?" asked Evelyn.

"I believe they're the ones who abducted Kathy and then took me to the Lloyd Hotel," he answered.

"But Tom!" Joshua exclaimed. "It could mean your life if they recognize you first.—And they could turn you in to the law, hoping for a reward."

Mandria rose abruptly. "I hope *they* collect it—if *they* even exist! *They* would certainly do me a favor."

"Mandy, how could you?" Evelyn uttered in dismay. "Surely Tom has explained—"

"Mama, Tom only explains things to his advantage," she retorted. "And as I don't care to hear any more of this, I'm going out to join the children." But on reaching the door, she turned with a parting shot, which unlike John's practice one, struck exactly where she wanted it to. "And after months of claiming to want this child—and holding me prisoner because of it—you might ask him to explain deserting… *it* now," she refused to include herself in the complaint. "Oh, yes, I defy him to explain that!" Then out she went with a resounding bang of the door.

The rest were amazed to hear Tom laugh. "One thing I'll say for your grandfather, Susan. He built some damned fine doors—and I'm afraid, they've been thoroughly tested around here."

"Indeed," Joshua, nodded, in awe of Tom's tolerance.

Evelyn's reaction was pique. "Well, Mandy may be too old for a spanking, but she is sorely testing my right to administer one! Tom, now she has added desertion to her list of grievances."

"…Still," questioned Susan, ever the independent thinker, "it sounded as if Mandy has been kept in the dark about this. She is quite intelligent, Tom, so why would you do that to her?"

"Oh, he has tried telling her truth, Susan—I'm certain he has," Evelyn said. "So did I every day before she left Savannah. But evidently, she isn't hearing a word in Tom's favor even now."

"Mamalyn, that is the very reason I have to do this," said Tom. "Without positive, undeniable proof, she won't ever believe me. I don't want to leave her now and I can't predict how long this might take. So, I'm afraid I must ask you to deal with her; …and should something delay me in Augusta, possibly the birth of our child."

"And the care of it," she reached for his hand. "After what you've been through to keep this baby, you're not to worry on that account. Just take care of your business there and I'll tend to mine here."

"But not here in this cabin," Susan came forward on her chair. "It's Mandy's first pregnancy and the delivery could prove difficult. No, sir,

I think they should move in with me while you're gone—and Joshua can just pack us all in his wagon and do that today."

"Yes—of course, yes," he agreed.

"Thank you, my friends," Tom said gratefully. "I was going to ask, but—"

"Hope-to-my-die?" Susan laughed.

"Hope-to-my-die," he laughed too. "—Oh, and Mamalyn, did you remember the gift for Mandria's birthday?"

"I did," she walked with him toward the back door. "And I've a story to tell about it when you've more time. But I'll see she gets it if you haven't returned—and that she knows you sent for it, too."

"Tom, are you going to tell her goodbye?" Susan followed, with Joshua close behind.

"I'll try," he said. "But I will speak with the children regardless. I don't want them thinking I'm a deserter too." And as he started across the yard, the rest stood crowded in the doorway, hoping for the best, as Tom met his returning family just at the corner of the stable.

"Look at our flowers, Tom!" Brittany danced about the bundle Mandria carried. "Mamalyn will love these, won't she?"

"Sure she will, Brit," said John. "Didn't I tell you they smelt good as perfume?"

"You and your nose," Tom smiled, ruffling the boy's hair, as he knelt and drew the youngsters to him. "Now, I've a big favor to ask and it will take some real grown-up behavior from both of you. ... You see, I'm going away—"

"No!" Brittany's eyes rounded. "You can't leave us!—What if them Short's was to come back? Oh, Tom," her lower lip trembled, "you can't leave;—you still love us!"

"Of course, I love you.—I love all of you more than my own life," And hugging them close, he glanced at Mandria above their heads. She looked so damn beautiful with her armful of early spring flowers. ...If only there had been love in her eyes, instead that set, cold stare. "Anyway, I'll try not to stay long and maybe I'll bring home some really good news."

"T…Tom," John fumbled around his own quivering lip. "You ain't lying; you will come back—and we can go fishing, like you promised?" And down his cheek slid a tear.

Seeing it, Tom felt elated and saddened at once. He'd never doubted Brittany's devotion for an instant, and now, when he needed it most, was evidence of John's feelings too. "Bear—son," he struggled to keep his eyes dry, "I have never made a promise I didn't keep. I will be back—hope-to-my-die!" Again, he looked at Mandria, and heard her exasperated sigh. Then rising, he took the flowers she held and handed them to Brittany. "Go, kids; deliver these to Mamalyn—and Susan might just give you another cinnamon bun."

"And I'm going with them," Mandria started to follow, only to be caught in the crook of a strong arm.

"No, you are coming with me," Tom countered.

"To Augusta?" she balked as he drew her toward the stable. "I won't unless you plan to deliver a baby on horseback!—Even for you, that is madness!"

"You are a ninny," he stated as they entered the shaded interior. "Your mother couldn't have put it better," he pulled her right into his arms; and in such a way, that her own were pinned beneath his while she was held nose to nose with him. "…Now then, pretty lady, one word out of you, until I've said what I must, and I'll close that savage little mouth with a kiss."

"You wouldn't dare!" she gasped and was quickly proven wrong. "Oh, you bastard!" she raled and he kissed her again. "Tom, stop—" and he claimed another. Then and only then, was Mandria silent— though her eyes fairly danced with angry green sparks.

"That's better," he smiled. "But, damn it, I should have thought of this months ago!" At that, Mandria's mouth opened to speak, but snapped shut when Tom leaned closer. "Now, I'm leaving as soon as I saddle the horse, but what I said to John and Brittany applies to you most of all. …Lady, I do love you more than my life and I've never—well, never knowingly broken a promise to you—and that does include our marriage vows."

"You did so!" the words escaped, for which she was kissed yet again.

"I didn't" he uttered from a whisper away. "And I'm hoping this trip will prove it to you, once and for all. Then what will you do with your fury, my love? It should prove an interesting homecoming."

"To say nothing of—"

"That's right: say nothing," he claimed her mouth once more. But this time, he kept it, kissing her thoroughly, possessively, unceasingly, until she stopped struggling and responded in spite of herself. "Just say nothing," he repeated against lips which had yielded to his. "It isn't necessary. You've said all I wanted to hear in that kiss."

"No, damn you—no!" she broke free. "It wasn't a kiss given, but taken!" And turning, she fled for the cabin.

Tom listened for the back door to slam. It did, and a few moments later, the bedroom door did too. "...Dear God, grant those good ladies patience," he sighed, throwing the saddle blanket over the horse. And as he finished the task, a smile crawled over his mouth. "Mandria does love me," he mused, mounting to ride away in the crisp morning air. "Now, to bring it to the surface again..."

"What?—We're going where?" And snubbing badly, Mandria sat up on the bed to face her mother.

"I said we are moving in with Susan until Tom returns. He wants us to do this, so we are. Now, kindly get up from there and help us pack."

"...Mama, how could you side with him against me? What if I don't want to move? Would it make any difference to you?"

"I'm sorry, dear," Evelyn said with primly laced fingers. "I know how you must love this cozy little cabin—"

"Love it?" Mandria retorted. "I hate it—oh, how I hate it!"

"Then we haven't a problem, have we? You hate it, so we'll leave. Come along now, we must get packed." And with that, and a sweet smile, she left the bedroom.

"Damn!" Mandria fell back on the bed in exasperation. "—Oh, that bastard!" she sank angry fists into the mattress. "Do this; do that; move here; move there!" she rose, and emptying a pillow case, furiously stuffed it with her meager collection of clothes, but left Tom's extra ones where they hung. "How dare he kiss me like that!" she fumed, yet still packed her vanity set. "Then he had the nerve to make something of it; *You said all I wanted to hear in that kiss*," she mimicked sarcastically. "Well, you are wrong, Tom Scott! One more month and I'll be free of any ties to you! Oh, yes, I'll expel them, right along with your baby!" So saying, she knocked his clothes to the floor, straightened her shoulders and marched through the door ready to defend her position with any who crossed her path.

And literally, everyone did. The cabin was aswarm with activity as the rest bustled about packing for the move. To and fro they scurried, laughing, chattering, stuffing things into boxes and bags, and no one bothered to ask Mandria a single question. Sinking onto a chair at the table, she clutched her pillow case luggage on her lap and wondered if she'd become invisible. She did not wish to help in any way, but they could have granted her the privilege of saying so;—of expressing her displeasure with the man whose orders they followed like a bunch of silly, cackling geese! But none did, so she rose and took her invisible self out the front door, braced with all the dignity and righteousness she could muster. And when the others came out to deposit various bundles in the wagon—including Tom's clothes—they found her within, still maintaining her silent posture of protest, and staring, very pointedly, at the cradle Joshua had placed at her feet...

Chapter 14

It was Midnight and a day and a half later when Tom reached Augusta. He was dog-tired and so saddle-weary he could hardly stand, but still he knew he'd get no rest until certain of Allen's whereabouts. That meant checking the registers of every hotel in town, which made it close to two in the morning before he sought a bed for himself. The next day, he checked the boarding houses, not finding Allen's name there either, and far too many Jacks and Harrys. So, come mid-afternoon, he turned to his one remaining lead, and paid a call on Miss Delilah Delightful, proprietress, madam and absolute boss of her own popular whore house.

When the maid brought word that a Mr. Thomas Scott wished to see her, Delilah was entertaining the owner of a local jewelry store. She wondered what she should do, for Donald Treadway had just given her a pearl ring, studded with diamonds and expected much in return. As a business woman, she knew she owed him attention. And yet, as a female who had found Tom a rarity among an eternal parade of uninspiring lovers…well, seeing him again was a treat she owed herself.

"Donald, darling," she took his hands and urged him up from a chair, "I know this is God-awful of me," she pressed those hands to her bosom, "but I'm asking you to leave now."

"W…what?" the portly man began to stutter, but did not withdraw his happily engaged fingers. "Delilah, not after the nice little bauble I brought you.—Honey, you can't mean it!"

"It's for your frigging enjoyment that I ask it, lover," she backed slowly toward the door with the grappled Donald in tow. "You see, sugar-balls, there's a man here to talk about a new batch of girls—a real fucking bunch of beauties, so I hear. Anyway, I have to see the bastard and try to get his God damn price down."

"Get his pants down first, Delilah, and his price will follow," Donald laughed at his own joke. "But new girls, you say?" he paused, wetting chubby lips with a thick tongue. "Any young ones, honey— real young ones?"

"Holy shit!" she gave a harsh laugh. "Donald, you and your craving for cherries is driving me damn-near crazy!" And this she said while opening the door. "But what the hell, I'll ask. And for being so sweet about this, by damn, you can have first pick of the litter. How's that, Mr. Puss-pounder?" she gently pushed him into the hall.

"…All right then," Donald pouted a bit. "—As long as I can return tomorrow for twice what I asked today?"

"You've got it," she agreed. "Lover, I'll fuck your rod so hot and so long—shit—we'll sell what's left for kindling." And she closed the door on Donald's delighted peel of laughter. "Stupid fat fool," she uttered, hurrying to her dressing table. "Tom Scott, huh?" she said, running a brush through her flowing mass of flame-colored hair. And remembering the nights he had spent in her establishment, brought a glow to her skin that rivaled the rouge she now applied to lip and cheek. "Wonder if he'll notice that I've gained a few pounds?" And opening her sheer violet wrap, she scrutinized the figure beneath. Her purple nightie, a mere slip of a thing, reached only to her thigh tops— and Delilah frowned at the dimples there. But her breasts were as magnificent as ever and truly caused the simple gown to hang like a work of art. Yes, and Tom Scott did appreciate good nipples and tits. "God damn, I'm anxious to see that stud-bastard again!" she smiled. And tying her sash snugly about her waist, she quickly sent a maid to fetch him from the front parlor. Then popping a mint in her mouth, she unstoppled her favorite perfume and enjoyed an expensive mini-bath.

When Tom entered, Delilah's hazel-brown eyes widened at his rugged, backwoods appearance. …How was it possible for a man to be equally appealing in a suit and this outfit as well? In more formal attire, he was everything a gentleman should be: ever conscious of his manners; ever mindful of keeping his virile masculinity subdued— which of course, made a woman hot for his pursuit. And now, dressed as he was, his primitive magnetism was blatantly stressed: untamed; undeniable; in every clinging inch of those buckskins—and this made a woman yearn to pursue him. But either way, the damnedest thing of all, was that he never seemed aware of his startling effect on females.

"Well, bless my puckered pussy," she murmured, circling him slowly. "Lover, I'd never forget a body like yours," she patted his bottom playfully. "And them skins show it off real good."

"Uh…Delilah?" Tom turned to face her—and the light dancing in her eyes made him realize she was going to present a problem he hadn't anticipated. "…I, uh—well, I need a favor rather badly."

"Fallen on hard times, sweet cakes?" she stepped closer. "Now, Delilah has a cure for anything *hard* and handsome as yours. Come on, give us a big juicy kiss and we'll just solve all your little problems."

"Please, Delilah, I'm serious," he held her slightly away. "I'm in big trouble and I haven't time for this." But seeing her disappointment and needing her cooperation, he added, "…Not now, anyway." And instantly, her attention was his again. "You see, I've been accused of raping a girl and trying to beat her to death—"

"You?" she laughed incredulously, running fingers across the breadth of his chest. "Listen, I know my girls didn't charge you a fucking cent—and I lectured them about it too. Of course, they laughed in my damn face, seeing as they knew I hadn't charged you either. But no, Tom Scott, rape wouldn't be possible;—not when every woman who lays eyes on you is so fucking ready to bed you."

"Thank you…I think," he nodded. "But I still need your help to prove I didn't do it.—And can I have a drink while we talk?"

"Help yourself—and pour me one too—but you'll have more than that, you great stud," she commented while going to the door.

And speaking to a maid in the hallway, she then returned to accept the glass Tom had waiting. "You know I'd gladly help you, Tom, but I hope you're not counting on the word of a whore to carry much weight. My knowledge of your...*abilities?*" she emphasized, while lowering herself on a chair facing him. "Well, it wouldn't sway no jury of upstanding citizens."

Tom chuckled, as he sat too, and stretched his legs out before him. "No, and it would make my wife madder than hell."

"Shit, I find that hard to believe," Delilah scanned him curiously. "Surely your wife enjoys your passion better—and more often—than any of us." Then her eyes widened perceptively. "Don't tell me the fool believes the rape charge?"

"She was manipulated, Delilah, and so was I. Her own father arranged for her to find me in bed with this girl, who happened to be a life-long friend of my wife's. The girl was severely beaten; I had been drugged;—but my wife still bought her father's story."

"Well...God damn," she uttered, rising to answer a knock at the door, whereupon a procession of maids entered with a tub and proceeded to fill it.

Tom watched uneasily. ...Were his *abilities* good enough to talk a woman out of, as well as into bed? Delilah had taken the existence of his wife as an everyday occurrence, probably assuming from his story and presence that he was seeking her brand of comfort. ...So, how was he going to convince her otherwise and yet be assured of her assistance? Especially when he was in need—dire need—of such comfort...

"Come, lover, and I'll scrub your back while you bathe," she smiled, removing her robe.

Seeing her scantily clad form; her full-to-bursting breasts; Tom groaned audibly, feeling each and every day he'd been without. But Delilah was not the woman he wanted so desperately and keeping to his chair, he nodded, at a loss for something to say.

"Thomas, I'm a whore, but I ain't no God-damn bitch. You're waging a hell of a war with yourself. So, you love your wife;—so what? I don't find that offensive, though judging your reaction to me, she's left you starving for a taste of pussy. Anyway, sweet thing, I don't know where you've been hiding, but you smell like a fucking horse—and that does offend me. Now, off with them skins and into this tub, or it's out the door you go!"

"Well, I'm sorry for the offense; and for having to refuse your favors, tempting as they truly—*truly*—are," Tom said and meant it. "But I do love my wife and betraying her now would only make me a liar;—and prove she was right about me all along."

"Oh shit!" she pointed sternly. "Get in that tub! If we ain't going to screw, then we ain't. But the least you can do is let me enjoy looking— *if* you want my help, as you said?"

"...Delilah, that is blackmail," Tom rose and began to undress.

"Yes it is. But you don't get something for nothing in this world, Tom. I learned that when my name was still Mary May Dredge." And as he turned to step into the tub, she gathered his clothes and handed them to someone who always seemed to be waiting beyond the door. Returning, she gave him a forward shove as she soaped his shoulders and back. "Damn it, would you just relax?" she said feeling his tensed muscles. "You're acting like a fucking virgin—and both of us know better than that.—Hell, more than half my girls know better than that!" And she allowed agitation to power her scrubbing. "Love!" she added, slopping a full sponge on his head. "God forbid it ever happening to me!"

Tom grinned up at her. "Well, that would be bad for business, wouldn't it? ...Not that it's done me a hell of a lot good either," he added with a sigh.

Delilah also sighed. Then rising to her feet, she handed Tom his drink, lit a cigar and handed him that too. "Lord, but you are a fine specimen," her voice mellowed as her eyes travelled over him. "...Is she worth it, Tom;—this stupid goose who makes you deny yourself a good piece of tail?"

"She must be. And don't ask me why," he nodded in honest wonder. "She professes to hate me; damns me for getting her with child; has made me the target of every temper tantrum imaginable;—and yet, I continue to want her like no other."

"Spoken like a man in love," she concluded. "And not like one who would betray it. ...So, why does she think you've put up with her shit, if not to prove yourself?"

"If only you knew her—"

"Hell, in my line of work, that would never do!" she laughed brassily. "And if I did know her, I'd just kick her pregnant fanny—because that's where her brains seem to be."

"...Almost," Tom chuckled, clinching the cigar in his teeth. He was remembering, that not so long ago, Mandria had made a similar pronouncement about the stimulation needed to stir her thinking process. "Anyway, I do need your help if I'm ever to prove my innocence."

"So, what can I do for you?" she took his cigar and puffed it herself.

"Delilah, there is a man who comes here, that I have to find. His name is Jack and he has a partner, Harry, who is suffering a groin injury."

"Jack Spidell," she injected. "Yes, I know him, and he's a fucking scum-bucket."

"But you do know him?" Tom straightened. "You could point him out to me?"

"I could, but the bastard ain't been around for a couple of weeks—"

"Damn!" Tom rose in aggravation. And aware of that too late, he accepted a towel Delilah was in no hurry to release to him. Then, wrapping it about his waist, he stepped from the tub, and looked about for his clothes.

"They smelled like a horse too," she smiled warmly, reclaiming her chair. "So, you're stuck in that cute little number 'til they've been powdered down and aired out—which could take a while. But hell, I'm not complaining."

"Well, I am!" Tom chuckled. "Surely, you've something more I can wear?"

"No, sugar-balls, I don't," she nodded mischievously. "And if I did, damn if I'd give it to you. I'm not fucking stupid—I'll keep you this way as long as possible. Tom, don't you realize you have a body that would cause pointy tits on a damn nun? Now, just sit down here, if you still want to know about Jack."

So, Tom sat facing her—awkwardly—because when he pressed the towel between his thighs, it came unfastened at the waist; and when he'd retie it, the towel would ride higher on his lap. "Delilah ... please?" he sent her a flustered look.

"Just forget about it," she shrugged. "I've seen it all in this place. I just enjoyed yours a hell of a lot—and as you've grown stingy about sharing, I intend to enjoy the God damn view!"

Tom leaned to the back of the chair with a sigh of resignation, and simply laid the towel across his lap. "So tell me about Jack," he began. "—But first, has anyone else come asking after him?—A young man in particular?"

"Not that I've heard," she nodded. "Who would he be?"

"My brother. I just want to make sure he stays out of trouble."

"In here?" she had to ask. "Hell, trouble is what the young ones come looking for!"

"I know," Tom agreed. "And you might remember him. Allen was in last August with Captain Herb. He was seventeen at the time, and anxious, so I heard, to try as many women as flavors of whiskey."

"So are they all, Tom. At that age, so are they all," she said philosophically. "But ain't that a damn coincidence? Captain Herb brought you in here too."

"Yes. ...Have you seen much of him lately?"

"And there's another coincidence. The Captain is in for the night—just down the hall with Ann Marie."

"Oh hell—of all the luck," Tom groaned. "Delilah, if I've had any good luck, I can't remember when it was."

"But you and him was friends. What happened there?"

"Nothing much," Tom said sardonically. "Mike was only engaged to the girl I supposedly raped and beat."

"Holy shit," she declared. "The old man sure did want your balls in a vice, didn't he?"

"That is why I have to find Jack and Harry. They worked for my father-in-law and I believe they helped him set me up."

"Well, maybe your luck is changing, sugar-lump. I said Jack hasn't come here, but I know where he lives."

"Where?" Tom came forward attentively.

And the towel receded farther, but of course, Delilah didn't care to mention it. "First, let me tell you how I know," she smiled appreciatively. "Like I said, he is scum—preferred taking my girls in the ass. And while he was about that—riding them like a dog—he enjoyed squeezing their tits real hurtful like;—like a frigging farmer would squeeze and draw milk from a cow. The bastard meant to hurt them too and wasn't satisfied until they were begging for mercy. It seems he can't finish a fuck unless his woman is in pain."

"…Then, why did you allow him the privilege?" Tom had to ask.

"I wouldn't have myself—and gave my girls permission to refuse him," she shrugged. "But he paid well and some of the stupid bitches still took him on. Anyway, I kept a boy here too—a pansy, who serviced my customers of that persuasion. And as Jack liked ass holes, one really busy night I offered Dexter to him, hoping to free up a girl. Well, he got fucking mad about it; proceeded to wreck the furniture in the side salon, so I had him thrown out on the street. Then, a few nights later, he returned with an apology, a big roll of money and a plan he considered a fine joke to pull on his partner, Harry. He said they'd had an argument; that Harry was jealous of the way Jack was spending their money in here. To get even, Jack wanted to take one of my girls and the pansy back to their boarding house—"

"Which boarding house?" Tom asked impatiently.

"I'm coming to that," her smile broadened, as the towel rode even higher. "You see, Jack meant to set up an orgy, where Harry was forced to watch him have sex with the girl and the pansy was to try and seduce Harry at the same time—"

"Delilah—damn it, when was this and where?" Tom insisted. "If this joke caused them to split up, I may never find them!"

"But it didn't—and that's what I've been trying to tell you. Dexter, by some miracle, was able to help Harry enjoy sex in spite of his injury, and that purely fascinated Jack. So now, Dexter is living there with the two of them—and I know this, because I saw Dex on the street yesterday and begged him to come home. But, he said he wouldn't as long as they kept paying so well for his service—and he didn't offer me a percentage either. Not the first God damn cent."

"Poor Delilah," Tom said dryly. "And once again, where is it they live?"

"Why poor Delilah? Just because I keep my purse between my thighs?" she laughed. "Well, I do—and it still wouldn't cost you anything to stuff it with that jewel between yours," she pointed, then wished she hadn't when Tom covered himself again.

"Believe me, I wish I could," he admitted. "The offer is damned tempting, much appreciated and truly needed, but Delilah, I have to go after these men.—Now!" he stressed.

"Well, they're at the Ulmer House on Reynolds Street, but you can't mean to go alone?" she questioned. "Tom, don't be a God damn fool! It would be three on one, because Dexter will side with them, and he is fucking good with knives—an expert, I'm telling you. He has killed more than once and sliced up a score of others. One night, I saw him take the ear off a man from twenty feet away—and the bastard near bled to death before he realized his ear was missing!"

"Nevertheless, I'm going to take Jack and Harry. And not only that, I'm going to deliver them to a plantation near Savannah where they can be identified."

"Now you're talking real shit!" Delilah rose before him. "You're on the run, right?"

"Yes."

"So you can't expect any fucking help from the law."

"No, but—"

"So how in the hell do you think you'll get both these bastards down there alone?—That is, if you survive their capture!"

"I don't know. But I haven't another choice, so I'll do it," Tom nodded.

"Like hell, you will!" she moved away. "If there is one thing I hate, its waste—and your dying would be one!" she went out the door, then locked him in. "Now, just stay naked and stay put, lover, until I've thought of a better way than sending you to a certain death," she called from outside.

It seemed to Tom he'd waited an eternity, though the mantle clock kept assuring him it had been just over an hour. "Damn the woman!" he paced the room, now wearing Delilah's bed spread. "Where could she be?"

In answer, Delilah entered, followed by another parade of maids. One brought his clothes; another carried in a huge supper tray; while the rest emptied the tub and drug it away. "So, get dressed, sugar-balls," she smiled at him. "Then we'll have a bite to eat."

Tom had no intention of staying, though he didn't say so as he hurriedly donned his buckskins. No, helpful as she meant to be, Delilah had detained him far too long. But when he started for the door, an unmistakable click froze him in mid step and he turned very carefully to face her.

"You might need this fucking thing," she laughed, waving a cocked pistol dangerously about. "If not for Jack and Harry, then to protect yourself from Captain Herb. He knows you are here now."

"Delilah, you told him?" he approached her cautiously. And removing the gun, he eased the hammer down. "Why for God's sake? I don't need another fight on my hands."

"No, but you do need his frigging help. Tom, his boat, along with his crew to stand watch, are your best bet for getting those bastards down river."

"True, but Mike would never agree to it. He'll go for my throat again.—And where is he, by the way? I'm surprised he didn't follow you in with a gun of his own."

"You're holding it," she grinned. "As I'm holding him. He is madder than hell, but is still in Ann Marie's room;—gagged, bound to a chair and almost as naked as you were."

"And?"

"And I think you should try talking sense to him. It's a chance, sweet thing—a fucking slim one—but the best I could do on short notice."

"Delilah," Tom drew her gruffly into his arms, "I'm going to kiss you."

"Well, I wanted more," her arms slid up and about his neck. "So make it a God damn good one, Tom?" And it must have been, because when Tom departed, Delilah sank onto the bed, allowing her reeling senses to settle. "Mrs. Scott," she nodded, "you have to be the stupidest bitch alive…"

Tom knocked lightly at the door to which he'd been directed, by that ever present hall maid. Ann Marie opened it, bobbed a satirical curtsy and left him standing there as she hurried away in a huff. She had, after all, given up a handsome customer good for the night and God only knew what was left downstairs! …But after a dozen paces or so, it dawned on her that the man at her door had been rather attractive too, and pausing, she looked back. He was very handsome indeed—and such a body he had! That alone had her sucking in her tummy and presenting her most seductive smile. The smile he returned sent tingles clear to her toes. …But it wasn't an invitation. And wondering how she knew that, Ann Marie turned again, compelled by some unseen force to be on her way…

Tom found the Captain exactly as Delilah had said: bound to a chair; gagged; wearing only his skivvies—and certainly, madder than hell. Anger blazed from his eyes and Tom had no doubt the sounds muttered against the gag were curses aimed at him. Taking a deep breath, he closed the door, fetched the chair from a dressing table and turning it backwards, straddled it as he sat directly before his one-time best friend.

"…Mike," he began, "I am not guilty of the crimes committed against Nicole. And I want you to help me prove it."

Further outraged, the Captain struggled mightily against his bindings, renewing his tirade of unintelligible curses.

"You might as well stop that," Tom folded his arms across the chair back. "You are going to listen, so just accept it."

But the Captain didn't and Tom had to wait until he had exhausted himself and sat panting in a quieter fury.

Tom began anew. "Did you ever listen to your Uncle's view of the case, as Allen suggested?"

Mike's nod was only slightly affirmative.

"...Yet, you weren't convinced."

And his nod became a very negative one.

"Well, up front, I want you to know, that Captain Pat can only prove part of this story. The rest is what we have pieced together and believe to be true. But as I said, if you will help me, I think I'll be able to prove it all. So, let's start with the how: You know Captain Pat suspects that Kathy's abduction and what happened to Nicole were connected. But it was a conspiracy with no apparent motive. And as all the evidence pointed my way, his theory carried little weight with most people. Am I right so far?"

Mike's nod was a definite affirmative this time.

"All right. Do you recall a conversation we had in my parlor? We were talking about Sam's influence on Nico and both agreed that he wouldn't hesitate to ruin her if it suited his purpose. Well, that is exactly what he did. You saw how severely Kathy was beaten for going against him, so won't you admit Sam was capable of doing the same to Nicole?—And especially, if she refused the cooperation he needed?"

Mike stared straight ahead, unimpressed with Tom's effort.

"Captain, you were at the Ball; you saw how furious Sam was about my marriage to Mandria—and he was no happier that Kathy had found a life of her own. I still don't know his reason for the original bargain with me, but I do believe this last maneuver was meant to destroy two marriages. It would have, too, had Kathy and I been discovered in bed together. ...And I'm afraid Nicole was his accomplice. We may never know how he persuaded her to it, but she was there, and if not to help Sam, can you name me one good reason she would be in a place like the Lloyd Hotel?"

At that, Mike gave Tom a look of pure accusation.

"No, it wasn't to meet me. I was still teaching school when she checked in. ...But I'm getting ahead of my story. I want you to see how cleverly Sam worked this out—and the mistakes he made. Now, sometime before noon, the hotel clerk said my red-haired wife took a room for us and one next door for a cousin. That wife was Nicole, wearing a wig—which was found in the room she rented. Just after noon, Iano dropped Kathy off at Hester's where she met Mamalyn, Mandria and Lucy for lunch. She was abducted on her way back around two o'clock, probably drugged, taken in a back way, and left in that second rented room—which she has now identified, as the place where she was held. Why Sam wanted us placed in two separate rooms, none of us can understand, but that's what happened," Tom shrugged. "Anyway, before school let out at three o'clock, I received a note saying a buggy would be waiting outside and would I please come by Sam's office for a peace conference. I didn't expect much, but for Mandria's sake, I went—and was also stupid enough to let him feed me a couple of drug-laced drinks. Again, the hotel clerk said I was carried in—drunk—a little after five. Carried, Mike, by two men; as Kathy was abducted by two. So now, with both of us there, Sam could complete his plan and would have, had Kathy not escaped first, leaving him with a problem. How was I going to be caught in adultery without a woman present? So yes, Nicole, who had been his accomplice, then became his victim—though, I believe he had to beat her into submission," Tom paused, noting Mike's ashen color.

"...Sam did a fine job tidying up the loose ends of his altered agenda, too. He knew Kathy hadn't seen him all day and because the henchmen he'd used were unknown to her, there was nothing there to link him to her abduction. As a safety measure, he must have paid the pair off and had them leave Savannah. He did the same to me—taking back the note he sent to the school. Without it, I couldn't prove I'd seen him that day either.

"And finally, he brought Mandria back to the hotel, sent for the law, and according to your Uncle, played the avenging, outraged father as he led the way in," he paused again, for Mike sat with his head lowered, his expression unreadable. "Think about it, Captain—think hard. You saw what Kathy suffered at the Seafest. Sam came close to killing her. Nicole would certainly have objected to this new plan, for the social disgrace alone. And I believe he did mean to kill her—left her for dead—with me to take the blame for everything."

Now Mike rolled his head from side to side and there was such pain and confusion in his expression that Tom had to look away.

"…Captain," he continued, "I don't intend to let Sam Lucas go unpunished. Those two bastards he hired are here in Augusta and I know where to find them."

With that, Mike became very still and raised questioning eyes to Tom's.

"I mean to capture them and take them to Iano's place. If Kathy can make a positive identification, then by God, they are going to talk. And I am just desperate enough—and angry enough—to resort to torture. But they will give me the truth." So saying, he carefully scanned everything about Mike. There was still confusion in his eyes, yet the knuckle-whitening grip he'd held on the chair arms had lessened a bit.

"Well?" Tom asked hopefully. "Have I gotten through to you at all? Will you help me take the bastards and get them down river?"

The Captain's expression then could only be called hesitant. "Damn it, Mike," Tom added, "if I were guilty, would I come out of hiding in a perfectly safe place and bother to track them down? And I'd have to be insane, as well, to ask your assistance.—Here," he added laying the pistol on Mike's lap. "You can have that back too. Then, if we fail, you still have the option of shooting me or turning me over to the law. So, now will you help me?"

Mike looked at the gun balanced on his knees and back at Tom for a long moment. And almost imperceptibly, one eyebrow lifted and a much missed twinkle surfaced to dance in his eyes. *Yes!* he nodded and mumbled incoherently. *Hell yes—all right, yes!*

"You must speak more clearly, Captain," Tom said seriously. "What's that you're saying?" How Tom had missed the animated bantering he'd once shared with this man, and as he removed the gag, he wondered what Mike's first words would be.

"Sir," the Captain grinned crookedly, working his sore face muscles, "after we've captured these two…would you mind sharing a bottle with an Irishman?"

"Not with the devil himself, if it's decent whiskey," Tom answered recognizing the dialogue. And he knew Mike was saying their bond had been renewed.

"Well, damn it, I'd ask you to shake with Satan if I had a hand to offer!" he reminded Tom of his hobbled condition.

"Patience, my friend," Tom smiled, untying him. And when Mike rose to his feet and their truce was indeed sealed by a handshake, Tom laughed. "Never in my life have I wanted to hug a man without pants, but damn it Mike, I'm going to hug you!"

"Well, hell," Mike complained, but hugged him back. "Has life in the wilds been that bad?" he scanned Tom's apparel.

"It wasn't so terrible," he answered, handing Mike his trousers. "No picnic either, but that story will keep. Let's go, Captain, a pair of bastards await our company!"

"A question first," Mike grinned lifting the pistol. "Is the damn thing loaded?"

"No," Tom chuckled, returning the bullets as he opened the door.

"Just thought I'd ask," Mike nodded as they went down the hall.

At the foot of the stairs, they encountered Delilah and without a word, each man took a turn at kissing her soundly before going out the door. She then turned, wearing a victorious smile, to face those in the main salon who had watched. "Well, what else did you expect?" she gave her brassiest, sassiest laugh. "Hell, the customers at Delilah's are always that grateful!"

CHAPTER 15

The knock on Jack and Harry's door was answered by Delilah's former employee. Dexter wore a mustard silk robe, mustard slippers and heavy mascara. His full, neatly brushed black hair was parted in the middle and held away from his face with tiny tortoise-shell combs. His ears were pierced with golden hoops.

Taking one look at the man, Mike turned half away and groaned audibly. Realizing he had neglected to say anything about Dexter, Tom hurried to cover Mike's reaction. "May we speak with Jack and Harry, please?" he asked politely.

Dexter scrutinized them thoroughly before answering. He didn't care for the rude fellow, who'd all but turned his back, but the taller one didn't seem so bad. In fact, he thought with a wistful tilt of his head and a second look at the fit of his trousers...not bad at all. "Well, they aren't here just now," he replied, matching Tom's pleasantness.

"Could you tell us when they will be?" Tom asked now.

"I could," Dexter made a pretty shrug. "But what's it to you, Mr. Buckskins?"

That earned him a look from Mike; and from Tom, a lie snatched from thin air. "Business. The boss sent us to see them."

"Mister Lucas?" his eyes widened with interest. "God, but I'd love meeting him. Is he as rich as Jack and Harry claim?"

"Probably richer," Tom nodded.

"…You know what?" Dexter struck a casual pose against the door frame. "You both seem familiar to me—especially you," he pointed daintily at Mike. "You've been to Delilah's haven't you?"

"I have," he straightened and considering his reason the normal one, his tone was almost indignant.

"You've been there too, Dex," Tom injected. "Yes, I know your name. And if I remember correctly, you were very popular the night I saw you."

A smile bared Dexter's small pearly teeth as he raised a hand to his brow. "Well, I do have my ways," he sighed softly.

Ready to leave, Mike nudged Tom with an elbow.

Tom wasn't. "I'm sure you do, Dex," he smiled engagingly. "… Aren't Jack and Harry worried someone might lure you away while they're gone?"

"It's always a possibility, isn't it?" Dexter's laughter tinkled down the hallway after grating across Mike's nerves. "But alas, I must stay until I get my share of the draft Mr. Lucas sent—and they didn't cash it before they left."

"Now, that's a real shame," Tom allowed regret to tinge his voice. "…But how long will they be gone?"

"Well, they said no more than a few days. And I know they'll return, because I insisted on holding the draft—clever creature that I am."

"And wise, knowing Jack and Harry as I do," Tom added. "So, where did they go?"

"On an errand for your boss. …But, why wouldn't you know that?"

"Just checking. You can never tell with those two," Tom nodded. "Mr. Lucas wanted to know if they've made any progress."

"Well, they only got his fucking letter yesterday, for God's sake!" Dexter declared. "What did he do: send you up here the same day he posted the frigging thing?"

"I didn't ask. I just follow orders—and collect my pay," Tom patted his rear pocket.

"…Yes. Well, I didn't like it much when they left me behind just to go looking for the boss's wife.—Who cares if she's still at her sister's? I don't enjoy being alone," he made a pouty mouth. "I get so…lonely?"

"Yeah, Lucas can be a real heartless bastard," Tom sympathized. "—Of course, you could ask us in," he added, hearing an intake of breath from Mike. "Couldn't you?"

"Why, yes I could," Dexter agreed, backing gracefully into the room with more than a little pleasure in his smile.

It was Tom's turn, now, to nudge Mike—and he had to, to get him through the doorway. "How is Harry, by the way?" he closed the door behind them. "I heard that red-head nearly ruined him."

"And isn't that just typical?" Dexter asked, hands clasped to slim hips. "A bitch will go for the balls every time! They have no real appreciation for the male anatomy—and Harry knows now, I'm right about that. He was in so much pain until I came along. Oh, yes, I showed him that attaining sexual satisfaction doesn't have to include the straining, grinding exertion demanded by females."

Mike stood no more than a foot from the door as he watched Tom cross the room to sit comfortably on a battered old sofa. Dexter watched them both, keeping a safe distance from each.

"Well, I'm glad you could help him," Tom said with approval. "Yes, you must be very good," he gave Dexter a slow once-over— which brought a sound from Mike that defied description.

"Oh, I am," Dexter said silkily, "and not terribly expensive when I find an appealing partner."

Tom met Dexter's questioning eyes—tried to avoid Mike's stunned expression—and reached for his wallet. "So, how much?"

"Uh…Tom?" Mike finally formed words.

"Oh, I haven't forgotten you," Tom replied and fought mightily to keep a serious expression. "I know you'll want some of this too—so hell, Mike, it's my treat."

"I…uh, well—Tom?" stuttered the Captain, looking so totally befuddled, Tom had to laugh.

"Dex, he is a bit bashful," Tom winked. "So, if it's all right with you, we'll let the Irishman watch for a while. Now, how much?"

"Depends on what you want," Dexter gently stroked his testicles. "Ten for an ass fuck; five for head—me to you or you to me. It's your choice," he smiled flirtatiously, "and my ever-loving pleasure."

"Well, here's a bonus for you. Forty dollars for the works. For both of us. Mike will come around—especially if you could do something to stir him up. ...Dex, would you strip for us? You know, give us a little something to start the blood pumping?"

"Certainly, sweetheart! I have a dance designed for that very thing. I'll just put this away," he quickly snatched the money, "then we'll get our fun little fucking party on its way!" And gliding toward a dresser, his hips swayed as enticingly as any woman's.

Mike was frantically vying for Tom's attention during all of this, but that one only watched Dexter as he opened a drawer and using a key that hung about his neck, locked the money in a small metal chest. He continued to watch as Dexter kicked off his slippers, most effeminately, and returned to the center of the room, where he slowly untied his robe sash.

Cemented to the spot by the door, Mike gasped as the silky garment slithered to the floor. "God damn!" he pointed. "Tom, he's armed to the teeth!" As indeed, Dexter was, for protruding from a sheath on the right hip of his sheer black lace pantalets, was a stiletto. Black lace garters, one riding his left thigh and one on each upper arm, held more of the wicked weapons.

"Dex...sweetheart, is that necessary?" Tom pretended shock, "Won't you put your little toys away?"

"Oh no, Mr. Buckskins; not just yet," Dexter glanced at Mike's holstered gun. "They've saved my life too many times—and on my chosen path, I'm sure you can understand why. ...Some men are such bigoted brutes," he looked Mike's way again. "Yes, I've had to protect myself more times than I care to remember."

"I do understand that," Tom nodded, "but frankly, the sight of those things has wilted a damn fine hard I had going."

"Believe me, darling," Dexter countered, stroking the swell of his own crotch again, "when I'm finished with you, you'll never remember my play-pretties were here. ...But first, you make the Irishman take off that gun or this goes no further."

"Oh, very well," Tom rose to stalk the Captain—and slapped his hand when he tried to deter disarmament. "There; now do we get your best?" he smiled at Dexter.

The man actually giggled, using both hands now to urge what looked to be an enormous erection. "What do you want first, sweet-meat? The dance—or maybe a quick little nibbling to get you started again?"

"Damn, if this doesn't promise to be interesting," Tom tried and failed to move the Captain forward. "Mike," he met his eyes, "would you *please* cooperate? Dexter *can take us both*," he stressed words that were lost on his confused friend. "—Can't you, Dex?" he tossed that one a hopeful expression.

"No problem, darlings," he still caressed his lace-clad genitals. "I've serviced as many as five lovers at once: jacked two, gave one head; and took one in my ass, while another sucked me off."

"B...but those knives," Mike was so astounded, he had to ask. "Didn't they kind of...well, get in the way?"

"Irish, I do wish you'd forget about them," Dexter sighed sweetly. "Why not think of this instead?" Whereupon he exposed a penis that would have done justice to a horse—and Mike really and truly blushed. "I knew you'd like it," Dexter laughed and started toward them. "Want to feel it, Irish? Don't be shy."

The Captain straightened and everything about him—from the clenched fists at his sides, the snarl on his lips, to the glare in his eyes—was threatening. And Dexter skittered to a halt, his hand resting conveniently near the stiletto on his thigh.

"God damn it, Michael—I will not tolerate your petty jealousy again!" Tom exclaimed, carefully stepping between them. He meant for Dexter to have ample time to judge his movement as non-threatening, even as the man nimbly angled for a safer distance. "Dex, I'm sorry about this," Tom apologized. "We've only been close a short time, but he is driving me crazy with his...his damn possessiveness! Just let me talk to him for a minute. If he won't behave, I'll make him leave us—and you can keep all the money just the same,"

Dexter nodded silently, but remained alert and ready with several razor-sharp responses should any hostility be directed at him.

"Michael, my love," Tom faced the puzzled, repulsed Captain, "you'd better listen—and *carefully*, this time. Now we've been through this before, you and I. Remember those very attractive Frenchmen we met on the docks in Savannah? There was one who wanted some of you, but would you let him have it? No, you wouldn't allow him past your damn belt buckle! We had a terrible fight over it too, and you ended up in bed alone.—Remember that?"

"Uh…yeah," Mike nodded.

"Well, if you don't *go along with me now*, the fight we'll have could be worse than before." And turning Mike toward Dexter he continued. "Damn it, look at him. He is *better* than the Frenchman who wanted your prick—*four times better*—and I'm telling you *Dexter can deliver the goods*. So don't be difficult, lover. I want him; —I *really need him*. And sweetheart, I want you beside me all the way. …Now, *do you understand* what I'm saying?"

Mike turned back to Tom wearing a wicked grin. "But must I share you with him?" he batted his eyes absurdly. "Oh, don't you want me anymore?"

"As much as I ever did, cupcake," Tom laughed. "Dexter isn't trying to separate us, but he could certainly add something to our day.—Isn't that right, Dex?"

"Well, it was," he said in exasperation. "But Irish purely scared the shit out of me, and now my beautiful hard-on is gone too.—Oh, damn; damn; damn!" he complained. "But before I do anything about this, are you sure he's in a better mood? These things can get messy, when all parties aren't agreeable," he fidgeted nervously. "Yes, I prefer voluntary participation. It's much more stimulating—and keeps me fucking hot just so much longer."

"Oh, Mike will participate now—to the fullest," Tom assured the hesitant man. "So, about that dance?"

"All right, I'll try getting it up again," Dexter began to fondle himself anew. "Just have a seat for a minute, will you?—But, yes, my dance is much more effective under a full head of steam."

"Then a *full head* is what we want," Tom grinned, aiming the Captain toward the sofa and goosing him when he seemed reluctant to go. "Meanwhile, I'll just be working on my friend here—with a few sweet nothings for his ear." And he yanked the surprised Captain nearly onto his lap.

"Say some goodies for me too," Dexter enjoined, both hands now sunk into his pantalets. "And do raise the lid on that darling little music box next to you. By the time it needs rewinding, I should be ready for anything!"

So while Dexter worked on himself, Tom did the same to Mike. "Sorry, Captain," he whispered, pulling him closer, "but this is important."

"Damn you, it better be!" Mike uttered back. "What the hell is going on here?"

"Later. First, we take care of Dexter—"

"God, I'd love to deck him!" Mike whispered in earnest. "—Let go; I'll do it for you!"

"Sit still!" Tom ordered aloud, tightening an arm about Mike's neck. And when Dexter looked their way, he forced the Captain's head to his shoulder and noisily reamed his ear.

"God damn it!" Mike yelled. "Tom, if you—"

"And shut the fuck up!" Tom barked another order, with a wink at Dexter. Then he was whispering nothings again. "Mike, he is an expert thrower and hasn't been close enough to get decked. Why should he? He can easily kill us from where he is! Now, damn it, act docile, will you?"

"…Oh," Mike nodded. And seeing that Dexter was watching, he cuddled his head back on Tom's shoulder. "So, what's the plan?" he murmured.

"We have to make him trust us. Then we have to get him over here between us—"

"Oh, hell—I don't like the sound of that!" Mike said too loudly. And realizing it, he added, "Why must your tastes be so jaded?—You big devil!" he swatted Tom's thigh.

At that, Dexter smiled and sidled a step closer as he continued to probe the nether regions of his panties. "Is he big, Irish?—Shit, from the fit of those buckskins, that was a stupid question. Why, I've hardly been able to keep my eyes from the snug way they flatter his ass. ...In fact, I simply must buy a pair for myself."

Tom smiled appreciatively and rewound the music box. "And I might buy them for you.—How about it, Dex? Ready yet? Maybe you could use a little help."

"Well, I did have a dreadful fright," he looked accusingly at Mike. "But yes, maybe it would help if you took off your clothes too.—Oh, yes, Mr. Buckskins, I'm sure that would inspire me."

Tom felt Mike go rigid, and he laughed as he dumped him on the sofa and rose to face Dexter. "I have a better idea," he began to unlace his shirt. "Why don't you do this for me? Come on, sweetheart, see for yourself what I keep in these buckskins."

Dexter's eyes widened in anticipation and yet, he hesitated when he looked at Mike. "So, what about it, Irish? You taking part or not?"

"I...uh, wouldn't miss this for the world," Mike's reply was somewhere between a question and a statement. And after a look from Tom, he added. "—Well I wouldn't! I want to please you ... angel foot," he smiled, getting up too. "So, uh...what do you want me to do?"

"Follow your instincts," Tom grinned. "*Between-us* we can have that nice big cock of his primed in no time." Then, making a bid for Dexter's cooperation, Tom made a to-do of unbuckling his belt, pulling it slowly from the loops and dropping it to the floor. "Your turn, Dex. Peel off those God damn pantalets and show me that fucker again."

"Shit, but I love games like this!" Dexter breathed. And hooking his thumbs into the lacy garment, he made a series of suggestive poses and turns as he slid it down and stepped out, coming closer in the process.

Mike even smiled in approval, for in doing this, Dexter had also left one of his weapons behind. "Oh-hell-yes!" he swore in pretended excitement. "Tom, I do want a piece of that tight little ass!—Can I have him first? Please—can I?"

"Now that's much better, Irish," Dexter saucily swayed his hips, causing his large penis to keep its own rhythm. "…But let's be fair," he paused thoughtfully. "I'll undress Tom first;…and then you can fuck me while I suck him off. That way, everybody gets some!"

"God damn it, Dex," Tom laughed, pointing to the floor before him. "I'm fucking ready for that, so get your dangling dick over here!—Now!"

And Dexter did, planting his dainty feet on the indicated spot, his tinkling laughter riddling the air. But that was the last thing he would be doing for quite some time.

"…Well, hell, Mike," Tom looked down at Dexter's laid out, unconscious body. "You didn't leave much for me to do."

"Sorry," he collected all four of the stilettos. Then he straightened and grinned. "Should I have waited until after the blow-job he promised?"

"Oh-hell-no," Tom nodded, binding Dexter's hands with his belt. "Get something to gag him and let's tie his feet too."

"Well, there's no gag in your mouth," he brought Tom a neck cloth and the robe sash. "Now, why was any of this necessary?"

"The draft, Captain—Sam's draft to Jack and Harry. He had to sign it, didn't he? It's evidence linking him to them."

"So, now we're going on a treasure hunt, right?"

"Maybe not," Tom retrieved the key from Dexter's neck and went to the dresser. "That's why I offered him money;—to see where he kept his valuables."

"Yeah, so why did you ask him to undress?" Mike sat on the sofa again.

"Obviously, to see where he kept the knives," Tom returned with the metal chest. "Delilah warned me about them, but I forgot to warn you," he chuckled, sitting too. "Sorry about that, friend."

Mike nodded as he gazed at Dexter's trunk-like penis. "You're sorry and I'm envious as hell.—Damn, he's hung! You ever see one like that before?"

"Once," Tom answered, while opening the box and retrieving his own money. "—On a damn buffalo."

"Well, it doesn't seem right," Mike muttered, thinking of Nicole. "With a cock like that, he could have satisfied...well, any woman. It's a damn waste, that's all."

"But this isn't!" Tom exclaimed. "Look, Mike, the check—and Sam's letter too." And scanning it quickly, he read a few relevant lines aloud. "...*believe my wife to be staying at her sister's; ... may try to contact my daughter or Scott; ...if so, report immediately; ...will have a bigger job for you.*—And listen to this, Mike: ...*Do not allow my wife to return to Savannah. Take all necessary steps.* And its signed *S. T.L.*!"

"Should be S.O.B.," Mike commented. "—But damn, Tom, if Mamalyn is in danger, shouldn't we be doing something about it?"

"She's not," Tom nodded, still too elated for long explanations. "And look at the check. It's to *Jack Spidell and Harry Tucker* and signed *Samuel T. Lucas.*—Hot damn!" he hugged the Captain enthusiastically. "This is great;—just great!"

"Look, I've had enough of your damned mauling," Mike laughed, getting to his feet. "Now, why don't we take your evidence and get out of here?"

But Tom didn't move. "It's not enough. I have to have sworn testimony from Jack and Harry, which means I can't leave until they return.—And that presents a problem doesn't it?"

"What problem?" Mike shrugged.

"They aren't expected for a day or so, and the Irish Mist is due to leave for Savannah tomorrow. Mike, I can't ask you to delay your run;—to lose more business and money because of me."

"But you could ask me to share a damn pansy with you?" grinned the Captain. "No, friend, any business or money lost before now, was my own doing," he stuffed his hands in his pockets. "So, I'm staying here. I've acted like a jackass just about long enough. And I kind of owe you this."

"It wasn't your fault—any more than it was mine," Tom rose and fetching Bruce's robe, laid it over the nude, unconscious man. "Sam Lucas did a hell of a job on all of us."

The Captain sat down again and his eyes came to rest on the silk-draped protrusion of Bruce's faded erection. It bothered him that, even in this state, the size was so obvious.

"Tom…about Nicole," he began hesitantly. "I really loved that girl—still do, I guess. But I was never able to satisfy her. It left me so damn full of doubts—about myself as a man and the marriage I wanted so badly. …And about you. I knew she had feelings for you;—I wasn't blind to the way she watched you. That's why I encouraged you to announce your marriage. I hoped Nicole would turn to me when she finally accepted that you were taken; that once she'd forgotten you, I'd be able to bring her some sense of fulfillment. And sure enough, she did accept my proposal. …I guess I went a little crazy when I heard she'd been found with you. I wanted to believe—because of our engagement—she had resisted your advances and that was the reason for her beating. …Tom, I felt so cheated; and at the same time, still unsure of things. Hell, it was just easier to blame you than admit it might never have worked;—that I wasn't man enough to make her happy. I'm still struggling with a lot of those doubts; … and it's damn painful," he paused. "But I know you're innocent and I wanted you to hear me say so."

"Thank you," Tom leaned to the back of the sofa, wondering how to reply. He was sorry for the terror and suffering Nicole must have endured, but he wasn't sorry Mike hadn't married her. Was there a way to console his friend without sounding critical of a girl he still loved? He could but try. "Captain, if Nico felt anything for me, it wasn't love. What she helped Sam do could never be called an act of love."

"I know—and I should have kept her away from his damned corruptive influence!"

"…You're blaming yourself for that? Mike, you weren't meant to be her keeper. That isn't a part of love either. Now, God knows, Mandria is head-strong, but Nico was worse. She did exactly as she pleased; saw whomever she wished; and no man on earth could have changed that."

"Yes, but if I'd spent more time with her; been more supportive or attentive; …been a better damned lover—"

"No. She never lacked anything she wanted and was never without attention. You, her father; her friends—all of you showered her with attention."

"You didn't. Maybe that's why she found you attractive," Mike said then. "And what did I do when she finally turned to me for it? I behaved like a bumbling idiot, with no staying power;—and one time I even hid, afraid of failing her again!"

"Damn it, that just isn't true!—Did she ever refuse you or turn you away?"

"Oh-hell-no! It was always the other way around. I just couldn't handle it, damn it!"

"Yet she kept coming back."

"Well, only God knows why," Mike laughed and the sound was coated with irony. "It's no wonder she dated Brown and listened to Sam's poison. Hell, she wasn't finding what she needed in me."

Tom hesitated. Painful or not, truth would be kinder than the demon of self-doubt that plagued the Captain now. "Perhaps there were no answers for Nicole. Sam knew it and using her weakness was exactly the thing he'd do."

"Yes, the damned bastard!" Mike said with a nod of ready agreement. "He did more than his share to keep her confused."

"Friend, you are shifting the blame again. Rather than admit Nicole wasn't perfect, you've blamed me, yourself, Brown and now Sam."

"But you said yourself Sam put her up to these things."

"Was Sam in bed with you? Did he order Nico to pretend her sexual appetite? Did he cause your failure to match it? Mike, you have had enough experience—and success—with women to face the damn truth. The fault—the terrible flaw—was not in you, but in Nicole."

"You…you're not saying she was promiscuous?"

"There's a fine line here, but no. I do believe, however, that as her mother before her, she suffered from nymphomania."

"Why?—And damn it, be more exact?" Mike pled.

"Well, if I could help it, I never sat beside her at any table, because she was constantly trying to touch me beneath it. Then there was the day she claimed she'd seduced Allen and said she'd give him up if I took his place. Supposedly, this seduction occurred the evening Allen took her to dinner;—an evening Sam arranged, by the way, and saw to it both drank way too much. And, Mike, he meant for a seduction to happen. But it was Nico who asked Allen to wait in her stable; Nico who returned wearing only a robe; Nico who tried to seduce Allen— knowing Willie Luther stood watching them all the while. And it was Nico who became furious when Allen refused her and left."

"Oh, God," moaned the Captain. "…But if they just had too much to drink—?"

"Damn it, stop granting her excuses! Nicole was sick—so sick she kept Joleen and Willie in terror of their lives. …Mike, she forced them to have sex in every way she could imagine, just so she could watch. Sometimes she fondled them; at other times, she whipped them or poked them with things while they were coupled and made to perform for her. And, friend, this started long before our trip to Tybee—the one where you *took advantage* of your *virgin*."

"So you think…Brown?—Even Sam?"

"I don't know, but I wouldn't bet against it."

Mike sat forward. "Tom, if I thought… I mean, if Sam was the first—Oh, God damn it, I can't bear the notion!" he pressed clinched fists to his forehead.

"Then you won't like this one any better. Lucas is totally without conscience, Mike, but he is not a fool. If he touched Nico, it wasn't by force. And if she allowed it…well, would Sam Lucas stop with less than having it all?"

Leaning to the back of the sofa again, Mike heaved a great sigh. "If she did have other affairs…would it have to be told? I'm thinking of Ransom here. I mean, first his wife and then his daughter—and with Nico the way she is now…?"

"I know," he laid a hand on his friend's shoulder. "Unless it becomes a deciding factor in my case, I wouldn't want it made public either."

"Thanks," Mike said gratefully, and looked away. "...But if proof exists about Nico and Sam, you would tell me, wouldn't you?"

There was something too calm about the hot-tempered Irishman's request. In the past, Sam's injustices had sent Mike into cursing fits, crying for blood and threatening to let it. Now, when he had the most reason, he wasn't angry enough. "Tell me something," Tom ventured. "Why did you buy a pistol?"

Mike took in a breath and laughed a bit. "Well, I was going to shoot you with it."

"And now you're planning to kill Sam Lucas if you find out he slept with Nico."

"Wouldn't you, in my place?"

"...Captain?" Tom said, waiting for their gazes to lock. "I'm sorry, but Sam Lucas belongs to me. Just back off." And eyes the color of blued gun metal reflected depths of unyielding resolve. "A bullet is too merciful for the man. I want him in a small cell, surrounded by vermin and the stench of his own filth. And I wish him a long, long life and a sharp memory, because I want him to spend every second remembering the pleasures he once enjoyed: fine rich foods; good brandy and cigars; the expensive cut of his clothes; the fat wallet he kept for a heart; the hunts, balls and clubs he attended with such pomp; every woman he considered a favorite.—All of it. And every day of his rotting existence, I want him to know he is there, not only for what he did to Nico, but the rest of us too."

"And what if he isn't convicted? That happens, Tom."

"Then I claim the right to challenge him," he said simply.

"Well, you'll need a second—and I claim that right," Mike insisted.

"Very well," Tom smiled slightly. "Your claim is duly noted."

"Yeah—but just be sure to finish him," Mike added a chuckle. "I've been practicing, but I still can't hit a damn thing with that gun."

Tom laughed too and rose for a much needed stretch. "Listen, we've talked enough about Sam Lucas. Pick another subject, Captain. What will it be?"

"...Mandy?" Mike said and Tom slowly turned to face him. "Uncle Pat told me she left you and what she planned to do. Did you manage to find her or change her mind?"

"I found her. And no, she is still determined to be free of me. But I'm keeping the baby, Mike—no matter how it ends between us."

"You convinced me of your innocence—and I would never have thought that possible—so, why couldn't you convince her?"

"Because Mandria is a damn, hard-headed, little goat!" Tom vented. "She is stubborn as hell and refuses to hear one word in my favor!"

"And you love her more than you ever did," Mike observed.

"Yes! ...Damn it all," he nodded, sitting again. Tom needed to talk about this and was grateful to have Mike's ear again. "I had hoped to sway her before now, but she is in her ninth month and it hasn't happened yet. So when Allen sent information about Jack and Harry being here, I decided the only chance I had left was going after them myself and helping Captain Pat clear my name."

"Her ninth month? Tom, you didn't leave her alone;—and where is Mandy anyway?"

"In Athens now. Some friends moved her into town the day I left."

"Into town from where?" Mike pressed. "Damn it, I'd like to hear the story from the time you left Savannah."

"You wouldn't believe it," Tom nodded.

"Well, I'm not half naked and tied to a whore-house chair, but give it a try," Mike grinned.

So, leaning to the back of the sofa again, Tom began. "Well, Captain, let's see. First, I went to her aunt's home in Aiken, South Carolina, kidnapped my own wife—who was madder that hell about it—and we headed for north Georgia, on horseback, riding double.

She tried every trick she could think of to escape me—including dire warnings that alligators were going to crawl out of a foothills lake and eat us. We survived, obviously, and have been living in a remote cabin above Athens—which I had to repair, top to bottom, trying to please her and seldom did. Then, I bought two orphaned children for the cost of a pack-mule, a few dishes and one hell of a fight—and she gave me the devil for that. I also adopted a pup, a cow, five laying hens and a rooster—that I've grown to detest, as he enjoys an active sex-life and makes a point of strutting and crowing about it whenever he sees me coming.—Oh, and I made friends with an elf of a man and caught a magic bear. But mostly, I spent my time arguing with a deaf woman and catching hell over monumental things like hair ribbons, night gowns, cradles, bath tubs, hairbrushes and cinnamon," he finished, while Mike wiped tears of laughter from his eyes. "And now, here I sit; hungry, in need of a good stiff drink—and after nearly six months of celibacy, I just propositioned a damn, naked pansy."

Laughing harder, Mike rose and handed Tom his pistol. "Here, you keep this. I'm going to the Irish Mist and leave instructions for the crew. Then I'll bring us back some supper and a bottle," he chuckled again. "—But damn, Tom, six months? Will Dexter's virtue be safe while I'm gone?"

"If Delilah's was, I can assure you Dexter hasn't a worry," Tom replied. "But don't stay long, Mike. If Jack and Harry show up, I'll need your help."

"Wouldn't miss that for the world," Mike started for the door. "Besides, we have a lot of catching up to do—and damn it, this time I want details."

"Such as?"

"Well," Mike paused, one hand on the doorknob, "such as why Mamalyn left Savannah; why Sam doesn't want her to return; how you know she isn't in danger from Jack and Harry; and how Allen learned they were here?" Then the Captain flashed that Irish smile. "And by damn, I want to hear more about the elf, the magic bear—and especially, that rooster!" So saying, he went out, laughing more than ever.

Tom stretched his legs out before him and smiled. It was good having Mike's company. Knowing he could depend on their friendship meant a hell of a lot to him. ...*But, Lord, please,* he closed his eyes in a silent prayer, *I want my wife back too. ...And if that's not possible, God, please make the baby look like her. ...Let me keep that much of Mandria. Please?* And the mist he wiped from the corner of his eye was not a residue of the laughter he'd shared with the Captain...

CHAPTER 16

"Mandy—for shame!" Evelyn exclaimed in surprise.

"Well, Mama, I'm sorry, but if I hear his name another time, I'll say worse. I feel like a prisoner in an enemy camp! You know the man betrayed me and yet you—and everyone else in this house—delight in singing his praises at every given chance! And for the ten millionth time, I *do* know what I saw in that hotel room!"

"Do you? Then let me tell you about something you didn't see. The night Tom escaped—"

"I know! He came to Marsh Haven and you told him where I was! …Why, Mama? How could you break your promise to me? If you hadn't, we wouldn't be in this miserable place now."

"And what do you find miserable about it? Susan has a lovely home and has done all she could to make us comfortable."

"I will not be comfortable until I'm back in Savannah," Mandria said impatiently. "—In my *own* room, wearing my *own* clothes and seeing my *own* friends again!"

"Dear, that is so…unlike you. I know you feel hurt, but I can't believe what you just said."

Mandria rose and went to look from the window of Susan's guest room. A few spring blooms graced the garden below and yet, the days were still chilly enough for a fire. April in Savannah meant a glorious riot of colorful flowers and warm breezy days. …*Not here, evidently*, she thought with a sigh. And homesickness was the least of her problems.

Now she had to placate her mother. "It's just that I had such hopes for my marriage and it turned out so badly, I find myself yearning for the simple, uncomplicated life I once had."

"And you'd settle for that rather than the happiness you knew with Tom? You were happy, Mandy—vibrantly happy—and so alive!"

"Until he betrayed me."

"Then please allow me to finish my story.—No! Let me finish," Evelyn held up a hand when Mandria started to object. "The night Tom came to Marsh Haven, I wasn't going to tell him where you were, but while we were talking, Nico came down the stairway behind him. She wasn't the least bit afraid and even wanted him to hold her doll— which she hadn't allowed any one else to touch."

"So? Maybe that just proves their affair. Maybe even in her damaged mind, she recalled other...*things* they had shared."

"And didn't remember the beating that nearly killed her? No, Mandy, if Tom had done it, Nico would have been terrified—the way she was when your father came."

"Mama, will you stop?" Mandria insisted. "Nico's reactions can't mean anything. Surely, you know that."

"You were ready to say they did a minute ago—when doing so went against Tom," Evelyn countered. "But your father isn't brain damaged, so how would you explain his reaction to Nico, I wonder?"

"Well, he had to be saddened. I was, when I saw her in the hospital. ...But what is your point?"

"No, Mandy, he wasn't saddened. It was more a state of disbelief. Nico was very afraid and kept repeating her little phrases right at him—as if trying to relay a message—and I think he knew what it was, because he left immediately. And a few days later, the second attempt was made on her life."

"Do you hear what you're saying? Mama, are you accusing Father of attempted murder!"

"Yes, I am. I think he tried to kill Nico—not once; but twice."

"Oh this is so ridiculous! It was *Tom* in bed with her; *Tom* covered in her blood; *Tom* still trying to—to hold her to him, right in front of me!"

"Hold her?—Or was he trying to protect her? Have you even considered that? Isn't that what the Tom we know would try to do? Mandy, you told me yourself that he always regretted being unable to stop the attack on his mother—and Patrick Herb said, drugged as he was, Tom thought his mother was there. Why can't you see another side to this, other than what your father wanted you to?"

"Well, let me tell you why," she said sarcastically. "Could it be because of Nico's cosmetic case and what was left of her negligee? Yes, Mama, that certainly says to me she went there prepared to meet my husband! And about the drugs? On the ride home, Father told me all about the things people can take; *to heighten their pleasure*, he said. But evidently, Tom took too much—though with his strong appetite, I don't know why he'd bother. Anyway, he did it; he was caught in adultery—and it is on his head and no other that the attempted murder charge belongs."

"Mandy, really—"

"Well, it makes as much sense as anything you've said!"

"I'm afraid not, daughter. Let me tell you about something else you didn't hear or see. I was standing right next to your father the night of the Harvest Ball, when yours and Kathy's marriages were told. He swore revenge for the fool we made of him. His exact words to me were, *You've only bought them time and precious little of it.* And, Mandy, he set out, from that moment, to destroy both marriages."

"...But how would an affair between Tom and Nico accomplish that?"

"The original plot was to have Kathy found with Tom—and it would have happened, had she not escaped her captors. But that escape must have forced a change in the plan."

"Father's plan, of course. Well, Mama, that is a nice little fairy tale—and just what Tom would have you believe—but I do not!"

"Then you'd place no significance on the fact that Kathy returned to the Lloyd House—with Captain Pat—and recognized the room where she was held? Or that it was right next door to the one where Tom was taken?"

Mandria began to pace, crying freely. "Then just explain one thing to me. What was Nico doing there? No, she came on her own, in disguise, *expressly* to meet my husband, or she wouldn't have brought the damn negligee!"

"I don't know her purpose for that, but don't you remember how upset you were when we learned Nico and your father were conspiring? Well, now we know what it was about. She helped him set this up, and then got caught in the middle when things went wrong."

"Mama, I understand why you are so willing to blame this on Father. He is a cad, and an unfaithful husband …but a murderer?"

"Need I remind you your husband is neither, yet you're willing to believe the same of him?"

"Listen, I know you want happiness for me!" her pacing and tears accelerated. "You want it so badly you can't accept what Tom did. No, it is just easier for you to blame Father."

"Mandria—sweetheart—I lived with that man for nearly twenty-seven years and no one on this earth knows what he is capable of better that I do. And when Tom suggested I leave Savannah—"

"Then he did cause your separation!" Mandria said in a fresh rush of fury. "Oh, that bastard! That liar! He wasn't satisfied with ruining my life!—Oh, no, he had to ruin yours too—and poison your mind against me! How I hate him—God, how I hate that man!"

Rising quickly, Evelyn grasped Mandria's arms and shook her. "Stop it;—stop this, do you hear? It's not good for you or the baby to get so upset. Now, calm down!" Then, she drew her sobbing daughter into her arms and held her. "…Dear, I could never turn against you. You are the only good to ever come of a marriage that never should have happened. There is no love between your father and me—and never has been. He married me for money, pure and simple. And I married him…on the rebound, when Ransom announced his engagement to Deborah."

"Ran…you were in love with Uncle Ransom?" Mandria pulled back to meet her mother's eyes. "Does Father know?"

"I don't think either of them does. From earliest childhood, Ransom and I were inseparable—forever sharing secrets and dreams.

I always hoped he'd return the love I felt for him, but to this day, he treats me like a dear little sister. And Mandria, I still love him. Can you imagine the pain of seeing the man you love almost every day and never, *ever*, being able to touch him? That is my point in telling you this—to warn you that if you aren't careful you, too, could lose something very precious in your life."

"What, Mother? Tom's baby? I don't want it—I don't!"

"That isn't what I was going to say, but if you continue like this, you could cause a miscarriage," Evelyn cupped her daughter's face. "Do you really want an innocent child to die because of all this turmoil?"

"…No," she answered meekly. "But I'm not keeping it. I could never love his child.—I'd just end up hating it too."

"Would you? I didn't hate you. Mandy, maybe you'll never be with Tom again, but think about the long years ahead. You do have love in you and who better to give it to than your own child?"

"Mama, you are so…wrong," Mandria snubbed, trying to dry her eyes. "I love you, and I thank you for telling me your story, but I am not going to love anyone, ever again. And if Tom thought he could bring you up here to convince me otherwise, then he was wrong too."

"No, Mandy, I asked Tom to let me come for the birth of your baby. He asked me to come early because he feared for my safety. … You see, I wrote down the words Nico said to your father and gave a copy to Captain Pat. And like Tom, he thought there could be meaning behind them. When your father found my copy, he not only twisted my arm, but threatened my life if I ever spoke to Patrick Herb again—and that is the reason I left him and Savannah as well."

"I…I'm not making excuses for what Father did, but what if he isn't guilty?—I mean, his wife went to the police behind his back!"

"And if he is guilty? Do you think he would allow testimony that might help Tom and cause the law to look elsewhere for a villain? No, he wouldn't, and I'm grateful Tom was wise enough to see the danger and offer his protection."

Mandria looked at her mother in genuine confusion, but was still unable to relinquish her doubts. No, her mother's case was based on the words of a brain damaged girl; the motives given for her father's actions just weren't strong enough;—and there was still the matter of that damned negligee! "Some protection," she scoffed, climbing onto the bed. "I'm about to have a baby, Susan is lame and John and Brittany are children. Yes, we are a lot of protection for you, aren't we? And where is this gallant gentleman—this knight in everyone's shining armor—who offered it?"

"Tom told you where he was going and why."

"Oh, did he? Or did he finally tire of the game he's been playing and leave all of us stranded. Mama, you seem to know the positive things about his case, but you haven't mentioned these mysterious men he claims to be chasing. And if Allen wrote about them, as Tom said, he didn't mention it to me!"

"Maybe because you wouldn't listen? ...Mandy, I saw the way you treated him at the cabin. When he tried to explain his mission, you stormed out and slammed the door. If you've been this way for six months, he's probably given up trying to tell you anything!—And about those two men? Kathy was abducted by two and Tom was carried into the Lloyd Hotel by two—which certainly says to me that locating them could be important."

"And it says to me, he stopped somewhere for a drink to brace his nerves; stayed too long and needed help to get where he wanted to go:—to meet Nico!"

"This is the same Tom who shouldn't need drugs because of his strong appetite?" Evelyn questioned.

"Well, he was drinking too, because I smelled it—along with a whole cess-pool of terrible things. Yes, so maybe he came in drunk and it started a fight between them that ended in the beating. Oh, the possibilities are endless, Mama—don't you see that?"

"Why, yes I do," Evelyn lost patience. "Now Tom is also a drunkard. So when did he use the drugs?—And remember, Kathy was just next door. Maybe you think she was going to join them and make it a real orgy. Or maybe, in Tom's drunken state, he had both women drugged and planned to go from room to room.—But why stop there? Maybe you think he meant to pleasure women up and down both sides of the hall!"

Mandria opened her mouth, but was so choked with revulsion she couldn't speak. Instead, she laid her head on the pillow and turned away. "I…I'm going to take a nap now," she uttered. "—And Mama, I do not intend to talk about this again. It seems you can't be rational where Tom Scott is concerned."

"Very well," Evelyn started for the door. "Take your damned stubbornness and return to Savannah. Yes, go live in your *own* room; wear your *own* clothes; and see your *own* friends. Oh yes, you and your father should be quite happy there, feeding off of each other's hatreds. But when Tom is cleared and Sam is sent to prison, that house will be very empty, Mandria—as hollow and empty as your life. And if you're wondering where I'll be, let me tell you. If Tom will allow it, I will spend every possible moment in *your* home, helping *your* husband raise *your* child!" Then going out, Evelyn took her turn at slamming a door.

Mandria looked over her shoulder in disbelief. "Now look what Tom has done," she nodded, for that was the first time she could remember such a display of temper from her mother—and she'd certainly not slammed any doors. "Dear God, we'll all be crazy if this doesn't end soon," she added with a sigh and closed her eyes…

Mandria remained in a black mood for the next few days, snapping at any who dared to intrude. It didn't help when she started down to the kitchen and overheard Susan and the children express concern about her to Evelyn. And her mother's reply sent her back up the stairs for another good cry. "Don't worry," Evelyn had said. "Mandy and I just had a few words over Tom. And as I told him once, if she thinks she is right, she will argue as long as you care to stand there. But my dears, once she has taken the time to consider all that was said—and that is what she is doing now—well, Mandy has never been afraid to admit an error in judgment. We'll just have to be patient and allow her to come that decision for herself."

"Never!" Mandria sunk a fist into her pillow. "I was not wrong!" she declared. …So what if she had been thinking about their talk almost constantly. So what if she admitted some parts of her mother's story made sense. There was still one thing everyone else seemed ready to overlook: the damned negligee! It said that Nico was expecting Tom; that the meeting was prearranged. Anything that *might* have happened before or after was immaterial to her. Mandria could even admit that Nicole had been the pursuer when she recalled the numerous times she'd caught her *friend* watching Tom—smiling so secretively and seductively; touching him whenever she could. Then there was the way she managed to place herself at his side at every given opportunity. And who could forget those thinly veiled remarks suggesting her interest was returned? …*Will you twirl me about the floor, or about your finger? …So you would like to hold me again. …Tom, you have always been crazy about me—and don't you dare deny it!* And finally, he'd succumbed to her persistence.

"Damn him," Mandria swore. He had even admitted to finding her *physically attractive,* and to cover that mistake he'd added that he *didn't like her very much* …to which Mandria now swore, "You damned liar!" And then she was in tears again…

April the eleventh was a Saturday and as usual, Susan had been baking for hours. Already, four trays of bread and pastries sat cooling on the opened window ledges. The delicious aromas filling the house soon brought Evelyn and the children to the kitchen too, and it wasn't long before all were chattering gaily while enjoying some of those hot from the oven treats. But this was also Mandria's birthday and when a cake came out of the oven, John and Brittany were eager to help Evelyn decorate it. Then, everyone helped to tidy the cottage and while Evelyn and Karen put a festive cloth on the table and wrapped gifts, the children gathered a bouquet from the garden and went upstairs to invite Mandria to her own party.

"…Well, thank you very much for the flowers," she tried to be gracious. "And you say the party is to be at noon?"

"Yes, ma'am," John answered.

"We fixed cake and everything!" Brittany said her blue-green eyes a-sparkle.

Silence followed, and Mandria felt compelled to fill the void. "…So, how do you like it here at Susan's?—Are you doing well in school?"

"Yes, ma'am," John repeated, folding his arms…much like someone else Mandria knew. "And Miss Rutledge, she's a pretty good teacher, but not so good as Tom."

"Yes," said Brittany. "We like it here fine, but our beds at home was better."

"At…home?" Mandria uttered. "…Did you really feel at home in that tiny cabin?"

John shrugged. "Best place we ever lived."

"But we had so little," Mandria pointed out. "It was cold and drab and we were always stepping over each other."

"Didn't seem that way when Tom was around," John smiled slightly.

"Maybe it was bad for you 'cause you never lived in no orphanage;—or with them Shorts!" Brittany offered.

"Yeah, nobody took care of us good as you and Tom," John added.

"…I'm afraid I didn't do much to help you," Mandria lowered her eyes. "There or here."

"That's all right, Mandy," Brittany patted her hand. "You're just pregernant. We understand, don't we, John?"

"Yeah," John sidled close enough to lay a hand on her shoulder. "And nice as Miss Rutledge and Mamalyn is, we wouldn't trade you off or nothing."

"No, we'd never!" Brittany vowed. "You're Tom's Mandy—and prettier than any princess in the world!"

Mandria sighed, but could not resist gathering them both in her arms. "Oh, you two little thieves. Now you're out to steal my heart, aren't you?"

Brittany giggled and the sound was like a tinkling music box. John only smiled, and she could have sworn she saw the glimmer of a tear in his eyes as he pulled away. "I guess we would; ...if we could," he said starting for the door. "Come on, Brit," he added without looking back. And giving Mandria a hesitant peck on the cheek, Brittany skipped along behind him.

Mandria felt miserable again. Those children needed love—wanted it from her—and yet, they sensed she couldn't give it. She had even hugged them and still they knew. ...*As hollow and empty as your life* her mother had said. And feeling a chill that had nothing to do with the early spring air, Mandria went to stoke the fire.

"Mandy?" Evelyn came in and gave her daughter a kiss. "Happy birthday, my dear."

"Thank you, Mama," she tried to sound cheerful. "...I hear you've planned a party."

"Oh, yes—and the children are very excited about it." Then she stood looking at Mandria as if trying to make a decision. "...How are you feeling today?"

"*Pregernant,*'" she laughed a little. "—At least, that's what Brittany tells me."

"Well, you do seem in better spirits," And she stood studying Mandria again.

"Mama, what is it?" she finally had to ask. Then her eyes widened. "What's wrong?—Have you heard something from ...Tom?"

"Would you care if I had?—Mandria, was that concern I saw in your eyes?"

"No!—For heaven sakes, no!" Mandria swore. "Now, please don't start that again."

"So you haven't changed your mind? ...Not even a little?"

"Not about Tom and Nico," she shrugged. "The rest doesn't matter."

"What does that mean?"

"Nothing!" Mandria insisted. "Mama, this is my birthday and I don't want to argue with you now. Please, can't we talk about anything else?"

"Well, yes, but Tom is what brought me up here this morning," Evelyn smiled, drawing the bottle of honeysuckle oil from her apron pocket. "Here, Mandy. Tom had me bring this from Savannah, especially for your birthday."

Mandria looked at the bottle in her mother's outstretched hand and couldn't move. ...*Why?* she wondered. It was her perfume—her essence—blended just for her and she had every right to claim it. But this was also the one luxury Tom had ever expressed a real fondness for—and the thought of him sniffing about, hoping for a pleasant whiff, caused her to rebel. Oh, no—anything that drew him closer to her person was unthinkable! So, snatching the bottle, she turned and flung it into the fireplace.

"Mandria!" Evelyn exclaimed as the shattered bottle spilled among the burning logs. "Why would you do such a terrible thing?" she fanned at the perfumed smoke the hissing fire spit back. "I really don't understand you—I just don't!"

Mandria wasn't listening. With the first puff of that sweet burning odor, her nightmare returned in brutal clarity. A whimper escaped her and spinning away, she had every intention of fleeing the room. But her foot caught on the cradle Tom had made and down to the floor she went with a heavy thud.

"Mandy?" Evelyn rushed to her side. "Oh, darling, are you hurt?— Here, look at me!"

"Mama?" Mandria uttered fearfully. "Mama, what's happening to me? I...I'm all wet!"

"Oh, my Lord—your water has broken!" And racing to the door, she yelled down the stairway. "Susan! Send for the Doctor—do you hear? Get the Doctor!" And waiting for only a word of Susan's reply, she hurried back to her daughter. "Come on, now," she managed to get her to her feet. "Are you in pain, dear?"

"...Yes," she nodded, looking back at the fire. "Oh, Mama, yes!" And she began to cry bitterly.

"Well, let's get you to bed," Evelyn urged her forward. "The Doctor should be here soon."

"It was my perfume, Mama," Mandria sobbed. "It was *my* perfume!"

"Yes, dear, I know," Evelyn sat her down and began to unfasten her clothes.

"No, you don't!—You don't understand at all!" And a pain wracked Mandria's body like none she ever known.

When it passed, Evelyn managed to pull back the covers and lay her down. "Now, Mandy, you must stay very still. Sometimes these things will heal themselves."

"But it was there, Mama—there in the flames!" Mandria nodded wildly.

"What was?" Evelyn asked, busily removing Mandria's shoes and stockings.

"My perfume!" she tried to sit up. "There with Tom—in the fire!" she fell back, biting her lip to keep from screaming as another pain stabbed through her.

Making no sense of the conversation, Evelyn went to the wash-stand and brought back a wet cloth.

"Don't you see?" Mandria moaned as her mother bathed her flushed face. "I didn't know it;—because of the fire!" And this time the pain bent her double.

Evelyn nodded in despair. Mandria was in labor, but her eyes looked so glazed and the pains were coming so hard and so fast it was frightening. "Try to rest, Mandy," she uttered. "The Doctor will be here soon."

"Oh, God—there they are!" Mandria's eyes widened. "Make them go away!" she screamed, clutching at her belly with one hand and flailing at her vision with the other.

It was then that the Doctor arrived and seeing Mandria's near hysterical state, gave her a small draught of laudanum. And after a time, that seemed an eternity to her, the vision passed out of focus and the labor pains were almost a welcomed relief.

"Well," Doc Lewis smiled at her through a velvet haze, "shall we get on with the business of birthing, Mrs. Scott?"

…Mrs. …is …is Scott …ott …ott the words seemed to come apart and echo about the room. Then another pain washed over Mandria, tearing at her body and filling her head with a crashing, tumbling roar. …It became the crash of sea waves and she felt herself diving into the sun-sparkled water; surfacing near shore; rising to walk from the sea, while her eyes remained fixed on someone in the dunes:—a man, standing with crossed arms and firmly planted feet, blocking her pathway home. He was tall, muscular, well proportioned, and unmoved by the strong wind that whipped his shirt and ruffled his dark curly hair. …It was Tom and she smiled at him, but it wasn't returned. Drawing closer, she tried to read meaning into his rigid posture and the granite blue eyes staring back at her. He was angry—so very angry—for never had she seen him look at her this coldly.

"Are you On The Chin Of A Giant?" she asked. "Is that why you're standing in my way?"

Now he smiled, but it was even colder than when he hadn't. "No, lady, this is my domain. You are On The Foot Of A Mountain, but you still can't tease at my whiskers.—Go!" he pointed. "Crawl back to the sea and leave me in peace."

Magically, then, Tom's cradle appeared in the sand between them. It was empty, rocking crazily in the wind…but Mandria could hear a baby crying and the sound seemed to come from the cradle. "Oh," she reached to search the covers. "I hear you. Yes, I hear you, baby." And the sound grew louder, though she was still unable to find the child.

"Go back to the sea!" Tom repeated sternly.

"…But where is the baby?" she asked, feeling frantic. "I can't see the baby! Don't you hear it? The baby is crying for me!"

Then Nicole stepped from behind Tom, clutching her little rag doll and singing. "Father, Mothers, Sister, Brothers," she looked sweetly up at him. "Time to feed the baby. Come on—one two; one two!" And she handed Tom the doll and a bottle of honeysuckle oil grotesquely capped with a human nipple, which he pressed to the doll's mouth. Instantly, it changed into an infant—Mandria's baby—and it choked on the perfume and cried all the harder.

ON THE FOOT OF A MOUNTAIN

"Stop! Why are you doing that?" Mandria started forward, ready to snatch the child away. Instead, she tripped over the rocking cradle and was falling...diving back into the sea; rising near the shore; and just as before, walking toward the tall man in the dunes...

Mandria's eyes flew open and she caught a breath while her eyes adjusted to the darkness of Susan's guest room. "...Mama?" she said, as Evelyn's face loomed into view. "Mama, is that you?"

"Yes, Mandy," she, gently smoothed her daughter's hair. "Sweetheart, you have a son;—a beautiful little boy."

"Where is he?—I couldn't find him!" she clung to her mother's hand. "Mama, I heard him crying, but I couldn't find the baby!"

"He's here, Mandy," Evelyn tried to assure her, "fast asleep in his cradle."

"No!—Oh, Mama, no!" Mandria tried to rise. "Take him out of there! Hurry, Mama—bring him to me!"

And because Mandria seemed so frightened, Evelyn did as she asked. "Careful, now," she said, placing the baby in her daughter's arms. And she watched with tears in her eyes as Mandria touched the tiny, sleeping face and cuddled the child against her.

"You're safe now," she murmured groggily. "You're safe, little baby." And closing her eyes, she drifted back to sleep still holding her baby close.

Susan rose from a chair by the fire and came to stand beside Evelyn. "What on earth was that about?" she whispered.

"A bad dream, I suppose," Evelyn turned, smiling beautifully. "Or maybe a small miracle," she was whispering too. "Susan, Mandy wants her baby. I don't think we'll hear another word from her about giving that child away."

"Well, there is something else we can toast. Shall we finish our mulled cider?" she led the way back to the fire.

"Indeed," Evelyn laughed softly. And settling back in her chair, she raised her cup. "To my new grandson; the miracle of answered prayers; ...and the mystery of dreams."

"And may the good Lord see fit to answer one more prayer, by any means He chooses," Susan added.

"Tom and Mandria?" asked Evelyn.

"Yes. Do you think there is a chance now?"

"I do hope so," Evelyn sighed. "Susan, I have never seen two people who were more in love. And this rift is just tearing them both apart."

"It appears more of a chasm than a rift, at the moment."

"I know and it's so sad;—so unnecessary!"

"Then we'll just have to pray a little harder," Susan rose, stifling a yawn. "And hope that God really does help those who help themselves—as Tom is trying to do right now. ...I wonder if he has found those men yet? I do wish we'd hear some news."

"So do I, Susan," Evelyn walked her to the door. "So do I..."

CHAPTER 17

"Damn, Iano, I thought we'd never put him down!" Mike panted, looking to where they'd dumped Tom on the bed. "He's strong a damn bull!"

"*Si,*" Rizza nodded, wiping the dampness from his brow. "And not in the arenas of *Spagna* have I seen one more *arrabbiato*…uh, angry.*"

"Well, he had a right, don't you think? Things were finally going his way. I mean, Kathy had identified Jack and Harry as her kidnappers; and after that damned clever stunt with the gourds, they spilled all they knew about Sam too—and well, Tom could really see an end to his problems. Then, this."

"It does not seem possible.—Think of it, *Capitano!*"

"Yeah, there we were in your parlor, enjoying an after-dinner drink—and I even made a toast to the coming down-fall of Sam Lucas—"

"Samuel *Trott* Lucas," Rizza corrected.

"Wasn't that the damnedest thing? It didn't surprise me when Tom offered to see the kids up to bed instead of joining us in a hand of cards. I knew he was tired;—knew he'd hardly closed his eyes while we waited for Jack and Harry to return. Hell, other than taking Dexter to Delilah for safe-keeping, he didn't relax his vigil for a second. Then, when we got the bastards here, it was that long again before they would talk. And besides all that, Mandy is due around the first of May and he's worried about getting back to her too."

"*Sí*, and when he comes down the stairs again, I did not notice his *tranquillita*...uh, his quiet—or that he starts to drink so much."

"Or that he brought Rob's belt and just sat there holding it," Mike added. "He was calm enough when he asked Kathy where the boy had gotten the belt too. And when she said Sam had given it to him...well, his next question confused the hell out of me. I knew his stepfather's name was Bob Trott, but I didn't understand why he asked if Kathy knew a man by that name—or if she knew if Sam did."

"And when Kathy says Trott is Sam's middle name—*Madre di Dio*! Tom is like *un matto*! ...Uh, the mad man! But imagine it, Michael: Sam Lucas and the step-father Tom detests, one and the same man?"

Mike nodded. "Damn, how a beating with that belt must have hurt. I mean, the buckle—the metal lion's head with fangs protruding from its mouth..."

"And with *un dente rotto*...uh, the one tooth broken, to make Tom know this is the same buckle;—broken during a beating his step-father gives to him."

"Yeah...but it does explain a hell of a lot," Mike said thoughtfully. "Tom may have been too angry and drunk to realize it, but Iano, Sam had to know who Tom was—and that Tom could expose him as a bigamist. He must have guessed Allen was his son, too—and it had long bothered Tom that Sam was always so friendly toward the boy. So...Allen had to be the reason Sam couldn't dispose of Tom right away—not even when he found out about Tom and Kathy.—I mean..." Mike paused, embarrassed by the mention of Kathy's past to her husband.

"It is all right, *Capitano*," Iano assured him. "My Kathy did not enter the affair with Lucas freely;—and Tom helped her escape this devil. *Pregore*, continue."

"Well, until Sam could get his hooks into Allen, he had to tolerate Tom and hope he wouldn't be recognized or remembered. And God, how he must have sweated that every damned day! It was probably Allen's presence that held Sam at bay the night we met him on the riverfront, too.—Hell yes, it was, because he didn't want to look bad to his newly-found son. …Anyway, from that point on, to keep himself clean in Allen's eyes, the bastard did his dirty work through Nico…"

"*Si,*" Rizza agreed, "and it comes to a head the night of the *ballo*— the dance. Sam sees a way to disgrace Tom; avenge his loss of Kathy; regain control of his *figlia*; and be there to console his *figlio* …uh, his daughter and son."

"The bastard nearly pulled it off too," Mike nodded.

"So, what do you think Tom will do about this?" Iano questioned.

"Murder is what he wanted tonight. And the hell of it is, he just gave me the words I threw back at him."

"*Si,* yet it was not words that finally stopped him, but our fists!" Iano grinned.

"Sorry about the mess," Mike shrugged. "We kind of wrecked your parlor, didn't we?"

"*Non fa niente.* Furniture can be replaced, but *non amici* such as this man. No, we had to stop him from leaving. Had he gone *ubriaco* …uh, drunk for Sam Lucas, Tom would now be *morto.*"

"It still took both of us to get the job done," Mike chuckled. "And I'll feel lucky to come away with only a black eye."

"*Si,* a real shiner, as my sons would say. But what will they think of me with only *una bruceata* of the carpet to prove my bravery? Uh… the carpet burn," Iano laughed too.

"Yeah, well, I'll stay with him for the night," Mike rubbed at his back, knowing it would likely be sore as well. "Tomorrow, when he's sober, we'll talk to him again. Uncle Pat should be here by morning too, and once he puts his information with Jack and Harry's, Tom should know have a truer picture of how this case stands.—Now, are you sure our two guests are still locked up nice and tight?"

"In chains," Iano answered, "with two of your crewmen and two men of mine to share the tack room. So, *buona notte, Capitano,*" he said, going to the door. "And sleep with the one eye opened?"

"I will," Mike said as Iano left. Then, removing Tom's boots and his own as well, he tried to decide which side of the bed offered the most room, for Tom lay sprawled exactly in the middle, where they'd let him fall…

The next morning, Mike awoke with all of the bed to himself. "Oh, hell!" he scrambled to pull on his boots and headed down stairs, only to stop in the front hall wondering which way to go. Should he check the house first or go to the stables to see if Tom's horse was missing? "Damn!" he circled the hall, changing his mind twice more. Finally, cupping his hands to his mouth, he yelled, "Tom Scott, if you're here, say so!"

No answer came, but from the morning room down the hall, Kathy did. "Mike," she said in a hushed voice, motioning him to join her.

When he had, she pointed into the room behind her, where Tom lay asleep on the sofa. "What in the hell is he doing down here?" he asked softly.

"Drinking again. ...Mike, this thing has really thrown him."

"Well, at least he didn't try to leave. Did he say anything, Kathy?"

"Yes, he said he knew the answer to Nicole's riddle—whatever that meant. And he said justice wasn't just if it ruined so many lives. ...Do you make any sense of it?"

"Not much. But hell, if he's thinking instead of acting out of anger again, I can only be thankful."

"So can we all, Captain," she smiled. "We haven't the furniture to spare for another brawl of that magnitude. But come to the breakfast room now. Iano has gone up for the boys and food is on the table."

After the meal, Mike and Iano looked in and found Tom still asleep. Then, Patrick Herb arrived and leaving Tom in Kathy's care, the men spent the morning observing while Jack and Harry were officially questioned and their written statements signed. Mike also turned over the letter and the draft they had found and told his uncle the latest discovery about Sam's past. And, as Patrick was curious, came the story of how Tom had asked Mike's help; which led to their visit with Dexter; and as is the want of the Irish to be generous with details, by the time Mike was finished, all present were crying tears of laughter...

Around one o'clock, they returned to the house for lunch. Kathy had it waiting, but going in to check on Tom, she found him missing again. That set all of them to searching and Mike found him back in the front parlor, slouched on a broken sofa, with yet another bottle in hand.

"Damn it, Tom!" Mike said in exasperation. "Look at yourself! What in the hell are you trying to prove?"

"Just celebrating defeat, Captain," he grinned crookedly. "Yeah, good old Sam has done it again."

"There isn't much he hasn't done," Mike said as the rest of the group filed in. "What particular thing are you celebrating?—And what defeat?"

Tom watched his friends perch awkwardly on broken pieces of furniture and somehow, that and their serious expressions, struck him funny. "Came to view the body, did you?" he laughed. Then he looked over the room as if just noticing its condition. "Damn, Iano, this place is a wreck! I'd choose a better class of friends, if I were you."

"Thomas…lad," Patrick nodded, "we need ta talk. Are you up ta doing that?"

"Sure, Captain Pat," he said cheerfully. "You want a drink?"

"No, but Oi do want ta know what's got inta you. Hell, we've nearly got Sam by the scruff of the neck."

"Do we?" Tom questioned. "You know, some years ago, I made three promises: I promised my mother I'd never let Bob Trott come near Allen; I promised her, too, that I'd keep Allen from learning the kind of man who sired him; and I promised myself if I ever saw my step-father again, I'd beat the hell out of him. So what have I done instead? First, I delivered Allen to Samuel Trott Lucas on a platter—so there went promise number one. And, if I expose his marriage to my mother as fraudulent, Allen will be branded a bastard—and there goes promise number two."

"Then forget the bigamy charge," Mike interrupted. "With Jack and Harry to prove Lucas hired them for what was done at the Lloyd Hotel, you don't really need it.—Does he, Uncle Pat?"

"Well...Oi would suggest presenting the strongest possible case. Showing that Sam's fear of having his past exposed, led ta the happenings at the Lloyd, would swing things more ta Tom's favor."

Tom held his bottle to each of the Irishmen. "Sorry, Captains Herb, but either way I still lose. Without the bigamy charge, my case so far, is weak. With it, shall I tell you what Sam's counter claim could be? Remember, in spite of any attachment he feels for Allen, he will be fighting to save his own damned skin. Remember, too, that he and Mamalyn are legally separated, so saving face in his marriage is also a dead issue. Anyway, he will just admit to being Allen's father. And he will say because he abandoned my mother that I—hell, that Allen too—tracked him down and likely that we were blackmailing him. He'll say I married his daughter to gain a toe-hold on his money from one direction, while Allen wormed his way in through the company. Blackmail, he'll say, kept him quiet when my marriage was told. Blackmail, the only reason he would promote Allen so rapidly too. ... And my wife, for one, would believe every damned word of it. Then there is Nicole: He can have his lawyer ask one question that would give reason for my being with her in that hotel room and rip a hole right down the middle of our claim she that worked with him. Under oath, I can not deny saying I was seeing her, because I told Sam I was that night on the river front—and I was married at the time. Oh, yes, you can bet your last dollar he'd bring that out," Tom paused for a leisurely sip.

"But Sam's letter and the check," Mike said, "—and the statements Jack and Harry just signed."

"Mike, he can just say what they did to Kathy was done without his knowledge. And remember, I can't testify they were the same two who hauled me into that place.—And neither Kathy nor I can place him at the Lloyd Hotel. So it would be the word of those two pieces of scum against the word of the prominent Sam Lucas.

And if the jury buys his version, they'd buy what he could claim about the letter and the check: that having no knowledge of their disgraceful treatment of Kathy, he did hire Jack and Harry to locate his missing wife because he was just-so-concerned; that he wanted to make certain she was at her sister's and remained away from the unpleasantness in Savannah, until he could settle it and affect a reconciliation. Therefore," he raised the bottle to all this time, "I celebrate defeat. And mostly because of Mandria, Mamalyn and Allen. Even if by some miracle, revealing Sam's past were to save me, what would it do to their lives;—to their pride and reputations? Winning that way, what would I have left of them?"

"Well...damn!" Mike looked about the group, who realized as much as he, that Sam could present such a defense. "—Uncle Pat, what do you think?"

"That we have more digging ta do," he answered. "Sam made other mistakes. Somewhere, there's proof he and Nicole instigated this plot—and by Jesus, Oi'll find it!"

"So why didn't I recognize the man?" Tom injected, but spoke more to himself than the others. "You'd think I'd know that voice; his eyes;—something," he nodded. "And his size baffles me most. I remember him as such a...a giant of a man."

"To a frightened child he would seem that way," Kathy answered. "But you are quite a tall man, and would have to look down on his height now—which would not bring those past impressions to your mind."

"I suppose," he shrugged. "...Still, I should have been forewarned. There were times when his presence—something about him—sent a chill through my soul."

"But all of us have felt this," Iano concurred. "There is much evil about the man."

"You know, Tom," Patrick said thoughtfully, "I still say exposing the bastard in every way is your strongest defense. So it might be wise ta prepare your brother for what could be said of him as Sam's illegitimate son."

"*Si,*" Iano agreed. "If Allen is to learn of the *passato*, it is best that it comes from you, *amico mio.*"

Tom said nothing, as he sat looking at his boot toes.

"Your brother would understand," Kathy added. "Tom, it isn't as if you kept him from knowing a worthwhile father."

Still, he said nothing.

"Oi'll be taking Jack and Harry ta Savannah this afternoon," Patrick urged. "Oi could tell Allen you're here, lad, and he'd come tonight or first thing Saturday morning...if that suits you?"

And when Tom remained silent, Mike took up the cause. "Damn it, Tom, you have to fight your best fight, so tell Allen the truth! What other choice do you have?"

"I actually have two," Tom finally replied. "I can let Sam win, which he seems destined to do anyway. Yes, as I told Mandria, after the baby comes, Allen and I could take the children and start over somewhere. ...Or there is the third promise I made. But it couldn't stop with a beating. I'd have to kill Sam Lucas and then none of this would have to be told."

"Now you're making no sense at all," Patrick argued. "Adding his death to the charges already against you wouldn't be wise. And neither would tucking your tail and running. Hang with us a bit, Tom. If we're not giving up, neither can you."

"Your choices wouldn't do your marriage much good, either," Kathy said. "If it came to killing her father—even in a duel—on whose side would Mandy be, feeling as she does now?"

"Not mine, I'm afraid," Tom nodded.

"Well, unless you expose Sam—fully—her doubts could linger forever," Kathy continued. "And you are not giving your loved ones enough credit. They can deal with the truth of a trial, but they could never live happily under Sam's domination, which they'd have to do if you pack up and leave.—And I know this better than anyone here. Now is that the life you want for them, Tom?"

"No—damn it all!" he rose and the sofa rocked back on its broken leg. "Hell, you're right, Kathy—all of you are," he began to pace a nearly straight path. "...And there goes promise number three."

"Then Oi'll send Allen on," Patrick gave Kathy an admiring glance. The Italian was lucky to have her. Besides being beautiful and Irish, she was such a sensible, level-headed lass.

"Si, and the news you give him, is not all bad," said Iano. "Tom, Allen now has a sister—one he is as much related to as you."

Tom stopped dead in his tracks. "...Oh my God," he uttered. "Do you realize what Sam could do with that? What he could inspire the gossips to whisper? We could hear incest and fornication on every damned street corner!—And won't Mandria just love the hell out of that?"

"But you aren't kin—not blood kin," Mike said. "How could anyone say so?"

"Because, Captain, we're talking about Sam Lucas—who would be that determined to keep everything he holds dear in his life. And wouldn't incest spice up the blackmail story considerably? Oh-hell-yes—and it would make me look twice the villain! What is bigamy compared to that?"

"Then the key ta defeating anything Sam might claim, remains establishing a definite conspiracy with Nicole," Patrick repeated.

"*Si*, but after you have spoken to Allen, it might also be wise to prepare Evelyn Lucas and your wife for each of these possibilities," Iano suggested.

"I'll have to, but damn, I'm not looking forward to it," Tom returned to the sofa, which rocked to its good legs again as he sat. "And if they can't endure the scandal this last revelation could cause, I won't ask it of them—especially Mandria. ...So, my final decision about exposing Sam's past will rest in their hands." Then, heaving a great sigh, he continued. "But I will tell Allen the truth of it, so send him on, Captain Pat. At least I can cheat Sam Lucas out of the son he wanted so badly. Allen may be mad as hell with me, but the truth will also keep him as far away from that bastard as he can get."

"Oh-hell-yes!" Mike agreed. "And Tom, if you've no further need of me, I think I'll help Uncle Pat get Jack and Harry stowed with my friend at Oglethorpe Barracks.—We didn't tell that, did we? Sam might get wind of their capture if they're taken to the city jail, so we're keeping them out there for a while. ...Anyway, I'd like to do some snooping of my own in Savannah."

"Yes, Captain, go," Tom nodded. "Neither can your crew run the Irish Mist forever—and they've had to for nearly two damned weeks. Sorry about that."

"Well, it wasn't your fault Jack and Harry took their sweet time in returning to Augusta—or that they were stubborn about talking, once we got them here." And wearing that Irish grin, Mike turned to his uncle. "We tried everything, you know, from friendly persuasion to roughing them up—just a bit!" he added when Patrick gave him a look. "So yesterday morning, Tom had them hauled outside in the sun and showed them two goose-neck gourds and strips of wet rawhide—something he learned from the Indians, he tells them. And if you turn that kind of gourd at just the right angle, it looks like ... well, a man's privates," he amended his description in deference of Kathy's presence. "Anyway, making that clear to the bastards, Tom knotted the wet rawhide around the base of each gourd; told them to watch what happened; and for most of the day, they sat in the hot sun doing that. Then, as the rawhide dried and tightened, they began to get real nervous. And by damn, when the gourds split open, they were ready to answer any question we asked. Especially, Harry, because he is still suffering from the foot Kathy put into him—which, by the way, was a very fine job, Mrs. Rizza," he finished quickly, seeing that his uncle's expression had gone from *a* look to *the* look.

But in spite of all Patrick could do to keep from it, he chuckled. "Not exactly standard police procedure—and Oi'll not admit ta hearing that story," he said, rising to his feet. "Now, shall we collect those two and be on our way, Michael?"

"No one leaves here without lunch," Kathy rose too. "I won't have it said that Iano's wife failed to treat his friends properly.—And you, Tom Scott," she drew him up and shoved him ahead of her, "are having a bath and a shave afterwards. You are going to look like yourself when Allen arrives." And she shoved him again.

"Well, damn!" Tom grinned, glancing at the solid wall of men marching in step behind Kathy. There was no doubt they backed her decision all the way. "Damn pushy bunch, aren't you?—The whole lot of you!" he laughed, as she shoved him yet again. But he knew a man had never had better friends...

Allen arrived at Pace the next morning, and having heard some of Tom's adventure in Augusta from Mike and Patrick, he came in high spirits. Yet, it was that very exuberance that made Tom's task harder. And if Kathy hadn't given him a bolstering nod, he might have backed away from it all together. Still he had little to say as he led his brother into the forest on the pretext of checking trap-lines for Iano. He just didn't know where to start and so, spent most of the morning answering questions, for like Mike, Allen was also eager to hear every detail of Tom's existence since fleeing Savannah.

About noon, they entered a glade and sinking into the lush, April green grass, Tom had to listen as Allen made the same hopeful deductions about the worth of Jack and Harry's capture, as his friends had the previous day. …And somehow, as Allen talked, Tom's thoughts focused on the letter their mother had given him from her deathbed. She had promised to guide him, and he prayed for that. He prayed, too, for her understanding of what he had to do; …and most of all, he prayed for her approval.

When a lull entered the conversation, Tom took a deep breath, and told Allen the circumstances surrounding his birth and all that was suffered at the hands of his brutal sire. It was awful watching the youthful enthusiasm drain from his brother's features. And the confusion that replaced it tore at Tom's heart. Then bringing the story forward in time, he revealed Sam's identity, and how the discovery explained their troubles in Savannah.

Allen grew silent after that and again, Tom watched his expressions change. Shock and confusion now became anger—and Tom prayed, as he never had, that it wasn't directed at him.

"So, the stories Mama told about my father, were really about yours?"

"Yes, little brother," Tom wished Allen would look at him.

"And the inheritance money?" he added. "That was yours too?"

"…As my father's widow, the money belonged to Mama—to do with as she wished," Tom hedged. "She had two sons, Allen, and she loved us equally. It's only right that we divided what she left."

"Maybe so," he nodded. "But it makes me glad that damned marriage was bigamous."

Now Tom took a turn with confusion. "…Why? If it comes to light, you will be called a bastard."

"But a *Scott* bastard, Tom, with the right to my mother's name. I *am* a Scott now—and damned proud to be one, bastard or not."

Tom's lips parted and then laughter just spilled out. "If Sam Lucas knew he had done me such a favor…but Allen, legally you're right. Damn it, you *are* a Scott!" And he felt so pleased with the notion, he lay back in the grass to enjoy it further.

Allen did the same, even to the laced fingers behind his head; unconsciously mimicking Tom as he'd done since boyhood. "Anyway, who'd want a father who would deliberately try and destroy a man's only…brother?" And his eyes widened, as he sat forward suddenly. "—Tom, Mandy is my half-sister!"

"I know," Tom sighed and then related his fears on that score.

"Well, damn Sam Lucas!" Allen exclaimed. "And you still want me to continue working for the bastard?"

"Until Patrick can nail him, you must. You are our only source of inside information.—And it was your information which led us to Jack and Harry."

"So where will you be, until Captain Pat can do that?—Back in Athens and staying out of trouble, I hope?"

"Yes, but don't envy me. I must repeat this lurid tale to a wife who already doubts every word I say. And to her mother, who doesn't deserve any of it."

"One down; two to go, huh?" Allen grinned.

Tom smiled too. "Yes—and thanks for taking it so well. The way my luck has been running, I was afraid you'd blame me for everything."

"Hell, my father might be a fool, but Mama didn't raise any," Allen lay in the grass beside Tom again. "…You've made me curious, though," he said after a moment. "Didn't Mama resent me a little—or fear that I'd turn out bad, considering the father I had?"

"Never, Allen—not for a moment," Tom answered. "In fact, you were her pet…"

So, for the rest of the afternoon, the brothers enjoyed reliving many childhood experiences; things from a time when they'd been in the care of a mother to whom they had never felt closer. Yet it was Tom's presence—his long depended upon assurances that Allen needed and Tom couldn't refuse when he asked to spend the rest of that weekend in his company. It was now, April 18th, and he'd already missed Mandria's birthday. But he reasoned, a day or so longer here wouldn't prevent him from arriving in Athens for the birth of his child. And he smiled, trying to imagine Mandria's reaction to his birthday gift of honeysuckle oil. Surely, she had been pleased...

Chapter 18

It was Wednesday, the 22nd of April when Tom arrived in Athens. Saturday would be their 9 month's anniversary, and he wondered if Mandria would raise her usual fuss over the small remembrance tucked in his saddlebag. ...But this time, even to him, it felt like a bribe. He had hoped to return with encouraging news and instead, brought only more dark prospects. And that Mandria might embrace the darkest was something he truly feared. Yes, the truth was, his visit with Allen and the reunion with Mike, had been the only bright spots in the whole episode...

The town clock was striking the noon hour as he dismounted before Susan's cottage and leaning his head against the saddle, Tom expelled a long sigh. He knew he'd been running on raw nerves the last few weeks—he knew that—and still the tolling clock gongs went through him like a death knell. Mandria's pregnancy was in its final days, and so, likely, was their marriage. The realization made his steps feel leaden as he trudged to the door.

"Tom?—Oh, Tom, I'm so glad you've come!" Evelyn drew him inside with tear bright eyes. And she hugged him with an urgency he knew to be dread.

"...What is it, Mamalyn?" he forced the words out. "Has something happened? Mandria—she's all right, isn't she?"

"Yes—I mean, no. ...Oh, Tom, I'm so sorry!" And she burst into wrenching sobs.

Panic fused every part of his being. He wanted to race up the stairs for the answers Evelyn was struggling with, but he felt rooted to the spot where he stood.

"They're gone, Tom," she managed now. "Mandria and baby left us over a week ago."

"Dead?" he grasped her arms. "Mamalyn, you're saying they both died?"

"No!—Oh, dear Lord, I'm telling this badly, but I've been so worried about them…"

Tom didn't hear much else, so great was the wave of relief that washed over him with a sea-like roar. And sinking on a kitchen chair, he could only wait for it to ebb.

"…But no, Tom, your wife and son are not dead," Evelyn finished.

"My wife—and son?" She had his full attention again. "…But it's not time yet! Mamalyn, was there something wrong with the baby? Is that what you're saying?"

Evelyn took in a breath and sat facing him at the table, determined not to mislead him another time. "The baby did come early—when Mandy suffered a fall—but he is perfectly healthy."

"And Mandria fared the birthing well?" he asked.

"Physically, yes," Evelyn nodded, "But I'd feel better about her mental state if she hadn't run away.—Oh, Tom, I just don't know what she was thinking or where she could have gone!"

"But she took my son—and she vowed to give him away!" his eyes flashed blue-flame. "Mamalyn, somebody in Athens had to see her leave, and I mean to—"

"No, Tom—no!" she interrupted. "…Oh, I've so much to tell you, but you must believe this one thing now. I don't think Mandy had any intention of parting with that baby. Something happened the night he was born—and maybe it was only a bad dream, but she wanted to hold her son and ever since, she has hardly left his side. Yet, that wasn't the only change in her. Before he came, she'd hardly allow your name spoken in her presence. Afterwards, discussing your case became an obsession. She wanted every detail I knew again and again—and instead of arguing, as she'd always done, she would only sit there and nod. Then one morning, I went shopping and returned to find her gone. And her note didn't explain much at all."

"Her note?—May I see it?" he asked, needing an assurance he couldn't even name.

"Yes, of course," she hurried to fetch her purse. "But it doesn't say much that I could understand."

Tom unfolded the single page and found that Evelyn was right:

Dear Mama,

Because I love you, I can not risk telling you my plans. Only trust me. Please remain with Susan until I contact you—and take special care of John and Brittany, as they will surely feel I have deserted them too.

Your loving daughter, Mandria

"...Well," Tom rubbed wearily at his temples, "what do you suppose she's up to?"

"As I said, I've no idea," Evelyn observed his telling gesture. "But you are in no shape to do anything about it today. You need rest, Tom—and you must speak with John and Brittany. Mandy was right on that account. Those children did not understand both of you leaving them behind."

"Where are they, then?" Tom asked.

"In school, of course, and they won't be home until three, so why don't you go upstairs for a nap?" And so saying, she rose and brought him a basin of water.

This caused Tom to wonder if he smelled like a horse again. He did seem to recall a shower of road dust when she hugged him at the door. "Yes, I could use some sleep," he nodded.

"And a bath," she added, handing him a towel, a razor and very pointedly—it seemed to him—a cake of soap.

"Mamalyn?" he chuckled. "...Is the need so urgent?"

"No, dear," she laughed too. "But I don't want you to frighten the children, and right now you don't look like the handsome man they know," she replied while tying on her bonnet. "Now, I'm off to do the marketing. There are some of Susan's cinnamon buns in the pie-safe if you're hungry. But after you've made yourself presentable, do get some rest?" And with that, she was gone.

"…Some homecoming," Tom grumbled to the empty room. "Mandria is gone, Susan and the kids are at school, and Mamalyn thinks more of marketing than talking to me.—Doesn't anybody in this house want to know how my trip went?" Nevertheless, he stripped off his buckskins and bathed. Then, opening the back door, he gave his clothes a vigorous shaking, in hopes of dislodging the grimy road dust. Out of curiosity, he sniffed them too, but could not detect any horsey or offensive odors at all. "…Well," he said in bewilderment as he returned to the basin to shave. Women were puzzling creatures at best—and especially his wife. Just where in the hell could she be? He was still wondering about it, as he climbed the stairs. It was only Evelyn's strong belief that Mandria wouldn't part with the baby that allowed him a measure of peace—enough, that he fell asleep almost as soon as he touched the bed…

Tom awoke around two, drawn from slumber by the smells and sounds of supper preparations. Yet he didn't rise right away. Instead, he lay looking over the room, as if something there might give him a clue to Mandria's whereabouts. Along with his clothes, her smocks and skirts hung on some wall pegs—but of course they would, as she wouldn't need the loose fitting garments now. So were her long-johns there, and recalling a night when the back-flap had come unbuttoned, cost him a smile. …But the gray dress she'd been wearing when he kidnapped her was missing, and hadn't she saved it all these months, vowing to return to Savannah dressed like the lady she was? …Hadn't she said again and again, she was going home?

Closing his eyes, Tom could almost see her smile as she looked upon the longed-for sights of the city she loved—and he knew with certainty she had returned to Savannah.

...But she'd also sworn to go alone. No attachments, she said. So why take the baby? How was she explaining his existence when she'd been adamant that no one know of her pregnancy? That she had kept the baby at all was becoming more of a mystery—and much less comforting when he realized she could have taken the child to her father's house. ...Sam Lucas raising *his* son? Instilling the wrong values; twisting the boy's mind beyond redemption?

Tom came forward in a cold sweat, repeatedly reminding himself the baby was little more than a newborn. "But damn!" he nodded. "—Damn her for having the baby while I wasn't here—and probably right in this room!" Then knowing he sounded ridiculous, he crawled from the bed to pull on his boots. "...A son," he uttered, unable to contain a smile. "—I have a son!" he said, as if just realizing it. And when innumerable questions arose, he hurried downstairs in search of answers. "Mamalyn, what did Mandria name the baby?" he began at once.

"So, good afternoon to you too," she smiled. "And I must say you look better."

"Thank you," he nodded, sitting at the table. "But what name did she give my son?"

Evelyn continued stirring her pots. "Well...John wanted to call him John Scott, Jr.—and it was some time before he understood why he couldn't. Then, Brittany came up with Zachariah Harold—"

"Mandria didn't!" And his expression was one of appallment.

"No, ...no she didn't," Evelyn smiled, bringing two cups of coffee. "I'm afraid Mandy didn't name him at all—at least she hadn't before leaving here."

"But you still think she meant to keep him?" he asked then.

"Yes, I do. Tom, whenever she thought no one was watching, she would cuddle that precious baby—and from the first, it was Mandy who got up with him in the night. And if you could have seen her expression when he nursed, you'd know I'm right."

Tom held Evelyn's eyes, reading the love she had witnessed between mother and son and expelled a pent-breath. He'd have traded his soul to see what she had. "So on what date was he born?"

"On Mandria's birthday; April 11th."

Tom gave a short laugh of irony. "At last! A gift from me she won't ever forget."

"I would say not—though it was her reaction to your birthday gift that caused this."

"The honeysuckle oil?" he sipped from his cup.

"Yes. You see, we were planning a party for Mandy and not wanting her to spoil it for the children, I took your gift to her beforehand. As I expected, she pitched a hissy-fit about it and flung the bottle into the fire. ...Then she tripped over the cradle and the fall brought on an early labor."

"...Dear God," he gave a helpless nod.

"Indeed, we all prayed to God that day. ...Tom, she behaved so strangely, making no sense whatsoever—and that was before Doc Lewis gave her the Laudanum. Over and over, she insisted it was *her perfume*. And she said, *It was there in the fire with Tom*. Then she would flail at the air, begging me to make something go away."

"It must have been her nightmare," Tom concluded. "She couldn't stop reliving that night at the Lloyd House."

"The night her own father forced her to see his evil at work!" Evelyn said bitterly.

"But speaking of Sam..." And as gently as he could, Tom revealed all that he had learned and each of the ways Sam might retaliate. "...Mamalyn," he said then, "I need to know how you'd feel if these things came to light. And I want you to consider the humiliation and damage it could do to your family. Also, I need to know how you think Mandria would feel about it. Because if it's too much for either of you, I won't allow it told—even if it means losing my case."

"Well...," Evelyn sat nodding, trying to absorb everything, "I can't speak for my daughter, but Tom, I don't see that you have another way to go. Either you use all at your disposal or Sam wins."

"So I've been told," he fondly recalled the lectures he received at *Pace*. "And thank you," he drew her hand into both of his. "But, I still have to know how Mandria feels. And as I think she returned to

Savannah, I'll have to go too. She may even have the baby in the same house with Sam…and well, it worries me, that's all."

"And so it should!" Evelyn's grasp on his hand tightened. "Now you listen to me, Tom. May God forgive me for saying so, but if Mandy allows Sam anywhere near that baby, she doesn't have sense enough to raise him. No, I'd rather see you raise my grandson alone than to let that happen!" Then, full of indignation, she rose and bustled after the coffee pot. "That goes for Allen too, by the way. He is your brother and more the gentleman for it than he'd ever have been under Sam's guidance. No, that man has ruined enough lives—damn him—so stop him any way you can!"

"…Mercy," Tom laughed. "And when did my mother-in-law become so plucky?"

"Arguing with your wife night and day helped a bit," she smiled while refilling his cup. "And I do believe some of Susan's notions are rubbing off on me. She is quite remarkable, you know."

"Miss Hope-to-my-die Independence? Yes, I suppose she is," Tom agreed.

"Well, it was Susan who kept this house running smoothly—in spite of Mandy's snits at every mention of your name. And while I dealt with that, it was Susan who could always explain to the children in words they understood."

"But you did say Mandria's attitude changed after the baby?"

"Along with her interest in John and Brittany, yes. Tom, she included them in everything, just as she did the baby and I felt … such hope," Evelyn paused. "Anyway, you can see why it hurt them so when she left."

"What could have caused this change?" Tom nodded. "You said she wanted to hear about my case, but did she say anything—or maybe ask questions you found unusual?"

"Nothing—except when it came to the honeysuckle oil. She said she had taken her last full bottle to Aiken and left a half full one on the dresser at your place. Then she said something about Hassie telling her there was none left at Marsh Haven either. I couldn't understand her concern, but as that was what she wanted to talk about, I told her what happened when I purchased this last bottle for you.—Remember, before you left for Augusta I said I had learned something?" she asked, going to stir her pots again.

"What I remember is Mandria slamming a lot of doors," Tom said beleagueredly. "But I'd like hearing your story now too—especially if she found it of interest."

"She must have, because afterwards Mandy went for a long walk. When she returned, I could tell she'd been crying—and that was the only time she did after the baby came," Evelyn reclaimed her chair. "Anyway, just before leaving Savannah, I went to the perfumer's shop, and in conversation, I mentioned that the order was for my daughter's birthday in April. Monsieur DuMont seemed confused, saying he'd recently been recording the birthdays of his customers and Mandy's was listed as November 1st. I assured him April was the correct month and he dropped the matter so quickly—and was in such an agitated state—it made me curious. So, when he excused himself, saying he'd check with his lab to see how soon my order would be ready, I stepped to the door to listen—and thankfully, I understand enough French to know what was said. Monsieur DuMont showed his book to the assistant he said had filled the last order and asked if he could explain why Mandy was listed with a November birthday, when her mother was standing out front wishing to make the same purchase for an April birthday. Well, the assistant hemmed and hawed, but finally admitted he had sold some to a beautiful blonde lady—a Miss O'Rourke—even though it went against policy to do so outside of Mandy's family. He even admitted to charging extra for her purchase—which she ordered, by the way, on October 29th and picked up the morning of the incident at the Lloyd Hotel."

"...And you feel Mandria found your discovery important in some way?" Tom asked.

"I don't know, Tom. All I can tell you is that for the next few days, she was exceptionally quiet and pensive. ...Then, she took the baby and left."

Whatever Tom had meant to say next was lost when the room was suddenly invaded by two very excited children. "I told you it was

Tom's horse—I told you!" John said to Brittany, as their hugs nearly toppled him from the chair.

"I don't care; I don't care!" she giggled. "He's home!—Tom, you came home!"

"And now we can go fishing like you promised!" added John. "We can go today, can't we Tom—just you and me?"

"Whoa, Bear—calm down, son!" Tom laughed. But there was no suppressing either of them and for a time, they talked incessantly each trying to over-speak the other.

Not even Susan's arrival slowed them down, but she did make a suggestion that restored some peace to her house. "Tom, for heaven sake, take the boy fishing!" she called after John repeated his request yet again.

"Yeah!" John hopped to his feet. "I'll get the poles!" And he raced from the room before any objection could be raised.

"And you, young lady, have thirty minutes to get ready for Melanie's birthday party," Susan spoke now to Brittany.

"But—but Tom's home!" she argued. "Besides, I don't like Melanie very much," she finished with a pout.

"You didn't feel that way this morning when you asked Mamalyn to buy her a gift." Susan countered. "And I'm certain Tom plans to spend time alone with you too," she sent him a look which said he'd better.

"Yes, of course, I will," he hastened an assurance.

"Then come along," Evelyn smiled, leading the little girl away. "And after you're dressed, we'll wrap Melanie's present together."

"Susan," Tom rose to give her a much-delayed hug, "how have you been?"

"Worried, mostly," she smiled. "Evelyn told you about Mandria—and your son?"

"Yes," he said, but nothing more, because John was back and ready to leave.

"Go!" Susan shooed them out. "We'll talk later—and make this a fun afternoon, will you? I think John missed you more than any of us."

So, the pair departed, not returning until dusk. And along with Evelyn's supper, all enjoyed a pan of fried trout—and John's happy retelling of their afternoon. But Tom was not unaware that a small pair of blue-green eyes in the gathering were more green with envy than blue…

By the time the children went to bed, he had seen another display of Brittany's jealousy. While helping them with their homework, she constantly answered questions put to John, trying to prove herself the smartest. Tom knew she was bidding for his attention and it saddened him deeply. The situation would never have arisen if he'd been able to give them more time and a normal home-life. He would too, and seeing to that was the way he explained to John why he had to leave again very soon. He was satisfied the boy had understood; … but how should he tell Brittany? Little girls wouldn't much care for the camaraderie he and John enjoyed while swatting insects and impaling fish bait on a muddy creek bank…

Over a final cup of coffee with the ladies, Tom was able to put aside the problem for a time. …In fact, it seemed he was even to be spared the depressing chore of repeating the details of his trip for Susan. And though he was grateful, he found her lack of curiosity strange. So he listened while both women went to great lengths in heaping praise on his *handsome, alert, and oh, so good* baby son. Then he was forced to conceal a smile of realization in his cup. Evelyn had already told Susan his news and in his mind, he could almost hear his mother-in-law's lecture;—her insistence that, for this one evening, they should only speak of happy things and allow him to enjoy himself. Watching Susan more closely, he decided he'd guessed right, for time and again she bit her lip on opinions she wanted to express. It was a special hug he gave each of them when it came time to retire…

With the closing of the bedroom door, however, Tom's apprehensions returned. He was more anxious than ever to leave; to find his wife and see for himself that Mandria had accepted his child. …But Brittany thought of herself as his too, and a good father would not place the needs of one child over another. No, he'd have to stay until he'd talked with her—a decision he accepted, though it left him too restless for sleep.

Going to an opened window, he gazed at the star filled night and inhaled the crisp air. It was scented with the full blooms of Susan's garden below; …and amongst the mixture he detected honeysuckle. "Damn it," he whispered, glaring at a section of the low rock wall which was all but strangled by the fragrant vine. …Would that scent and the woman who wore it always have such a strangle-hold on his heart? He was afraid they would. "Think of something else," he murmured, turning away. "—Anything thing else…"

Then, he seemed to see the clothes pegs he'd been staring at so blankly. …Was it the dimness of the room that made his suit and dress shirt appear clean and pressed? For months, they'd hung at the cabin in the same sad shape as the day he'd escaped from jail. And Mandria had never touched them, other than the time she dressed Brittany in his shirt while her clothes were laundered.

Out of curiosity, he turned up the lamp for a closer inspection and found all his clothes had been cleaned—and mended, for the button missing from the cuff of his Christmas shirt had been replaced. That Mandria could have made such a concession—even to relieve the tedium of her final days of confinement—was too much to accept. More likely, Susan or Evelyn had done this, and over his wife's strong objections.

What he didn't find, when looking through Mandria's things again, were her buckskins or boots. "Well, she must have burned them," he decided, because he couldn't imagine one reason she would take them. *The ladies of Savannah* would be appalled.

…Or maybe she intends presenting them in evidence, he thought now. …Yes, as proof of the primitive existence she'd had to endure. And certainly, any divorce court would then award her custody of the child—especially, if the judge happened to be married to one of her high and mighty lady friends!

Tom had worked himself into quite a state, and spotting the cradle, he knelt to grasp the edges as if the piece had become an ally by virtue of the fact that it had been able to stop Mandria from running, when he never could. …Thankfulness that mother nor child had been harmed in the fall, tempered his thought. "But the danger was there;—and look what she's risking now," he imagined the future once more. …There was Sam Lucas, driving about Savannah wearing that cold, intolerant sneer, while beside him a small boy took great pains in imitating his Grandfather's every expression. "Damn it, Mandria—no!" Tom said into muffling hands raised to block out the vision.

Then, expelling a great sigh, he admitted the cost of the last several weeks. He was physically and emotionally drained. After all, the baby was just a few hours older than the last time he'd allowed his tired mind too much range. And it was a certainty Mandria wouldn't be leaving Savannah no matter how long it took him to get there. She was home and how had she put it? Oh, yes …*Everything I love is in Savannah.*

Scanning his attire, Tom realized a further foolishness to his urge to pick up and leave. Had he ridden headlong into Savannah, dressed in buckskins, upon his avenging—and stolen—steed, he would have been spotted and immediately jailed or hung. "No, lady," he nodded. "Better to rest up here first; better to arrive there blending with the night, until I know what in the hell you're planning. …Meanwhile," he smiled, "there's a lady here too—and as our lives seem destined to entwine, I'm going to do my damnedest to re-enchant her." Then, he sat gazing at his suit with new interest…

Tom checked his watch as he left the stage office the following day. As he suspected, the agent had little trouble recalling the beautiful green-eyed lady—in a gray dress—who bought passage south, for herself and a small baby. So, with that question settled, he was ready to keep a more romantic appointment. It was nearly three when he stopped at the school-house gate and brushing a piece of lint from his suit sleeve, he straightened his tie, ready for the moment Susan would dismiss her students. It was important that his appearance be impressive, for more than his own future happiness hung on this meeting.

Then the door opened and the slippered feet coming toward him ahead of the crowd of students, faltered to a hobbling stop. But her eyes never left Tom, even while stooping to remove a pebble from her shoe. "Good afternoon," he made her a grand bow.

And Brittany's smile, even for an eight year old, said she found him the handsomest man in the world. "You look so…different," she circled him slowly. "Better even, than Miss Rutledge's preacher!"

"Why, thank you," Tom chuckled, enjoying her admiration. Yet, with the approach of certain class-mates, her expression darkened and Tom noticed. "…Brit?" he leaned close. "What's the matter?"

"Them," she whispered. "They tease me and John something awful. They call us white trash and say we live with Miss Rutledge 'cause we don't really have no family."

"Do they now?" Tom straightened. "—Pardon me, young ladies," he turned to address the group with a charming smile. And the girls, ranging in age from nine to fourteen, blushed and broke into tittering giggles. "My *daughter* tells me you're her classmates?" he asked, making a to-do of patting the small hand he held.

"…Yes sir," heads bobbed and eyes went from Tom to Brittany and back.

"Well, I've been away from Athens for some time now, and I wondered if you could direct me to the finest dress shop in town?"

"That would be Miss Wren's up on the main street," they agreed among themselves.

"Why?" one, bolder than the rest, dared to ask.

"Because I have neglected this beautiful child's wardrobe shamefully," he sent Brittany an adoring look. "So, shall we see what Miss Wren has to offer, dear daughter?"

"Oh, yes!" she said, with a pride that reminded him of Mandria.

"Of course, your mother won't approve of ready-mades," he added as they turned to leave. "She will want you fitted by her own dress-maker—and Lord only knows what that will cost me! But for the present, perhaps we can find…well, something passable."

After a backward glance, Brittany paused, turning shining eyes up to Tom. "Then maybe we should only buy pinafores and matching hair ribbons—something like Melanie, Leslie and Morgan are wearing," she pointed to the open-mouthed girls. "That would be passable. For the present," she added, with lift of her small chin.

"Whatever you say, daughter," Tom laughed as they left, "whatever you say."

They returned to Susan's with three new pinafores, a score of ribbons, a pair of shiny, black patent shoes—and after their talk, a very happy and understanding little girl...

CHAPTER 19

Sam Lucas was a man with a problem. It seemed his wayward wife was allowing her lawyers to proceed with finalizing their legal separation. And that was costing him. Not that his wallet was suffering anything terminal. He'd protected funds against that years ago. But his pride was certainly bleeding badly and he thought, perhaps, that was worse. He assumed, after years of courting favor with Savannah's elite, he would have been shown more support. But that wasn't the case and he'd even begun to look about for another residence, should Evelyn return and insist on retaining her family home in the settlement. ...If she returned; and it was still possible to prevent that if Jack and Harry could locate her first. It was about time he heard something out of them too, but as always, the dim-witted bastards seemed to be moving at a snail's pace.

In earlier years, he might have pulled up stakes and left Savannah all together. But his son was here now and Sam was not going anywhere, as long as their relationship continued to progress, ... though this was also moving at a maddeningly slow pace.

Then, out of the blue, his daughter returned. Sam still wasn't certain what to make of it, but somehow, was going to take every advantage afforded to him. For with Mandria's return, her ruined marriage reigned supreme among the gossips again—as well as his chosen suitors for her, all of whom felt she should now be eager to make a proper marriage with one of her own kind. Sam thought so too, especially since a bidding war could once again win him favor from men of influence…

⸺◈⸺

"Really, Father," Mandria put down her evening purse. And the rattle of her jet-beaded cloak as she removed it, clearly bespoke her agitation. "I haven't been home even two weeks—and still you persist with the same boring questions!"

"Yes, because you've yet to answer them satisfactorily. Instead, you've spent nearly every waking moment re-acquainting yourself with Savannah, as you put it. So what, pray tell, are you saying to our friends about your sudden reappearance among us?"

"The same as I told you—and I had hoped my own father would accept my explanation as graciously as our friends have."

"Missy, it's because I *am* your father that I want the whole story. Can't you see that if I'm to guide and protect your best interests, I must have facts?"

"My best interests are my only concern now," Mandria said coolly as she entered the front parlor. "But I have outgrown the need for your guidance and protection," she added, pouring herself a sherry. "Believe me, Father, if I have learned anything from this entire experience, it is putting what is best for me ahead of all else."

Sam settled on a chair facing her. "Before you refuse my help, need I remind you of your disastrous choice in husbands—*again?*"

"Hardly. I am aware of all my mistakes—and I do credit you with making me see that one quite plainly."

"So why do I detect bitterness between us? You should be grateful— and certainly more open."

"Father, I am bitter at the entire world," she sighed. "You just happen to be a part of it.—But I did come home, didn't I?"

"Yet you are still avoiding some very important issues by refusing my questions."

"I told you what happened. The rest is of no consequence," she made him a pretty, but disinterested shrug.

"You only said Scott abandoned you shortly before you gave birth; that you didn't want his child and *took care of the problem* before arriving on my doorstep. But where did your husband go, Mandy—and who delivered his child? We both know your mother has always supported the bastard, so why no mention of the part she must have played in this?"

"Stop it;—just stop!" Mandria banged her glass to a table. "Isn't it enough for you that I'm here; that I've learned a hard lesson and now want my rightful place in this society?"

"Then what of the marriage you should be anxious to dissolve?" Sam tried a new tact. "You've yet to move in that direction—and there has been much interest expressed about when those proceedings will be final."

Mandria smiled, but there was little warmth in it. "Frankly, Father, it's because of that *interest* that I've delayed divorce. It would seem a married woman is allowed much more freedom, which I intend to enjoy fully.—Not that I'm adverse to an advantageous match, but I mean to take my time about it. And if that means moving in with my brother-in-law to escape your constant badgering, then I'll do it."

"…And what does Allen say about that?" he wondered aloud.

"He, at least, treats me with dignity and understanding. Allen was hurt just as badly by his brother's behavior, but still agreed to escort me everywhere in town I've wanted to go—and not once has he condemned my position or questioned what is dead and gone."

"Is it, my dear?" Sam's eyes narrowed. "Allen resides in Tom Scott's house, where you also lived for the few short days your marriage lasted. …Is the past dead, or do you still feel an attachment for the owner of that place?"

"There are not enough words to tell you my feelings for Tom Scott," Mandria rose as calmly as she could. "And I didn't return to *his* house—I came to *yours*. But one more session such as this and I will leave. Where I live in Savannah, matters little as long as I'm allowed to get on with *my* life!"

Sam watched as she started from the room and knew from her rigid posture she was apparently serious. But he couldn't allow her to move out, when for the first time ever, she had not immediately squashed consideration of the suitors he intended her to have—and when her presence under his roof was half of what it would take to force a final confrontation with Tom Scott. "Mandy, wait," he called, concealing purpose in placation. "…Listen, you didn't have to give up the child. He does have my blood in him too, and if your future husband—when you chose one—will not accept another man's baby, given time I think I could raise him as a true Lucas grandson."

"That can never be," she nodded adamantly. "The boy is a Scott and too much a part of something which shouldn't have happened. No, Father, I had to put all the distance between that child and myself that I could."

"Well, it is your decision, of course, but I wanted to make the offer. And should you wish to reconsider—"

"No! …Thank you," Mandria interrupted. And being too choked with emotion to say more, she proceeded up the stairs.

"Good night, then," Sam said, listening for her bedroom door to close. "…But I will change your mind, daughter—somehow," he muttered, issuing a sigh of frustration. She was right about one thing, though. Badgering her for the whereabouts of her mother or son had netted him exactly nothing;—and he'd gleaned little of value from elsewhere.

Sam had questioned the driver of the stage Mandria claimed to have ridden and could only conclude she'd left the baby somewhere in Augusta. The man did recall a lady fitting her description, with a baby, in the depot up there, but when his passengers boarded for Savannah, the only woman with a child he could remember was a meek half-breed Indian in buckskins. And as she spoke no English, that one had ridden cowering in her shawl the whole way. So why the lie about how she'd returned? Maybe she'd come aboard the Irish Mist? Who knew?

He'd even questioned Allen, because he and Mandria had become almost constant companions—as his own children, by all rights, should have been had they any inkling of their true relationship—but Allen had only advice to offer, and no new information.

"Give her time to heal, Sam," Allen said. "When she is ready to confide in us, she will. It's just going to take a while for the hurt and betrayal to fade—as it has with me too."

But Sam's knowledge of Tom Scott made time a thing to be feared. First, because holding Mandria to protect his unborn child was something Tom would do. Secondly, because deserting her at a critical period was not—unless she'd been in the care of someone he trusted, which had to be Evelyn, of course. Thirdly, it still had to be a matter vital to his case that forced him out of hiding and not knowing what that was or the outcome was enough to drive any man insane! And, fourth, because Tom Scott wouldn't go to such lengths and then passively accept the disappearance of his wife and son.

No, the child had to be found, making certain that all trails ended at Sam's door. "But damn, the aggravation of it!" he swore. Tom should have been hung while the whole city was in a zealous uproar. Now, time had elapsed; anger had subsided; there were far too many tales of *friends* relentlessly working to clear the bastard—and such persistence must also be stopped.

It would be, too, once Tom had drawn a final breath. For as Sam had already seen, Savannah courted only the living. Wasn't Nicole all but forgotten by the society which spawned her? Indeed she was, while Savannah swished merrily on to the next ball, seeking new interests. But Sam did approve of this attitude. Yes, if he played it just right, that new interest would be found in his heroics. Who wouldn't admire a father protecting his only daughter? A grandfather who shot dead a cowardly bastard trying to rip a baby from its mother's arms? A husband who bravely carried on, though news of their daughter's tragic lot so upset his poor misguided wife, she'd have to be confined in a mental ward indefinitely?

"So come to Savannah, Tom Scott," he invited. "Come true to character, with all those upright morals marching before you—and we'll see how well they can stop a God damned bullet!"

With an itching kind of impatience, Sam rose to fix a brandy. Surely the people he'd sent to Augusta would return with his grandson quickly. It was vital that the boy be under his roof, whether Mandria approved or not. Likely, she wouldn't; likely they would argue loud and long, but her character was also predictable. She would hardly put an infant out on the street.

"And this time, there will be no Nicole to foul things up," Sam uttered as he started upstairs. "—Nor idiots like Jack and Harry," he added, idly wondering why he'd heard nothing more from them. They'd needed money badly enough to come begging once—and he'd made it clear they'd get no more without earning it. Yet, the letter he'd sent concerning Evelyn went unanswered and the draft uncashed. Sam shrugged. Knowing that pair, they were either dead or long gone from the area. Then putting his theories aside, he entered his bedchamber and disrobed. A man needed to unwind from the stress he was facing; to reward himself pleasurably.

From a shadowed corner of the room, a young Negro girl rose, trembling visibly as Sam approached. A single tear slid down her cheek and it amused him. Kneading fingers pushed into her nude breasts and she swayed slightly, revulsion causing her knees to buckle. His hands moved to her shoulders, playing on that moment of weakness; forcing her downward until she knelt before him. He cupped her face and her eyes closed. He drew her forward, tracing his swelling penis across her full lips, but she kept them sealed. Again he presented himself, tightening his grasp on her head, and again her mouth remained closed. How Sam did enjoy such useless resistance, and the proof pulsed ever so pleasantly in the thickening rod of his offering. "You can't win, Gladys Ella," he said huskily. "It's this or an ass fucking." At that, her eyes flew to his in silent pleading. "And I would have to bind and gag you. It's a damn nuisance, but my daughter wouldn't understand your painful screams." Then probing her lips once more, he found them softened enough to be parted. "Better; …much better," he inserted the throbbing head of his member, sighing at the lush, wet warmth of her mouth. "Now, a bit of suction," he suggested, going for deeper insheathment. "And lets put that little tongue to work, shall we?"

In answer, the girl convulsed, her whole being trying to reject the thing pushing toward the back of her throat. But even in the dimness, she saw the rage in Sam's eyes; felt the thumbs he pressed into her windpipe; and knew if she disobeyed, he would strangle her. So, clinging to his legs, she drew herself closer and began to suckle in sheer desperation.

Slowly then, Sam's hands left her throat and reclasped on her head. He made a few testing thrusts, adjusting the fit between them until the most comfortable angle of entry was his. There he paused, enjoying her hold on his thighs; the nails digging almost painfully into his flesh; the mouth which continued to invite him more deeply within. He smiled and accommodated, allowing his movements to take on a regular, steady rhythm…

The girl prayed it would be over quickly and concentrated on the one way she had of surviving with any dignity—and her life. When his final, frenzied moments arrived, she managed to let his spewings drain from the corners of her mouth and back over him. It was a small victory, but swallowing it would have meant she accepted his debasement. A small victory, indeed—and short lived.

Sam panted heavily when he released Gladys Ella, allowing her to fall backwards at his feet. But she made the mistake of showing her triumph, by wiping the back of a hand across her mouth in disgust. "Just a damn moment!" he hauled her forward and into lamplight. The milky cum, clearly visible on her dark skin, lay on her chin and in dribbles upon her breasts. "I do not appreciate this," he said with deadly calm, his eyes piercing her like knife points. And easing himself down on the bed, he sat facing her with folded arms. "Eat it," he said. "I will see you eat it."

The girl was trembling badly, more terrified by this mood than she'd been before. So lifting his spilled remains on her fingers, she ate. It was that or certain death, for his eyes were focused on her throat, watching for each accepted swallow.

"Now, bitch, you will bathe me with your tongue—and you may begin with my feet." Sam caught her wrist, pulling her along as he moved to lie in the center of the bed. "…However," he said, bringing her face to his, so there could be no misunderstanding, "since you didn't care for the taste of my cum, I would advise you to pay special homage—*with your tongue*—to my ass hole. Perhaps that will teach you to treat my attention with more respect." Then shoving her against the footboard, he propped leisurely in the pillows and lay spread-eagle before her.

What had happened in the shadowy corner was far preferable to this. Here in the light, the girl could hide nothing from him. Here in the light, she could also see more than a murderous glint in his eyes. He was going to become aroused by her actions and she would be forced to pleasure him again. And this time, he would observe the deed closely, making sure she accepted all he gave. ...Was it her fault in some way? Should she have forgotten her dignity and simply allowed him to use her? There didn't seem to be any right or wrong in her world—and fewer answers. So, in total dejected defeat, she lowered her mouth to his toes and began to lick and suck on them, one by one...

CHAPTER 20

It was late Friday afternoon, Joleen had supper simmering over the fire, and keeping her company, Mandria sat rocking a very sleepy baby. Then a noise on the stairway brought her to her feet, ready to flee toward Joleen's nursery.

"Allen?" she stopped, recognizing his boots before the rest of him came into view. "Did you see him?" she asked, jiggling the baby when it stirred. "Please, what did he say?" she finished in a hushed voice.

"Ask him yourself," Allen grinned, stepping aside as Mike came down behind him.

The Captain gave her a subdued version of his wide Irish smile and his manner was just as hesitant. "...So who is this?" he tugged back the baby's cover.

And Mandria had to laugh at his shocked expression. "This is Tandy—Joleen and Willie Luther's beautiful little girl, Captain."

"Yeah—uh, yes, she is beautiful." he stammered awkwardly. "But where is Tom's baby?" And it sounded close to a demand.

"*My* baby is still napping," she replied with a lift of her chin. "Now, please sit down while I put Tandy to bed too. We need to talk, Captain Herb."

"Coffee," Joleen brought full cups when the men were settled at the table. "And here some Hassie-cake, do you want it."

Mike did. "My God, that's delicious," he stuffed large bites in his mouth.

"Hassie don't make nothing that ain't," she said, bringing another cup as Mandria returned. Then gathering her sewing basket, she stepped on to the back veranda, allowing them the privacy of her kitchen.

Mandria paused to sip her coffee, feeling a bit hesitant herself now. What she wanted from Mike wasn't going to come easily. "…So, how have you been, Captain?" she began lightly.

"Fine," he nodded. "And maybe a little curious about your brother-in-law, here. I haven't seen much of him since you returned to Savannah."

Mandria nodded. As she suspected, Mike resented Allen's association with her. "Well, Allen has been a good friend…and Captain, I always considered you one too."

"So did I. Yet, you are living with your father, which obviously puts us on opposite sides. Mandy, I don't even know why I agreed to come to this meeting."

"You feel you've walked into an ambush," she concluded.

"Sort of, yes. But this is still Tom's house. And Allen's—though I don't understand a willingness to escort his brother's wife while she does the town every damned night."

Mandria glanced at Allen, who shifted uncomfortably. "Then you must also have heard that I've been swamped with attention by Father's same old friends. Honestly, he's lining up suitors faster than I can count them—"

"And you're bragging about that?" Mike injected. "Damn, Allen, do you just sit there while she chooses Tom's replacement?" his temper flared brighter. "What happened, boy, did Sam finally win you over?— Or maybe what you learned at *Pace* made you want it all: money, acknowledgement—"

"Captain!" Allen interrupted. "Mandy's point was that it's been my presence that keeps those suitors at bay—and *Pace* is something for Tom to deal with, not you or me. But knowing what we do, you must realize I love this lady…as a sister? So even if I don't understand everything she's doing, I find one of them most admirable: Mandy brought my nephew here and not to Sam's house. Now, let's hear her out, shall we?"

Mike gave Allen a long look before turning to Mandria again. "…Well, get on with it, then," he said, apparently mollified.

Mandria knew she had missed something that passed between them, but had to put it aside for now. "As I said, I don't appreciate what Father is doing any more than I ever did, but it pleases him that I haven't rebuffed his suitors this time, and therefore he has allowed me a great deal of undisturbed freedom every night—and more importantly, every day. That is when I'm able to spend a few precious hours with Seph—"

"And just who in the hell is this Seph?" Mike bristled again.

"That's my nephew, Captain," Allen chuckled. "Joseph Phillip Scott."

"Oh," Mike uttered. "But that doesn't explain a hell of a lot—like why he is living apart from his mother and why she feels it's necessary."

"Because, above all else, I must protect my son;—and because I do know my father. Even before all this trouble, he was never honest or kind to another living soul, including his wife and daughter. I just will not have Seph exposed to his cruelties or raised the way I was."

"Now that is the first sensible thing you've said," Mike admitted grudgingly.

"There's more, Captain. If Father suspected that I love—and intend to keep the child of an enemy—he would give me no peace at all. So, I told him I gave the baby away and made the best arrangements I could to keep him believing that."

"By living in his house and pretending an interest in the rich old fools he'd have you wed," Mike gave a negative nod. "…Why, Mandy? Why put yourself through all this?"

"I must, because the answers I need are here in Savannah; …and I'm hoping Father will lead me to them. So, I gave him back the daughter he thinks he lost;—a bitter, betrayed woman whose only dream is recapturing her place in his world."

"And do you still feel bitter and betrayed?" Mike dared to ask.

"Yes, but I'm no longer sure who is responsible," she admitted. "Mike, don't you see? I've been left somewhere in the middle of all this—which doesn't put you and I on opposite sides at all."

"Then what about Seph? Aren't you putting him in the middle too? You are, Mandy, and it isn't wise. You should have left that baby with Mamalyn."

"I...well, Mama couldn't nurse him," she grasped for a believable excuse. "But Joleen has a baby too, and when I'm unable to be here, she can at least feed him."

"Now there had to be wet-nurses available in Athens too," Mike argued. "...So did your reason have something to do with Tom, maybe?"

"We needn't go into that," she straightened defensively. For Mandria knew her attachment to Seph would have been easy to explain compared to her feelings for Tom. It was best just to stay clear of the subject. "Listen, as I said, I don't know yet who is guilty or who is innocent. But frankly, I've come to a point where I need help."

"From me?" he shrugged. "My views are biased. I believe in Tom."

"And I believe in truth. I can't build a life on doubts. I must know exactly what happened—either way—and for Seph's sake, learn to exist in spite of it."

"You will forgive me if I see your doubts in a different light?" And Mike's smile now was the one she'd always found charming. "I see them as hope for you and Tom."

"...Captain, please?" she focused on the hands pressed palms-down before her. "Couldn't we just pool our information; put the puzzle pieces here on this table, and possibly fit them together?"

"We already know how they fit—and why," Mike answered as he and Allen exchanged another of those odd glances. "In fact, the only missing piece is the one showing that Sam and Nico did this thing together."

Mandria gave both of them a look of her own. "I could tell you something about that—if you would stop keeping things from me. Now, what is going on between you two?"

Mike looked at Allen again and saw his slight nod. "She is a grown woman," he carried on the verbal side of their disagreement. "And hell, when Tom left *Pace*, he said he was going back to Athens and tell her anyway."

"That's twice you've mentioned that name," Mandria said impatiently. "What or where is *Pace*—and for God's sake what was Tom doing there instead of Augusta?"

"*Pace* is the Rizza's place upriver, where the men we captured in Augusta were taken for questioning," Mike answered. "Mandy, Kathy identified them as her kidnappers and they confessed to working for your father—even signed statements to that effect for Uncle Pat. ... But a problem arose and Tom asked that everything be put on hold until he could discuss it with you and Mamalyn."

"What problem? I can't imagine anything that would keep Tom Scott from throwing the smallest bit of favorable proof right at my head."

"Captain, don't," Allen made a plea when Mike started to speak. "You know how Tom felt. He said rather than put Mandy through any more, we'd just leave for good."

"He'd do what?" Mandria shot forward in her chair. "Damn him—he can't leave until this is settled! Does the idiot think anything could be worse than believing..." And there she curbed both temper and tongue. "That—that he didn't want his son after all?" she finished the best way she could.

"Allen, Tom can beat the hell out of me if he wants to," Mike stated, "but I'm telling her."

"Oh...damn," Allen rose and went to the window. Perhaps Mike was right, but if Mandria reacted the way Tom feared, he couldn't bear seeing it.

"Well?" Mandria insisted, though Allen's withdrawal did make her uneasy.

"Well...how much do you know about Tom's childhood?" Mike began.

"I know it wasn't always happy," her eyes went to Allen. "But what could that possibly have to do with the present situation?"

"Everything—and don't worry about Allen," Mike read her concern correctly. "The secret Tom kept from him is out."

"...Allen, is that why you're upset?" she asked. "You can't believe it matters. The truth doesn't make you a different person—not to me."

Allen's laugh was a short bark of irony. "Oh, but it does—and especially to you," he continued to gaze from the window. "Mandy, truth isn't always a cure-all."

"But in this case, truth revealed one hell of a motive," Mike countered. "It was at *Pace* that Tom learned why Sam wanted to disgrace and discredit him; why he wanted everyone who cared to turn their backs. Because with Tom out of the way, Sam would be free to develop a very important relationship...with his own son."

"His son?" Mandria repeated dumbly, her mind not seeming to take in the implication. But hadn't she just said she knew her father—and didn't that make an illegitimate son entirely plausible? "One of Kathy's children!" she leapt swiftly from acceptance to a wrong conclusion. "And Tom could know that—damn him! They were lovers, after all."

"No, it's none of Kathy's children," Mike barely masked bemusement—which prompted a question. "Why is it women think a simple affair would privy a man to information of that nature—or that he'd even be interested in knowing it?"

"Captain..." came an objection from the other side of the room.

"Never mind, Allen," Mandria said with deepening curiosity. "All right, Mike, who is my father's son?"

"Who has Tom spent the better part of his life protecting? And more importantly, who was the man Tom feared would try to claim that son?"

Mandria's thoughts took flight like a stone skipping across the surface of water—and she felt each jarring bump of realization. Then came the final splash and down sank her already weighted spirits. "Oh my God," her fingers pressed temples which suddenly throbbed. "You think my father planned to acknowledge Allen?"

"I don't know that, but whatever he had in mind, Tom was a definite threat. Don't you see? At any time, he could have recognized Sam as his stepfather. Tom, alone, could tell Allen how their mother was treated and turn this newly found son against his real father. And Tom could have disgraced Sam too, by naming him a bigamist. ...So, with Nico as his accomplice, Sam simply rid himself of every one of those possibilities."

Mandria nodded in confusion. It did make sense and yet the thick walls of resistance she'd erected and maintained so diligently were not crumbling. ...Was it because she had learned too much too quickly? Even now, she didn't seem able to grasp one thought before another dawned. "—Allen?" her eyes widened. "This makes us half brother and sister!"

Allen returned to the table and took both of her hands in his. He'd been wrong to avoid his share in telling this story, for Mandria was, indeed, his sister and already loved dearly as such. "That is exactly what had Tom so worried;—why he wanted to speak with you and Mamalyn before allowing any of this used in his favor. ...Mandy, I am the same kin to Tom as I am to you. And if cornered, Tom fears Sam would have your marriage called incestuous—anything to shift public condemnation away from himself."

"And Sam would do it, too—in a damn flash!" Mike agreed.

"B...but it isn't true!" Mandria declared. "Tom and I are not related!"

"No, but think what the gossips could do with the story," Mike continued. "And Sam would have to keep it alive. Then, he would become the poor errant husband, blackmailed for an eighteen year old mistake in his youth. And Tom more the villain:—after Sam's money and his daughter with full knowledge of the crime he committed against nature. Seph would be watched closely too—for those *abnormalities* to appear?" Mike painted the worst possible picture, because Tom deserved his best effort. "The eyes set too close together; the slack, weak jaw; the slobbering lip—"

"Captain, that is disgusting!" Mandria expressed all the revulsion he could have hoped for. "Has my father actually threatened to do this terrible thing?"

"No, because we haven't yet been able to corner him. But Tom saw the possibility coming—and who would know better than he, what his step-father is capable of? Yet, as Allen said, he's refusing to use anything we learned if you or your mother would object. And to date, without this information, his case is not the best in the world."

"Unless we can find that missing puzzle piece," Allen turned questioning eyes to Mandria. "I believe it's your turn to share information, isn't it?"

"So if Father and Nico are linked in conspiracy, the past wouldn't have to be told," she said thoughtfully. "And Seph needn't suffer the slurs of unfeeling, ignorant people…"

"Possibly—but for God's sake, Mandy, more is at stake here than preventing gossip!" Mike's tone took on an edge. "Either Tom goes free or your father does—and which would you rather see walking the streets of Savannah? Uncle Pat feels Tom should present his strongest stand and damn it, so do I! Hell, your family has been subject to gossip for as long as I can remember—and all because of Sam. So why not give Tom everything it will take to bury the bastard once and for all?"

"He won't though. Not without permission from you and Mamalyn," Allen repeated, his gentler tone softening Mike's reprimand. "…But I can tell you one thing, sister-of-mine. Allen Scott will never call Sam Lucas *Father*. If Tom is convicted, I'm gone from here. Or if Tom is forced back into hiding because you don't want to face the gossips, this time, I go too. That much of Sam's victory I can take from him."

Mandria lowered her eyes, unsure of what she was feeling. She hadn't meant to sound uncaring, but Seph was her first concern. … The walls, it seemed, were still holding… "Well, here is what Mama discovered," she said noncommittally, and repeated the story of the visit to the perfumers. "And Nico picked up her order the very morning she registered at the Lloyd House," she finished. "When I was in…in that room," she struggled, "I smelled my perfume too. That means Nico was expecting Tom—had planned on his arrival, from her negligee down to the honeysuckle oil she knew he liked," she stated and both men missed that she was not saying Tom hadn't been a willing participant.

"Mike?" Allen asked hopefully. "Isn't this what we've been searching for?"

But the Captain was more cautious, perhaps because he, too, was still smarting from betrayal. "The bottle—Mandy, was the perfume bottle among her things?"

"I didn't look, Mike. I could hardly stay on my feet, much less go sorting through Nico's belongings," she said bitterly. "But I believe the bottle was broken—spilled in the fire, for whatever reason—because it wasn't until I did the same thing myself in Athens, that I recognized that charred, burnt fragrance as my own honeysuckle oil."

"Damn!" Mike swore. "Another blind alley. I don't know that an odor would be considered tangible evidence without the bottle. And any fledgling lawyer could argue that you were mistaken; that it is impossible to correctly identify a substance altered by fire."

"Yet, I did exactly that;—and did it twice," she pointed out. "And what about the date of purchase? It does coincide."

"Well, anyway, we'll pass this on to Uncle Pat and see what he makes of it," Mike shrugged.

"Yes, what we still need to tie all of this together, is a reputable witness who saw Nico and Sam together that day," Allen said.

"What about the men you captured in Augusta?' Mandria questioned. "You said they had signed statements."

"He also said *reputable* witnesses," Mike injected. "As Tom pointed out, their scruffy words against your father's well-tailored ones, wouldn't sway many jurors."

"Hell, I would just like to find a witness who *ever* saw Sam and Nico together," Allen sighed in frustration. "I mean, the plan was too good for a spur of the moment thing. As we suspected earlier, they had to meet and discuss it. And someone, somewhere in this city, had to see them!"

Mike didn't like what he had to say—had, in fact, tried to avoid even thinking about it. Yet, the possibility did exist and now was the time to face it. "...Maybe no one saw them because they weren't meeting in public," he uttered. "If Tom's theory is right, they may have been lovers too."

"Michael Herb—no!" Mandria turned from him. …Would it never stop? Was there no limit to the vile things her father could do? And if it was true, how could Tom be so insensitive as to even suggest such to Mike, knowing he still loved Nico?

"You're saying then," Allen phrased his words carefully, "there might have been a place where they met privately…for whatever reason."

"There was," Joleen said from the doorway. She hadn't meant to, but Mandria looked so unhappy. Her friend never laughed any more, or showed the least interest in the conversations they once enjoyed. Even while holding her son, her smiles never reached her eyes… Then Joleen burst into tears, realizing she had involved herself in a serious matter. "Oh, Miss Mandy, Ah done told—and Willie, he going be so mad with me, Ah bet-ya!"

"Joleen, no he won't," Mandria went to comfort her. "…Please, won't you tell us what you know?"

"Can't! No, Miss Mandy, can't do no harm to my husband! Can't tell what he seen!"

"Then go get him!" Mike insisted. "We'll ask Willie ourselves!" he shooed Joleen from the door.

They waited in tense silence, but when Willie came in from the coach-house, all began hurling questions at once, and in turn, Willie remained silent, staring blindly ahead—and not even Joleen's repeated elbow jabs were going to make him speak.

"Damn you, Willie Luther!" Allen swore. "Right here in this room, Tom offered you freedom—and gave both of you work and a home where your daughter will always know her parents. No, you won't be sold off. Thanks to Tom, your family is safe. So how can you stand there and refuse to help him?"

Willie Luther finally lowered his eyes. "…Ah wants to, Mister Allen. Ah'd lay down my life for Mister Tom—and that's the truth. But Hassie done vowed me to silence and she the onlyest one can unloose that."

"Then let's send for Hassie," Mandria nodded. "Willie, will you please go for her?"

"Better do it," Joleen urged, when he seemed reluctant to move. "Cause Ah done vowed me something too, Willie. Done told Miss Mandy Ah find me a way to repay her for getting us married—and this here could do it."

"Ah's going, woman—just got me something to say first," he replied before turning to the others. "Joleen, she mean good, but don't go pestering her 'til Hassie gets here. She say more than should be, could end up costing our lives. Hassie the best judge over things this important." And with that, he turned and left.

"…Well, you may as well have your supper while we wait," Mandria turned to place napkins and flatware before the reseated men. And following her lead, Joleen brought two filled plates and more coffee.

"Help yourselves from the pots if you want more," Mandria added, starting down a short hallway.

"But aren't you hungry?" Allen called after her.

"Course she is, but don't you men got no ears?" Joleen said as she also headed for the nursery. "Them babies been fussing for a while now and we be feeding them first."

"…I didn't hear anything. Did you?" Mike asked.

"Not a thing," Allen shrugged, digging into his food, which tasted better than usual. "Anyway, Captain, it's Hassie I want to hear."

"Oh-hell-yes!" Mike exclaimed, also finding Joleen's stew exceptionally flavorful.

It was wonderful what special seasoning could do for a meal—especially one as palatable and coveted as hope…

CHAPTER 21

"So what going on in this kitchen?" Hassie bustled in before Willie Luther.

"Just finishing up the dishes," Mandria hugged the old woman in greeting. "But there's food left if you want some."

"Done ate," Hassie answered. "Done heard the questions put to Willie too. Now what this about?"

"It's about bringing Tom home to stay," Mike replied. "But to do that, we need to know if Nico and Sam Lucas had a...well, if they might have had a private place to meet," he finished the best way he could.

"Please, Hassie?" added Allen. "What does Willie know that might help us?"

Ever the spokeswoman for her people—and an absolute dictator—Hassie took a seat at the table where she gauged each one of them with the eye of a hawk: Joleen and Willie awaited her permission to speak; Allen was eager to help his brother—as was the Captain, though he was hurting deep over Miss Nico yet. "...And you, Mandy-chile?" she questioned. "You come to Marsh Haven last week and bring that sweet baby boy for Hassie to see. But wasn't no talking to you then about Mister Tom. What make it different now?"

"Nothing is different, Hassie," Mandria's defenses clicked into gear. "My husband may still be guilty of an affair. But, I'm learning things about Father, too—and no matter how it goes with my marriage,

Sam Lucas has a lot to answer for. Then…maybe…I'll be able to sort through the rest and—and make a home for my son."

"Funny thing about homes," Hassie glanced over the room. "Not the walls outside what make it, but the loving and laughing; the sharing and crying inside, in good times and bad—"

"And my son will have it all," Mandria injected. "Now, please tell Mike and Allen what they need to know."

"And you don't?" Hassie persisted.

"All right, for heaven's sake—tell *us* what *we* need to know!" Mandria conceded.

Hassie's chin rose smugly. "Done mentioned this to Mister Tom, but so much happening the night he left Savannah, don't know as he remembered to relay it on. Anyways, Willie he drive some for Miss Nico, and one night, he take her to your boat, Captain Mike. She wait, getting madder and madder 'cause you wasn't there."

"Oh, hell," Mike groaned, remembering the night all too well.

"Yes, it's that meeting place we want to know about, damn it all," Allen said hoping to spare Mike all he could.

"Hush up that cussing—there's ladies present!" Hassie ordered. "Now Miss Nico, she leave the riverfront and have Willie drive her to a house on St. Julian Street—the Tabby House—and Ah ain't never knowed nothing nice goes on there. Then she have Willie wait whilst she go in and write her a little note. He takes it to young Mister Brown and brings him back to see her. And Willie wait some more—didn't drive her home 'til nigh-on to midnight."

Mike was forced to turn away, unable to contain another oath, though this one was, at least, garbled.

"…Hassie?" Willie Luther asked and received her consenting nod before continuing. "You gentlemans might want to see what Mister Bernie keeping in his wallet. Ah find him to the Brown's Sunday-house, out on the walk and too full of drink to get his key in the door. Even too drunk to read Miss Nico's note, but he smell it and laugh. Say he know what she wants and he got it. Then, Ah gets him in the carriage and he pulls out his wallet to fold that note into a pack of others. Say Miss Nico giving him a right sweet-smelling collection of them things."

Mike could not help himself—the words were out before he could stop them. "That God damned bastard!"

But Hassie saw his pain and her reprimand came with understanding. "Ain't no use in that, Captain Mike. You be lucky not to marry with that one—and we just hitting the tip of this nail—"

"I know;—I know that! Just tell us about Sam, will you?" Mike made a swift interruption, for more than anything—for Joleen and Willie's sake, as well as his own—he didn't want to hear the story of Nicole's treatment of this couple repeated.

"Yes, Hassie," Mandria nodded in puzzlement. "Where does my father fit into this?"

"Well, somebody got to tell Miss Nico about that place—and it one of Mister Sam's favorites," she replied. "Lot of years back, when Ah live to the town house, he buy him a brass-ankle girl to the slave market. Brought her home too, but Miss Evelyn, she see what he want with that uppity gal and she wasn't having it there; —not with you being just a little girl and all. So Mister Sam, he move his woman to the Tabby House. Take me along, to see she gets settled in nice and comfy. It ain't no usual cat-house neither. It high class; for folks what can afford the best. And that's where he keep his brass-ankle, 'til she get pregnant. Then he sell her off to some people heading out west."

Mandria's laugh was not gleeful. "Allen, do realize we could have brothers and sisters from one coast to the other?"

And Allen could only nod in agreement.

"…So?" Mike asked Hassie now.

"So nothing," she shrugged. "But Mister Sam, he keep women in that house, on and off, ever since. And just maybe, Miss Nico be one of them. Captain Mike, you knows now, she wasn't so innocent, but she was still too young to make these kind of arrangements all by herself."

"Well, it does sound like something Sam would do," Allen speculated. "I mean, Tom told me about the fancy place he had for meeting Kathy…" And seeing Mandria's down cast eyes, he paused.

"Hell, you know what I'm saying, don't you?" he said to everyone in general.

"Then, what about Brown?" Mike countered. "I can't see Sam Lucas happy about sharing a nest with him. Remember how he went after Tom when Kathy…" And he paused now, as Mandria's eyes suddenly lifted to meet his. "Well, you know what I mean, too," he also spoke to everyone.

"When Tom was sleeping with Kathy?" she finished it for all. "You people needn't avoid saying so. I've come to expect no better from the man I married."

"That was before Tom even met you—and you know it!" Mike argued.

"And he was single then, Mandy," Allen added. "So, are you really being fair?"

Hassie rapped the table sharply, silencing all three of them. "Listen, Ah knows this kind of stuff pull at the heart strings; twist them up crooked 'round the brain—and arguing betwixt yourselves be the outcome. But Ah don't see no need in straying from what brung me here. Now, we done put Miss Nico in the Tabby House and 'pears to me, that's where you going to find answers to all these questions you asking each other."

"…How, Hassie?" Mandria shrugged. "If the place is as exclusive as you said, no one could just go to the door and say, *Pardon me, but I'd like the room number where Nicole O'Rourke was seeing men.*"

Mike shot to his feet. "No, Mandy, but Brown could give us that information—damn his rotten soul!" And he stomped out the back door.

Hassie caught Allen's sleeve as he rose to follow. "That Captain Mike a man with a festering sore. But he got to keep his head on—and it up to you to see he does."

"I'll try, Hassie," he said hurrying away. "But damn I wish Tom was here. He could always handle that hot-headed Irishman!"

In the silence which followed, Mandria looked at those who remained, but her eyes returned to Hassie's quizzical expression. Unless she left too, and quickly, there was a lecture in store for her thoughtless statement to Mike. "Goodness, it's after six o'clock!" she stood, checking a lapel watch. "And I have a party to attend in less than two hours, so Hassie…?" she paused, "I'll talk with you later?" And giving the strangely quiet old woman, a final hug, she also departed.

Then there was only three left in the kitchen and as Hassie had yet to say anything more, Joleen did. "…Is you mad with me? Ah didn't mean no harm getting us all involved."

"No, girl, you done the right thing," Hassie nodded, but continued to sit there gazing at the tabletop.

"So…you wants me to drive you home now?" Willie asked.

"No, Ah going to stay the night—maybe longer," Hassie nodded again. "Working on me a little notion, but Ah needs to hear what they learned from young Mister Brown first." Then, she smiled. "'Sides, this give me a chance to play with them sweet little babies…"

Mandria wasn't sure how she'd get through the evening ahead. It was hard enough resisting the urge to throw the past in her father's face. But knowing Mike and Allen were out searching for Bernie Brown, she felt the least she could do, was keep Sam Lucas happily occupied for the evening. So, after refusing to attend this particular party every day of the last week, here she was, beside an unusually jovial sire, on a carriage ride into what promised to be a thoroughly miserable experience, held at the country estate of Oscar Shurling, one of Mandria's most ancient—and undesirable suitors. The man was an incorrigible lecher, who could never keep his eyes—or hands—where they belonged. And still, her father had always wanted them to marry.

"Think of it this way, missy," Sam was saying just then, "you've been wed and bedded—even given birth—and to some that would make you damaged goods. But not to Oscar—who is nearing seventy, after all. Your reward, when he dies, would be a vast fortune, and with wise management, I could make you an even richer young widow."

Again, Mandria resisted an urge. She wanted to ask who he planned to have her marry then—for if scheduled *wisely*, she could go through a whole string of wealthy old men. Instead, she forced a smile, saying it was certainly something to consider, and pretended thoughtfulness as they rolled through the property gates.

Mecca Dawns read the gaudy, gold painted letters—and Mandria cringed. *Revulsion Dawns* would better describe her life on these grounds had she been foolish enough to ever think of marriage to Oscar. She could credit herself with some intelligence and that was before she'd learned what loving a man should make a woman feel. ... *What Tom made me feel, damn his soul!* she shouted inwardly, banishing thoughts of him away.

Comparisons were inevitable on this night, however, for there was Oscar, ready to greet them and immediately attaching himself to her arm with the tenacity—and the stickiness—of a leech. Making it worse, he smelled as old and unwashed as he always had. ...And Mandria found herself remembering days when Tom had come in from hunting or repairing the cabin. He had been sweaty too, but it was the scent of warmed skin which he never allowed to ripen, layer upon grimy layer, as Oscar did. Then she was remembering the fresh, crisp scent of a shaving talc and unable to handle the memories that evoked, she fended them off with a deep, determined breath. But her reward was a stronger whiff of Oscar, even amid a room full of powdered and perfumed guests.

Thankfully, the night was only mildly warm and as the tall windows and doors stood open, Mandria was able to stem her feeling of near suffocation. She merely kept them moving, stopping to chat, very pointedly, with those who stood near an open portal. Still, her displeasure with the man so adamantly stuck to her side, lent heightened color to her cheeks, which he, of course, mistook for a blush. Encouraged by this, Oscar repeatedly asked if she'd care to view his gardens and wild animal collection, while she refused with as many excuses. It was bad enough having the smelly old ogre hang onto and ogle her so possessively, but to go alone with him into the shadowy night? Unthinkable!

Then Sam joined them, intent on discussing some business matter with Oscar, and Mandria quickly joined a group of ladies on their way to freshen up—needing, more than anything, a few peaceful minutes away from her torturous performance. But when she returned, her father waited at the bottom of the stairs.

"Come, my dear," he took her arm now. "You must see something truly rare in this part of the country." And in very few steps, they were through a set of French doors and out on a rear veranda.

"...Father?" she questioned nervously, not having seen Oscar inside. "Please, I'd rather not be out here."

"Oh, but you must see Shurling's latest acquisition," he proceeded at a crisp pace. "A Mountain Lion—or Puma, as some call it." And when Mandria nearly stumbled, he jerked her onward, down steps, along sloping paths, ever deeper into the rear of the gardens where only sparsely spaced torches lit the way.

...*Why a Puma?* she wondered, now following blindly. ...*Why the very animal I likened to Tom?* And her vision of him in those tawny, well-fitting skins grew so vivid, her knees almost folded again.

"There," Sam stopped before one of the cages in a long row. "You must admit Oscar made a fine choice in this one. Look at his sleek muscle tone; watch how they move as he prowls on those silent feet." And Mandria was looking—recalling times she would turn to find Tom gone on his silent feet; or turn again, to find him there before having seen or heard his return. Oh yes, she was watching the beautiful creature, but she wasn't enjoying the eerie feelings it caused one little bit...

Oscar broke the spell. "So here you are!" he cackled his way toward them. And the Puma paced more furiously at the grating sound of his voice. "Changed your mind, my lovely Mandy? Then you must allow me to show you my birds too. I've just acquired several peacocks you will admire—especially the male, who enjoys strutting about with his favorite lady too.—And did you know they make excellent watchdogs?"

"N—no; no I didn't" she took an involuntary step back from his nearness.

"You are ever the elusive one, aren't you?" he cackled again. And the Puma issued a low, warning growl. "But never mind. If the years have taught me anything, it's that persistence rewards itself. Now, shall we have a look at my fine peacocks?" he grasped her arm with strength that surprised her. "Come, they're just down here—away from the more vicious breeds."

Once more, Mandria was to be towed, and with each resisting step, she grew more leery—as did the Puma, who was now snarling loudly. She glanced over her shoulder, even ready to ask her father's assistance, but was shocked to see him walking in the other direction. It became clear to her then, that she had just been delivered to Oscar Shurling; that her father cared little about the situation she was certain to face;—and Mandria was furious!

"Stop!—You must stop!" Anger brought her to a balking halt. "I—I'm allergic to feathers of any sort," she lied without guilt. "And when the sneezing begins, I'll be no good to anyone for weeks.— Which means I could not accept any of your very kind invitations."

"So sorry, my pet. I didn't know of your ailment," Oscar panted, the exertion of trying to drag her telling on him. "Here, do sit beside me, while I catch my breath," he led her to a bench facing the Puma cage, where she was forced to sit when he did, because he'd yet to release her arm. "I must say I'm disappointed, though," he slid his grasp to her hand. "I had a special place erected for viewing the birds—very private, you see, so as not to disturb the tom while he performs for his ladies."

"The ...*tom*," Mandria uttered at the irony. It mattered little that he spoke of peacocks and not turkeys...but the *tom*, of all names in this world?

"The male—yes," Oscar nodded, regretting the coincidental use of her husband's name. But that was over, wasn't it? Yes, and now her father said she was looking for better. Then a smile touched his lips, for he'd just thought of the cleverest way of presenting it. "Indeed, my peacock is an extraordinary specimen—but spoiled, I'm afraid. He rather enjoys attention and pampering from all his hens."

"Really," Mandria commented, sending the quieted, but still pacing mountain cat a look of accusation.

"Oh, my yes!" Oscar laughed raucously, which drew an irritated hiss from the Puma.

"You really should see what a fine, big fellow he is. Able to get it up and hold it—much to the pleasure of his chosen mate."

"…I see," Mandria hesitated, paying closer attention now. If Oscar was describing the bird's fan of tail feathers, he'd certainly phrased it oddly. But her suspicions came too late.

"Well, of course, you see!" he began to pull her hand further up his lap. "You're no innocent—you know what I'm offering, don't you, sweetie?"

Mandria did manage to gain her feet, and yet her hand was steadily drawn toward his crotch, where he held it pressed against his swelling penis. "Sir, I am still married!" she fumed, knowing her bent posture was also affording him an excellent view down the low neckline of her dress. "You will release me this instant!" she demanded.

In answer, he only laughed, sliding his free hand into her dress to fondle her breast. And the Puma snarled menacingly, rattling his cage with violent swat of powerful, bared claws.

"Oh, you stupid, filthy, old—" But Mandria didn't get to finish her tirade. Instead, she was falling backwards; thrown off balance when his grasp suddenly went slack. It took a few moments to untangle herself from a shower of her own skirts and petticoats, but she came up fighting mad. "Oscar Shurling, if you ever touch me again—" And there her second tirade ended. "Mister Shurling?" she asked, eyeing his strange, limp posture. "…Sir?" she stooped for a closer look, certain now, that he was unconscious—or maybe, dead? "Oh, dear God!" she straightened, holding clinched fists against her mouth. … Could the fool have suffered a heart attack? …And what if he wasn't dead;—shouldn't she be doing something? "Oh damn! I'll have to go for help—but you don't deserve any, you foul smelling old buzzard!" And with that, she turned and fled.

What followed was a great deal of excitement. The male guests, armed with lanterns and blankets, rushed down through the gardens on a rescue mission, while the ladies hovered about offering Mandria comfort. "Eat this," or "drink that" they advised, pushing an assortment her way. "But do be brave and try not to faint."

Mandria did accept some water, because her sprint to the house left her thirsty—but faint? She had never fainted in her life. …Well, except when Tom made her pregnant.

Then the men were returning, carrying Oscar in the folds of a blanket. And over the hub-bub of getting him upstairs and sending for a doctor, Mandria heard that he was alive, if still unconscious.

"Talk about freak accidents," nodded Mr. Watson as he and Sam approached. "A tree limb, of all things;—a damn tree limb!"

"Father—what happened?" Mandria raised questioning eyes.

"We found a tree limb, my dear, lying on the ground behind the bench where Oscar sat," he answered.

"Big around as my arm—even saw where it broke from the tree," added Mr. Watson. "Just fell and hit Oscar over the head. Knocked him cold, it did."

"And weren't you fortunate?" Sam looked at her curiously, his words sounding more of an accusation. "Had you been sitting beside him, you might have been injured as well."

"Yes…well, I wasn't sitting," she nodded in confusion and resentment of her father's tone. "I mean, we were…talking there, but I got up from the bench, and the Puma was making a lot of noise,—but you'd think I'd hear a tree limb as big as that when it fell."

"Truly a freak accident," Mr. Watson repeated. "Just one of those damned odd things that happen."

As soon as the doctor gave his assurance that Oscar would recover, the guests began to leave—and Mandria was more than ready. But she wasn't even seated in the carriage when Sam made a suggestion. "You know, daughter, you could stay the night and look after poor Oscar," he held the door open as if she might leap at the offer. "You almost owe it to him—and I'm certain the gesture would be much appreciated."

Appalled, Mandria sat with a determined plop. She had about reached her limit with Sam Lucas. "Well, *I* would *appreciate* going home to my *own* bed, thank you!" she snapped. "And another thing,

Father: when and if *I decide* to sleep elsewhere—or with another man—*I'll* make the damned choice!"

"Mandy!" Sam hurried into the carriage, signaling the driver to go. "Kindly lower your voice," he glanced about to see if she'd been overheard by other departing friends. "I know the accident must have upset you, but there is no reason for this behavior."

"Isn't there?" she asked, building a fine fit of temper. "Maybe this accident wouldn't have happened if you hadn't abandoned us out there!"

"So…is that an expression of concern for Oscar? If it is, he'll be pleased."

"No!" she exclaimed. …*Why wasn't he hearing her?* "I am not concerned for him in the least," she retorted distastefully. "I'm glad he is alive, but you had no right to subject me to a mauling by that filthy, unwashed old man!"

"Come now, a mauling?" he laughed. "Oscar has always wanted you for his bride. And not three hours ago—right where you're sitting—you said it was something you'd consider. I am certain Oscar was just overwhelmed and only wanted to show you how deeply his feelings run."

Mandria knew then, her father had told Oscar she'd shown signs of weakening and that between them, they'd decided the time was right *for persistence to reward itself.*

"Listen closely to me, Father," Mandria said calmly and wondered how. But she did know why. Sam Lucas had to be pacified or off he would go on his nightly prowl of the city, and she didn't want him happening upon Mike and Allen if they were still questioning Bernie. "Now I will consider any serious offers of marriage. But not to Oscar Shurling—*never!* And one thing more: if you ever—*ever*—put me through another ordeal like that, I will leave Savannah and never return."

"And go where?—Perhaps to claim your son?" he shifted the subject to one of his liking. "You know, Mandy, that is why Scott held you. He wanted the child and it wouldn't surprise me if he comes looking for it. Yes, you should have kept that little draw-card. We'd have Scott then. Back in jail—or hung—and you would be free of him all the sooner."

"That is a closed subject," Mandria stubbornly folded her arms and looked away. "As I said before, I put all the distance I could between his child and myself—and I'll have it no other way."

"Well…we'll see," he nodded sagely. "But don't close doors too tightly on the past, missy—not when you may have left something of value there," he said, thinking of his long separation from Allen.

"Meaning what?" Mandria fought off a prickling sense of uneasiness.

"Oh, lessons learned; decisions wrongfully made under emotional stress;—that sort of thing," he shrugged. "Some you may even come to regret, such as giving away the baby—"

"Father, this is getting tiresome!—And far too philosophical for me," she interrupted. "I like facts. And it is a fact that you arranged my time alone with Oscar Shurling. It is also a fact that you'd better *not* do it again, so perhaps you should reflect on your own mistakes— No!" she lifted a cautioning finger when he started to speak. "Don't say anything more. We'll just drop this matter and leave it at that."

Sam leaned his head to the back of the seat and sighed. There went a profitable deal down the drain. Oscar had wanted Mandria, and their marriage would have brought Sam half interest in a stretch of land along the river that was being heavily sought by the promised railroad. But that was not to be now. …*Unless Oscar would settle for another kind of woman. There was something to think about…* And Sam had time to ponder many things on the ride back to town, because Mandria didn't utter another word all the way…

So now, here she was, ready for bed, yet still sitting at her dressing table, wishing she did have someone to argue with—even Tom. At least she could have yelled at him and rid herself of this pent anger over the events of the evening. Instead, she lifted her hair brush, spending some of it in the lengths of her tresses. But soon her scalp began to hurt and realizing her strokes had become nearly maniacal, she forced herself to stop. "…So your father set you up," she spoke to her mirrored reflection. "So Oscar behaved like a jack-ass. Is that reason enough for yanking out your hair? …I mean, nothing that matters has changed. Your son and your future are still yours. And no one was really hurt—except Oscar," a small smile touched her lips as she recalled his timely and well-deserved thump on the head. Then the smile faded. …*Tom claimed Sam had set him up too. And if Nico had cooperated as readily as Oscar…*

Well, just suppose the situation had happened in reverse. What if Tom had found her with a hand pressed to Oscar's crotch, while he rummaged about in her dress? How innocent would she have looked of wrongdoing? Of course, she did try to get away…but if Tom was drugged, as everyone insisted, he couldn't have. "…So it is possible," she uttered, not understanding the rush of color to her cheeks. "It could be possible…" But she couldn't finish it. Too many thoughts were descending on her now; too many claims and counter-claims—all of which she'd have to re-evaluate, and the task seemed so impossibly overwhelming, she ended up just sitting there idly toying with the things on top of the dressing table. …Until her fingers closed on a glass perfume stopper.

"Now, what is this doing here?" she quickly replaced it on the bottle. She had purchased more of the Honeysuckle because she needed an excuse to go by the perfumers and check out the story her mother had related. But she hadn't used any because it reminded her of… "Well, who could have left this bottle unstopped?" she asked, chasing unsettled matters away. All women knew how rapidly perfume evaporated so that ruled out the maids. No, this is something a man…"

"Father?" she guessed with narrowed eyes. *Snooping about for clues to Seph's whereabouts?—Or a burglar?* her eyes widened again, as she made a quick search of her jewelry case, only to find nothing missing. "… Well," she puzzled, "first a limb falls to earth without making a sound, and now a stopper that leaps from a bottle all by itself…"

Mandria was still trying to unravel these mysteries when she finally crawled into bed. It was enough to keep her mind occupied as she drifted toward sleep. But the next morning, she awoke tired. Who wouldn't be, after dreaming of a stalking Puma all night long…?

CHAPTER 22

It was nearly one in the morning when Allen came home. And Hassie was not the only one waiting up for him in the parlor.

"Tom?" he stared. "Damn, but I'm glad to see you!" he added a bear-hug. "But is it safe for you here yet?—And listen, has Hassie told you what's happening now?"

"As long as I stay out of sight, its safe enough, I guess. And yes, Hassie filled me in, little brother," he settled to finish a plate of supper. "I've seen my son, too—at long last," he said with less joy than Allen would have expected. "So, what did you and Mike learn from Bernie Brown?"

"Well, we found him down on River Street and early as that was he'd already been drinking. He didn't want to talk about Nico at first, and I thought maybe he was scared of something or someone. But Mike kept feeding him whiskey and after listening for a while, I believe Bernie was as much in love with Nico as Mike, because it really hurt him to talk about her.—And I mean to the point of tears."

"I know the feeling," Tom nodded. "But did you learn anything more?"

"The most important thing was that Nico did have a suite at the Tabby House. Bernie said he knew because he'd given her money for part of the rental. ...He said more—things I don't know how Mike managed to sit there and hear, but he did it."

Hassie patted his arm. "Then you done good at keeping his head on straight," she gave her approval.

"Anyway," Allen continued, "I told Bernie I might be interested in keeping a woman there too, but wouldn't want my boss-man to know I could afford it. I asked if that was a danger;—if he'd ever seen Sam Lucas hanging around the place. He said he hadn't, but did know Sam owned the building because Nico had told him so."

"And?" Tom urged.

"And that's when Bernie got emotional and started crying. He was loud with it, too, and Mike cold-cocked him—which surprised the hell out of me, because I didn't see the blow coming anymore than Brown. Then, we put him in a cabbie and told the driver to take him to his mother out at Hollow Oak."

"And?" Tom repeated, knowing the Irishman would be doing something more with what they'd learned.

"And early tomorrow, we're going to the Tabby House ourselves, and one way or another, we're going to have a look at Suite D," Allen finished.

"But you will return and tell me before doing anything more," Tom said in that same listless tone. "I want Patrick Herb to see the place too, and then you're to bring him by to talk with me."

"He is still taking pressure for time spent on your case, Tom," Allen replied, "but Mike says he can do as he likes when he's off-duty, so we'll get him there." And when Tom only nodded, Allen had to ask, "...Brer, what's bothering you? You might as well tell me, because I know something is wrong."

"The only thing that isn't wrong is sleeping downstairs in the nursery with Joleen and Willie's baby," he answered as he rose. Then looking from Allen's concerned expression to Hassie's, he expelled a breath. "Listen, I'm just really...tired now. Maybe tomorrow I can make more sense of things." And without another word, he went up the stairway.

Allen turned to Hassie. "Did something happen before I came home?—Or do you know why his mood is so...so somber?"

"No, he come like that—in the back way about midnight, all dog-tired on the outside and angerful inside. Say he got one question: do Ah know where his baby is? So Ah go fetch the boy and he look him over real good—top to bottom. That onlyest time Ah see him smile too. But must have calmed him, 'cause after Ah puts the baby back in bed, he full of questions. So, Ah tell him what went round the kitchen table today. He surprised my Mandy-chile' stay to listen—ask if we have to tie her down," Hassie nodded. "…But he still plenty upset, and likely it about her, 'cause he did some grumbling 'bout her flitting over-town."

"Well that's just great," Allen commented. "His first night home and he has to hear some big mouth gossip.—And I'll wager he *didn't* hear, that most of the time, I've been with her."

"Never you mind, Mister Allen. Hassie's going to remedy some of this real soon now;—and maybe some other things too," she stood, signaling their conversation was ending. "So what time you meeting Captain Mike to the Tabby House?"

"Nine o'clock. …Why?" Allen also rose.

"Then you'll need breakfast about eight," she answered, without really answering the question asked. "Good night to you, Mister Allen," she finished, taking Tom's empty plate toward the kitchen stairs.

"Good night, Hassie," he replied, feeling something like a child who'd been sent to bed. So he went…

But Hassie was up with the sun the following morning—and not by choice, so was Willie Luther. "Come on, boy," she whispered, prodding him down the back steps, "got us a little scavenging to do." And they left by the back gate…

Allen had the breakfast he was promised, and just after he left the house, Hassie sent Willie up to Tom with coffee and bath-water, while Joleen fed Seph. When Willie had also deposited the spare cradle at the foot of the bed, cleared away the tub and returned to the kitchen,

Seph was asleep. Next, carrying Seph with her, Joleen was sent on a mission that included fibbing.

"Mister Tom?" she said entering the bedroom. He wore only his trousers as he sat on the edge of the bed, sipping coffee and ruffling his damp hair with a towel. "Excuse me, sir, but you got to mind this baby for a spell."

"...All right," he nodded, setting his cup aside. "What's going on?" he asked as she placed the boy in his arms, at which point she hushed him. "Has something happened?" he said more softly.

"Fixing to," she smiled. "He still asleep, but my baby raising the roof downstairs. Has to separate them, or they both be hollering before long."

"Oh," Tom nodded again. And seeing his son for the first time in daylight, he smiled too. "...Joleen, I forgot to ask Hassie, but did Mandria ever give him a name?"

"She calls him Seph," Joleen shrugged. "Don't know what that short for—'cept Ah don't think it Seph-a-lis, 'cause that ain't no nice name."

"Syph—no; no, that's not so nice," he chuckled. "No, Seph is short for Joseph...my father's first name and Allen's middle one," he said, wondering at the stroke of luck that caused Mandria to choose a name from his family.

"Yes, sir.—Know what Tandy short for?" she beamed him a wider smile. "It a mash together of Tom and Mandy!"

"Well, that's quite an honor, Joleen," he said, truly touched, "...Did my wife like your choice?" He couldn't imagine Mandria approving any linkage to him and hoped she hadn't given Joleen and Willie her usual grief about that.

"Sure did!" she said, surprising him. "Anyway, Ah appreciate it, if you keep Seph 'til Ah gets my baby quiet," she said moving away. "And welcome home, Mister Tom."

"...Thanks, Joleen," Tom said to a closed door. And after a moment of indecision, he placed the sleeping child on the bed and laid down beside him. He traced a finger across the boy's open palm and tinier fingers closed about his large one. "Well, how do you do,

Seph?" he grinned, making an introduction of it by gently wagging his extended appendage. "—And you're plenty strong too, aren't you?" he said, approving his son's grip. But his pleasure in finally finding this baby—even in lying there quietly watching him sleep—was lessened by thoughts of Mandria. That one had a hell of lot to explain…

⸻◈⸻

"Captain, I'm not sure this is going to work!" Allen kept pace, but moved with far less enthusiasm.

"It worked for Tom and me in Augusta and it will work now," Mike insisted. "Hell, I'll do the talking—you just play along. But come on, will you? It's important that we get into Nico's suite."

"I realize that, damn it, but I don't know how to act like a—a damn pansy!"

Mike came to a halt on the sidewalk in front of The Tabby House and faced him. "Allen, why else would two men want private accommodations? And what woman could we ask to act our whore? Oh, I know some good ones—real drawer-droppers—but none with the class to live in this place."

"…So, what about Sam's brass-ankle? Why was she accepted?" Allen stalled the inevitable.

"Damn it, little brother, stop asking useless questions and let's get on with this!" he stepped up and rang the bell. "And by the way, while we're here, you are Dexter and I'm Harry," he grinned at Allen's beleaguered expression.

Granny answered the door and smiled sweetly. "May I help you?" she gracefully adjusted her gold rimmed glasses.

"Uh …yes, ma'am, I think you can," Mike replied, seeing that Allen was equally taken aback by her genteel appearance. "—If you are Granny Geeter, that is?" he added, wanting to be sure.

"I am," she smiled on. "And may I ask who sent you?"

"Bernard Brown," Mike answered. "He told us you are most selective and that we might find just the place, here, we're seeking."

"We?" Granny glanced from one to the other. And Allen lowered his eyes, unable to meet hers.

Not so with Mike. "We—he and I," he charged boldly ahead. "So you see the need for discretion?"

"I do if you have the money to pay for it," she continued unruffled while Allen turned a deep crimson. "And I certainly am selective. My clients—of all persuasions—are both well-heeled and well-bred. I do not allow riff-raff to wander these premises."

"If you did, we would not be here," Mike retorted with equal haughtiness. "We will meet your price and certainly your standards. Now, may we see your rooms?"

Impressed, Granny allowed them entrance. "His first encounter?" she nodded toward Allen, who walked a pace behind, fidgeting with his hat brim.

"Almost," Mike grinned. "He's not a virgin, but close enough to be pleasing—with enough innocence left for blushing, as you can see." And they both laughed when Allen flushed again.

"Yes, well, we all have to start somewhere, dear," Granny patted Allen's arm as they went into her office, where she offered them chairs and sat at her desk. "There is paper-work to do, but first, let's see which suites are available," she ran a finger slowly down a ledger page.

"Forgive me, Granny, but not just any suite will do," Mike nodded. "You see, Dexter is an avid Numerologist and has proven himself right so many times I've come to trust his guidance in all things. Anyway, he insists that we have suite number 4—or any combination of numbers equaling four. Is that possible?"

"I'm afraid not, sir," she nodded too. "My rooms are lettered and not numbered."

Mike made a grand sigh. "Well, Dex, what to do now? I so wanted to please you, but you heard what Granny said."

Allen had no earthly notion what he was supposed to say—much less where Mike was headed with this load of garbage. "...Well, I—that is, what about suite D? It—I mean, D is the 4th letter...?" And when Mike cackled out a laugh, and squeezed his thigh, Allen wished he hadn't figured that out.

"Granny?" Mike turned back to her—and much to Allen's chagrin, kept that hand on his thigh. "What about it?—Is suite D available?"

"My heavens!" Granny said in amazement. "There might be something to your Numerology. The lady who had this suite paid me several months in advance; right to the last day of April—which was yesterday!"

"Now, Dexter, don't get your hopes up," Mike rose and stood casually at Granny's side. "I mean, what if the lady wants to renew her lease?"

"No, her sponsor told me some time ago that she wasn't going to. But she did pay me and fair being fair, I held her rooms anyway," Granny advised them. "Besides, had *that* young woman returned to find her things disturbed, she would have caused trouble."

"Now what sort of person would ever give you trouble?" Mike hugged her shoulder, thereby, positioning himself for a closer look at the ledger. Then, he emoted a gasp. "By damn, look at this!" he held a restraining hand on the page while motioning Allen to come with the other. And ignoring Granny's startled expression, he plunged head-first into his act. "Dex, count the letters—just count them! And wasn't the set you gave me this morning: 4,7,5,4? Well, there it is plain as can be: Suite D—or 4; 7 letters in Deborah; 5 in *Scott*; and her lease was up in April—which is the 4th damn month!"

Allen was so amused with that bit of non-sense, he burst into laughter; then so did Mike, which left Granny looking from one to the other doubting her sanity for allowing the pair into her establishment.

"Didn't I tell you Dexter was uncanny?" Mike tried mightily for composure. "Granny, I swear to you, since we met, my luck has been phenomenal—on the job, at the gaming tables—just everywhere! And if he likes suite D—resides under *this* roof—your luck will change for the better too!"

Allen was still chuckling as he, too, studied the ledger over the old woman's head. "And Harry, look at the letters in the reference column beside Miss Scott's name: S.L.—now what does that tell you?"

Mike immediately began counting his fingers as if calculating a magical sum. Then, smiling broadly, he drew Granny to her feet before she had any notion of rising, and hugging her close, spun joyously about the floor. "Oh-hell-yes!" he chortled. "It's time for the final test, Granny! So would you please show Dexter to suite D?"

"...But my paperwork," she steadied herself in confusion. And it grew when Mike returned to his chair and sat.

"The test first," he insisted. "Dexter must be completely at ease here or his readings will become garbled—and heaven forbid *that* ever happening!"

"...You're not coming with us?" Allen now shared Granny's confusion.

"In a moment, dear thing," Mike replied. "I wouldn't want my presence to sway your decision. ...Because of our closeness?" he gave Allen a lusty, roving gaze, which brought on yet another blush as he turned and ushered Granny from the door. Mike then took out a pin knife and made some damaging adjustments to the desk locks, just in case he might need to pay Granny's office an uninvited visit...

In suite D, Granny watched as Allen circled the room repeatedly, his fingers pressed to his temples. "Well?" she finally asked. "What say you, sir?"

"I say...the woman who lived here was very beautiful," he stalled, hoping for one of the loony inspirations that came so easily to Mike. "...And Deborah Scott was not her real name," he continued, seeing he had caught the woman's interest. Then, quickly counting the letters in Nicole's first and last names, he said to his own amazement, "She was a 13, Granny.—And 1 plus 3 equals 4! Isn't that exciting?" he exclaimed, allowing the wonder of it to whisk him behind the curtain concealing the bedroom alcove. There, he swung open the wardrobe doors to find an array of expensive negligees and a dress he hoped Mike might recognize. Then, he moved to the dressing table...

Mike sauntered in and found Granny still nodding her head. "Here you are," he smiled, glancing casually about. "Seems cozy enough to me," he gave her a wink. "But does Dex like it?"

"Dex requests you presence;—now, Harry!" the command came from behind a blue wall of curtains.

"Uh…Granny, excuse me for a moment," Mike said politely. "He can be so damned temperamental!" he added confidentially.

"I'm sure," she sat primly erect on a chair, knowing that she too must humor the strange young man.

As soon as Mike entered the alcove, Allen handed him a perfume bottle containing Nicole's heady, rose essence. Then, he pointed the Captain to the wardrobe, and Mike clutched the skirt of a dress he knew well.

"What now?" Allen whispered.

"Now we take the damn suite, and get Uncle Pat over here for a look-see," Mike whispered back.

"But what if she wants to clear this stuff out? Selling off the goods of former tenants is a common practice."

"Not if we buy them first," Mike grinned, liberally dousing Allen with Nicoles perfume. "Just bring one of those negligees. I'll handle the rest." Then, whipping the curtain aside with dramatic flare, he returned to Granny wearing his best Irish smile. "Good news! Good, good news! Dexter loves it here—and especially wants to keep that lovely collection of negligees, so how much for the lot, Granny? And I'm afraid he has already been into her perfume, so we'll keep that too."

Granny opened her mouth in new surprise. "…*He* wants them?" she watched as Allen caressed the sheerness of the gown he held. "He is a Numerologist, a Homosexual—*and* a Transvestite?"

Mike had never seen a man blush so repeatedly in his life and could not help laughing hardily as he pulled out his wallet. "Oh-hell-yes! This one has many, many talents, Granny. So why don't I just buy everything the lady left here? Dex is worth every cent of whatever you want to charge."

"…Well, $50.00, I suppose," Granny accepted the amount, but was still gazing at Allen in amazement. "Then, we must take care of the paperwork and get each of you a key."

"That we can," he offered her an arm, then turned them both toward Allen. He just had to see that blush one more time. "But lambkins, if you wish, stay here and try on your new nightie. …Just for me?" he added with enough meaning to bring it forth in blazing clarity. And on reaching the door, the Captain paused yet again. "Granny, would you believe Dexter is hairless, with skin as soft and smooth as a babe?"

And looking at the young man with the flaming face over the rim of her glasses, Granny said, "Sir, after today, I would believe anything."

Alone now, and vowing Mike would pay for this miserable experience, it took several moments before Allen could motivate himself and begin a more in-depth search. But he found nothing that belonged to Sam Lucas. "Damn," he uttered, hoping Patrick Herb might see something he'd missed...

On the street once more, Allen came to realize how hard the morning had truly been on Mike. "...Listen, little brother," he began, "I know I should go by and see Tom, but just tell him what we discovered and that I'll come later on, will you?" he looked away. "I'm going to visit Nico now. ...Somehow, I just need to see her today."

"All right then," Allen nodded. "But, Harry—dear—you did get our room keys, didn't you?" he batted his eyes, trying to lighten the Captain's mood.

"Oh-hell-yes—lamb-chop," Mike presented one to him. And as he headed off down the street, he did chuckle a bit.

But Mike hadn't been entirely honest about his plans. He was going to visit Nicole, but then, by God, he intended to visit suite D for a thorough search of his own...

CHAPTER 23

W hat a Busy Saturday morning it was all around...
"Good morning, Joleen," Mandria said as she breezed into the
kitchen. "...Well, good morning to you too, Hassie," she added,
surprised to find her still there. "So what news is there? Did Allen and
Mike learn anything from Bernie Brown last night?"

Hassie continued to cuddle and rock Tandy. "Learned Miss Nico
did have rooms to the Tabby House and they gone now, to check that
out.—But its nine thirty, girl, and you should be worrying 'bout your
baby. That little boy going to need feeding again real soon now."

"Don't I know it," Mandria started for the nursery. "Hassie, I'm
full as a tick!"

"Might as well come back. Baby's not in there," Hassie called.

"Oh?" Mandria returned, noting that the spare cradle was also
missing from its usual place by the hearth. "So, where is he?"

"Had to put him upstairs—so Tandy's hollering wouldn't wake
him," Joleen retold her fib.

"Alone?" Mandria asked, unable to believe they'd do such. "He
could be crying now and you'd never hear it down here!"

"Been checking on him," Hassie shrugged. "But you making a
real good point there, Mandy-chile'. That baby boy needs his mama
here—and you sure can't hear him cry living way over there to your
Daddy's house. That just ain't natural."

"Well, this is no way to make a point!" Mandria spun and hurried up the kitchen stairway. And, a nod from Hassie sent Joleen up too.

Mandria went straight to the study, as it was the closest room to the stairs and surely that was where they'd put Seph. But not finding him, she rounded on Joleen. "Where is my baby?" she demanded.

"In your bedroom," the girl answered. "'Cause it's quieter?" she finished, not at all comfortable with lying when Mandria looked so upset. But Hassie did know what was best...didn't she?

"Upstairs;—another floor away?" Mandria's hands flew to her hips. "Joleen, how could you?" And not waiting for a reply, she raced up the front hall. She couldn't remember being more frightened and furious at the exact same time. And yet, she took the stairs in silence, listening closely for Seph's poor helpless cries from the emptiness above. And Joleen followed as instructed.

Mandria reached the bedroom and froze.—They had even closed the door! Now she wished Seph would cry, for every awful thing she'd ever heard about babies, smothering in their blankets, passed through her mind. "It's a dream—it's must be a bad dream," she murmured, forcing herself to turn the knob.

Immediately, her eyes fastened on the cradle sitting at the foot of the bed. It was so still—too still—and again, she forced herself forward, willing the cradle to move. ...And now, she knew it was a dream—the same horrid dream she had the night Seph was born—for the cradle was empty, yet she could hear her baby. He wasn't crying, as he had then, but she knew every sound Seph made and this one meant he was beginning to get hungry and needed his mother.

"Seph?" she whispered, lifting teary eyes from the cradle, only to refasten them on the bed. And so great was her shock, she had to grasp the footboard to remain erect. For there was her son, noisily sucking his little fist, and beside him, lay his sleeping father.

Mandria's first impulse was to take Seph and leave; to find Hassie and deliver a lecture of her own! ...But she had never won an argument with the woman in her life, and realizing how cleverly all this had been arranged, her eyes went to the door—which, of course, was closed again. ...*She wouldn't!* Mandria thought, hurrying to try the knob. It was locked, just as she suspected it would be, and from the outside. …*Oh, dear Lord, what to do now?* she looked heavenward. When no answer came, Mandria sighed, and moved quietly to a chair before the hearth, where she sat looking at the matched pair of sleeping males on the bed.

The sheet lay draped across Tom's waist, its whiteness contrasting sharply against the darker skin of his shirtless, muscular arms and chest. Then, the baby stirred, and even in slumber, up came a large hand to draw him closer. And Mandria found herself struggling with a new set of emotions. For though she wasn't yet aware of it, the re-evaluation she had postponed the previous night had begun…

She remembered wondering once, if Tom could be violent with Nicole and ever gentle with her; if, in his own warped way, he did love her…and now the baby too, because there had been only gentleness in the protective gesture she'd just seen.

But what was she thinking? She no longer believed Tom had beaten Nicole. It was only their affair she was unsure about—and she sent his handsome form and features a look which said he'd yet to explain *his* presence at the Lloyd House to *her* satisfaction! …Or had he, and because she remained mired so deeply in the gore she'd been shown that night, she could not—or would not—hear him?

All along, Tom had insisted her father set him up.—And didn't the fiasco at Mecca Dawns prove Sam Lucas could create any situation he wished—even to placing his only daughter in the free hands of a man like Oscar Shurling? It did, indeed.

All right, so with that and what she'd learned yesterday from Mike and Allen, her father's motives and actions were perfectly clear. And yet, a tightness in her chest said the walls about her heart were still intact. …Had resistance become a habit she didn't know how to break? Or maybe the walls remained, not to keep Tom out, but to buffer a pain from within, far worse than any she'd yet to experience…

"Mandria…?" Tom said, questioning his own eyesight. And when she looked his way in surprise, he felt it right to the bottom of his soul. Dear God, but those green eyes were magnificent; and apparently their effect on him had not lessened a whit. "…You're looking well," he finished inanely.

Mandria scanned him closely, her defenses right back in place. "You're not. You need a haircut."

"Damn!" he propped on an elbow. "I'd have settled for a simple hello."

"Hush, will you?" she rose, when Seph registered a cry of protest. "And you needn't yell. It upsets him, as you can see," she added gathering the baby in her arms.

"I wasn't yelling," he nevertheless, lowered his voice. "…Was I?" he asked when the baby continued to fuss.

Unfastening her bodice as she sat down again, Mandria offered Seph her breast, which he greedily accepted. "No, I suppose you weren't," she nodded. "He seems to have had his own reason for waking up."

Never, had Tom seen a more beautiful picture; …nor a more painful one. And unable to watch longer, he fell back in the pillows. "…So, what color are my son's eyes?" he stared at the ceiling, in search of distraction.

"Blue—as most baby's are," she replied. "…But why do you ask?"

"I don't know," he nodded. "I guess I was hoping they'd be green."

"They might be. It's too early to tell," her answer came with soft laughter.

And Tom looked in time to see a tiny hand rewarded with a kiss.

It brought him to a sitting position, wondering why he felt so miserable. For months, Mandria had denied wanting his child and here she was, not only tending the baby's needs, but obviously loving him very much. For as many months, he had prayed for her change of heart. …So maybe, seeing it only made his own exclusion from her warmth hurt worse. He tried to dismiss the feeling in a shrug. "Yes, well, he does seem to be burdened with my hair, though."

Mandria didn't reply, but she did send Tom a curious look. She'd always considered his hair one of his best features—when it was cut properly, of course.

"So, what is Seph's full name?" Tom continued. "—And as you hadn't bothered to name him before leaving Athens, when did you decide he needed one?" he added with an edge on his tone he didn't mean to make so obvious.

"His name is Joseph Phillip—after Allen and you—*if* that meets your royal approval," Mandria's chin lifted, in retaliation. "And I didn't name him at first, because I thought his father might want a say in that. But you didn't come back, did you?"

"Lady, if you'd waited where I left you—"

"Oh, all right, so you did return. So, let's not get bogged down in that," she interrupted. But it was herself she wanted to un-bog, for she'd slipped back into the habit of blaming him for everything. "Anyway, you asked and I'll tell you. I named Seph the second day into my journey home, because literally everyone asked what his name was. At first, I just said Scott, hoping people would accept that and leave me alone. Then, I was caught off-guard when two old maids asked my name too. *But that makes your boy Scott Scott* one said, as if I'd committed a crime. And down her long, nosey nose, the other said, *Such a poor unimaginative choice, my dear. You may have scarred the child for life.*"

Tom chuckled, thinking Mandria had actually earned the put down for waiting so long to choose a name, but he didn't say it. Instead, he decided to catch her off-guard too. "And what did you call my son when you left Augusta disguised as an Indian woman?"

"Well, Toma-chi-chi was the only Indian name I knew, but no one..." she paused, her eyes widening. "How did you know about that?"

"First, because your buckskins and boots were missing from Susan's guest room. Then, because your trail ended in Augusta, where the Indian woman's began. And lastly, because I found your buckskins in the bottom of that wardrobe," he pointed. "...And I also learned from the stage agent in Augusta, that I wasn't the only one who'd been asking questions about you."

"My father's people, of course," she nodded. "So now do you see why I took such precautions?"

"No, I don't. Is Sam no longer *poor Father?*" Tom asked as she rose and placed their sleeping son in the cradle. "If not, then why are you living with him instead of where you belong?—With Seph," he hastened to add, before she could accuse him of obscene suggestions or something. Besides, so far, their conversation had failed to reach its usual vocal heights, and even if that was because the baby slept, he wanted it to continue.

Mandria turned away on the pretext of adjusting her dress, but mostly, it was to keep from looking at him when she said, "I am only doing what is best for Seph, until I am free to make a safe home for him. ...Somewhere."

That brought Tom off the bed, the baby's sake forgotten and his own remembered. "Lady, Seph has a home! And you might have the decency to wait until a divorce is finalized before looking elsewhere— Especially if its safety you want!"

"Hush!" she hissed, stooping to soothe the startled baby. And this sent Tom across the room in exasperation, where he stood, one fist on his hip, the other hand gripping the mantle top. But it wasn't until Seph slept again that Mandria followed. "Now, what did you mean?" she asked, idly rearranging things along the narrow shelf before him. "I haven't begun divorce proceedings. ...Yet," she added, wondering why.

"But damn it, Mandria, that only makes what you're doing worse!" he exclaimed. And again, he was quickly quieted.

"I assume you're referring to my nightly excursions," she reasoned. ...But why was she bothering to explain—and how had he put her on the defensive? "What you don't know—very obviously, sir—," her chin came up, "is that Allen has been my escort."

Tom folded his arms and glared. "Really? ...So where was Allen last night—while you were cavorting in the moonlight with Oscar Shurling?"

Mandria's lips parted, but she couldn't say a word—and not because of anything Tom just said. His manner, his stance, his tenseness, even the fire in those blue eyes—everything about him— screamed of jealousy. Beautiful, wonderful jealousy! ...And the walls about her heart simply collapsed, enabling her to see in every direction at once. It had not been a lack of favorable evidence that kept her from accepting Tom's story, but fear that her lack of faith in him for all those months, was something he would never forgive. Now, she knew he was innocent;—knew he did still love her too. "Oh!" she spun on her heels. And with her smile concealed from him, she directed her thoughts to Seph. ...*Sleep, little son;—please sleep! Mama has a job to do for both of us...*

But seeing guilt in her refusal to face him, Tom grasped her upper arms. And as he turned her, for one confusing instant, he would have sworn she leaned into his grasp. "Well?" he demanded, meeting her eyes—which only furthered his confusion. He had just accused her—and wrongfully—of choosing to be with that Shurling bastard alone. Why then, did she look so...pleased?

"You were the tree limb," she stated matter-of-factly. "You were there and I thought it was the Puma."

"...What?" Tom nodded, now at a total loss.

"And you only got here yesterday, didn't you?" she began to pace back and forth before him.

"Late yesterday, yes; just in time to see you and Sam leave for the evening—and hell yes, I followed you to Shurling's party, just hoping to overhear where my son might be."

"By sneaking from window to window around the house..." she guessed. "Well, no wonder I felt so uncomfortable! And you followed me down through the gardens and saw that whole disgusting thing?" She had come to a stop, and Tom braced. For her pacing usually precluded an angry outburst. ...And yet, as he studied her lovely features, he saw that she was only curious.

"Yes," he answered, still cautious to a fault. "I saw the whole damned thing."

"Well, how *did* you manage it? I knew if a limb that large had fallen, I would have heard it."

"It was an afterthought," he shrugged. "I banged Shurling's head back against the tree. And when you went for help, I broke the limb above him...and just let it fall."

"Then you beat us back to town, because you were in my bedroom too, weren't you?" she asked now.

"Still looking for my son, yes, I was. ...But how did you know that?"

"Because you like my perfume," she said smugly. "And because clever as you think you are, you left the bottle unstoppered."

"Anyone could have done that. What made you think it was me?"

"I didn't, until you admitted being at Oscar's," she replied. "It was just a feeling and it stayed with me all evening—especially when I looked at the Puma. And I even dreamed one was chasing me last night."

"...Mandria, what in the hell are you talking about?" he asked, making no sense of her story. But instead of answering, she went to the wardrobe, her musical laughter dancing in the wake—and Tom was not unaffected. He hadn't heard that delightful sound in months. ... There was something different in the way she moved too.

"I believe it will be an early summer," Mandria conversed, while deftly removing her dress and slippers and putting them away. "Don't you think it's very warm for an early May morning?"

And as if Tom's mind weren't boggled enough, she started toward him wearing only a lacy chemise and pantalets. ...Then he was remembering an occasion when she had deliberately taunted him, claiming her advanced pregnancy would prevent him from doing anything about it. And she was just as safe today, for Seph was not yet three weeks old. But if that was her game—to arouse him, simply for the pleasure of rejecting him—then he'd be more than happy to repeat a lesson on *manual stimulation* she'd evidently forgotten. ... Even if she was already accomplishing her primary purpose, because he couldn't seem to keep his eyes from roving her, top to bottom.

"Well?" Mandria stood before him, arms akimbo, her expression challenging. "Thanks to Hassie, we're locked in here, with time to ourselves, so what are you going to do about that?"

What he was *not* going to do was leap into one of her traps. "Lady, what would you have me do-about-that?" he asked skeptically.

"I would hope, what you've done for nearly six months: Stand and take it," she replied with a pensive nod. "…You're not a runner, are you, Tom? You took it all and kept coming back for more."

This was a new tact. Her observation sounded almost complimentary, and that sure as hell couldn't be real. "Listen, come to the point, will you? What is it you want?"

She smiled, beguilingly. "What I want most, I can not have yet. But meanwhile…" her sentence drifted into oblivion.

If it hadn't, Tom wouldn't have known—not when she reached for his trouser buttons. Then, instinctively—defensively—after eons of rigid conditioning, he warded her off. "If this is another of your safe plays, lady, you'll fare no better than before," he warned, wishing he was certain of his own words. And Mandria followed when he took a backward step, reaching for him again. "Stop!" he hissed as loudly as he dared and continued to retreat. "I don't think this is funny—and you can't afford to!" he added more sternly. But Mandria paused only long enough to put a hushing finger to her lips, before coming at him another time. Then, he grasped her wrists, anchoring them securely behind her;—a mistake that cost him a groan, for he'd only managed to bring their bodies together. "Oh, hell! Mandria…"

"Quiet!" she whispered, looking toward the cradle.

"All right," he said more softly. "But you can not…"

"Hush!" she repeated.

Tom heaved a frustrated sigh and glanced toward the cradle too. Seph seemed sound asleep to him, but nonetheless, he tried to lower his voice a bit more. "Lady, you can't just…"

"Oh do shut up," she laughed softly. "Honestly, Tom Scott, I have never seen a man try so hard not to have what he wants."

"…Meaning?" he asked, still leery of freeing her wrists.

"Meaning, I never thought I'd have to force you to put your arms around me."

She looked serious—and sincere—but Tom wasn't convinced. "You want me to hold you," he remarked suspiciously.

"For three or four weeks yet, it will have to do. But you could kiss me all you want—or must I force that too?"

Tom didn't mean to sound sarcastic, but he just wasn't sure of her. "And you are going to kiss me back, right?" he drew her closer, expecting rebellion. When it didn't come, he lowered his mouth to hers for a tentative taste. Neither did she object to that. So, cupping her face, in his hands, he kissed her more deeply. "…You are kissing me back," he looked at her in honest surprise.

"Yes," was all Mandria got out before he was devouring her mouth, behaving like the starved man he was.

"…Three weeks?" he finally managed words against her much-kissed mouth. "Lady, I'll never survive the wait."

"You don't have to—I do," And because she was cupping his face now, obviously wanting to say more, he found the patience to listen. "…Tom, I'm trying hard to think of this as penance—though what I have in mind is certainly no punishment for me."

"But I don't want you in sack-cloth and ashes," he nodded. "Truth be told, I don't want you in anything, but my arms."

"I know," she sighed. "But you were so patient and I treated you so badly! …So, until I'm able, I intend to do the love-making for both of us."

He had to laugh at that. "If you expect me to refuse such an offer—"

"No, because I wouldn't let you," she laughed too, stroking the rigid fullness of his loins. "…Still, when I think of wasting this, I could cry," she added softly.

"Oh, damn," he swore. "I think it was easier when I knew I couldn't have you. And now that I can—but still can't—well, *three weeks*, Mandria?"

"Or four," she reminded him, moving toward the bed. "…Aren't you coming?" she asked when he hadn't followed as closely as she wished.

And Tom, who'd been happily watching the sway of her hips, somehow complied, snagging her hand as he went. "Whoa, pretty lady," he swung her to face him as he settled on the edge of the bed. "Your chemise is lovely, but I've looked at it as long as I care to." And catching the shoulder straps, he slowly peeled it away, revealing the newly ripened fullness of her breasts. "…So what are these?" he asked, finding folded pads of cloth on her nipples.

"Let's just say your son is well-fed—so much, I tend to overflow at times," she smiled as he placed kisses on each of her breasts.

"I could suggest a remedy," he allowed his face some wallowing time there too. "I believe I told you I was never weaned?"

Mandria hugged him closer. "For the next few weeks, sir, you may suggest anything that pleases you," she unfastened his trousers, and worked them down and off.

"Lord, but I've missed the feel of you," he said then. And lying across the bed, he drew her upon him, enjoying the notion, once more, that her body was created to fit only his. The moments that followed, were beautiful and bitter-sweet as hands reacquainted themselves everywhere; lips and tongues sought each other; and even through her layers of protective under things, their passion for each other kept building. In answer, they began to move together, never imagining the rhythmical mime would reap such a whirlwind of emotion. "…Mandria?" Tom sought her eyes, and seeing they were easily as fevered as his, he rolled her beneath him, where parted thighs welcomed more of his mock invasion. And soon, stunning them both, it ended in a very real and mutual climax.

Mandria looked at him in astonishment. "I don't exactly know how you did that, but I'm so glad you did."

"Well…maybe this is the time to say, *it's bigger than both of us,*" he shared her fascination. Then, settling beside her—happy just to look at her—he smiled contentedly.

Mandria, however was far from it. There was so much she wanted to say and wondering where to begin, she started twice to speak, but didn't.

Tom chuckled. "I will never tire of watching you think. Did you know your eyes change color every time you change your mind or mood? It's like watching a kaleidoscope of different shades of green— And right now, you're trying to decide something, aren't you?"

"Yes," she answered. "Tom, haven't you wondered what brought this about? Have you no questions?"

"Only about a million," he said lightly. "Then I thought: what the hell;—why ruin a good thing? You can ask in three weeks—or four," he added, feigning a shrug of indifference.

"Mister Smug-mouth," she cuffed him playfully.

"You can hardly blame me for being distracted—and loving it," he caught her hand and brought it to his lips. "In one day, it seems, I've become a father and a husband again. ...Lord," he nodded, "I may never recover fully."

"Yes, you will," she rose on an elbow above him, "because you are a fine decent man. You're going to teach again, too—right here in Savannah—as soon as we can settle this awful mess."

"Lady, I wish I could share your confidence. ...But I recently discovered something from your father's past—"

"I know all about that," she interrupted, her chin rising. "Mike and Allen told me the whole ugly story—which gave Father a motive for framing you that I'd have to be blind not to see. Mama kept saying he did it because he objected to our marriage; that she heard him promise revenge the night of the Harvest Ball. But I've never mattered that much to him—not enough for such an elaborate plot and attempted murder. No, it was you, standing in his way to a natural-born son. And for that, I know he is capable of every crime he saw you accused of."

"But should it be told at trial—that your father is my step-father; that Allen is half-brother to us both—you do realize what he could make of that publicly? ...What could be said about Seph?"

"Tom, don't be ridiculous. Now, I will admit being upset the first time I heard that, but it only took the trip to Oscar's last night for me know there is not one redeemable thing about my father. So I don't care what is said, by him or anyone else—and if I know my mother, she told you the same thing."

"She did," he grinned. "It was very unlike the dear lady, but she said—and with a great deal of pluck—*just stop the bastard!*"

"And you will—especially if Mike and Allen are having any luck this morning. Tom, do you realize if they can prove a connection between Father and Nico, it will show a continuing pattern of violence toward the women in his life? Your mother, Kathy, Nico, me—even my mother. Each went against him in some way and suffered for it."

"Love, maybe I should hire you as my lawyer," he traced a finger across her lips. "And isn't it strange that the thing I feared would send you further from me, is actually what brought you back?"

"...Actually, it wasn't," she admitted, nonetheless enjoying his compliment. "I am a woman, after all, and the things which proved your innocence to me were seen through those eyes."

"Such as?" he looked at her with interest.

"Well, it started with the honeysuckle oil you had Mama bring for my birthday—"

"Which, I hear, you smashed in a fit of temper," he laughed. "Let me guess: did your reason have anything to do with bathtubs, cinnamon or cradles?"

"...More than you know," she replied, recalling her sea-dream again. "And I'll tell you why, sometime. But Tom, breaking that bottle, when and where I did, was the smartest thing I've ever done. You see, the night Father took me to the Lloyd House, there was a scent in the room I couldn't identify. I knew it and yet I didn't. But when I threw the bottle into the fire at Susan's, there it was again—that very same smell."

"And according to your mother, Nico picked up a bottle of your honeysuckle, just before registering at the Lloyd House. ...But even if she did—even if she had it with her—what does that prove to my woman and her beautiful eyes?"

"Well, first of all, no woman expecting an affair, would take along everything needed in a cosmetic case except her own favorite perfume. And she certainly would not bring the favorite perfume of her lover's wife—unless the lover had been drugged and she thought he might respond more readily to it. And I even know why," she added sagely. "Because, sir, you happen to love your wife to obsession. Therefore, you have a passion for her scent—which you proved again last night, when you left the bottle in my room unstoppered."

"Yes, ma'am, I do," he grinned at her confident expression. "And damn, if your theory doesn't make some sense."

"Well, it does to me—and there's more," she informed him. "Last night, not only did Father deliver me to that garden, but he also twisted my words so that Oscar Shurling would think I welcomed his attention. I truly believe Father hoped the man would seduce me—by force, if necessary. Then, he could have come charging in to defend the family honor by insisting on a quick divorce from you and immediate marriage to Oscar. And," she paused for breath, "if he is capable of so horrid a deed to his daughter, what he did to you is entirely plausible. And—"

"And," Tom gathered her to him, quieting her busy mouth with a kiss, "climb down from your soap-box, lady. You said we have time to ourselves, and right now I'm more interested in exploring the lovely proposition you made. Now, what-are-*you*-going-to-do-about-that?" he quoted her.

"'What-would-you-have-me-do'?" she quoted him back.

"Anything!" he pled. "Do as you damn-well please!"

"…Well, it would please me to touch you," she ran caressing fingers over his chest. "To just let my hands enjoy the shape and the feel of your body again."

"And?" he encouraged.

"And it would please me to find that I can still awaken my beautiful beast," she replied, drawing those magical hands and herself down his belly.

"…And?" he repeated.

"And it would please me to tame him," she smiled, fondling the swelling proof of his interest. "With kindness, of course," she added, placing a series of feathery kisses upon its velvety head.

"Oh, damn, lady!" he hauled her up and into his arms. "…Mandria, I'm sorry," he whispered shakily. "It's been too long. Another second of that, and I'm gone."

"Then go," she insisted, manipulating him now with her hand. "I want you to go," she teased at his ear with her tongue. "Just go and go and go!"

And claiming her mouth, pressing her closer to him, Tom found he still enjoyed it when she tried to order him about…

CHAPTER 24

On returning home, thanks to Mike, Allen hurried upstairs to change from his perfumed clothing. Joleen had told him lunch was being served and that everyone was already at the kitchen table, but he had blushed quite enough for one day, thank you, and knew there would only be more if he had to explain literally smelling like a rose. No, that part of his story could go unmentioned—forever!

"So that's about the gist of it, Tom," he finished a preferred, and much tamer, version of his morning while they ate. "Keys and all, we are now in possession of Nico's rooms and all she left there.—But you could pretend more interest," he laughed. "Instead, you've done little more that poke at your food and ogle your beautiful wife."

"Oh, he's interested, Allen," Mandria assured him, only half-wishing Tom would behave. "So, you and Mike are to meet Captain Pat at the Tabby House later today?" she added, as Hassie handed over Seph and removed her plate.

"At five o'clock, yes. That's what he told Mike;—said he was tired of arguing with his superior and was going to do what he knew to be right."

"And where is the Captain of the Irish Mist now?" Tom asked, reaching to ruffle the baby's hair.

"Well, he said he wanted to see Nico—no, that he *needed* to—and will come by later," Allen answered. "...Brer, do you think he'll ever get over her?"

"Humph!" said Hassie, having heard all she needed to. "Some folks got more to do than feel sorry for a man who don't know when he's better off. Now me, Ah got dishes to wash here, so go do your talking in the parlor. Shoo, younglings!—Get!"

But soon after, Willie Luther was left with both the dishwashing and Tandy to tend, while Joleen and Hassie made an exit too. And along with the suite key, taken from Allen's room, each carried a small covered basket…

Dressed in civilian clothes, Patrick Herb turned onto St. Julian Street at a little before five and saw his nephew and Allen approaching from different directions. There didn't seem a need for greetings. But what followed their search of suite D had Patrick chattering excitedly and the other two totally baffled. "By Jesus, we've got him!" Patrick expounded as they stood looking over an assortment of things on the coffee table. "Now Sam Lucas will not be able ta deny knowing Nicole—and very well indeed!"

Allen toyed with a ring—one he'd seen Sam wear often—and wondered, *How could I have overlooked this among the trinkets in Nicole's jewelry box?*

Mike glanced at an end table, wondering much the same thing. *How could I not have seen Sam's initialed cuff-links in such a small drawer?*

Then there was the monogrammed smoking jacket found wedged between the hanging negligees—and both were puzzled about missing something as obvious as that.

"And lads, if this Brandy isn't from Lucas' private stock, Oi'll be eating the bottle!" Patrick said now.

"Yes, sir, I—uh, have a feeling it is too," Allen nodded. *…Was it possible Mike had planted all these things? He did have a room key and the time to do it, but how in hell had he come by so many of Sam's personal possessions?*

"So, what happens now?" Mike struggled with similar conclusions about Allen. "Will you arrest Lucas or what?"

"First, Oi'll be getting an order ta pick up these things—and that ledger of Granny's you told me about too. It shouldn't be long in coming either, not with the rest of the case we've been building," Patrick said with much satisfaction. "Then, Oi'd say Sam Lucas will be looking at the world through a whole lot of barred windows and doors."

So bright a prospect brought a smile to every lip—and some reconsideration from the two younger men. Sam Lucas was guilty, after all, and loading the room with false evidence was just a tad underhanded when compared to the things he'd done to Tom and Nicole. ...So, perhaps, it was time for a show of support?

"I know my brother will be happy to hear that," Allen met Mike's gaze steadily. "He deserved a break, and Lord knows, I'm glad to see him finally get one."

Not to be outdone, Mike had a ready reply. "Well, I'm happy about this too.—As any friend of Tom's would be." ...*But why ask approval after the fact?* he wondered. *I would have greatly enjoyed helping to set this particular trap. ...Yes, Allen should have included me;—and now that I think about it, damn if my feelings aren't hurt!*

So, Allen just realized, were his, which now had the pair close to glaring at one another.

"Oi'll be going by ta tell Tom what we're about," Patrick said. "But first, hand over the room keys, if you would. Oi want this suite sealed, so as not ta contaminate the evidence."

Mike complied readily, but Allen still searched his pockets. "I must have left it on my desk when I changed clothes, Captain Pat," he apologized. "But if you're going by there, ask Joleen to go up and get my key for you."

...*Now, that was a timely bit of forgetfulness, wasn't it?* Mike decided. "Meanwhile, Allen and I have some unfinished business to discuss—*don't we*, Allen?" he all but dared the boy to disagree.

"We *certainly* do!" Allen retorted, heading for the door. "I believe I could use a damn drink too."

Mike followed, his pace showing the same agitation and Patrick couldn't resist a comment. "Are Dexter and Harry having a spat already?" he chuckled. "Take heart, then. It happens ta the most loving of couples."

"Oh, hell!" Mike tossed his uncle a disgusted look. And mumbling an excuse he'd never remember, stomped down the hallway after Allen.

It was a brisk, silent walk to the nearest ale-house and now, drinks in hand, the two sat facing each other across a table.

"Tom has to be thankful for a friend like you," Allen said abruptly.

"Would that his brother felt the same," Mike remarked.

"What does that mean? I'd go just as far out on a limb as you would for him."

"I know that, Allen—and because you are his brother, this is at least understandable."

"…So you're saying I'm too closely associated to be trusted or to think straight?—Is that it?"

"Well, it wasn't exactly legal, was it? And knowing Tom's strong sense of honor—as we both do—you have to admit he'd never have given his approval—"

"So?" Allen injected. "It netted positive results—and you'll never hear me argue legalities." *…There. Now Mike would have to know he was capable of keeping a secret of such importance.*

"Nor I. And I've never meant anything more." But Mike, too, waited in vain to be taken into confidence. And for a refill. When neither seemed forthcoming, he expelled an exasperated breath. … *Surely*, he thought, *with just a few more drinks, Allen's tongue would loosen as readily as had Bernie Brown's.* "Damn, the service here is lousy!" he said. "Let's go down to the Boar's Head, shall we?"

"You've never had much patience, have you, Captain?" Allen vented his own exasperation as they rose to leave. "—Even when your intentions were good."

"So?" Mike puzzled. "What does that have to do with poor service?"

"Nothing," Allen shrugged. "I was just making conversation—*if* you'd care to discuss anything."

"I'm ready when you are," Mike said hopefully. But again, both were left waiting.

The walk to River Street was also brisk and silent, worsening their growing resentment. Then, because the service at the Boar's Head was always excellent, they had downed several rounds before conversation resumed. And as emotions ran high, it was on less than a sober level.

"Tom Scott is the best damn friend a man could have," Mike managed to focus on Allen. "But, damn it, boy, your attitude about this could stand improvement."

"Meaning what?" Allen retorted, missing the table with his elbow, but recovering nicely—he thought—by stooping further to brush off a shoe.

"Meaning *trust!*" Mike leaned downward too, hissing out that all important word at Allen's ear. "Trust—yes, a valuable thing between real friends," he also followed Allen back to a sitting position.

"Oh, I agree—I truly do!" Allen nodded to the point of exaggeration.

More silence, and this brought Mike forward in anger. "Are you saying, then, that I'm not to be trusted?"

"I didn't say that!—When did I say that?" Allen met him nose to nose. "But there is a definite lack of trust around here!" he said with equal heat.

"Have you bothered to ask yourself why, Allen Scott?" Mike was close to yelling. And as that had several patrons looking their way, each slunk to the back of his chair again. "…Listen, little brother," the Captain continued in a more subdued tone. "I need some air, so let's finish this outside. And I do mean finish it—done; gone; once and for all; over and done; finished!"

"That's fine by me," Allen led the way. "It's past time for some real straight talk!"

Walking straight was another thing, but one to which neither attached importance while waiting in vain for the other to speak. So, midway into the next block, Mike turned them into an alley, where settling on a crate, he twice-folded his arms before they would remain where he wanted them. "Well?" he said, deciding he wasn't going to get any closer to a Father-Confessor pose than this. "I don't think we could ask for more privacy. Do you?"

"There's always suite D," Allen chuckled, then shrugged away his amusement. "But yes, this will do fine."

"So?" Mike urged.

"…Yes?" Allen did the same.

Completely out of patience, Mike grasped Allen's lapels. "So about suite D: What happened there will stay between us, you jack-ass! Do you understand that?—Can I make myself any plainer?"

"Damn you!" Allen bristled, trying to pull free. "Damn you for thinking it necessary to threaten me!"

"I am not threatening you!" Mike yelled as their off-balanced tussle continued. "But I sure as hell will have truth!"

"And what would you know about that?" Allen swung at the Irishman and missed, which sent him careening into a wall, then sliding down it, where he sat rubbing a bump to the head he'd taken along the way. "…Captain, are you trying to kill me?" he asked. "I mean, false evidence or not, I believe we're supposed to be on the same damn side."

The boy was ready to talk, Mike decided and he—being the adult—would see that reason prevailed. So, setting a nearly even course across the alley, the Captain of the Irish Mist dropped anchor in the dirt beside Allen. "Little brother, it has been established that the clues found in suite D were planted and that there were some hard feelings, because *one* of us forgot to include the other in his plans. But as you said, we are on the same side and it was all for Tom's good.— Now, what the hell are we fighting about?"

"Damn if I know," Allen shrugged. "…So, how did you manage to steal those things from Sam?"

"Me?" Mike asked in surprise. "I thought you did!"

"No, Captain, I didn't," Allen nodded. And a different kind of silence ensued. "…I mean, this morning, when you escorted Granny back to her office, I did look through the room. That's why I knew things were put there afterwards. And I thought you did it because you had time today and the other room key."

"And I knew they were planted because, after I saw Nico, I went back and searched the suite too, but found nothing belonging to Sam. …So who else had the opportunity—and knew how vital such evidence could be?"

"Just Captain Pat," Allen had to say. It was a somewhat sobering thought for both.

"Oh-hell-no!" Mike nodded adamantly. "He would never—and I mean *never*—tamper with the law!"

"Wouldn't he? Captain, he helped Tom escape;—even provided a horse. I'd call that tampering and thank him for it."

"He didn't!" Mike said in renewed surprise. …But then, Mike had been leading a lynch-mob that night, and he realized his uncle may have bent a few rules to prevent his involvement in a hanging. And though they had discussed Tom's case many times since, here was a part yet to be mentioned…

"Anyway," Allen was saying, "this is a lot more serious. If it's ever learned the police had anything to do with planting evidence, Sam Lucas will never be brought to trial."

"But we can't let Uncle Pat know what we suspect either," added Mike. "—You want to talk about noble? I think he'd throw himself on a sword if he thought I knew he'd ever broken a law."

"So we aren't to have the pleasure of revealing this fun evening of interrogation to him?" Allen grinned.

"No!—Oh-hell-no! Not to Uncle Pat!" Mike nodded again.

"Well, even for us, this was kind of stupid," Allen scanned their surroundings. "Here we are, half-drunk, sprawled in the dirt of some alley, ready to throttle each other to prove what good friends we are."

"Yeah," Mike chuckled, "allegiance to your brother extracts some strange tolls, doesn't it?" Then, struggling to his feet and helping Allen to his, Mike voiced another thought. "…I wonder if we should tell Tom what Uncle Pat might have done?"

"Lord no, Captain!" Allen objected. "They're cut from the same damned cloth—honor and nobility; nobility and honor. And it wasn't either that put old Sam's tail in a crack."

"No, *lambkins,* it wasn't," Mike made a to-do of linking Allen's arm through his.

And batting his eyes absurdly, Allen asked, "So it's to remain as secret as our torrid love affair?"

"Oh-hell-yes—forevermore!" Mike chortled as they headed off down the street...

Just after noon on Monday, as Mandria was preparing to leave, Tom caught her hand at the front door. "...Lady, you don't have to go through with this."

"You know that I do," she insisted. "After what Patrick Herb told us, we must keep Father unawares—just as I was trying to do, the night of Oscar's party."

"And look how that worked out," he reminded her. "So now you're blithely off to hostess his dinner party, fully aware it will be ... well, little more than a damn auction for your favors."

"Tom, please," she reveled in another display of his jealousy. "Father can hardly sell me off while I'm still legally wed to you."

"He wanted to give you to Oscar Shurling—and who knows how many others like him are lurking about?" he grumbled. "You can not expect me to enjoy the notion that other men want to court my wife."

"No, but you should enjoy knowing they won't get anywhere," she smiled.

And he didn't. "Oscar tried," he pointed out.

"Then let me assure you, Oscar is the worst of the lot—and as he is still nursing his battered head, he won't even be there tonight. Now, don't be difficult," she laid a hand along his cheek. "—And for heaven sake, don't come sneaking through any more bushes." Then she was cupping his face with both hands. "Tom, look at me. You are safe only as long as you remain inside this house, so promise me you will not leave?"

"Well, I won't if you promise to return just as soon as possible," he said unhappily.

And Mandria had to laugh, because she'd seen that identical expression on Seph's little face when she couldn't give him her breast quickly enough. "You son makes that an easy promise to keep. When it comes to his dinner, Seph is an absolute piglet!"

"I can understand why," Tom drew her closer. "Yes, remind me to have a talk with that boy. I've only made him a loan of you and I won't allow him to monopolize my lady forever."

"Why, Thomas Phillip Scott," she feigned dismay. "Are you envious of your own son?"

"You're damned right I am," he smiled at last. "Let him get his own woman. Mine should be busy enough tending me."

"Soon, my husband; very soon," she kissed him. And because his eyes said he'd like nothing more than hauling her back up the stairs, she quickly freed herself and left.

So there stood Tom, alone with his amorous feelings and jealousies in spite of Mandria's assurances. "Damn it," he muttered, envisioning that dinner party. Of course she wouldn't allow any unseemly behavior, but the guests were still invited for one purpose. And seeing her through their eyes, collectively, brought him no peace whatsoever. Why, every male present would be imagining himself her husband; anticipating the delights of her lovely body; wanting badly to touch her and… "Damn you to hell, Sam Lucas!" he muttered, going in search of a good strong drink, no matter that it was early afternoon…

———⦅※⦆———

When the door closed behind the last departing guest, Sam turned to his daughter and smiled. He had helped himself to a liberal share of the liquid refreshments and his mood was pleasingly mellow "Well, I must say that went well. To the man, they were enchanted with you, Mandy."

"I'm glad you approve," she forced the returned pleasantry, but could not resist adding to it. "I hope you also noted that when I want to charm a man—even a roomful of them—I can do so without your assistance."

"Indeed. And quite delightfully too. But which do you favor? I'm damned if I could tell."

"Now, don't rush me, Father," she dredged up a laugh. "That was the mistake I made the last time, don't you think? Just allow me to become well-acquainted with each at my own pace."

"But you've known this group for years—"

"Yes, though I've never seriously considered marriage to any— which does lead me to see them in a different light," she turned and sauntered toward the stairs, weary of his unrelenting persistence. "But don't worry. When my choice is made, you'll be the first to know— and I do look forward to seeing your reaction."

"But you'll give me no hints;—no hints at all?" he chuckled, following a step behind.

"None," she nodded, "—or you might feel inspired to create another scene like the one last Friday night."

"Mandy," he drawled, covering his heart with a hand, "how could I know Oscar would show such enthusiasm?"

Mandria paused at her door and turned to face him. "As you said, Father, I have been married and have certainly learned, the hard way, just what I want—and do not want—in a man. Perhaps, that particular *enthusiasm* is something I'd rather discover for myself?"

Too much drink or not, Sam was purely enjoying himself. This was as close to a real conversation as he'd ever had with his daughter. It occurred to him, then, that in spite of Evelyn's stifling influence, Mandria's true nature might be closer to his own: hot blooded and passionate. ...And since they were being so open, she shouldn't mind answering a question that had long plagued him. "Yes, daughter, you were married, but was Scott an adequate lover?"

Taken a-back, Mandria didn't know how she could answer without betraying herself. "...Well, I believe that is a matter of taste," she uttered, finally. "And far too personal for casual discussion."

"It shouldn't be," he shrugged. "You are finished with the bastard, are you not?"

"That is why I don't wish to talk about him—or our relationship," she insisted.

"I'm not asking for details, my dear," he laughed. "I'm just curious about the fascination he holds over so damn many women. And as you knew him that well, humor me. Was Scott an adequate lover?"

Now Mandria understood. Nearly every woman important to Sam Lucas had been strongly attracted to Tom—and he was envious! The thought brought such pleasure, she decided to give him a reply. "All right then: as a man—a lover—Tom was much more than adequate." And watching him frown slightly, she continued. "Yes, I may be done with him, but the intimate moments will not be easily forgotten. If you want the truth, Father, I fear that lovers like Tom are extremely rare in a woman's life—and what came before or what follows, will never quite compare—"

"That will do, missy!" he said sharply. "There's no need for a dissertation when a simple yes or no would have sufficed," he slowly mastered his temper. "…So, tell me: did you accept any invitations from tonight's guests?"

"Yes," her smile remained constant.

"Good;—very good," he said with approval. "…But you still haven't been to the lawyers about that divorce."

"No" she answered now.

"…Well, shall I make an appointment for you?"

"No," she repeated, still smiling.

Sam lost patience after all. "You could let me in your plans a bit more, damn it all!"

"No *dissertations*, remember, Father?—Not when *a simple yes or no would suffice*?" she laughed, stepping into her room with a graceful twirl of her skirts. "Good night—and do sleep well," she added sweetly before closing the door in his face.

So there Sam stood, alone with his darkened mood and because of Mandria's less than comforting admission—complete with conjured pictures—it worsened with each passing second. …There was Tom, surrounded by adoring women—Sam's women, until that bastard had come to town. …Tom, with his hard, muscular body—and as Sam had seen while helping Nicole disrobe him, with more than his fair share of cock. "…But I will see you in hell, Tom Scott," he vowed anew. And sending a withering glance down the hallway, he followed it to his room. Someone had to pay for his misery—and if Gladys Ella gave him any of her usual resistance tonight, she would be eternally sorry and eternally dead…

Some time later, Sam wandered down to his study for a brandy. It was a warm, moonlit night and not bothering with a lamp, he sat before an open window to cool off. His mood now was more calculative than envious. In part, this was due to an enjoyable—yet sobering—session in his bedroom. The girl would be nursing some rope burns and sitting in pans of hot water for a time, but the torn flesh would heal, wouldn't it? Besides, an abundance of dark meat wasn't healthy and he had been neglecting his favored whores of late…

The other thing on his mind was Mandria. Since when had she been willing to speak so plainly about sex? Too much brandy had prompted his questions to her. But as she'd had only one small glass of wine all evening, what was her excuse for replying as she had? … And he wasn't mistaken about her expression, either. She had enjoyed watching him suffer through her little speech. "So what is really going on here?" he murmured into the surrounding darkness. The night yielded few answers other than the chirp of a cricket; a futile puff of wind that died after rattling a palm frond; and a creak on the staircase as the house settled deeper into slumber. … Then came a second creak and Sam glanced up to see a shadowy figure pass his open study door. He knew who it was in spite of the light summer cloak and hooded hair. Tensing, not daring to twitch a muscle or expel a breath, he listened as she moved down the back hall. Hearing the rear door quietly shut, he rose with a stealth born of deep fury and followed…

It was several days later and Sam had a brand new set of prospectives. Mandria had returned to her husband's home with a frequency that explained itself. And it only took a day to obtain visual proof. He'd simply bribed a vegetable street-vendor and sent her around to the back door. Yes, Tom Scott—and the child—were in residence. And the greatest blow was that Allen—his own son—knew of and apparently condoned this deception.

Then, as if he hadn't enough to absorb, worse news arrived with his spy from Police Headquarters. Never mind that Sam had used identical tactics to entrap Tom, it was simply intolerable that he was being framed to substantiate a forthcoming charge. Who would sympathize or understand that he'd only used Nico to further establish his claim on Allen? Was it so wrong wanting to share his life, wealth—even the respect of his name—with an illegitimate son? …Again, the pain ran deep, for Allen knew of and did condone this deception against him.

Sam Lucas, however, was not a man to let sentiment stand in the way of survival. He'd lived his entire life on the flat side of a two-edged blade. If he toppled in either direction, the leap would be clear of danger and the landing comfortably cushioned by sizable stashes of cash money—more than enough to begin again elsewhere in style. … After he'd tidied up a few debts, that is, for when he left Savannah, his enemies could not be allowed to consider themselves victorious.

The first step in his grand finale had already been accomplished. And going to his study window, he watched in amusement as a band of policemen made yet another futile search of the neighborhood and the shrub-laden square. But they would not find Nicole O'Rourke as they had the unconscious body of her hired guard. No, she had been used in barter, the one toy that would keep Oscar Shurling amused and quiet until the next step was completed. That would happen today: after Allen left for work; after Mandria returned from a morning visit with her dear little family; after she left again to keep a luncheon engagement he'd conveniently arranged for this very occasion…

The scream was blood-curdling, bringing Tom from his desk chair in an instant. A second one had him racing down the kitchen stairs. "Joleen, what is it...?" he skidded to a stop, frozen by what he saw. Willie Luther lay sprawled on the floor, knocked senseless from a viciously bleeding blow to the head. With trembling hands, Joleen knelt over him, applying pressure to the wound with a tea towel. It was then he realized both babies were crying and that Joleen's attention was riveted in that direction. ...Tom had to force himself to look over his shoulder.

"Good morning," Sam smiled, his pleasant tone accompanied by the sound of a pistol being cocked. And Tom knew a moment of sheer terror, for it wasn't aimed at him, but into a willow basket hooked over his arm;—a basket that held both infants.

"Lu—Lucas, please," Tom stammered helplessly. "I'll do anything you want, but for God's sake, move the gun away from those children!"

"Not in what's left of your lifetime," Sam nodded toward the table. "I know we've done this before, but pen and paper await your use this time. And I would suggest you write exactly what I tell you."

"All right, damn you!" he readily complied, as Sam seemed to be growing upset with the yowling babies. And so, as dictated, he recorded lie upon lie, in his own hand:

Mandy,

I have denied my feelings for Nicole as long as I can. Having admitted this, I also admit my guilt for her present condition and my latent, but sincere desire to set things right. I am taking her away from here, knowing there must be a place we can start a new life together. Understand that I owe her this.

I am sorry, Tom

His hand shook with anger as he turned the page for Sam's inspection. But the hand holding the pistol hadn't wavered, and that kept Tom in check. "…So you are responsible for Nicole's disappearance," he commented. "I suspected as much—as does Patrick Herb."

Sam finished checking the note before bothering to answer. "I'm aware of Patrick Herb's activities—and that he's likely part of your scheme for framing me, but none of that matters now."

Tom heard a sharp intake of breath from Joleen, and wondered if Willie had awakened or died, but he didn't look. No, it was best if he remained the center of Sam's attention. "Anyway, Mandria won't believe a damn word on that paper," he said then. "She is not that gullible;—not anymore."

"But she will have years to wonder about it, won't she?" Sam said, giving the basket a shake. "Girl!—Get over here and quiet these brats!" he demanded of Joleen.

And as she went, Tom dared a look at Willie. …Had his eyelids fluttered, or did he only wish they had? He wasn't given time to do more than guess.

"Let's go, Scott," Sam ordered. And seeing his intention, Tom's heart all but stopped. For with the gun still aimed into the basket, which Joleen now carried, Sam was backing her toward the door.

"Lucas!" he said rising to his feet. "You don't—you can't mean to take them too?"

"Not originally, no," Sam graced him with a smile. "But you've behaved so nicely because of them, I've decided to do just that. Come now, my buggy is just down the alley and as I will be otherwise occupied, you are to do the driving."

"May I ask where we're going?" Tom sought to leave any clue Willie might hear.

"Back to jail, of course—but a far better one than you managed to escape before," Sam answered. "Now move, you bastard!" he added, propelling the gun muzzle deeper into the wicker.

It was a command to be obeyed…

CHAPTER 25

Tom was sweating profusely. It had little to do with the warmth of the day, the airlessness of the hooded buggy or the close proximity of those within. Where they were going or what was to happen had long passed from his thoughts, as well. He could only worry about the continuing pressure of Sam's trigger finger on the gun still held to the basket in Joleen's lap; of what that could mean as they bounced over pot-holes and ruts along a river-side road. Repeatedly, he tried to avoid them and when he couldn't, to slow the horse and ease the buggy wheels through. And each time, Sam would become irritated and insist on more speed.

But Tom was not going to abet a senseless, preventable accident that would take the lives of these children, and the best solution he could devise, was distracting the man from the precautions he had to use. "…Samuel Trott Lucas," he said with a nod. "It has been a few years, hasn't it, Step-father?"

"So you finally remembered!" Sam gave a bawdy laugh. And Tom used the moment to ease back on the reins. "But I am curious. How long have you known?"

"Is that important?" Tom asked. "The thing is, I'm not the only one who does;—and all agree it lends proof to your motives."

"Proof—by false means!" Sam repeated an accusation Tom had yet to interpret. "But that is neither here nor there. After today, efforts on your behalf will cease."

"So will your efforts to sway Allen," he dared a counterpoint. "He knows the truth now and wants nothing to do with you."

"That is his loss," Sam managed smoothly, though it rankled beyond the telling.

"Well, your plan with Nicole didn't work out so well. What makes you think this will end better?"

"Because I don't repeat mistakes—like depending on incompetents," Sam waded into an area more to his liking. "Yes, Scott, I will admit, enlisting Nico's aid was the worst one I made—though I did enjoy her young, supple body. But this time, I work alone."

"…Not quite alone," Tom finally recognized the route they travelled and now understood Sam's reference to a *better jail*. "Oscar Shurling may lend you the use of his cages, but involving himself in murder is something else again.—And if you haven't told him that, I wonder why?"

"Let's just say Oscar has been delightfully compensated," Sam gave an ugly snort. "Yes, for the present, he couldn't be happier with our arrangement."

"Meaning what?" Tom had to ask, remembering Shurling's fondness for Mandria.

"Why the lovely Nico, of course," Sam answered, as if it should be obvious. "Her mind may be gone, but it always was her body that served my purpose best."

"Damn you," Tom uttered, experiencing disgust and relief at once. "I didn't think you could sink any lower, but—"

"But now you do?" Sam made a smiling interruption. "Well, Nico chose her own fate. The bitch readily agreed to help me put you and Kathy in the same bed. She hoped once Mandy divorced you, to be the next Mrs. Scott."

"A notion you fostered, no doubt," Tom stated.

"Most certainly. It was what she wanted to hear. And in return for her help, I promised a session with you beforehand. Yet, when it became necessary for Nico to replace Kathy, she refused—clinging to her futile dream of winning your eternal love and devotion. Quite touching, don't you think? But most ungracious, as only I could come

ON THE FOOT OF A MOUNTAIN

anywhere close to slaking her appetites for all things carnal. Yes, Scott," he paused to enjoy a sigh, "she was nearly the perfect lover—and it's too bad you can't remember the sterling effort she made to arouse you. I enjoyed it from across the room."

"…Then, you did mean for her to die," Tom nodded. For though Sam's words and tone were glib, Tom now suspected the viciousness of Nicole's beating stemmed from a warped kind of jealousy or possessiveness—or what ever the hell it was that drove this man.

"Oh yes! You see, she wanted you to remain in Savannah—in my damn way—and that was never my intention. After all, it was you who denied me a son all these years."

"You have a daughter too," Tom commented. "Did you ever consider her feelings for one minute?"

"Mandy is a fool—and was repeatedly warned against becoming involved with you. Look what it got her: A common brat and soon to come, widowhood."

The question came hard, but Tom had to know. "…So, what about these children? Do you really mean to murder two innocents as well?"

"Like the reins of this buggy, their fate could be in your hands," Sam answered. "You will continue to do as you're told, or believe me, I'd have no compunctions about killing them right in front of your eyes."

"I do believe you, Sam Lucas," Tom made the only reply he could. Then, as the buggy swung through the gates of Mecca Dawns, conversation ended. It was just as well, for Tom couldn't risk saying more; fearful that some word or action of his might cause Sam to prove his threat. He stopped, when directed, in a lane that had led them to the rear of the gardens; went into a barred cage, as directed, and then watched, helplessly, as Joleen and the children were locked into the next one down. No, it wasn't until Sam departed for the main house, with no explanation, that he dared a decent breath. For the moment, it seemed, they were safe.

Not that he was willing to accept a moment-to-moment existence, for almost immediately, he began an inch by inch inspection of the space. It was then he became aware of Joleen's sobs. He saw that she slumped dejectedly on the far side of her cage, the basket cradled and rocking against her, while tears streamed from her eyes. He considered repeating something Mandria once said: that personal matters were often discussed before slaves, because they weren't considered capable of understanding a white man's business. ...But Sam Lucas was planning murder. Sam Lucas would leave no witnesses. It would have been cruel to raise her hopes falsely, when she knew death was inevitable. It would have been insulting, as well, to suggest otherwise.

So, Tom resumed testing the strength of the cage, bar-by-bar; top to bottom; and wondered if Willie Luther had been able to hear what was said about a jail—and if so, would Mandria make the connection? He hadn't until they were nearly on top of Shurling's place. Or would she catch the only other clue he'd managed to leave? As Sam dictated, he'd begun her note with *Mandy*, but would she realize it was coerced because he'd never before used her nickname? Then he had to nod. It seemed he wasn't above indulging in false hopes of his own...

Hassie strode determinedly down the street—a woman with a definite purpose. It had been near on to one o'clock when Old Jed located her in the market place and by the time they reached the Scott house, she'd learned the state of things. Jed told her, that earlier in the morning, he'd helped Sam load a trunk on the rear of his buggy and that it was much too heavy and large for the overnight business trip he'd claimed to be taking. Afterwards, Jed discovered nearly all of Sam's belongings to be missing from his bedroom and study, and finding this suspicious, had gone in search of his sister, whom he knew was still staying with Joleen and Willie. When he got there, it was to find Mandria and Allen in the kitchen, assisting a Doctor summoned to tend Willie Luther. And seeing no sign of Joleen, Tom or the babies, Jed had doubled his efforts to locate Hassie.

Her shoulders straightened with pride when she recalled Mandria's behavior upon their return. Of course, the girl was frightened, and of course, she took a spell of crying in Hassie's arms. But for the most part, she was holding up bravely, certain as they all were, that Sam was behind this. Not for a moment did she believe that contrived note, and only worried for the safety of those missing from her household.

Once revived, Willie Luther suffered the same fears, but was given little time to dwell on them as Police Captain Herb had also been summoned, and continued to batter him with questions he couldn't answer. Growing impatient with this fruitless endeavor, Hassie signaled Jed and they left to work out a scheme of their own. "Going to do me a little fox hunting," she said to her brother. "Old fox, he wily and ain't about to show his fine bushy tail while everbody looking for the chickens in his mouth. But Mr. Fox, he ain't dealing with no fool here—no sir-ree! He dealing with a little black weasel who want the same chickens and don't mind being sneaky in the getting!" Jed could only nod in agreement, for Hassie in this mood, was not to be denied.

With that, they entered the Lucas home and called a meeting with the entire staff. A while later, all took to the streets in small groups, fanning through the city in every direction…

Feeling as discouraged as Joleen's unceasing tears made her look, Tom now sat in the corner of his cage. He had not been able to discover one weak point in the entire structure. Also, gauging from the angle of the sun, it had to be nearing five o'clock, and with each passing hour, hope of rescue was fading. Joleen knew this too, but God love her, she continued to do what she could for the babies. Crying the whole time, she had fed them, crooned them to sleep—and even fashioned dry nappies from torn pieces of her petticoat. At one point, Tom did attempt expressing appreciation, teasing that Willie Luther might have questions about her tattered undergarment. But Joleen just continued rinsing the soiled cloth squares in the animal trough—which had also been her sole source of drinking water—and nothing could have stressed his failure, more than the look she gave him. Plainly, it said, *What need has a dead woman to fret over such?* And with a fresh rush of tears, she turned to hang her wash on the few twigs of a shrub she was able to reach from her cage.

Since then, Tom hadn't found it in himself to try again, fearing he'd only upset her further. He was so disheartened, in fact, that he didn't bother to rise, or even to look, when footsteps sounded on the path from the house. He felt them, however, vibrating through his body like the beats of a hammer, for he didn't doubt who was coming. But why allow the bastard any show of anxiety? No, that he wouldn't do—and knowing all the while, it proved nothing to his life-long enemy.

"Well, Scott," Sam drawled satisfactorily. "I must say I've enjoyed the afternoon. Did you enjoy yours?"

Assailed by the strong smell of whiskey, Tom's eyes remained fastened on his boot toes; the reply he would have made, filled with profanities he sorely needed to express, left unsaid. For experience, from long ago, warned that Sam was here to gloat; and Sam, less than sober, was at his brutal best. ...Yet, he also sensed the presence of others and almost magnetically, his gaze was drawn upward. Yes, Oscar Shurling was there too ...and held between the two men was Nicole. Tom would not forget that moment, though he'd never remember rising to his feet, or what, if anything, was said at that point.

Rags were all that covered her nakedness, emphasizing the bright bruises of repeated sexual abuse too numerous to count. ...And her eyes told a worse story. Long gone was their once vital, if cunning, sparkle. Gone too, was the girlish innocence they'd held after Sam's savage beating. Now, there was no light or life left. And Tom found he was grateful;—grateful, yes, for though Nicole's body might *serve*, further rape of her mind was beyond Sam or Oscar's control. The rhyming child she'd become had simply retreated another step...

"Lucas; Shurling, I have a question," Tom said in true wonder. "...What possible pleasure could you get from molesting this poor, pitiful shell of a woman? Surely, even a damned goat would show more response."

"How little you know!" Sam said haughtily. "Now remove your clothes, Scott, and be damn quick about it!"

But his mind still reeling from Nicole's appearance, Tom could only utter, "Not again." ...*First Delilah, then Dexter, and now—hell, what was this compulsion of friend and foe with separating him from his clothing?*

"Yes, *again!*" Sam applied his own connotation. "And I find it interesting that you recall the last occasion."

"Meaning what?" Tom tried following the conversation more closely.

"Meaning, perhaps all your dead-weight was a farce; that you enjoyed having Nico undress you;—and the splendid foreplay that followed."

"Go to hell, Sam Lucas," Tom said off-handedly. But he was growing uncomfortable with the direction of things and wanted no more surprises as stunning as Nicole. "For what reason should I undress?" he asked pointedly.

"Because you were told to!" Oscar responded, his detestable cackle raking the air. And from somewhere down the row of cages, the Puma registered a complaint. "You see, we have a bet—Sam and I—and you are to settle it for us."

"But do hurry," Sam added. "Once the drug reaches its peak, Nico becomes most anxious for the feel of a nice hard cock." Stressing this, he began to massage her genitals, and breathing a guttural sound, she embraced his arm, drawing herself closer to the pleasant sensation.

"No, Lucas—stop!" Tom managed as bile rose in his throat. "Stop!" he repeated, but Sam didn't. "Damn you, I won't be a party to this—so stop!" he was yelling now.

"Bastard, you weren't offered a piece of this sweet little tid-bit, but you'll settle our bet all the same," he laughed as Nicole convulsed in climax. Shurling took her over at that point, adding breast suckles to repeated massage. "You see, Oscar says no living male can watch a good fucking and resist arousal," Sam continued. "And oddly, this time my money is on you. I say the too-moral Mister Scott would not permit so obvious a display of lust."

"Sam..." Tom began, but was unable to find words vile enough. "Well, just forget it. I'm not playing your damned sick games!"

"Aren't you?" his eyes slid menacingly toward the next cage. "Of course, the little ones would go without supper, but perhaps you'd rather see Oscar satisfy his craving for breast milk? He isn't getting any from Nico, as you can see, and should be quite thirsty when we're done with this. The choice is yours, however," he finished with a shrug.

"Oh God," Tom turned away. He'd never felt such loathsome contempt—nor been more aware that his *choice* would make little difference. Neither woman would be spared defilement—and a wrenching sob from Joleen said she realized it too. Wildly, he sought arguments, but could think of only one thing: If there was no weakness in Oscar's cage, he had to find one in Sam's scheme and quickly exploit it. "...So the plan allows time for indulging perversions?" he turned and began to unbutton his shirt as slowly as possible. "That can only mean one of two things. Either you've established an alibi for your time here, or you're not returning to Savannah."

"Of course, I have an alibi," Sam sent Oscar a glance that Tom didn't miss. "My—uh, whore is likely in another's arms as we speak, but she will swear to being with me."

Tom permitted himself a smile. "You are lying—which, again, means one of two things. We are on Shurling's land and when finished here, either you will leave him to answer for your murders or you plan to murder him too."

"What's that?" Oscar lifted his head from his favorite obsession.

"Enough!" Sam ordered his surprise at having truth revealed playing havoc with the conciliatory tone he wished Shurling to hear. "Let me assure you, Oscar and I have no quarrel. After all, I brought him this pretty play toy—and we have yet to discover her full potential."

"Besides," Oscar intoned with his nasally whine, "you won't be found on my property. You and Nico will go floating down the river: a lover's escape gone wrong."

"A drowning?" Tom gave an incredulous laugh. And dropping his shirt, allowed his impressive size to explain that. "So where is your damn army, Shurling?—For that matter, where are all your slaves? You know it would take more than the two of you to get the job done.—

Think, man: why has Lucas told you to keep your people away from here?"

"Shut up, Scott!" Sam snapped.

But Tom waged ahead. "He did because he has sworn not repeat the mistake of involving a partner. No, Shurling, he will leave no witnesses to this.—None!"

Then Sam was laughing, determined to show Oscar how ridiculous Tom's scenario was. "You are such a fool! Don't you realize you haven't eaten today? When you're properly weakened, we can do with you what we wish.—Right, Oscar?" he asked for and received an eager nod of agreement. "Meanwhile, yes, we've plenty of time for perversions" he smiled at Tom now. "So remove those trousers, if you please." And this time, cocking the pistol, he aimed directly at the basket in the next cage.

"Starvation takes a good long time—time you don't have!" Tom muttered, shedding his remaining clothes with furious jerks. "You won't wait for me to starve or drown. More likely, you'll just go on a shooting spree—leaving the gun in Shurling's dead hand!" And now he stood grasping the bars wanting desperately to rip them out and mortally attack Sam Lucas.

"…My, my, my" Oscar nodded, his whiskey-dulled, sensually-heightened brain failing to heed Tom's repeated warning. He was, instead, admiring the well-built man before him—and glad for the money he'd spent on the sturdiness of his cages. "Such a pity," he said. "That cock will be missed snaking its way up the softness of a thigh."

Sam's envy was vented more cruelly. "Not for long, old friend. There is more pleasure to be had from a living man than a ghost. Your chance to prove that to my daughter will come then—even if I have to drug her too."

"Yes!—Oh yes, that prize alone is worth getting rid of her husband!" Oscar laughed loud and long. And again, the Puma voiced all the resentment Tom couldn't. "All right, Sam," Oscar began fondling Nicole again, "how was this to go? While I screw the bitch, you're to make certain he watches.—Wasn't that it?"

"I believe so," Sam answered obligingly. "—And remember, Scott, take your eyes from them—just once—and the colored girl belongs to Shurling for a thorough draining." Then as Nicole was led to a near-by bench, he added more confidentially, "I've seen the slave women he keeps here for nursing. Their nipples are not too attractive—stretched, some as long as your thumb—to accommodate a most voracious appetite." And as if he hadn't said enough, he added, "…You know, it has just occurred to me that Mandy should still be nursing your son. A bonus for Oscar, wouldn't you say?"

Tom clinched his teeth on the rage he felt. He knew—reason told him—this was only a taunt; that Sam was not returning to Savannah and had no intention of keeping promises made to Oscar Shurling. Still, the very thought of Mandria or Joleen being so horribly used was nearly his undoing.

"Is he watching?" Oscar called, standing before Nicole, who sat lifelessly where he'd placed her on the end of a stone bench. And he made a grand to-do of drawing his exposed penis across her cheek.

"He is, my friend," Sam replied. "Proceed as you wish. I'll inform you if his interest manifests itself."

"Then I'll give her a little taste;—gets us both good and hot, you know." And Oscar laughed as Nicole's mouth opened to accept him with no resistance. "That's the way, girlie—lick, lick, lick," he encouraged. "Oh yes, you're doing so fine…"

A roaring sang in Tom's ears, thankfully blocking those cajoling words and the wet slurping sounds from Nicole, but he could not look away—didn't dare—or *the little ones would go without supper*. No, he had to keep watching; keep believing this did not make him a participant in the unholy orgy being fostered on Nicole. …Or *the little ones would go without supper…*

After what seemed an eternity, his voice elevated with excitement, Oscar posed another question. "Anything yet, Sam? He must be stirring, because I sure as hell am!"

"Nothing yet," Sam nodded, trying to quell his own stirrings. How was it possible to see and hear such and not feel it? Had it not been for the number of women at Tom's disposal, Sam would say it proved he wasn't much of a man. ...*So what would it take to arouse Tom; to force out the baseness in every man's soul;—and most of all, to humble him?* An idea began to form and he walked to where Oscar now had Nicole kneeling on the bench and was just inserting himself from behind with a pleasurable quiver. "Have you any rope stored near these cages?" he asked softly.

"In the shed," Oscar answered huskily, too involved to do more than point.

But Sam gained his full attention on the return. "That is quite a hard-on, my friend," he said next to Oscar's ear, startling the man. "Oh, now don't lose it, for God's sake!" he laughed. "I've decided to change our wager, and you'll need that cock primed more than ever."

"Say what?" Oscar grinned, keeping his member massaged to readiness.

"Come along," he waved the rope. "You hold the gun on Scott, while I do the honors."

"You—you're not opening the cage?" Oscar stammered, which necessitated a more vigorous rubbing. And behind them, Nicole remained on all fours, as she'd been placed.

"Hell no, but you do have my permission to shoot the bastard if he causes one bit of trouble.—Or better yet, shoot the brats." Then turning to Tom he said almost pleasantly. "Hug the bars, Scott—and press yourself tightly against them."

And because Oscar did aim toward the basket and his grip on the pistol was a nervous one, Tom assumed the position he was told, while wrists first, then waist, thighs, knees and ankles, Sam trussed him securely to the bars.

"Now, Oscar, bring Nico closer," Sam directed "I think it's time we included our guest in the festivities."

"God damn it!" Tom realized his intention and began to struggle with his bindings in earnest. "You had better kill me, Sam—because if I get out of here, I am going to dismember you with my bare hands!" he yelled, and continued a frantic attempt to pull free.

"What is his problem?" Oscar asked in confusion. "—What are we doing here?" he came dragging Nicole behind him, while waving the pistol dangerously about.

Sam relieved him of the weapon, with a groan. Why were his adversaries always so much brighter than his associates? It was a puzzle. "Watch and see," he positioned Nicole a few steps in front of Tom, and bending her from the waist, he locked her fingers about the bars for support. "There," he turned to Oscar. "Now do you see the point of this?"

What Oscar saw was a woman, her head hanging low between her shoulders, but in an excellent stance to be taken from the rear, as he intended doing at the bench. "Yes, well, I suppose Scott will see much better from here," he surmised. "So no wonder he's raising a fuss— now he'll be forced to respond, heh?"

Groaning anew, Sam sharply pulled Nicole's head up by her hair and presented the coil to the stupid man. "Your reins, sir? Mount up and ride. She will do the rest for us."

The light finally dawning, Oscar exclaimed, "You want her to eat him!—And you don't care if I win the bet!"

"Let's just say it isn't every day one is privileged to see his own values proven by an enemy," he looked back to Tom's diligent struggle with the ropes. "Scott claims to love my daughter and if that is true, nothing we do can affect him. But do keep Nico's head up—and coax her forward a bit? It could take a while to break this one's resistance."

"Yes, nice and slow," Oscar breathed contentedly while easing himself into place. "Oh yes, Sam, we'll have this little filly going for the carrot in no time."

"No!" Tom roared at the first brush of Nicole's lips. "No, God damn it—I won't!" But there was no way of stopping it; no give in the rope, in spite of his struggle. And when Oscar quickened his strokes, so quickened Nicole's appreciation for the service she performed. ... Then betraying everything he held sacred in the world—his integrity, his intellect, the woman and love of his heart—Tom's body began to respond.

"Let her go, Oscar—now!" Sam knocked the man aside, when on her own, Nicole moved up to wrap her arms about Tom's legs. And kneeling beside her, Sam used his fingers to stimulate a wet, ready vagina. "Take him, Nico—do it!" he encouraged, feeling no small amount of arousal himself. "Eat him—gobble it down! It's yours, Nico, take it!" And ever obedient to the suggestive properties of Sam's drug, her effort to please intensified...

Time and place vanished for Tom. Thought ceased, his senses mellowed into liquid non-existence. The ropes lost their bite, freeing him to ride the spinning edge of a huge, inescapable whirlpool. He was going down; being sucked ever deeper into a spiraling funnel toward oblivion. It wasn't unpleasant. It wasn't pleasant. It was merely just. He had no will. He had no strength. He was weak; yielding; expelling both soul and spirit; ...right along with his seed...

"Good girl!—Good, good girl!" Sam hugged Nicole appreciatively. "You did it, Nico—you really did it!"

A less enthusiastic Oscar tapped Sam's shoulder. "I believe you owe me twice what we bet! You ripped my nightshirt—to say nothing of robbing me of a ripe piece of tail!"

Laughing, Sam looked at Tom, who hung gasping in the ropes and laughed harder. "Gladly, Oscar! I'll gladly pay double—and remember, Nico is always receptive," he handed her into that one's keeping. "And now, I'm in the mood for some myself, so take her back to the house, where the beds are softer and I'll join you shortly. Yes, I do believe she has earned a very special evening, and we are going to see that she has it."

"...How?" Oscar licked his lips in anticipation. "Sam, what can we try that's new and different?"

"Well, just look at her perfect little body," he said enticingly, "and imagine how two men might dip into it at the same time?"

"By God!" Shurling's eyes widened. "That is something I've not tried—but you'd better come soon! I'm fucking hot just thinking about this!" he prodded Nicole before him. "And I get her ass—you owe me that! Yes, you do!"

The grate of Oscar's laugh and the responding snarl of the Puma were drifting echoes for Tom. But the sound of Sam's taunting words reached him clearly. "So, Scott, now you are an adulterer. It's just as well you'll never see Mandy again. This time you can't claim innocence. This time you allowed Nico to have what she wanted—and filled her sweet little mouth with your hypocrisy. To hell with your high and mighty morals.—Oh yes, Scott, now you *have* betrayed your wife!"

The moan that escaped Tom was not a denial. It was an expression of deep self-loathing. He wasn't a man. He didn't deserve Mandria. He wasn't strong enough to be husband or father. He deserved death. He wanted to die…

It was with a great deal of pleasure that Sam lifted the pistol and delivered a stunning blow to Tom's bowed head. Then, cutting him free of the rope, he watched him absorb a painful impact with the floor; watched as he welcomed the added punishment; curling his body about it before growing still.

At last—boy and man—Sam had seen Thomas Phillip Scott brought to heel. "Indeed it will be a special evening," he laughed while sauntering back to the house. "And tomorrow will be even better." Yes, tomorrow he would destroy this entire cast of characters and move on to new adventures…

CHAPTER 26

It was fully dark when Tom opened his eyes. …Why wasn't he dead? He'd tried very hard to die, yet here he was alive and his head hurt; alive…and cold and hungry. "—Oh, God damn it!" he uttered a further disappointment. Sam should have remained to see this. Sam would appreciate knowing his first thoughts had been for a few creature comforts. …But he was a creature—a rutting animal—with no right to call himself more.

The cooling air blew over his flesh and he shivered badly—shame being the name he gave it. Nonetheless, he rose in search of his clothes and as he shrugged into them, realized how dark it had grown, the only light around filtering down from the upper windows of the main house. And it was quiet; …so deathly quiet. Panic sent him rushing to the side of his cage. "Joleen?—Are you there? A…are the children all right?" he grasped the bars, desperate for an answer. Out of the darkness, two hands stretched forth to cover his. "Yes sir, we here," Joleen replied, with no trace of the tears she'd been shedding the entire day. "Babies done fed and asleep now."

"Well…good," he nodded, confused by her calmness. The danger she faced had not passed, so what was this show of bravery? One answer—that she wanted to comfort him—was unacceptable, and he tried to withdraw from her touch.

"No, Mister Tom," her fingers tightened. "While there's time, Ah got to thank you."

"Thank me?" self-hatred returned in full measure. "Joleen, you shouldn't even be here! None of this was your doing.—All you can thank me for is involving you!"

Still she clung to his hands. "Lawd got His very own reasons—His own ways—and He pretty good 'bout looking after His lambs."

"Right," Tom retorted. And pulling away he began to pace. "Acceptance?—Is that your advice? You've made peace with God and now you're ready to take mistreatment from those mad-men?" Inwardly, his thought went further. *There can be no such moment for me. Put to the test, I failed—and if I can't forgive myself, why should God?*

"Don't know as Ah said that," Joleen answered. And Tom could have sworn her words were softly underlined with mirth. "Just saying the Lawd don't get in no hurry and we sometime meant to suffer a passing doubt while He getting ready to move."

"Like hell!" Tom declared, out of patience. He wanted to physically shake Joleen back to the reality of what was in store for them—and would have had he been able to reach more than her fingertips. ... Then, he paused in mid-step, shamed by his harshness. ... *What right do I have to criticize her faith? It is likely her only remaining strength.* So, expelling a breath, he returned to where she stood, determined to show more compassion; to do all he could to get her through the agony of waiting to die. "...I didn't mean to take my anger out on you," he reached for and received her hands into his. "I'm sorry, Joleen."

"Got plenty of reason for anger," she nodded. "Just don't go forgetting it righteous—and might be of help pretty soon."

Tom's confusion grew. *Was she contradicting herself;—preaching acceptance and retribution together?* "I won't forget," was all he could think to say.

"Yes, sir, Lawd get mad once and clear out a temple," she went on. "Now, don't that prove when it right, we got to do the same?"

"Joleen, if I could escape this cage—and damn it, I've tried—I'd gladly do that very thing," he felt, but could not put reason to her growing excitement.

"'Course, the Lawd might had a little help from upstairs," she added. "But we'd take some too—from anywhere! ...Wouldn't we, Mister Tom?"

"Yes, from anywhere," Tom answered with sadness. ...*Have I misjudged the depth of her terror?* he wondered. ...*Is Joleen resorting to delusion, hoping for deliverance by a band of avenging angels?*

"And if things got put to right, you'd have to go along with it; 'cause you know the Lawd behind it."

"Yes," he nodded, "I guess I would."

"Glad to hear that," said a voice from the night;—a voice Tom recognized, though it startled him badly.

"Hassie!" he went now to the front of the cage, watching as she materialized before him. "Hassie, how did you find us?—Can you get us out of here?"

"Wait, Mister Tom," she raised a hand, while unsteadily lowering herself on the bench across the path. ...And once again, Tom sensed the presence of others. Yes, there were many eyes watching; ears listening; and a great deal of tension in the surrounding darkness. "We got to talk," Hassie continued, as Old Jed came to stand at her side. "Long and serious."

"...All right," Tom agreed, his heart beginning to pound. Hassie and whoever accompanied her had come from the direction of the house. Now, there was time for talking—and worse, Joleen's rambling dissertation was beginning to make sense...

"'Bout your questions," Hassie began now. "We find you by the grape-vine—talked to folks all 'round Savannah: them working in yards; coming and going on errands;—even the field hands along the road out here. Ask who seen Mister Sam today? What time? Which way he headed? And open or closed, everbody knows his fine buggy— that why he pay so much for it. ...Next thing, is can Ah get you out of there? Well, sir, Ah got the keys right here, but you got to understand how...and maybe, help us a little."

Tom thought he'd never force the words out. "A... are they dead, Hassie?—Lucas, Shurling; ...Nicole?"

"Miss Nico all right as she ever going to be," Hassie had the same problem with a reply. "...But yes, sir; ...them other two gone."

"Well...how?"

"Start with, one young girl, but all us took a hand 'fore it done. ... See, Mister Sam been using this girl, real ugly-like, back to his own bed. And when she see what they doing to Miss Nico—hear her cry like a hurt, tortured kitten—she put a knife in them both. Quick and clean, she stick their throats. ...Then, we all take a turn. Lot of hatred built up over the years. Lot of suffering 'cause of him."

"So Sam's own slaves did him in," Tom concluded.

"Mister Shurling's people take part too. Those men was demons of the same sort."

"But Nicole;—you did say she was spared?"

Yet again, Hassie hesitated before speaking. "...Put the knife in her hand and she just lay there looking at it. Then she growl like a dog, and start stabbing them too;—still was when we leave. ...We just close the door and leave."

"Dear God," Tom uttered, pressing his forehead against the coolness of an iron bar. He couldn't imagine a gorier tale—and it had to be the bloodiest: pierced throats; multiple stab wounds; ... Nicole mindlessly mutilating the bodies further...

"Mister Tom?" Hassie vied for his attention. "Got to know how you thinking. That real important to us here." And he could almost feel a collective intake of breath as all awaited his reply. But Hassie hadn't finished. "Had a word with Joleen while you still knock out. Heard what was to come. We help you, you got to help us back. If the law say those men die by our hand, they going to call it a uprising. ... Know what that means?"

Tom took in a breath of his own. Indeed he did know. Raising a single hand against the Master, was enough to cost a slave his whole arm. This deed would end in mass slaughter;—death for the very ones who took the time and trouble to rescue him. And Joleen;—even the children? Yes, until now, he hadn't been able to include them in his death sentence, the thought being too awful. But it would have happened. Sam wouldn't have burdened himself with their care, or left

Mandria with anything to hold dear. So his son and Joleen's daughter would live because of these people—and if he could prevent it, not at the cost of their lives. "…Hassie, are Shurling's servants here too?" he asked.

"Yes, sir, we all here," she replied. "Done our talking, and ready to hear what you think the best thing."

"In other words, you're in a hell of a mess," Tom acknowledged the irony, "And expect the one locked in a damn cage to keep all of you out of one."

Hassie's chuckle was a mixture of relief and wonder. …*Why was it she never found Tom's cussing offensive? …Maybe because in spite of all he'd endured from Sam Lucas—and yes, from her Mandy-chile'—he still remained one of the best and most honest white men she'd ever known.* "Don't like admitting Ah'm stumped, but yes sir, we in a mess, and Ah done promised you'd help. …So what's to do?"

"First, open these doors, Hassie, and then get some torches lit. Because yes, there is much to do," he replied, and with a single nod from the old woman, his orders were swiftly obeyed. But as Tom stepped from confinement and had his first clear look at the blood-spattered group in the blaze of torchlight, more instructions immediately followed. "Clothing. Have everyone pair-up in size, then have Shurling's people bring a change of clothes for each of the Lucas servants; nightclothes for themselves; and meet us down at the marsh.—And bring more torches."

"Tend it, Jed," Hassie said with a second nod and that brought about the scurry of departing feet. And a question. "So, Mister Tom, what we doing besides getting shed of these ruined-up clothes?"

Before answering, Tom stopped for a peek into the basket Joleen carried; to ruffle a tiny head of hair so nearly the color and texture of his own; to pat Tandy's smooth little cheek too. And it was with a lump in his throat and mist in his eyes, that he picked of a torch and led the way down the path. "Yes, the clothes will have to be burned," he said. "And we can't forget to have every one wipe down their shoes, top and bottoms."

"Then what?" Hassie puffed as she and Joleen hurried to keep pace with Tom's longer strides.

"Then once you've locked us back in the cages, and returned the keys to the house, you will take the Lucas servants home and put them to bed, where they must be when news of Sam's death reaches Savannah."

"What if we get stopped on the road—or in town?" Hassie worried.

"Let's hope you aren't;—though should you be, you won't look a bloody mess. And maybe you could claim to have been to a church meeting—a gathering, or whatever."

"But what about the people here?" Joleen asked. "They just going to bed too?"

"All but the best actor among them—and Hassie, you'll need to find out who that is from Shurling's people. Anyway, he will go for the law. He'll say he heard strange noises from the bedroom and because of Shurling's recent head injury went in to check on him, only to discover the killings. He will say no more and no less. When the law arrives here, Nicole's condition, plus testimony that she'd been held here for some days, will be enough to convince them of what happened. If not, Joleen and I can, because we saw them take advantage of her."…*And I did too, damn it all*! he added inwardly.

They had reached the river marsh at that point and Tom searched until finding a blackened pit where refuse was regularly burned. But Hassie still had questions. "…So Miss Nico going to take blame for all of us?"

"Yes, but she won't be punished, and her father will see that she gets the best possible care," Tom said with assurance. "Hassie, this might be twisting truth a bit, but Nico did help Sam start this trouble and it's only right if she can help us end it here and now."

"…Just hope this truth-twisting work out better for everbody than it did for me," she said with unusual timidity. "Ah done stole things and lied and been where Ah shouldn't, trying to help catch Mr. Sam. …See, it was me and Joleen what put his belongings in Miss Nico's rooms to the Tabby House."

"You two?" Tom looked from one shame-faced woman to the other. "But why—how—and to what purpose?"

"The how done after Captain Mike and Mr. Allen rent the place. We steal Mr. Sam's stuff from the house; then steal Mr. Allen's key and put it all around in her place. The why cause Mr. Sam guilty as sin, and white man's justice just moving too slow! ...We only poke it little, that's all." Then Hassie nodded. "But my Daddy always say two wrongs don't never make no right—and we like to got you killed with our meddling. Joleen tell me Mr. Sam say he blame you for what we done more than once today. ...Then look what it lead to out here: death and more wrongs."

Tom nodded too. Hassie was a good woman with a bothersome conscience; a leader, taking responsibility for the actions of subordinates. She was beginning to feel guilt for Sam's death—and that was dangerous. "I don't see it that way," he countered. "Hassie, where the rest of my friends never could, you forced Sam Lucas to show his true colors. And cared enough to track him down here;—you and your *band of avenging angels*," he added, not quite smiling. "So, for the little its worth, you saved my life and I can only thank you for everything you did."

Hassie's shoulders straightened perceptively, while Joleen's posture clearly became indignant. "For the little your life is worth? You making me mad, Mr. Tom! It all right for you to give thanks;—go 'round making everbody feel just fine. But wouldn't let me thank you. No, you rather believe Mr. Sam's lies;—rather think you party to things your body didn't let your mind have no say-so 'bout!"

"What's this?" Hassie's interest sharpened. "Same as happen to Joleen and Willie;—what Miss Nico make them do. You saying they wasn't wronged if you wasn't."

"I didn't say that, Hassie," Tom replied. "But they were slaves, with no rights whatsoever, and—"

"Like you was a slave to them ropes!" Joleen interrupted.

The women reminded Tom of a pair of warring hens now;—feathers bristled and circling for attack. "Yes, but Nico was the one with the power. A white woman—"

"Like Mr. Sam a powerful white man," added Hassie.

"Yes, but they—and especially Willie—could have been hanged for even mentioning the sexual behavior of a white woman."

"Didn't stop us from feeling dirty," Joleen countered. "Keep us thinking we worthless and weak to let that she-devil use us so bad."

"I can certainly relate to that, Joleen, but you *were* with the man you love!" Tom said, knowing immediately how heartless it sounded. "—I mean, at least you never had to *betray* Willie because of Nico."

"Now we down to the bottom of the pot," Hassie folded smug arms before her. "You less of a man to your way of thinking; less able to trust your decisions; you just ain't no more good."

"Hassie?" Joleen's eyes rounded. "Why you go and say such a thing? Quick as a rabbit, Mister Tom think of a way to make all of us safe here;—safe from the hangman too!"

"Onlyest one don't know that is him," Hassie sent Tom a look reserved for the stupid. "Don't know all he lose is a piece of male pride; don't know he save you and them babies keeping them demons amused 'til we can get here; don't know he been tortured, same as they burn him with hot fire. Joleen, he don't even know that was the work of a strong man;—a fine, strong man!"

"Yeah," Joleen giggled. "He ain't bad to look at, neither. Next to Willie, he just ain't bad;—and Miss Mandy, she think so too!"

"Ladies..." Tom injected, but Hassie continued as if he no longer stood there between them.

"That not all my Mandy-chile' thinking. Her crying real bad this morning—feeling guilt of her own. Say it been over six months since she sleep with her husband. Say it her own silly fault. Say they been reunited in spirit, but it too soon after the baby for more. Say she wish she gone ahead and done it anyway. Say if Mr. Tom end up dead before he know how much she love him, she ain't never going to forgive herself for waiting."

"Six months?" Joleen said in awe. "...Lawd, Hassie, ain't no wonder he couldn't hold back.—Holy preacher-man couldn't have. Have to be made of rock did he!"

"That ain't the point, girl!" Hassie retorted when Tom turned away. "Point is, he got a wife who love him much as he love her—and if he go messing that up 'cause of some hurt pride, then he crazy."

"Well, he won't, Ah bet-cha," Joleen nodded. "Not ready to risk another six months without neither. Miss Mandy, she feel pretty strong 'bout him and Miss Nico before, so best he just keep his mouth shut on this, or it could happen again—and that would be crazy!"

Age did have its advantages and Hassie heaved an indulgent sigh. The girl was young and as was the ilk of the newly-wed, greatly impressed with the physical side of the marriage bed. Joleen couldn't see Tom's abstinence for the greater act of love that it was; couldn't appreciate that he'd been willing to wait until his wife's faith in him was restored. "Listen now, telling or not, that Mr. Tom's decision— something between him and my Mandy-chile'. ...Course, was it me, Ah might let it slide on by for a while. She going to need comforting while the town buzzing over the bad things Mr. Sam done out here. No, just ain't sensible adding pepper to a stew what already hot."

"Sides that," Joleen tacked on her bit of wisdom, "takes a fool to climb out of quicksand, then turn around and jump back in—a misery-loving fool!"

Listening to all this, it bothered Tom that they placed no importance at all on his failure to withstand Sam's tactics. Of course, he'd been called crazy and a misery-loving fool, but not for the reasons he would have chosen. ...So what point were they trying to make? As always, Hassie wanted what was best for Mandria—and still seemed to think he was. Joleen wanted the same, but insisted he should protect himself too. *Best keep his mouth shut; ...not ready to risk another six months without...*

Tom groaned—miserably. ...*What of a lifetime without?* Yes, all would be better served if he took himself off and stayed. ...And yet, Hassie was right about one thing. Mandria would need support getting through the gossip, the funeral and a whole ton of legal matters yet to be settled. And in good conscience—if he had any left—he could not relegate this duty. No, he had to go home, at least for a while yet.

...And meantime, what of the marital relationship Hassie said Mandria wished to resume? Well, he could confess his sin and surely she'd mete out the punishment he deserved. ...Although, adding stress to an already stressful time in her life wasn't fair either. So how could he keep the truth from her and still avoid a situation she was certain to encourage?

...Of course, she had given birth less than a month ago, making this decision of hers unwise, if endearing. And if all else failed, wouldn't concern for her health seem a viable excuse? A deep aching sigh followed.—But no, he couldn't soften on this. If he couldn't stay strong on this one point, he shouldn't return home at all!

...Then what would become of the son he hardly knew? The brother he'd promised and wanted to be there for? The home he was so proud of? ...And there was also John and Brittany, awaiting their trip to Savannah and inclusion in the family he'd promised to give them. Tom nodded again, but now in wonder. How in the hell had he come by so many obligations? He started to pace then, as the war between heart and mind continued, and was unaware the two women watching his every gesture, prayed they had said the right things.

...*So you aren't the tower of strength you wanted to be, but does that relieve you from commitment?* he thought. *Certainly not. ...But what if your shortcomings cause more harm than good?—Damn, and still you have to go home, because deserting your family is not the answer either...*

"People coming back, now," Hassie's voice pierced his confusion. "Want us to start them stripping and washing off some, maybe?"

"Yeah, nice little tide stream right over there," Joleen pointed.

"In a moment," he took in a breath and let it out slowly. Then turning, he gathered both of them to him. "Let me just say I appreciate your concern. And no matter what, I'll know I can depend on your loyalty to Mandria. ...I still have some things to work out, but believe me, I'll do what it takes for her happiness." And with that, he went to address the growing assembly, his orders crisp and precise; his attention to detail exact.

Still watching him, Joleen grinned joyfully. And Hassie cringed. Tom hadn't fooled her with that smile that didn't reach his eyes—or words that circled 'round decision.

No, this was a man with a duel left to fight. One whose enemy was more his equal than Sam Lucas ever had been. For now, he fought himself…

CHAPTER 27

The grandfather clock was sounding a quarter past the hour when Mandria rejoined Allen at the kitchen table. She'd gone in to check on Willie Luther, who tossed fitfully in spite of the dose of Laudanum left by the doctor, and he wasn't to have more for some time yet. It had taken dozens of sutures to close his wound and she was told, he might suffer severe headaches for a while to come. But none of that caused Willie's restlessness. There just wasn't a medicine on earth that could ease the endless wait they both endured…

Once, during the evening, Allen had offered to fix her supper, but she couldn't eat, and noted, he didn't either. Then, he suggested moving their vigil up to the parlor, where the chairs were, at least softer, but neither could she do that. She needed to stay close to Willie, for they prayed the same prayers—and maybe, because they did, there was twice the chance they'd be heard by a God who was supposed to be merciful.

She watched now, as Allen made yet another attempt to school his features; to keep worry from his expression; to become the strength she might soon need. She reached for his hand then. There was nothing she could say. Mandria just wanted him to know she was grateful to have him there;—so grateful, because she'd spent most of that terrible afternoon alone…

She remembered meeting Allen on the front walk and the laugh they'd enjoyed. It had been close to one o'clock and he was coming in from work for a quick lunch. She had just returned from lunch with one of her father's would-be suitors, and was anxious to join her husband and son. Yes, laughing and teasing, they'd entered the house and gone straight down to the kitchen, which was fast becoming a favorite family gathering place. …And there they discovered Willie Luther lying unconscious in a pool of his own blood. There they found that ridiculous note. And nowhere could they find Tom, Joleen or either of the babies.

Allen had immediately gone for the doctor and then for Patrick Herb. And by the time Willie had been revived, tended and questioned, she was in quite a state. The note told them more than Willie could, because though it was in Tom's hand, the words, meant to hurt in the cruelest of ways, were her fathers—and that had her crying on Hassie's shoulder, when she and Old Jed appeared from nowhere. She felt a brief flare of hope when Patrick Herb and Allen agreed with her about the note and left to seek-out Sam Lucas for questioning. But she couldn't maintain that hope, because after giving Willie a scheduled dose of his sedative, she'd returned to find Hassie and Jed had departed as well. And she was totally alone. It was dusk before Allen came home again and his news was more than depressing. After a trip to the Lucas home and several between his office and favorite clubs, it seemed that her father had also gone missing.

Mandria's grip on her half-brother's hand tightened, for all this was eons ago, and still they'd heard nothing. …Then, as simply as that, Joleen just came walking in the back door, lifted Seph from a willow basket and placed him in Mandria's arms. Relief went beyond joy and happy tears accompanied her questions while she and Allen both cuddled and petted the baby.

"First off, your husband fine too," Joleen said, re-tucking a blanket, as Tandy still slept soundly in the basket. "…Is mine?" she asked, having to know.

"Yes!—Yes, Willie is fast asleep, which the doctor said would do him the most good," Mandria nodded. "Now, what happened, Joleen—and where is Tom?"

"Send this message: Mr. Allen, he want you to join him to the Police Station right away. And Miss Mandy, he say for you to please—*please*—stay here and wait." Then she hesitated. "…Mr. Sam, he dead."

"Tom didn't…" Allen shot to his feet. "…Did he?"

"No, sir—no!" Joleen answered. "Miss Nico been held prisoner out to Mecca Dawns, and it was her stabbed him and Mister Shurling both." And with that, Allen made a hurried departure.

Mandria could not quite absorb such news. "My father…and Oscar Shurling?" she prodded. "But how is Tom involved?—The Police haven't arrested him again, have they?"

"No, Miss Mandy," Joleen rummaged about for something to eat. "He doing his turn at what they call a statement, but then he'll come on home—just like Ah got to. See, we witness to some of what happen. Both us locked up in Mr. Shurling's cages and seen bad things done to Miss Nico." And as if starving, Joleen began to eat from a cold pan of cornbread and a bowl of red beans.

"By Oscar?" Mandria could still almost feel his unwanted fondling. "And my father took Nico—all of you—out there, didn't he?" she tried very hard to not to ask that.

"Not Miss Nico. She already there…," Joleen put down her spoon. "Maybe you shouldn't hear this. He was your daddy, even so.—Or maybe Mr. Tom ought to tell it."

"No, I'd rather hear it from you," Mandria straightened. "For almost a year now, my father has put Tom through every possible hell, and he shouldn't have to come home from a police investigation and repeat the latest thing all over again. Please, Joleen, just start from this morning and tell me everything."

"…Everything," Joleen repeated, knowing she couldn't. "Well, Mr. Sam come in the back door here, while I fixing to give Willie some food. Hit Willie over the head with a gun and Ah scream. That bring down Mr. Tom," she paused for another bite. "They would of fought too, Ah bet-cha, 'cept Mr. Sam hold his gun pointed on these babies—"

"The babies?" Mandria exclaimed. "Oh, Joleen, you had to be terrified;—Tom too!"

"Was. That why he write what Mr. Sam say; then drive where Mr. Sam want to go;—'cause he never onest took that gun off them. Anyways, get to Mr. Shurling's, your daddy lock me and the babies in one cage and Mr. Tom in the next. After while, them two men come back and Miss Nico with them," she nodded over the memory. "…She a sorrowful sight, Miss Mandy, all bruise-up and wearing neigh-on to nothing. And, not excusing your daddy, but Ah think Mr. Shurling done most of that, 'cause Mr. Sam say she the prize for getting to use them cages."

"Dear Lord," Mandria nodded too. And this was the man her father had long wanted her to marry;—the one he'd tried giving her to, not a week ago.

"Done bad, ugly things to that girl right before us—both of them," Joleen continued. "And much as Ah used to hate her, Ah got to say Ah'm glad she act like a zombie. Didn't say nothing sounded like words; just keep looking through them big empty eyes. … When they finish, they take her back to the house," Joleen made a purposeful skip in the story. "Go there, 'cause beds be softer, Mr. Sam say."

"Wait! …Wait," Mandria insisted. "What else did my father say? For God's sake, didn't he even bother to explain why you were brought there and locked in cages?"

"Well, heard Mr. Shurling say Mr. Tom and Miss Nico going to be found in the river. Say it would look like they was running off together and drowned. But Mr. Tom don't believe it and he warn Mr. Shurling he going to die too. Say your daddy won't leave no witness—and he did say that, 'cause Ah heard him 'fore we even got out the buggy."

"…But you and the children?" Mandria asked now.

"Don't know 'bout them," she answered, "but, Miss Mandy, Ah heard it all and seen it all, and he couldn't have let me live."

"No, I guess not," Mandria had to agree. "…So, then what happened?"

"Heard say it was in Mr. Shurling's bed where Miss Nico get hold of a knife and stab them. …Heard say the men be naked and both going at her at onest. …Heard say she crying in real bad pain. …

Heard she start stabbing and wouldn't stop. But heard when the law come, she give up the knife meek as you please."

"Yes, but who sent for the law; and where did they take Nico? Surely, she's not in a jail cell," Mandria hoped not.

"No, her put back in the hospital, and Mr. Tom say law won't punish her or nothing.—Oh, and it was Mr. Shurling's house-boy what find them dead and run get the law."

"Then it was the law who let you out of those awful cages too," Mandria surmised. "…And so, finally, ends a long, dreadful saga."

"Yeah, it finally done," Joleen said, but noted Mandria's somber expression with concern. "…You not going to cry, is you?—Not over Mr. Sam?"

"Oh, no, Joleen;—not one tear!" Mandria vowed, hugging Seph close. Then she rose, going toward the stairs. "Instead, I'll wait in the parlor for my husband and let you get in there to yours. …And Joleen," she paused to look back, "as bad as it was, thank you telling me the truth. Once again, you've proven to be my very good friend."

Joleen sat where she was a while longer and tended to Tandy's feeding, but she was at odds with a twinging conscience. Mandria was her friend too—the best friend she'd ever had. And she hadn't lied to her…exactly. Joleen just hadn't said Sam and Oscar were already dead when Nicole was given the knife. Neither had she lied by omitting Tom's experience at their hands—and she still hoped he wouldn't tell it either. Hassie said that was a matter best settled between husband and wife; …but Hassie didn't live in the house with those two. When things went peaceful, their relationship was near as happy as hers and Willie's. "When they fighting, though," she rolled her eyes, "—oh, Lord, everybody walk on tipsy-toes."

Up in the parlor, Mandria was also feeding her baby. She was thankful to be holding him again;—and more than thankful Tom would soon be joining them. At long, long last, they could be a family. "It was a struggle, Seph," she murmured softly, "but now you will have a home with a mama and daddy who love you."

…Then, unbidden, questions arose. Why hadn't Tom wanted her at Police Headquarters?—Was there something he didn't want her to know or to see? …And unbidden too, she envisioned the scene in Oscar's bedroom: blood spilling, nudity affording no protection as a slashing blade descended again and again… "Stop it!" she admonished. And afraid of waking Seph, she lay him on the sofa and rose, searching about for diversion. "…This is really a lovely room," she mused, "where friends and neighbors will come to call, once this business is forgotten. Yes, soon the Scotts will be accepted members of the community.—And that's only right. We are respectable people, who were at the mercy of a very amoral man, that's all."

…*So why this deep sadness for a father who'd never treated her like more than a bargaining chip?* she wondered. …*A father who twice tried to kill her husband—and likely, would have murdered her son as well? A man notoriously unfaithful to her mother and no kind of parent at all?* … But the sadness remained and for that, she was beset with two shames: one for having a father capable of these awful deeds; and the other for ever having loved him—which the sadness said she had.

"I must be insane," she pressed fingers to her temples. She couldn't have felt guiltier had she'd been caught in another man's arms. Tom had shown her what real love was. Tom was a good man, a good father and would never put his children through the things her father had. "So, no!—I will not dishonor my husband by mourning you, Father! No, you don't deserve it;—and Tom deserves better!" Then, drying tears she hadn't known she was shedding, she composed herself and sat sedately upon the sofa again…

When Tom and Allen arrived Mandria's greeting was all she thought it should be. She hurried into her husband's arms, saying right away, that Joleen had told her the worst and assuring him of her love, she asked no questions. She would have been happy just to hold him forever; to forget the world outside and bask in the warmth of her feelings for this one man. But too soon, Tom gently freed himself and asked for something to eat.

Of course, he has to be hungry! Mandria thought as she went down to the kitchen. *When Joleen came in, didn't she eat enough for two women?* But Mandria did not want to dwell on the way they'd been mistreated in captivity;—no, she only wanted to feed her husband as if it were any normal day. And yet, it would have been nice had he held her a while longer… "Silly goose," she muttered, climbing the steps with a ladened tray. After all, there was the rest of the night and the privacy of their bedroom for that;—and every night thereafter. So, she waited, patiently, while both Tom and Allen wolfed down the food. She listened, patiently, to their small-talk. She carefully showed no reaction when they spoke seriously about the day's events and the probable steps for having all charges against Tom dropped. And she didn't miss the measuring glances that Tom repeatedly sent her way.

…But why measuring? If Tom expected her to break, she wasn't going to do so. She was no weak, weepy female. She only wanted to be a warm, loving wife—and the looks she sent back conveyed this. Then finally—finally—the men had talked themselves out and the time Mandria longed for came. They said good-night to Allen and while Mandria returned the tray to the kitchen, Tom carried Seph up to their room. How anxious she was to join him; how her feet flew over the stair steps and sent her all but running through the bedroom door—which she closed too loudly in her haste, for Seph awoke with a startled howl.

Already in bed, Tom had been watching the baby beside him when this occurred. "…Lady?" he looked Mandria's way. "…Is something wrong?" Slamming doors usually meant there was.

"No, Tom," she gave him one of those melting smiles. "Just pacify your son until I can get there," she hurriedly removed her dress, then slipped into a gown. "And let's hope this feeding will keep him happy for the night?"

Tom said nothing as he drew Seph upon his chest and busied himself with quieting the boy. He knew what Mandria was suggesting— he knew, and God help him, he did want her badly, but until he'd made some sort of peace with himself over the incident with Nicole, it couldn't happen…

"I'll take the baby now," she came crawling up beside him. "And you, sir," she added with a look from those beautiful green eyes, "had better not fall to sleep on me."

Never before had Tom swallowed a groan. It left what felt like a rock in his throat. ...But she had given him an idea, and when she drew his hand into hers, the effect was so powerful, he decided to act upon it immediately. So to keep her from seeing the heartache he suffered—and himself from seeing her tempting face and form— he drew a forearm across his eyes while pretending a yawn. Then concentrating mightily on his breathing, he gradually slowed it to a steady rhythm, punctuating the effort with light snoring sounds. Lastly, he allowed the grip of the hand she still held to go slack. And prayed all was convincing...

Mandria had sworn she wouldn't cry again; that she'd show Tom her strongest self. And being strong did not allow selfishness. No, Tom had to be as exhausted as he'd been hungry, and expecting romantic vigor after such a day, was entirely selfish of her. He loved her—she knew that—and once more, she reassured herself that they would spend the rest of their days as passionately involved as they liked. So, easing his hand down on the bed, she cuddled their baby between them. She had nothing to weep about anyway. No demons,—imagined or real— could come between them ever again...

--------⬥⬥--------

Only Seph shared her bed come morning, but Mandria thought little of it. Tom had always been an early riser—and so it seemed, was his son. Already sucking his little fist, Seph was working himself up for a good cry if breakfast didn't soon come. "You, my fine boy, are much like your sire," she smiled while changing his nappies. And gathering him to her breast, she laughed at the eager way he sought it. "...Oh, Seph," she drew a finger along the smoothness of his plump, rosy cheek, "what sort of girl will you marry? Will you make her as happy as I am with your father? ...I don't want you to have the troubles we've had, but will you handle your own as well and bravely as he?"

"Morning, Mandy-chile'," Hassie said from the doorway. "Brung you up some biscuits and hot tea."

And not having heard the door open, Mandria laughed at her own startlement. "So, good morning to you too, Hassie!—And just where did you disappear to yesterday?"

"Like everbody else, Ah went looking for the peoples what supposed to live in this house and be happy about it," she answered. But not before giving Mandria the same measuring look Tom had.

And Mandria began to feel a niggling discomfort she couldn't name. "Well, we are all here now, safe and sound—which, of course, you know already."

"Safe and sound," Hassie nodded.

Mandria did too. Why had that sounded more a question than a statement?—But she was being silly again. The days of looking for covert meanings in everything said died with her father, and only bright times lay ahead. So, she smiled—brightly. "Have you seen that husband of mine this morning? I've been wondering what he could be up to so early."

"No, he gone 'fore Ah gets here," Hassie replied. "Lots of business need tending, Mandy-chile'—like Mr. Sam's funeral, for one."

Mandria's smile faded. "...Dear Lord, I hadn't thought of that falling on Tom. It doesn't seem fair, does it?"

"It ain't.—Now, how you going to make it easier on him?"

"Well, I am going to be strong—which means I won't go to that funeral. No, I will not honor a man who wanted my husband dead," Mandria vowed again. "...I've said my good-byes," she added. "And Tom will never see me mourning a father like that."

"Might be better if he did," Hassie commented, taking Seph to his cradle. And noting the un-mussed covers there, confirmed her belief this was still a troubled marriage.

"Hassie, how could you say such?" Mandria puzzled. "Hasn't enough been done to Tom already?"

"Maybe too much," Hassie came to sit on the edge of the bed. "...Mandy-chile', sometime it not wise to show a husband too much strength. Sometime you got to show you depend on his strength and can't make it day to day without him."

Mandria nodded. "For you, of all people, to preach weakness is laughable! Everyone depends on your strength—and how often have I heard you criticize feminine wiles? Surely you don't expect me to take up fits of the vapors!"

"No, smarty, Ah don't," Hassie replied. "All Ah saying is that, right now, Mr. Tom need to be needed around here."

"Well, of course he's needed. But what has that to do with my going to the funeral—or not?" Mandria asked in exasperation.

Hassie sighed, and it too, was in exasperation. Without revealing cause, she had to make Mandria see that Tom was troubled and get her to do something for it. "…You know, men funny creatures. They hold things in what should come out—and 'cause of it, they heal lots slower than women. Now, Mr. Tom going to the funeral, 'cause it's the right thing to do and you can't let him face it alone. So what if you cry for your daddy? It not disloyal to your husband if you got human feelings. …Thing is, he might need to cry too, and strongest thing you can do is give him the chance. Go girl—and cry together. Then the healing can start."

Mandria's lips parted in realization. Never—not during the worst of their experiences—had she seen even the sheen of a tear in Tom's eyes. Of course, she had cried by the gallon buckets, and had to admit it helped. …What did Hassie know of Tom's feelings that she didn't? Why, when the bad times were finished, would he need to cry? The notion was close to frightening. Yet the stubborn line of Hassie's mouth said she wasn't going to reveal anymore; that if Mandria wanted answers, she must accept the challenge as presented. "All right then," Mandria said with her own bit of stubbornness, "If I go—and Tom would understand if I didn't—and if I should cry, it will not be for my father, but in relief that this is over and done."

"Tears is tears," Hassie shrugged as she rose and started from the room. "Somebody ought to bottle them for doctor's use. Good dose can sometime loosen things up better than black-strap and molasses." And without looking back, she was gone.

"…What on earth?" Mandria wondered, leaving the bed to dress. There were times when Hassie's mysterious wisdom made no sense at all—and still managed to be as unsettling as if it had…

⸻⟨✤⟩⸻

When Mandria came down stairs, she paused in the front hall to wind the grandfather clock. She could hear the laughter and chatter of the reunited family below stairs, and not wanting the mood Hassie gifted her with to dampen their spirits too, she remained away from the kitchen. But soon, the morning began to drag, and to keep busy while Seph napped on the sofa again, she resorted to housework. As she was watering the ferns in the front window, she noticed two neighbor women conversing on the sidewalk across the street. Smiling, she raised a hand in greeting…but it wasn't returned. At first, she thought perhaps sun-glare on the glass panes had prevented her from being seen. Yet, they did seem to be looking right at her, and the longer she stood there, the more positive she became they were talking about her—or, at least, the family who resided in her home. …And why did they keep glancing up the street?

"The newspaper, of course!" she said, when they stopped a boy who was selling them. Then, she had to watch as the women devoured the story with several expressive gestures of shock and dismay. … And why had their unthinking rudeness set her heart to pounding? She was behaving as if she were guilty of her father's crimes and that wasn't true. She was Mrs. Thomas Phillip Scott, wife and mother, with a household to run—which that pair across the street should be doing instead of gossiping! "Why how dull their lives must be," she turned with a dismissing flip of her skirts. "—Especially in the bedroom," she added cattily and with great enjoyment.

However, two steps into her grand departure, Mandria came to a halt, her heart pounding again, for there on the table by the sofa, was a folded newspaper. "…Well, so what?" she asked, and with a lift of her chin, she passed it by. "I have more to do than that!" she dusted the room with a vengeance. The same was given to the sweeping she gave the front hall. Then she proceeded to the study and straightened up in there too. But always and from everywhere, that dreadful paper kept drawing her eyes…

Some time later, Tom came in and Mandria's nerves were stretched to the limit, though she did manage a warm greeting. Yet now Tom was leading her to the very spot she had tried to avoid; seating her right next to that damned paper. As Seph still slept, beside her, Tom sat on the coffee table at her knees, and even so, her hand began to inch toward the folded news sheets.

"We have to talk about funeral arrangements," he said as she lifted the paper to peek at the headline:

NICOLE O'ROURKE GONE MISSING

But instead of feeling relieved that it was an out-dated issue, Mandria felt anger. Had Tom taken today's copy out of the house? Did he think she couldn't handle an account of her father's actions? "The funeral," she repeated. …*Well, I'll just show him differently right now!* she decided.

"Yes, I contacted your minister about the church and the service is to be in the morning—"

"He wasn't my father's minister!" she interrupted. "Father never attended any church that I know of, so you can just contact Reverend Szabo again and tell him I want nothing more than a graveside service. Tom, I want no eulogies either—and just the briefest form of the burial rites."

"…I ordered flowers too," he said next.

"Well, I don't know why!" she snapped. "For God's sake cancel them. We do not owe the man any such tribute!"

Tom sat thoughtfully drumming his fingers for a moment. "Then it will be as you wish," he nodded. And placing a kiss on her forehead, he rose and left the house again.

Her little tirade had awakened Seph, and while holding him close, a feeling of disquiet descended. "Oh, damn," she uttered. Where was the sense in what she'd just done? She had been angry with Tom for trying to protect her and so found fault with all he'd done. Now he would have to return to nearly every place he'd been that morning; exchange his instructions for hers;—and that reminded her of what Hassie had said: *Sometime you got to let him know you depend on his strength and can't make it day to day without him.* "Well, I was upset," she reasoned. "…But I will make amends," she added as an idea took shape. "Yes, Seph," she rose and started for the stairs, "by tonight, your daddy will know how much he is needed." And reaching their bedroom, she laid the baby in the cradle and began a thorough rummaging of her wardrobe…

CHAPTER 28

T om returned just after six and the sound of Mandria's laughter drew
him to the parlor, where she and Allen were enjoying a sherry.

"There you are," she started toward him, smiling beautifully, for
the success of her close attention to dressing was reflected in his eyes.
She'd chosen a spring-green gown—his favorite color. She also chose
to rise on tip-toe and kiss his mouth—allowing her favored perfume
to wreak its desired havoc on his senses. "Join us, won't you?" she drew
him into the room. "We're dining formally tonight, but you've time
for a drink first." And when Tom made no objections, she proceeded
at full sail.

Gaily, she chatted her way from the parlor to the dining table and
right through the meal—always asking Tom's advice or opinion on
whatever topic they happened upon; and encouraging him to assist her
in all the gentlemanly ways.—Oh yes, she was scoring points against
their un-named estrangement, for his dark blue eyes seldom left her...

But once retired to their room, Mandria had cause to look back
on the evening more closely. Tom had been the perfect attentive
husband...yet wasn't it Allen who laughed most; who freely returned
her banter? Allen, whose smile showed a lightness of heart? Allen,
who gave more than two or three word responses to conversational
questions?

Of course, only moments ago, Tom had had plenty to say. He
suggested that Seph share their bed for another night, quite persuasively

explaining his reason: the fear he'd suffered for the baby's life during their ordeal at Mecca Dawns. He said he wanted Seph near enough to touch should a nightmare need chasing away. He said he knew she would understand, as hadn't she spent that terrible day fearing the same thing? He finished by kissing her good-night—on the forehead again—then rolling to the far side of the bed.

And while Mandria lay awake in the darkness, she was now as certain as Hassie, that something was troubling her husband;—and it wasn't about them, for he looked at her with heart-rending love. ...But where was the fire;—the passionate nature that had always prompted him to kiss her without notice; to hold her close for no particular reason;...to want her with a frequency she found both breath-taking and eternally exciting? ... *Good dose of tears can sometime loosen things up...* she remembered more from Hassie. And closing her eyes, she vowed Tom would cry at her father's funeral, if only in sympathy for her. Yes, and once those tears were shed, they could be buried right along with the sorry man who caused them...

Mandria had no idea how soon and how easily her tears were going to surface. From the moment they stepped from the carriage the next morning, she was struck by the large crowd that had gathered in the cemetery. A few family friends were present, but only they wore somber clothing befitting the occasion. The rest were drawn by morbid curiosity;—and some, not having finished the more sensational accounts, brought their newspapers with them and stood avidly reading, as she passed. Others whispered their own sordid versions of the gossip—and not one seemed to care that she heard or saw.

But Tom cared. "Ladies and gentlemen!" he exclaimed in a tone which said he used the term loosely. "This is not a tea-party and we are not here for your entertainment. This is a funeral and you will show my wife the consideration and respect she is due, or I will bodily escort you to the gate!"

"And he won't do it alone!" Allen stepped forward to say. "Amen," chanted both Captain Herbs, doing the same.

Backing a distance away, the crowd grew waitingly silent. Even a reprimand from one of the principals in the juiciest tale of the year, was better than anything they could have hoped for. They had been noticed, and now felt included in the scheme of things…

"…Mike?" Tom extended a hand, but could not quite meet his eyes. For this time, hadn't he truly betrayed the Captain as well? And should he—or could he—tell him about it? "…When did you get in?" he finished lamely.

"Yesterday," Mike answered, a little troubled by the question. Had things been so bad Tom had lost track of what day it was? "Yeah, this isn't the way I expected to spend a *Saturday* morning," he said in a lightly informative way.

"Saturday, yes," Tom nodded. "Well thank you for the back-up; —you too, Captain Pat; Allen." And turning to his wife, he placed her hand on his arm and led her forward again.

Hidden in dark layers of veiling, Mandria's silent tears worsened. They began in mortification, over things whispered about her father. Then, her wonderful Tom had come to her defense and the tears warmed to ones of pride. But she hadn't missed the exchange between Tom and Mike and wept now for the vulnerability beneath her husband's soldiered demeanor. Tom wasn't only troubled; he was in pain…and suffering badly.

So curious was she about this discovery, the words spoken over her father passed from notice. Tom was hurting and Hassie said he needed to cry. …Well, it wasn't evident in the steady arm on which her fingers rested—and the hand covering hers was strong and soothingly deceptive. It didn't show in the way he stood—so quietly straight and erect. It wasn't visible in his handsome, stonily-set features, nor in his eyes—his dry eyes—which never left the casket before them. It occurred to Mandria then, she was looking upon that perfectly chiseled statue to which she'd once compared him. Her partner, husband and protector for life—neatly placed at her side for all the world to see. …

But what of the man within this splendid shell? What feelings raged there, waiting to spring up and choke him?

…Tears is tears, Hassie promised.—*And please, God, let mine beget some from him,* she prayed, moving aside her veils. Then lifting Tom's hand, she held it against the wetness of her cheek. She watched his lips part slightly and not caring if it was in surprise or because he struggled with hidden emotions, she raised tear-drenched eyes to his. "Tom… hold me," she whispered. "Please? I've never needed you so badly." And oblivious to the crowd or the solemnity of the service, she nestled against his broad chest, crying as if her heart were breaking—which she greatly feared it would, until his arms closed about her.

When she heard his ragged intake of breath, how her heart soared. She reached to touch the tears on his face and her joy increased. Why they cried lost importance. It only mattered that they were turning to each other for comfort. …And now, feeling no guilt or disloyalty, she could cry for a father she'd always wanted and never had. Now, she could say these things to her husband, and hopefully, he would feel free to discuss what was bothering him too. Yes, now, the healing could begin…

On the ride home, Tom remained deep in thought. And for some time afterward, he paced restlessly about the house. But Mandria didn't mind. She was glad just to have him there; hopeful too, because wherever she happened to be, he came to look in and give her half a smile. Yes, and when he was ready to talk, he had to know she was there for him.

Soon though, Mike and Patrick Herb arrived and along with Allen, Tom invited the men into his study, where they shut themselves away for nearly an hour. That Mandria had been excluded did raise her curiosity—especially when the Herbs, with Allen close behind, made a hurried exit via the hallway without stopping by the parlor to say their goodbyes. …And hadn't Mike's eyes looked suspiciously red?

"He still loves Nico," she murmured sadly. "…And whatever was said had to be hard on Tom too," she glanced toward the tall and still closed study doors, wondering if she should go in and talk with him. But before she could decide, the doorbell rang again.

"…Lucy?" Mandria looked at the girl in true surprise.

"Yes, Mandy, it's really me," she nervously clutched her purse. "May I come in?"

"Well, of course," Mandria replied, showing her into the parlor. "…And please, have a seat," she added when Lucy seemed reluctant to do so.

"Your home is very pretty," Lucy perched rather than sat on the offered chair. "It really, really is!"

"Thank you," Mandria said on another sad sigh, for they'd been friends forever, and now the distance between them had never felt greater. "…So: what have you been doing with yourself? I came by, several times, when I first returned to Savannah, but—"

"I know," Lucy injected. "You were told I wasn't home, but I was. …Mandy, it's what my parents wanted and I couldn't go against their wishes."

"Then why are you here?" Mandria had to wonder. "It's a little late to offer support when the whole city knows now, that Tom was innocent. Or is it me they don't wish you to associate with now—because of my Father? …And who will it be next week?"

"Oh, Mandy, you have every right to be upset with me," Lucy brought prayerfully laced fingers to her chin. "I was not a good friend to you and Tom.—Or to Allen," her eyes grew misty. "Instead, I let my parents tell me what to do. And now, there is nowhere else in Savannah I want to be;—nowhere else that might understand what a bad daughter will do when pushed over the edge of a cliff!"

"…What does that mean?" Mandria tried and failed to make sense of the declaration. That much about Lucy hadn't changed.

"Well, from the first, I kept telling Mama and Papa they were wrong; that they shouldn't be so ready to judge people. And when the truth was learned, I thought I deserved an I-told-you-so—and I even made so bold as to suggest we come as a family to apologize. But Papa became very angry and…I don't know, Mandy," she began to cry in earnest. "Maybe he is just too old to change—or too darn stubborn! Anyway, then I got really, really mad too, and I left and I'm here now because you've always been my friend—though I wasn't yours—and I had to tell you and hope you'd understand and everything."

"Oh, Lucy," Mandria hurried to console the sobbing girl. And as she took her hands, all resentment melted away. "I'm so sorry our troubles affected you too. It was kind of like a snowball rolling downhill, gathering more and more lives into it than I ever realized."

"Then, I'm forgiven?" she cried on. "We can be friends again?"

"Yes, Lucy," Mandria smiled. "You are very dear to me and always will be."

"Thank you;—oh, thank you so much!" she exclaimed. "…But what will Tom say when he learns I've come to stay with you?"

"I…well, I—I'm certain he'll be…surprised," Mandria used the word best describing her own reaction. "And cordial, of course," she added, praying she was right. She was not even going to try guessing what Allen would have to say. "…But yes, you are welcome to use our guest room."

"Then I think I will," Lucy rose unsteadily and dabbed her eyes. "Mandy, I've been walking the streets since early this morning, carrying a satchel with all the clothes I could get into it. …I went to the graveyard too, but I didn't know if you'd want me there, so I watched from the fence, and then walked some more—until I found the nerve to knock on your door."

"Lucy…you must be exhausted!" Mandria said in amazement.

"I could use a nap—and maybe a cold cloth for my eyes," she snubbed. "…My bag is on the porch, if you don't mind my getting it now."

"Of course, and the guest room is on the front here, just over this parlor. Go now, and I'll bring up some fresh water," she urged. "—And maybe something to eat?"

"No, just water, thank you," Lucy turned to leave, but halted sharply. For there, filling the doorway stood Tom.

"Hello, Lucy," he said—cordially. And looking at Mandria with an expression she couldn't name, he added, "Your analogy about snowballs was quiet correct. ...And did you know, at last count, Brittany had adopted two kittens into this growing menagerie?" Then, with an arm about Lucy's shoulder, he steered her toward the stairs. "Go on up. I'll get your bag," he directed.

Mandria was still puzzling over what was said when he came to the door and spoke to her again. "You'd best hurry with that water. Your kitten looks as if she could do with some attention—especially if the weight of this damned bag means anything." Then he was gone and her puzzlement grew.

"...Was he complimenting or criticizing me?" she asked. He hadn't smiled this time—not even half-way—and yet, he had managed to put together sentences of more than a few words, so that was an improvement. ...Wasn't it? Yes, it had to mean he wanted to communicate; that he was trying. She would simply have to be patient a while longer...

As the day wore on, however, Mandria began to wonder at the ways human patience could be tested. It began when Lucy rose from her nap and came upon Allen in the front hall. No one had thought to inform him of her presence and turning his back, Allen abruptly left the house without speaking a single word. Visibly shaken, Lucy returned to her room for a good cry.

It took a while, but she was finally coaxed from hiding, and hoping to cheer her, Mandria invited Lucy to her own bedroom for Seph's afternoon feeding. "So what do you think of my son?" she smiled, propping comfortably in the bed pillows.

"He is just...precious," Lucy said, looking quickly away from Mandria's gaze, as if to appreciate the décor. "You did all this yourself, didn't you, Mandy?" she asked with too much exuberance. "—And now you have it all: a husband, a baby and a really beautiful home!"

"Yes, I suppose I do," Mandria answered. ...*Maybe,* she added inwardly. The home and baby, certainly, but her husband continued to wander the premises as if searching for the place where he fit into their lives. ...*The fool!* she thought in annoyment.

"I'm so jealous," Lucy said as fresh tears sprang to her eyes. "I ruined my chance for this—ruined it for ever and ever!"

"No you haven't," Mandria said. "Why would you think so?"

"Because I turned my back on Allen—as he just did to me—and I still love him. But you saw how famous I am with him now. He hates me;—he really, really does!"

"Now, I don't believe that's true," Mandria proceeded carefully. "Of course, Allen hasn't confided in me, but there is something you should already know about the Scott brothers. Loyalty to family and friends is strongly ingrained in them both. Even when they've been wronged, you can trust them to do what is right. Lucy, I gave up on my marriage. I failed Tom far worse than you failed Allen. But he knew we belonged together and chased me half way across two states and back, just to prove it. …So, if you're asking my advice," she added, now ashamed of her moment of pique with Tom, "I would say, give Allen time to adjust and believe in his sense of fairness." Then a smile tugged at Mandria's mouth as she realized something of importance to her own situation. "If the Scott men have a fault, it's that they demand more of themselves than they do of others. And it's only when they think they've failed in some way that a problem arises…"

"I…I'm not sure I know what you mean," Lucy shrugged.

And Mandria had to laugh. She'd started this to bolster Lucy's spirits, and now felt amazingly better herself. "I guess I'm just saying how much I love my husband—even if he isn't the god he expects himself to be. Allen won't disappoint you, either, though the wait can be maddening. But Lucy, a Scott is well worth it."

"Oh, Mandy, if I could only hope…" And rising on the crest of a new flood of tears, Lucy again fled back to her room.

Naturally, Mandria was distressed, but there was little she could do while Seph continued to nurse so greedily. "Dear Lord," she sighed, closing her eyes, "if there is a purpose to any of this, I do wish You would make it known to me."

"Do you now?" asked Tom, as he stood leaning against the door jamb with folded arms.

"Were you eavesdropping—again?" she quelled her surprise in a smile, hoping to coax one from him.

"No," he lowered his eyes to examine the toe of his boot. "Nevertheless, I do keep running into your pearly words of wisdom everywhere I go."

"My pearly words...?" she started, stopped and began anew, vowing to remain calm and reasonable. "Tom, are you angry because Lucy is here?"

"Not at all," he nodded. "—As long as these little scenarios aren't being staged for my benefit."

"Would you care to explain that?" her eyes shot green-tinted arrows in spite of her recent rededication to patience. She had just been accused of something—she knew not what—and by a husband she adored, but could not, for the moment, imagine why!

Then Tom did the one thing that wasn't expected. "Pull in your claws, little cat," he teased, but sobered almost at once. "...I just find it strange that in one day, you've managed to say so much of importance."

Somewhat mollified, Mandria eased back into the pillows again. "Why don't you join us, here, and we'll talk about it."

"...Not just yet," he said—and she didn't miss the yearning in his tone. "...Mandria, when we lived at the cabin, do you remember the hours I spent in the workshop?"

"Yes, but I suspect it was because you needed a place to escape my fits of ill-temper," she offered.

"Well...that may have been 2nd or 3rd on my list of needs," and this came with another of those half-smiles. "Anyway, I had to stay busy—to keep from dwelling too much on the number one need—and I discovered that building things really did help me to think through my problems more clearly."

"...And?" Mandria wondered where this was leading.

"And I saw some tools out in the carriage house, so I'm going out there for a while. ...I just thought I'd tell you, in case you heard the noise."

Mandria nodded. "All right. But what do you want to make?"

"I don't know yet," Tom shrugged as he turned to leave. "But it will have a hell of a lot of nails in it."

And for a second time that day, Mandria could only utter, "What on earth…?"

———◈———

That had been over an hour ago, and after placing Seph on a pallet beside Tandy, Mandria stood looking from the kitchen door.

"He still at it?" Joleen asked. And Mandria sent her a look of astoundment. No one could miss hearing that continuous pounding. But at least it helped to muffle Lucy's snubbing—and she sat right there at the table.

Then the door bell rang—again—and Joleen went up to answer it. She returned much pleased with herself. "That was Captain Mike and Ah sent him 'round to the back, so now maybe that racket going to stop!"

It did. And as there was only Lucy to contend with, Mandria put her to shelling a pan of butter beans, which soon quieted her too.

However, it didn't last. Now both Tom and Mike were hammering away—and on top of that, Allen came home. He had almost reached the bottom step before spying Lucy, and then he marched straight for the back door, slamming it, as he also proceeded to the carriage house.

"Reckon he going to start that too?" Willie Luther rubbed his head, which was already pounding enough from within. "If he do, think Ah'll take some more medicine and lay down for a while."

Again the hammering ceased, leading Lucy to a conclusion Mandria couldn't refute. "They're talking about me," she said meekly. "Allen is telling Tom he doesn't want me here!" And up the stairs she went, crying harder than ever.

Mandria had to follow, of course, and against a trio of hammers, she managed to calm Lucy by reaffirming her welcome and promising to speak with Allen on her behalf. While returning to the kitchen, Mandria made herself a promise as well. She was going to add a word or two about Allen's lack of manners!

"Oh, Lawd," Willie moaned, heading for his bedroom, Laudanum bottle in hand. "Don't know how them babies sleeping through all that."

"I don't either," Mandria had to agree as she looked from the window this time. "But it's getting dark and they'll have to stop soon, for the sake of the neighbors, if nothing else. ...So, let's do something about supper, shall we Joleen?"

The preparation presented no problems and soon the freshly shelled beans and a pot of potatoes were simmering over the fire. But how many they were to serve—and where—certainly did.

"Captain Mike going to eat too?" asked Joleen, counting as she sliced off pieces of roast beef.

"He'll be asked to stay," Mandria nodded, adding another plate to her stack. "And that will make seven of us."

"No, Willie done took his medicine and he'll be asleep, so that's six," Joleen corrected. And Mandria returned a plate to the cabinet. "So, what about Miss Lucy? She going to feel like coming down?"

"Well, she hasn't eaten all day—so yes, I'll insist that she join us," Mandria gave a determined nod and began setting the table.

"Better not put her close to Mr. Allen," Joleen advised. "Do and she going to take another run up them stairs."

"Damn!" Mandria sat with a bump. "Joleen, is there no way—no *peaceful* way—we can all just enjoy a meal together? This is worse than trying to feed troops on a battlefield;—and those hammers couldn't sound more like cannons if they tried!"

"...Miss Mandy," Joleen came to sit beside her, "lots of us feel like we been in a war. All carrying wounds too—some inside, some out. Maybe, you just trying too hard. Maybe, a peaceful meal have to wait for the dust to settle."

"And the healing to begin," Mandria cited words that had kept her going all day. And after a moment, as hard as it was, she managed a smile. "Joleen, do you remember when those terrible sisters came here to sew? We were both crying that day. But we survived them, and we'll survive this."

"Well, we did have some help from Miss Evelyn," Joleen smiled too. "But Ah think we done growed up some since then. Likely, we could handle most anything now."

"...Mama," Mandria lowered her head on folded arms. "Lord, I miss her—especially when I'm this tired and confused. She could always tell and there she would be with a hug and some good common sense answers. You know, even when we disagreed—and we certainly did about Tom—I knew she still cared. Once, she was so angry with me, she stomped from the room and slammed the door. ...But that, too, was done with such love."

"Yeah, Ah bet she missing you too..." Joleen glanced up as a shadow crossed the doorway. And listening, hard, she realized the trio of hammers was a duet again. Looking, hard, into the fading twilight, she saw Tom in retreat, but then he turned and went up the steps to the level above. And she wondered, hard, on what he'd overheard to change his mind about coming through the kitchen.

"I'm sure Mama does miss me," Mandria rose and began collecting the plates from the table. "Listen, we'll just leave these by the pots and I'll take Lucy up a tray. We can give ourselves that much peace anyway."

"Kind of a informal buffet," Joleen nodded, going to the window. And at once, she franticly motioned Mandria to join her. For there was Tom heading back to the carriage house with a bottle and three glasses. "Yeah, for those of us going to feel like eating," she added, turning to stir the butter beans. Mandria said nothing as she watched her husband. It would have been impossible to speak anyway, with her heart fluttering so wildly. ...She was now remembering a night when Tom had taken a bottle to the stable while she had a bath. What happened when he returned was as close as she came to giving in to him. Of course, they'd both had a few drinks at that point—but it could happen again tonight. And this time, she wouldn't stop it...

But time passed and though the hammering did finally cease, no one came in for supper. ...Or anything else. "Well," Mandria gazed at the lighted windows across the courtyard, "...should I go out there, Joleen?"

"Ah wouldn't want to myself," she answered. "Men what drinking for fun, usually get to talking and laughing out loud. Haven't heard a peep from them, so must be something serious going on."

"And my presence wasn't requested," Mandria uttered, realizing she'd been excluded yet again. Disappointment and a liberal pinch of resentment were such that she no longer had an appetite. "Joleen, do me a favor, will you?" she started for the stairs with Seph. "Take a tray to Lucy and tell her I said to stay in her room for the night. Tell her I'll explain tomorrow—when I've thought of how to do that," she added sardonically.

"But where you going?" Joleen called.

"To bed," Mandria answered. ...*Alone again!* she thought and she was really growing unhappy with that...

CHAPTER 29

More time passed. Mandria was now dressed for bed, but couldn't relax enough to lie down. It had been hard enough sitting through Seph's feeding. "Well, at least he can sleep," she tucked the baby into his cradle, "—even if I'll be pacing the floor until dawn, evidently!" But midway into her second lap about the room, she stopped. "I'm being silly—I know I'm just being silly," she tried shaming herself. It wasn't working, though. "Then do something!" she imparted a stomp to the carpet. "Go tell your husband how you feel about these secret talks—and if nothing else, demand equal time."

...But dare she? Could she face down three troubled men who were obviously seeking solace from a bottle? Obviously so, for she'd put on her robe and was already marching down the stairs. ...*Am I sure?* she wondered. And apparently she was, for her slippers were taking her over the veranda, down the steps and across the courtyard. ... *But is this the right thing for Tom?* she halted and lowering the hand which had already reached for the carriage house door, she stood there undecided...

"Allen, how many times must I repeat this?" she heard Tom say, in a less-than-sober voice. "Mandria just buried her father today—and there is enough damned pressure on her without you causing more. Now, if she can forgive Lucy, so can you. Lucy is young, after all, and was only following her parent's orders. That isn't something to condemn her for. It's to be admired...sort of."

346

"Oh-hell-yes!" slurred Mike. "And coming here today was a clear choice—an adult choice—in spite of her damned old gouty papa."

"Maybe, but listen to who is giving advice," Allen pitted his garble-voiced argument against theirs. "This one carries a torch for a woman who never loved him enough; and the other has all the woman he wants, but is letting a dead man keep them apart!"

And with a hand now pressed to her heart, Mandria slid into the shadows next to an open window...

"Enough, Allen!" Tom declared. "There is no use bringing that up again. It was hard enough telling Mike the true story—and damn if I enjoy being reminded of this particular failure!"

"One time—just one time—when you were not in full command of a situation and your entire life is a failure?" Allen continued. "Who named you God, Tom? Who said just being there made you responsible for what Sam did? Never mind that it was done to you—no, that can't matter. Tom has to be at fault!"

"Well, damn," Tom remarked. "That is twice today I've been accused of playing God. But I'm not God—and no one knows that better than I do."

"Yeah, well, welcome to the human race," Mike raised his glass. "So, here's to a whole world full of failures; to all men who sought the unattainable and fell flat on their God damned asses!"

"That's a bit fatalistic, Captain," Tom countered. "You acted in good faith, even if Nico never could—and somewhere out there is a woman who will appreciate the fine man you are."

"And your woman would probably appreciate you taking your own damned advice, Brer," said Allen.

"Well, I have some for you too," Tom said in rebuttal. "At least give Lucy the courtesy—"

"Quiet, both of you!" Mike demanded. "Now, I'm the only one here to have loved and lost—so damned far. And because—so damned far—Tom has preferred hammering to hearing what I came to say, I now claim the right to arbitrate between the Scott brothers: You, Allen, are treating Lucy as if listening to her parents was an unpardonable sin. But God knows, if Nico had listened more to her father, things might be very different for me. Think about that, boy. Lucy is a good girl who is crazy about you—and you'd better wake up and see it."

"Amen," Tom muttered—which drew Mike's attention to him.

"And you, Tom Scott, are a bigger damned fool than your brother."

"Oh, amen; amen; amen!" injected Allen.

"Shut up!" Tom and Mike chimed, precisely together.

"So," Mike continued, "when you told me what happened between you and Nico, I didn't take it well. Then Uncle Pat and your bad-ass little brother, here, made me see why you told me. You knew I loved Nico as much as Mandy loves you. And gauging my reaction to the story, gave you an idea of what to expect from your wife."

"No, Mike…at least, I don't think that was the reason," Tom nodded, unsure now. "If so, it was damned selfish—which makes me twice the bastard."

"There he goes again!" Allen said in exasperation. "All the evils of the world resting right on his shoulders."

"Nonetheless, let's just suppose I'm right," Mike over-spoke him. "Tom, in spite of what you told me, I came back, didn't I? And that's because it took a lot of guts for you to admit the truth; guts you wouldn't have if you'd purposely betrayed me—or Mandy. For God's sake, man, you were bound hand and foot—and bound by nature to react as you did."

"But it made me part of the things done to her," Tom argued. "I didn't want to be, but damn it, I was!"

"Don't you think Sam Lucas knew how you'd feel?" Allen asked. "He was a master at using people."

"This time, Allen's right," Mike added. "The bastard couldn't be satisfied with killing you—oh-hell-no! He had to destroy your dignity;—to make you believe you were capable of the same unspeakable acts he and Shurling enjoyed. Tom, his victory wouldn't have been complete without bringing you down to his level."

"And you're letting Sam win as long as you keep debating this with yourself," said Allen.

Then in unison, the three men scrambled to their feet as Mandria swung the door open and came in. She briefly glanced their way, but said nothing as she turned to look over the place. Still without a word, and nodding in wonder, she approached a tree-thick rafter support column, bristling with shiny nail heads, and circled it slowly. The silence continued as she went now to her husband, took his hand and towed him toward the door. But once she had ushered him out, she turned to impart some information to the other two. "Allen; Mike; supper is in the kitchen—should you be hungry," she gave the near-empty bottle a look. "Allen, lay out a pillow and sheets, if Mike cares to sleep over on the sofa." And these words were said in tones ranging from stern to gracious. "Now, good-night, gentlemen…and thank you," she added, which brought wide smiles from them both. For this came with an expression of unquestioned fondness.

"As for you, sir,—upstairs!" she turned again to prod Tom forward. "No! Not one word, just move!" she insisted when he attempted to speak.

So Tom went, thinking it had been a number of years since he'd heard such stricture. Then it came from his mother and usually meant he was in for a spanking…but what could it mean now? Mandria's eyes were sending green tinted shards sharp enough to score leather, and if she'd heard too much out there—oh, hell, was he in for it! … Yet, why had she thanked Allen and Mike; and why, in turn, had they felt imitating a pair of grinning idiots was in order? Some friend and brother he had! Oh-so-ready with advice but let the real trouble start and on whose side had they come down?

He braced as they entered the bedroom, waiting for the door to slam, for then he'd know just how angry Mandria was. But all he heard was a soft click and reasoned, of course, that Seph's presence accounted for that. Then followed the sound of the key turning in the lock, and he felt a beading of sweat on upper lip.

Mandria was coming toward him now, and Tom watched as she began to circle him—slowly—much as she'd done the support column. "Well?" she finally paused to look him in the eye, and standing close so their hushed voices would not wake the baby. "Would you care to explain your behavior?" And as Tom couldn't fathom her direction, he didn't dare a reply. "I mean it!" she went on. "Do you realize you've given everyone in this house a splitting headache?—And what for? So you could pound hundreds of nails into a perfectly good post, which didn't need one bit of help to hold up the carriage house roof!"

"I—well…I couldn't find any lumber," he offered, expelling a breath he'd been holding forever. Perhaps she hadn't heard over much. …But why, then, had she locked the door? "And I'm sorry about your headache.—Maybe a good night's sleep would cure it?"

"No-it-would-not!" her arms flew akimbo, but remembering to keep the volume down, "Thomas Scott, I demand an apology for that suggestion alone!"

"I said I was sorry," he nodded, "I didn't mean to give you a headache."

"Oh, please!" she said in exasperation. "Would you please stop playing the imbecile? *You*, sir, are purposely excluding *me* from *your* life, and *I* want it *stopped!*" she ordered, each emphasized word accompanied by a poke to his chest. "—Or am I to assume you now prefer the company of males to mine?"

"No! You have to know I love you more than my own life, but Seph is not yet a month old and—"

"And," she interrupted, "before your trip to Mecca Dawns, it was *I* who had to keep reminding *you* of that! Since, you have not even hugged me unless I forced myself into your arms."

So much for that excuse, Tom thought, …*but where to go from here?* "Well, what happened that day," he paused, lowering his eyes, "…well, I've had a few problems with it, that's all."

"Ones you'd rather confide to Allen or the Herbs," she returned. "…Of course, that is my fault, so maybe I should apologize to you instead."

"Lady, *you've* nothing to apologize for," he met her eyes instantly, his inflection implying it was definitely the other way around.

"Yes, I do, Tom," she insisted. "Your reluctance stems from the way I treated and doubted you the first time Father tried to separate us. Had I believed in you then, you'd be able to trust me now. In your heart, you would know there is no problem we can't solve together."

Tom nodded. "You can't blame yourself for your father's expertise," he borrowed a line from Allen, "He was a master at using people."

"The way he used you; knowing you'd blame yourself?" she countered. "And as Allen also said, you are letting him win if you keep debating this with yourself."

"You're quoting from the carriage house?" Tom's heartbeat accelerated. "…So, how much did you hear?"

"All of it. You don't hold a corner on eavesdropping," she folded her arms smugly. "And if you expected me to go screaming about the room like a banshee—well, I haven't, have I?"

"…No," he answered, but not before bringing everything about her under close scrutiny. "I just wish you hadn't heard it that way," he sank on the edge of the bed.

"But had I waited to hear it from you, when would that have been?" she questioned.

"I don't know," he admitted. "Soon—maybe; …someday."

"And meanwhile, our marriage could have fallen apart."

"Mandria…what do you want me to say?" he shrugged. "That what happened is excused because I wish it hadn't? Or maybe you think pretending it didn't happen makes me the husband you deserve and everything will be just fine again?"

"Oh, no, Thomas Scott, you *are* the husband I deserve—and the only man I will have," she lifted his face in her hands. "Pretending is for children," she placed a kiss on the edge of his mouth. "I am a woman, fully grown, who isn't about to lose you to some off-the-wall game with your conscience." And this time, her lips lingered hungry and sweet upon his.

"Lady, for God's sake stop!" Tom demanded, but contrary to the words, his arms pulled her with him as he fell back across the bed. And Mandria laughed, for the fit of their bodies could not have suited her better. "Oh, damn," he groaned, quickly turning her to lie beside him. "Mandria, please be serious—please?" he asked, with a definite strain in his voice. "Now, you started this talk, and I think we should finish it."

"All right," she agreed, "as long as you will concede a few points to me—and meet one term."

"What points?" he eyed her impish expression suspiciously, "—And what term?"

"First, admit that you want to be with me; and then that wild horses couldn't drag you away from your home and family."

"Done. ...But you haven't heard the details...and you may feel differently once you have."

"Well, I intend to prove you wrong—which leaves only my term," she sat up to unfasten her robe. "You may as well join me, Tom. As you said to me once, I want nothing between us now, but truth."

Tom also came forward, stilling her hands. "Mandria, I won't make love to you, if that is what you're hoping—and on this, I will not budge. Even if I'd never been to Shurling's place, I wouldn't. It's too soon and might endanger your health."

"...But I feel fine;—truly I do," she smiled, touched that he cared.

"You feel *too* fine—which is precisely the point," he forced his eyes from nipples shadowed beneath her thin lawn gown. "Lady, you didn't escape this ordeal unscathed—not when you are so willing to behave unwisely. Now, Lord knows, I appreciate the offer, but I will not budge on this."

"All right," Mandria nodded, knowing he meant it. "...After the better part of a year, another week or two won't matter, I suppose." Then her eyes came into play, disarming Tom completely. "There is nothing to keep you from stripping, however." And her hands danced over his shirt buttons, undoing them easily. "So, I guess you'll just have trust me, as you've never been able to before, and allow me the use of your body."

"...I don't know as I've ever had a more tempting proposal," he uttered, going back into the pillows, where she moved the material aside and spread fingers warm and wide across his chest.

"This body belongs to me—no matter the restrictions we must place on it just now," she said, guiding her hands into a downward slide. "There," she added as they came to caress and to hold the most volatile and vulnerable part of his being. "...If I could only stir the inner man so easily. Don't hide him from me, Tom.—Please don't. Bad or good, I need to share your thoughts and feelings about everything that happened. I want to touch you as intimately within as I'm doing here."

Grasping her arms, Tom drew her up until she lay stretched along his length, his arms wrapped and holding her pressed as closely against him as was possible, her head tucked beneath his chin. "I'm going to say this quickly, Mandria, because I can still hardly stand thinking about it: ...Your father and Shurling wanted me to settle a bet. Oscar said any man would become aroused watching a sexual encounter. Sam bet him that I wouldn't. Anyway, when I refused to go along, they found a way of forcing it. It seems Oscar had a craving for breast milk and Joleen was offered to satisfy that. As he put it, if I didn't co-operate *the little ones would go without supper...* So, I disrobed and I had to watch every filthy thing done to Nico. But that bet was never the point. Sam was out to prove something else; —something I helped him do, damn it! I was tied to the cage, and Nico was placed where Oscar could take her from behind...while she was to take me in her mouth. And it happened—I fought it, but it happened. ...So, now you know. And this time, I wouldn't blame you for leaving me for someone with more courage or morals—or whatever the hell it is that I'm lacking."

There was a terrible moment of silence, followed by a deeply distressed moan from Mandria. "...Let go of me," she finally managed in a strangled voice. And Tom ached as she rolled to sit on the edge of the bed, her quaking shoulders, proving the wretched effect of his tale.

"...Lady, I'm so sorry," he nodded, not daring to touch her. "But you wanted to know the inner man and now you know there isn't much of value here."

"I'm sorry too," she inhaled, looking his way with tear-bright eyes, "for all you've suffered for loving me.—And Tom, if you dare to suggest we separate one more time, I am going to smack you right in the mouth!"

Confused, he nodded again. "But you pulled away—and surely in disgust."

"I did no such thing!" she said, holding her side. "You were just so into your story, you squeezed too hard and I couldn't breathe," she laughed a bit. Then, leaning over him again, she said, "Now, would you please kiss me?—And I'll accept no more pecks on the forehead, damn you. I want to be kissed like you mean it; and I want your hands everywhere else!"

Tom looked at his wife—his beautiful, green-eyed, tan-haired wife. And for the first time since leaving Mecca Dawns, he felt something other than depression. It began almost like a bubble rattling about in his chest, rose up his throat as if suddenly released from mooring, and spilled from his mouth as laughter. "Oh, yes ma'am!" he laughed, harder, marveling at how wonderful it felt. Then, he was kissing her deeply, and his hands were, literally, everywhere else…

"Good morning, ladies," Mandria smiled coming down to the kitchen. "Here, Hassie, hold Seph while I get some coffee, will you?" And depositing the baby, she hummed her way to the hearth.

"Somebody mighty chipper this morning," Hassie observed. "Must have had a good night's sleep—or something."

"As a matter of fact, we hardly slept at all—which is why we saw you arrive a while ago," Mandria returned to choose a fresh sweet-roll from the box Hassie had also brought. "Anyway, Tom and I are making a trip, and there were so many plans to make, we talked nearly all night."

"A trip?" Joleen smiled. "So where you going?"

"Back to Athens for the rest of our family," she answered.

"When?" Allen asked, coming down to join the conversation. "Because if you don't mind, I'd like to go too. I could use some time away from…this house," he finished sourly.

"Well, of course you're welcomed to join us," Mandria had to point out, "but Allen, *this house*—and all in it—will still be here when you return."

"Except for me," Mike joined them too. "Thanks for the use of the sofa, Mandy," he yawned. "Now may I have a cup of that coffee And Joleen went to get it, but poured an extra cup, on hearing Tom on the stairs too.

"Morning, people!" he beamed a smile and going straight for his wife, placed a kiss on her mouth that left her blushing. "I'm sure Mandria told you our plans," he swung a leg over a chair and sat next to her, "—so Mike can we book a cabin for tomorrow morning?"

"No problem," he nodded, but gently, for he and Allen had finished that bottle the previous evening. "I must be getting too old for these drinking bouts," he said, amazed that Allen's eyes weren't the least bit bloodshot, while his felt like one of those little red pin cushions from a sewing box. "Yeah, maybe I need to take a trip somewhere too. It might be good to see new things; …to think new thoughts."

"Then, why don't you come with us too?" Mandria offered, knowing he spoke of Nicole…and, perhaps, a need to move on? "Athens is really a pretty place, and I know you'd enjoy it."

"More than you did on our first trip there, I hope," Tom teased her. "But yes, Mike, do come. We might even get in a day of fishing— and to tell you the truth, I could use your help getting my family, their pets and all their belongings back to the Irish Mist. Matter of fact," he sent his wife a covert look, "it might take two wagons and Allen and I will need spelling from time to time, because I doubt either Mamalyn or Mandria has ever driven one."

Mandria nodded appropriately—and in wonder. Her mother had a trunk, of course, but belongings for the children would have fit in a pillowcase. Tom's speech, then, went to show he'd also sensed Mike's desire for change in his life.

"I'll think about it," replied the Captain. "I have until we get to Augusta, so I'll let you know."

"…Excuse me?" said Lucy, who stood on the bottom step, fingers primly laced, and for once, dry eyed. "Allen, I wish to speak with you, please. In private?—In the parlor, please?" And she turned and went back upstairs again.

"Well, what nerve!" Allen's color deepened. "How dare she come down here—uninvited—and think she can order me around!"

"Don't be the fool that I was, little brother," Tom said, as Mike tried to ward-off a grin. "Go up and talk to the girl. Tell her your feelings—even your resentments—and let her tell you hers."

"Do it, Allen," Mandria presented the motivating point, "if nothing else, you can tell her what you think of her."

"Well, that I can do!" he rose, taking the stairs in twos. "And hold your ears, ladies. I don't intend to mince words!"

When the clumping of his boots had died away, it was replaced by a chuckle from Mike. "He won't be too rough on her, will he?"

"He'll try to be," Tom answered. "But like his older brother, once in love with the right woman, always in love with her." And the look he was giving Mandria had her wearing a most becoming blush...

"All right, Miss Lucille Donnita Love, you asked for this and you are certainly going to get it!" Allen stormed into her presence. "And I don't want to hear tired excuses—like you were only following your parents' orders!"

"But I was, Allen," she looked at the hands folded in her lap. "In my entire life, I have never disobeyed them once...until now. They fed and clothed me; sick or well, they were there to care for me and I wouldn't want to hurt them for the world. You loved your mother that much, didn't you? I mean, had she asked the same of you, wouldn't you have done it?"

"I didn't know my mother that long—which is beside the damn point!" he snapped. "But I don't think she'd ever have asked me to stop seeing someone I loved;—not over a dirty bit of gossip about the family!" Allen added self righteously. "And stop sitting there staring at your hands," he turned away. "...That is just the way you looked the last time I came by your house—like a timid mouse, even afraid to squeak!"

"I was afraid...then and now," she said softly. "Whether you know it or not, Allen, things haven't gone smoothly for me either. I knew my parents were wrong and though I obeyed them, we've done nothing all these months but argue about it. I was so miserable, I hardly left the house at all, except for church every Sunday, and I only went there to pray for us—and for Tom, of course. Over and over, I asked God to help Tom prove his innocence, because that was the only way I could see of changing Mama and Papa's minds about you. ...But it didn't, when it should have and our last argument ended in bitterness. I left them both in tears," she snubbed back some of her own. "And that hurt me so deeply, but I'm not going back and if you reject me too, I don't know what will become of me. I can't impose on Mandy forever and I've nowhere else to go and no way on earth of maintaining myself alone—and I know I'll just end up starving to death in some gutter. I really, really will!"

Allen still stood with his back turned, but he didn't need to look to know she was crying—not, sobbing exactly, for she hadn't the breath after that non-stop confession. And much as he hated admitting it, he had been impressed. ...*Imagine*, he mused, *all those months I felt so alone, Lucy was arguing on my behalf—and praying for us every Sunday.* '...*Think about that, boy,*' Mike had said. '*Lucy is a good girl, who is crazy about you—and you'd better wake up and see it*' ...*But I am awake!* he thought then. *And not some weak-kneed boy to be swayed by female tears!* ...*Yet, a lot could happen to a good girl waiting to starve in a gutter.* ...And glancing over his shoulder, he knew this little mouse wouldn't stand a chance on the streets. *She's too damned gullible; too trusting;— and what she really should do, is go home!* "Lucy," he turned with every intention of telling her so. "...Where are you going?" he asked instead, for she'd risen and started from the room.

"To get my things," she answered without pausing. "I think your silence explains your feelings well enough. You've none left for me. But thank you for listening, anyway. It was most kind of you, really. ...Really, really kind."

"But you're going home—aren't you?" And for unexplained reasons, that was now the last place he thought she should be.

"No," she replied, moving up the stairs.

"…Well, what kind of answer is that?" he yelled, following behind. "You can't just up and leave with no where to go!"

"Allen, there is no use hollering at me—there really and truly isn't," she turned in the doorway of the guest room to face him. "Only a gentleman would show this concern, but I won't burden you any longer than it takes to pack my valise." Then she quietly closed the door in his face.

"Damn," Allen muttered. "Well…damn," he began a furious bit of back and forth pacing.

From the bottom of the stairway came a deep familiar voice. "Little brother?" Tom called softly, and waited for Allen to look over the railing. "May I have a word with you? Come down here," he added, sitting on the steps. "I don't think I'd want any of the ladies to hear this."

Heaving a sigh, Allen went down and claimed a spot beside Tom. "Well, what is it?" he asked, his manner showing a depth of frustration.

"A question first," Tom began. "Before all my troubles started, when you first came to know Lucy well, were you falling in love with her?"

"I…uh, I suppose I thought I was," Allen's answer came grudgingly.

"And you do realize she still cares very much for you too?"

"Too?" Allen objected. "I didn't say I felt that way now!"

"But you do, or you wouldn't have chased her up the stairs. Lucy wants to stay—to be where you are. And she gave you every chance to ask, which you muffed royally."

"So how would my ever-wise big brother have handled it?" Allen's attempt at sarcasm was over-ridden by the curiosity in his eyes.

"I wouldn't pretend to know how to handle your woman," Tom planted that little seed nicely. "I only came up to tell you the Captain just left and the rest of us are leaving now, to drive Hassie home—including Joleen and Willie."

"So?"

"All the way out to Marsh Haven. …And all the way back."

"So?" Allen repeated, impatiently.

Tom looked at his brother in wonder. "So, I did not hear the door lock when Lucy closed it. And unless I've missed my guess completely, she would not be adverse to a visit from you."

Allen's astonishment appeared on a flush of color—and a hushed voice. "But we've never—I mean…you're not suggesting—Tom, if I just walked into that bedroom…why, she'd slap my face!"

"Just the type of woman we Scott's seem to prefer, mores the pity," Tom nodded. "I will remind you, though, this is a respectable house and we never take unfair advantage of our ladies—especially one who feels as lost and vulnerable as Lucy does at the moment. And remember: you can not go where you aren't welcome; you can't take more than you're willing to give;—and nothing that isn't given freely."

"To Marsh Haven…and back," Allen uttered.

"Yes, but only if you really love her, little brother," Tom said as he rose. "Just go slowly and perhaps, when we return, things will be more settled around here?"

"Maybe so," Allen rose too. And as Tom disappeared down the kitchen stairs, Allen gathered all his nerve and started upward. … Should he knock and ask admittance or just go in and catch her unawares?—And what was he going to say? …Was a declaration in order, or would she know if he simply took her in his arms? And kissed her? And… Then, standing before Lucy's door, he looked at the toes of his boots. This was the hardest step he would ever take—one more, and his future could be decided…

"Tom! Come here—come quickly!" Mandria said from the guestroom doorway. "Look, she isn't here!" she added as he joined her. "Lucy is gone and so are her clothes! There's not a note, either. She's just gone!"

"That damned fool bungled it again!" Tom muttered, marching toward Allen's room, his wife close behind. "We'll see if he has any idea where she is and then—" He bumped head-on into a locked door. "Allen!" he shouted at it. "Open the damned door!"

"…Just a moment—I'm coming," came a muffled reply. And after what seemed an unusually long moment, Allen peeked from a partially cracked opening. "I'm not dressed, if that was Mandy's voice I heard," he said almost sheepishly. "—And you're back earlier than expected too," he swiped at his much-tousled hair.

"But Lucy—Allen, where is Lucy?" Mandria pled.

"Yes," Tom said looking angrier by the minute. "Did you just turn her out on the street? You probably didn't have the decency to carry her bag down either—or did you, and then just throw it out behind her?"

"No, Brer, I carried her bag. From there," he pointed to the guest room, "to here, because—because we got married this afternoon, and the trip to Athens will be our honeymoon."

Silence followed, bracketed by two shocked expressions. "You're married?" Mandria finally managed, as her hand crawled to her cheek. "To Lucy?"

Then Tom was laughing and extending his hand in congratulations. "Well, maybe you aren't such a bungler after all!—Open up, Allen, we'd like to welcome your bride!" And a frantic squeal from within said Lucy had just buried herself beneath the covers.

"Tom—stop that!" Mandria tugged at his arm, laughing too. "Come on, now. I'm sure we'll see them at supper.—Won't we Allen?"

"Probably so," he glanced toward Lucy for confirmation. But she was just sitting up again and the sheet fell away from her beautiful large breasts, stirring him every bit as much as the first time he saw them. "Oh, or maybe not!" Allen said slamming the door shut abruptly.

And returning to the bed, to take her in his arms again, he couldn't help smiling. He loved Lucy for the delightful person she was. But to capture such a prize as those lovely, huge breasts into the bargain— and without having knowledge of it—was truly amazing! …*No*, he thought as she snuggled them closely against his bare chest, *we won't be down for supper.—Later, maybe, so we'll know when to be ready for the trip…but no, supper is definitely out of the question…*

"Mandria," Tom chuckled as they descended the stairs, "…do you suppose there is some sort of mark on our door that only the orphaned and homeless can see?"

"I don't think so," she smiled. "Maybe it's just that the happiness here shines from the windows like a welcome beacon."

"Well, I'll tell you something I'd welcome," he nodded. "I hope Mike does decide to go with us, because that brother of mine is going to be less than useless now."

"Oh?" she teased. "So, Allen doesn't know how to drive a wagon either?"

"He knows, lady," Tom stopped in the front hall to pull her to him. "But he is a Scott—and we do adore making love to our women." Then he was kissing her, proving the truth he spoke…

CHAPTER 30

$\mathcal{S}$usan Watched as John and Brittany skipped far ahead on the road home. "Left behind again," she sighed, wondering why it bothered her so. This was a daily ritual, for the children were anxious to play for a while before starting their homework. …But since Tom's letter had arrived last week, being left behind seemed to apply to more in her life than the distance between school and home.

"So you have a crippled foot," she tried shaming away her mood. "But few other women have managed as well—not alone, and not on two good feet. Susan, you support yourself adequately and can hold your own with *any* man, on *any* subject he cares to discuss!" … It wasn't her fault that most men were as intimidated by her quick mind as by her deformity.

And then, there was Tom, who'd never been bothered by either. Tom, the one man she had known worth having and whom she'd sent away when the treasured control over her life began to slip under his spell…

"It was for the best," she nodded, again recalling what he'd written. Apparently, he and Mandria were reconciling their differences; promising evidence had been found in some boarding house; and soon, he hoped to clear his name. "Well, that's only right," she declared. "He loves his wife and child and I want him to be happy—so, enough of this poor-me business!"

Then, as she went through the front gate, her attention was drawn to the yard, where the children were usually at play. "Now, where are those rascals?" she murmured, heading around the side of the house. She'd warned them to stay away from her flowers, for though she and Evelyn were gifted with many a lovely bouquet, her carefully tended gardens were beginning to look quite bare. But neither were they in the side or back yards and curious, Susan started for the kitchen door. …Perhaps Evelyn had a chore needing attention, and expecting to find the children hard at it, she entered, only to come to an abrupt halt in the doorway. For there, lounging at her kitchen table—gobbling down a plate of her cinnamon buns—sat a stranger. … And what was it about his attire that seemed so out of place?—The hat! He wore a Captain's hat and Susan nearly panicked. Savannah was on the coast— and this man could be a bounty hunter if Tom was on the run again! "Excuse me," she managed the sternness of her teacher's tone, but was still unsure of how she should treat him.

Mike had looked up when the woman came in, and watched in amusement as her expressions went from surprise, to fear, to suspicion. "All right, you're excused," he chuckled, taking another bite from a confiscated bun.

"I beg your pardon!" she added anger to her expanding display of emotion. "Who are you and what are you doing here?" And furthering her pique, the man rose with a backward scrape of his chair and made her a grand, but insolent bow!

"Captain Michael Leonard Herb—at your beck and call, ma'am. And who, may I ask, are you?"

"Oh dear God!" she gasped. "—Out of what port, sir?"

"Savannah, of course," he replied as a twinkle danced merrily in his eyes. "—Is there another?"

"Not this far inland," she retorted. "So you can't be much of a seaman, to have veered this much off-course."

"You're right there. I'm no kind of seaman at all—"

"What then?" she interrupted. "A pirate—or someone's hireling, who would rob an innocent person of their…their possessions?" she quickly amended. To have said freedom, would have warned she suspected his true purpose.

"Oh-hell-yes!" Mike exclaimed, enjoyably. "If taking these cinnamon buns qualifies me for a pirate, a hireling and a robber, then I must plead guilty!"

Heaving an exasperated sigh, Susan stepped forward—and Mike, not knowing about her limp, reached out to steady her. "Take your hands off of me!" she snapped, angling backwards now.

"…But I thought you were falling," he recoiled in surprise of his own.

"I certainly was not!" she informed him. "—And even if I was, your assistance would not be needed!"

"Yes ma'am!" he saluted smartly. "Anything else, ma'am, before I'm sent to the gallows?"

"There certainly is! You can tell me what you're doing here—besides stealing food—and then, sir, you may leave."

"*And-then-sir-you-may-leave?*" Mike bristled at her imperial tone. "So from whose royal presence am I being dismissed? I was polite enough to introduce myself, but who are you—other than a hoarder of buns from a hungry man?" And with deliberance, he gnawed off another bite, smacking over it loudly.

Susan was furious! …But certainly, his actions just proved him a low-life—and possibly dangerous? "My name is of no consequence," she decided it best to remain calm. It had to be safer. "You are the intruder and I'm asking you, kindly, to leave."

"Well, I'm so very sorry," he responded in a like—if mocking tone, "but until the others return, I can not do that."

"…What others?" she asked, imagining a whole posse of men as arrogant as this one. "—And what have you done with the rest of the people who live here?" she demanded.

"Nothing, damn it!" Mike swore, losing patience. He was beginning to regret volunteering to remain behind while Seph finished his nap. And where was that teacher—the old and dear friend of the Scott's—he was told to expect soon? Surely, she would know how to deal with this nosey neighbor, or whoever the hell she was. …Still, as she said,

he wasn't known to her, so maybe some explanation was in order. "…
Listen, Miss, I'm not an intruder. Tom Scott has—"

"So you are here for Tom!" she interrupted him yet again. "Well,
he is not even in Athens, so now will you go?"

"Yes, he is," Mike insisted, "and I'm here to help get him back to
Savannah."

"In chains, no doubt!" Susan threw caution to the wind. "Oh, you
filthy despicable, mercenary!" she spat, arms flying akimbo.

Mike stared at the angry female—and suddenly began to laugh.
"Is that what all this hostility is about? You think I'm here to capture
Tom or something?"

"Well, aren't you?" she demanded.

"Oh-hell-no, lady!" he laughed on. "Tom Scott is my very best
friend!"

"…Mine as well," she nodded, though she still wasn't certain she
believed the man. "Then why did you say you'd come to take him
back?"

"To help get him back is what I think I said," Mike corrected.
"…He came to collect his family and take them home," he added,
wondering if every woman on earth was ready to defend Tom so
valiantly.

"So, it's safe now?" she asked, her voice and manner much gentler..
"The law no longer wants him?" she said hopefully.

And for the first time, Mike realized she was quite beautiful—a
raven haired beauty, with an olive complexion, big dark eyes and a
figure as ripe and lush as any man could want. That, in turn, made him
curious about her interest in Tom, for it seemed so…intense? Fired
by more than friendship? "Mandy came with us," he stressed that,
watching for her reaction. "And their son, Seph, is asleep upstairs," he
added. "That's why I couldn't leave the house."

"Oh, I'm so glad they came too," Susan smiled.

And Mike felt it. It was as if he'd been standing in shadow and
suddenly stepped into light. It also made him uncomfortable, though
he couldn't imagine why. Regardless, his next response came out
sounding critical. "But no ma'am, the law no longer wants him. Simply

put, the villain is dead and Tom can now return to being everyone's hero."

"…That was an odd thing to say," Susan straightened—defensively, of course. "A real friend of Tom's would know better. This wasn't a tale from a dime novel, Captain Herb. Sam Lucas really was a villain—an evil man, capable of ruining many lives. And if Tom—or the hero— was able to foil him, I say more power to him!"

"I…well, I meant nothing derogatory," Mike nodded, searching now for his own defense. "I just wasn't sure how much of the story you knew.—Or wanted to know. And that was the quickest version," he finished inanely.

"Then begin another version by telling me where everyone is," her tone softened again. "And by letting me apologize for my inhospitable manners," she extended a hand. "I'm Susan Rutledge and this is my home."

"Susan…?" Mike all but swallowed his tongue. There wasn't one damn thing *old and dear* about this teacher friend of the Scott's—both of whom, had forgotten to mention a lot of her outstanding attributes. But recovering nicely, as the Captain always did, he turned the hand she'd offered in forthright greeting, and lifted it to his lips. "Susan— from the Hebrew, meaning *lily*—and God never created a lovelier lady to carry the name of his favorite flower."

"Balderdash!" she drew her hand away, refusing to admit she found that compliment bothersomely pleasant. "And Michael means *he who is like God*—which is another far cry from the truth. So drop anchor, Captain Herb. I'm not some wide-eyed little twit and I won't go sailing off on any of your seaman's blarney."

"If you had, I'd have been disappointed," he chuckled. "And I don't even know why."

Neither did Susan know why she was blushing. His attempt to flatter had failed, but his honesty was affecting her most strangely— and she didn't know the why of that, either. "…Now the matter is settled, may I offer you a fresh cup of coffee?" she asked, not feeling settled at all.

"If it comes with another cinnamon bun, yes, you can," he smiled, sitting down again. "And as I tried telling you before, I'm not a seaman, but Captain of the Irish Mist—a riverboat running between Savannah and Augusta."

"I see," she said, going to swing the pot over the fire and wishing, for the first time in many years, that her limp weren't so noticeable—which, in turn, made her feel more off-balance than her foot did.

"As I also tried to tell you," Mike continued, "Tom took his family to see the house where he and Allen lived as children."

"Yes, I told Evelyn this morning the people there had moved away," she said bringing cups to the table. "But speaking of children, did John and Brittany go too? They ran ahead of me coming in from school."

"They got here as the others were leaving—so, yes, they went," Mike said with a laugh. "And I must say, once they had finished dancing around Tom and Mandy, they took a shine to their Uncle Allen and Aunt Lucy."

"So Allen came too?" she said happily. "—But who is Aunt Lucy?"

"That's Allen's new bride of less than a week!" he announced. But noting her frown, he added. "…You seem bothered. Do you have a problem with that?"

Indeed she did. A child she'd helped raise was now married, and yet again, she felt left behind. That, however, was not something she cared to explain. "No problems," she fibbed. "…I was just wondering where to bed everyone down."

"…Oh?" Mike drawled, and that thoroughly wicked twinkle returned to his eyes.

"Yes, Evelyn can now share *my* room." And because she had stressed that too strongly, she became flustered and rushed on. "Tom and Mandy will, of course, have the guest room, as Seph's cradle is already there; you and the children can sleep on pallets in the parlor; …but that leaves the newly weds—"

"Your coffee is boiling over," Mike said out of nowhere.

Unheedful, she continued. "No, that won't do. The newly weds must have the parlor and you and children can move in here—"

"Susan, your coffee is boiling over!" he repeated more forcefully.

"Oh—drat!" she hurried to tend it. Why was she behaving this way? But she knew why. This roguish male was…well, disorienting, at best. He'd forced her to say there was no room in her bed for him, without his having actually asked to be there!

"You know, I was proud of Mamalyn when Mandy told her about Sam's death," Mike took a turn at being unheedful. "She said her whole marriage had been a death waiting to happen. And that if she had tears left to shed, they'd be for Nico," he paused to nod. "That touched me. It truly did."

"…Bun?" Susan pushed a plate his way—and wondered how she knew there was more behind what he'd said than was evident. "Anyway, Captain Herb, with that sorry man gone, Tom, his family and friends can now enjoy the happy lives they richly deserve."

"Yeah, I'm sure they will," he said, selecting a large sticky, sweet confection. "—And it's Mike; Susan—please call me Mike."

"Mike, then," she agreed. "…But I am curious. Why did you say *they* would be happy, as if you don't count yourself among Tom's friends?"

"Well, there was a time, when Mandy wasn't the only one who doubted him. …I wanted him dead."

"You can't be serious?" her eyes widened appealingly.

"I've never seen… I mean, you have the most—your eyes are onyx," Mike stammered. "And very beautiful."

"Listen, you—thank you—but you just said… Why would you want your—our—best friend dead?" she stammered back.

"You're welcome," he gave his head a shake. …*Best to keep a focused mind here.* "I was deeply in love with the girl Tom was accused of beating nearly to death," he finished.

There was such pain in Mike's eyes, it prompted an observation. "And you love her still," Susan said aloud. Then, she felt embarrassed. *This is none of my business,* she thought,—*though he does have a strangely flirtatious way of mourning a lost love.* "Which only proves how fickle men are!" the words were out before she knew it.

"Damn," Mike swore in confusion. "Did I pass out and miss something here? I must have, because I can't find a sensible connection in your last two statements."

"Well...,"—*Well, what, Susan Rutledge?* she thought now. ... *You can't say he loves another and therefore the pleasure you find in his company and compliments has been lessened. ...Nor can you say, because of your enjoyment, you hoped there was no one else.* "It's really quite simple," she latched onto middle ground. "When you obviously still love this girl, it makes me resent your blarney all the more." There. That should put it back on him, rather nicely.

"Yes, but love—like blarney—must be returned if it's ever to work. In my case, it wasn't, so I guess I'm doomed to become a dreary old maid." And he finished with the ultimate in pitiful sighs.

Not an hour before, Susan had also been feeling sorry for herself. *...But Lord, I hope I didn't sound so ridiculous!* she mused. *This man is simply impossible—and spoofing a charm he's very sure of, too.* It went beyond her usual distain and spilled into the outrageous. She tried hard to keep a straight face, but when he uttered another of those pitiful sighs, she laughed. And now, he was laughing—enjoying the fool he'd made of himself. So, perhaps—just perhaps—there was more of worth to Captain Herb than she'd first thought...

"All right, Mike," she began, "would you kindly fill the gaps in this story? I want to know what changed your opinion of Tom; all that happened on this last trip to Savannah—and you and your blarney, I'll deal with later." That last part led Mike to rise to the occasion in his usual way. And he was soon regaling Susan with lavish embellishments of the story.

It was into this merry scene that the others returned. Yet, as they too gathered about the table, Susan was soon indulging in more sobering observations. ...Yes, Mandy and Tom were happy together now, and an example arose when it came time for Seph's feeding. Mandria's departure from their midst was preceded by a kiss to husband's forehead—which, to Susan, seemed an unnecessary thing. Nonetheless, had it not been for an active youngster on each of his knees, she was certain Tom would have accompanied his wife. As it was, he kept an on-going watch of the stairs, for her return.

...Then, there were the newly-weds, who held hands as if their fingers were glued together. And though they took part in the ongoing conversations, numerous and amorous glances said they'd really prefer being alone. Susan nodded. Yes, they would definitely be given the privacy of the parlor. ...*But dear Lord*, she thought cynically, *such turmoil over a piece of flesh!*

Precisely as this thought passed, Susan discovered a gaze of questioning perusal coming her way from Mike and she looked back in distaste. No man was going to mistake her for a glob of putty to be molded—or fondled—into conformity. But instead of retreating from her glare, as most men certainly did, Mike laughed aloud. And at a time when nothing said by the others merited it—which left her blushing again and mortified beyond the telling. Absolutely, here was a man who needed to be taught a lesson—and she was the woman who would see he learned it well. And soon!

Then Mandria rejoined the group, and as the women had already started supper, setting the table was relegated to her. Weaving her way in and among the men who continued to chat there, Mandria began to notice how Mike kept leaning around her from several points, for a clearer view of Susan. She also noted Susan pretending to ignore Mike, and when that didn't work, to send him scathing glances. But look at him she did and Mandria couldn't resist involvement. "...Susan, have you seen Joshua lately?" she posed an innocent sounding question. "I do believe he was sweet on you."

And when Mike straightened attentively—in the mode of a hound on-point—Susan decided that here, at last, was a way of ending this game. "No, Mandy, I haven't seen that dear man since we moved you down from the cabin. But he has written—and such lovely, intelligent letters, full of news from all over the state." Now, he'd assume her interest lay elsewhere.

"Nothing more?" Mandria persisted. "No promise to call when he returns to Athens? Surely you've answered and encouraged him."

"Yes—no!" Susan floundered. She didn't want her name romantically linked with anyone—and that had to be made clear too. "I mean, yes, I've written to Josh, but not to encourage the impossible," she said to Mandria, though the words were directed at Mike. "And thankfully, he is a sensitive soul who would never suggest anything to ruin our lovely friendship."

"Good for you, Susan Rutledge!" Mike purposely misconstrued her message. "Those intelligent, sensitive souls don't amount to much anyway, so why waste time when I have just waltzed into your life?"

If Susan could help it, the collective laughter—at her expense— would not go unanswered. Oh no, this unseemly display of male ego was going to cost Michael Herb a mighty guffaw from this same audience. "Sir, I do not waltz to any man's tune. The foot, you see," she mimed a few awkward steps about the floor. "But then, some men don't even need a partner, such as I to look the fool. They have only to open their mouths."

Susan received the laughter she expected—and something she did not. For not only was Mike laughing as much as anyone else, but he wore an expression of true admiration. At a loss, Susan turned to stir her stew—and to stew over this turn of events. Was there no way of besting this thoroughly incorrigible Irishman…?

CHAPTER 31

"Tom?" Mandria said in the hushed darkness of the guest room. ...And turning in the bed, she smoothed caressing fingers over his chest. "Am I wrong for wanting everyone to be as happy as we are?"

"No, lady," he smiled, pulling her closer. "But I can feel another question coming, so what is it?"

"Well, what if we asked Susan to come for a visit? I mean, she has done so much to help us and leaving her here, all alone, seems very sad."

"And?" he asked, knowing there was more.

"...And nothing," she shrugged. "But school will be out for the summer next week and she'd be free to return with us."

"And?" he insisted.

"And if we're taking two wagons back anyway, there would be plenty of room. ...Also, I've been thinking about giving a party and maybe Mike could escort her and then—"

"And then," Tom placed a finger on her busy mouth. "And then we come to the truth of the matter. You want to play match-maker again."

"Well...it worked out well for Allen and Lucy—and for Joleen and Willie. And I think it is adorable that Tandy is named for the two of us."

"So now you want to populate the world with our namesakes?" he chuckled.

"No, of course not," she laughed too. "But there is an attraction between Mike and Susan—and I know you saw it."

"Yes, I saw, but as I told you before, Susan values her independence. And Mike…well, besides being among the walking wounded, he is much his own man too. Likely, they'd butt heads more than is healthy."

"So did we for nearly six months," she reminded him, "and look at us now."

"Love, I'm just saying Nico left a deep gash in our Captain, and he has nothing to fall back on. I don't know if he's ready to risk that hurt again."

"I hurt you, and you risked it."

"Not by choice," he teased, lifting her palm to his lips. "As I recall it, you locked me in our bedroom—not once, but twice—and I had a devil of a time salvaging my honor."

"But I persisted and won you over, didn't I? I mean, we've yet to consummate our reunion, but when the time comes, you will risk your honor for that too, won't you?"

"Yes, pretty lady—yes!" he rolled her beneath him. "And as long as you continue to persist with me, do as you please with this business of match-making. …Just be careful. As I said about Joleen and Willie, if it's meant to be, it will be. If not—well, don't get caught in the middle."

"Then perhaps you should remove yourself, sir," she smiled up at him. "As that is where I seem to be now: caught in the middle— between you and the mattress."

"And you want to be here, which is my whole point in a nutshell. Susan and Mike must want the same thing or it won't work."

"Oh, no, Tom," she said sweetly, "Your whole-point-in-a-nutshell is seeking entrance at another door—you great rutting stag!"

"Lady, when opportunity knocks? Open, damn it!"

And she did, aching as much as he for more than the beautiful mockery they endured…

In the days to follow, the men enjoyed a fishing trip, made arrangements for a second wagon and spent the rest of their time completing some needed repairs around Susan's house. Of course, she thanked them as each task was completed, but insisted again and again that she could have done it herself.

"Not the leak in the roof, surely," Mike dared to suggest. "Susan, you have to admit that was work for a man."

And, in a tone as crisp as her starched white blouse, she retorted, "Captain Herb, it's only because men have the muscles and scaling ability of monkeys that you were able to make quick work of that job. But given time, I assure you, I would have devised a method of repairing it too."

"Yeah, but not before the damned roof caved in," he laughed at her declaration. Then, infuriating Susan further, he scampered away doing an excellent imitation of an ape that included hooting and scratching his way across the yard…

Meanwhile, the ladies began to pack for the trip home and Mandria and Evelyn made a special project of convincing Susan to accompany them. It began with a discussion about the party Mandria wanted to give.

"Especially for Tom," she said. "It will be my way of thanking all the close friends who stood by him through that whole ordeal." And she got the nod of approval she expected from Susan. "So, as you have been his staunchest ally and dearest friend, of course, you must come too."

Once again, Susan gave thanks, but politely refused. "I have been thinking of tutoring a class of slow learners over the summer," she fibbed. "And that takes preparation, you see."

Mandria and Evelyn wisely said they understood, but by no means abandoned their quest. And when the next opportunity arose, Mandria related the story about the day Tom took her to see their home for the first time, and stressed how hesitant he'd been over hosting a party properly.

"Tom?" Susan asked in surprise. "I have never known him to lack confidence in any area."

"Well, he does in this one," Mandria appealed to Susan's loyalty now. "That is why I want you to come. You have known Tom longer than any of us and he has often said you were a stabilizing influence on him," she resorted to a fib of her own.

"Yes," added Evelyn, "Tom even came seeking my advice once. He wanted to be certain what was socially acceptable in announcing his marriage to Mandria. Susan, he wants to fit comfortably into his new life, but is still a bit unsure about it, poor dear," she finished with a sad little sigh.

"And I remember that huge plate of food he fixed down at Tybee," Lucy injected, having no notion of what the other two hoped to accomplish. "Mike called it a mountain! ...But I didn't think it was so bad. I mean, he doesn't eat as much as my Papa, and no one would dare call him socially unacceptable. ...Would they?"

"Of course not, dear," Evelyn hugged her. "Other than the way he and your mother have treated you lately, they are fine people.—And when I get home, I mean to have a word with them about it, on your behalf."

"Mama?" Mandria smiled. "Since when did you become so ... plucky?" she borrowed Tom's description.

"Since I've known Susan," Evelyn said with pride. "And she could certainly teach the ladies of Savannah some valuable lessons too— which I would see she had the chance to do. Yes, Susan could stay with me and I'd introduce her to those who need to hear her valued opinions."

There the matter was dropped again. For this time, Susan had not refused their invitation so quickly. And too, Mandria wanted to mull over a new approach which had inadvertently presented itself. Yes, when they talked again, she had to remember to boast about Susan's resourcefulness as a single woman...

"Honestly, Miss Rutledge," Mandria nodded when shown a safe way of packing the cornflower dishes among the clothes in Evelyn's trunk. "I've never known such a clever woman. Is there anything you don't know how to do?"

"Not much," Susan answered appreciatively. "It's been learned through trial and error, but I've always enjoyed a challenge."

"Then you should write a book on what you've learned—or give lectures about it. There are so many women who would like doing more for themselves and you could tell them the easiest ways of going about it."

"…Not in Athens," Susan said. "No, here I am, and ever will be, *that poor lame schoolmarm.*" With that, she hobbled from the room— and they did nothing to stop or console her, because Susan's expression of discontent was a good indication she was seriously considering their invitation…

Praise came her way again when the women wanted to move a heavy box across the parlor to the door, where it would later be loaded on the wagons. Under Susan's direction, they managed to slip a throw rug beneath it, and while Evelyn and Lucy tugged from their end, Mandria and Susan sat on the floor behind, pushed on the box with their feet, and it slid along as easily as if on wheels.

"Now, that was truly ingenious—and there isn't a mark on the floor either!" Mandria said to her partner, who sat in the same extended-leg, dishevel-skirted position as she. …And while the others were busily adding their compliments, Mandria saw Susan's crippled foot for the first time. Laced into a flat heeled ankle boot, it wasn't badly turned at all, but rather, that leg seemed a bit shorter than the other.

Mandria's heart fluttered with excitement, recalling that Mrs. Littlejohn had suffered a similar condition, which was greatly improved with a special shoe! …But would Susan agree to visit the same cobbler, or would she consider the idea a foolish act of vanity? Well, she had been vain enough to purchase expensive night wear, so wasn't it possible she could be persuaded to try this too? *Just be careful,*' Tom had said. And Mandria decided the first step was still getting Susan to Savannah. *Yes, take one step at a time,* she thought,—*and then, maybe, some with a less noticeable limp!* "Susan, you simply must come home with us now," she laughed, finding it hard to stay her elation. "Because at Mama's next club meeting, you and I could get down on the floor and repeat this amazing maneuver. Oh yes, we'll show the ladies of Savannah exactly how much a woman can do when she really puts her mind to it."

Along with the others, Susan laughed at the notion. Then she sighed. "Let's be realistic, shall we? Mandy, I do appreciate your admiration for my small suggestions, but you all come from a society where the women have maids by the dozens. What could I say that could possibly interest them?"

"Dear, don't sell yourself—or our ladies—short," Evelyn advised. "They admire spirit in any woman—and we have a monthly tea for the sole purpose of honoring the achievements of the city's outstanding women. Also, there are plans for asking Lucretia Mott or Elizabeth Stanton to come speak—"

"The suffragists?" Susan interrupted, clearly expressing her interest. "...I mean, I've read of their work in the north, but it's not a popular subject among the women here."

"Well, it is in Savannah and I mean to make it more so," Evelyn continued. "Susan, had it not been for my father's will and good family lawyers, Sam would have had total control of my money—and even more control over my life than he did. In the last few months, I've come to realize how fortunate I was;—and how wrong it is that other women are suffering a plight I was spared."

"So you, too, believe in equal rights for women," Susan nodded thoughtfully.

And while Lucy stared at the pair as if they'd just admitted belonging to a coven of witches, Mandria looked at her mother with new respect. "Think about it, Susan," she turned her way again. "With your spirit and Mama's influence, you could help make this issue a force to be reckoned with—and not just in Savannah, but all over the state."

"Well, I would like to attend your party for Tom," she hedged, "... and perhaps, a few of Evelyn's meetings."

"Then you *are* coming with us!" Mandria scrambled to her feet and pulled Susan to hers. "—Come on now, we'll just go upstairs and start packing for you too!" And they all went, before Susan could change her mind.

However, there was a down-side to Mandria's success, because with women's rights even more prominent in Susan's mind, her patience with Mike's constant teasing became increasingly short…

---·◈·---

"Mandria," Tom asked the following night, "…did it seem to you that Mike and Susan nearly came to blows over which of them would go for a damned bucket of water?"

"No," she fibbed, "I think we're all just a little excited over the trip home. Besides, Susan has a lot on her mind: getting the house closed; finding people to water her gardens; tending her animals and such."

"But we don't leave for another three days," he pointed out, "and frankly, I'm already tired of refereeing their duels. …So, while she is in school tomorrow and things are relatively calm around here, would you care to ride up to the cabin with me?"

"Just the two of us?" she asked hopefully.

"Yes, love—if Mamalyn wouldn't mind keeping Seph for a few hours."

"…And may I choose the route?" she asked now.

Tom laughed, pulling her spoon-fashion against him. "I think we're of one mind on that. It will be through the hills on horseback. Now sleep, lady, we'll need an early start."

As Mandria snuggled closer, trying to quench her excitement, her eyes came to rest on Tom's buckskins, which she had yet to pack. Then they traveled to her valise and she smiled secretively. "…On one horse, Tom?" she asked then. "Please, just as we did last time?"

"If that's what you want," he chuckled softly, glad she was looking forward to a trip she had not enjoyed before. "But I haven't any ribbon for tying up your hair this time."

"And I've no harsh words to give in return," she drew his hand into hers. "But I'll think of something to keep you alert. See if I don't."

"I'm scared to death," he yawned. "Now, will you please go to sleep?"

"Yes, sir," she answered. And yet, it was quite a while before she could, because Mandria was making some careful calculations and devising an extraordinary plan...

Tom awoke the next morning to find Mandria sitting at the dressing table in her robe, while arranging her hair. And lying across the foot of the bed were his buckskins. "...I assume you want me to wear these?" he sat up to ask sleepily.

"Yes—you did say they made travelling easier," she shrugged, gathering her tresses into a bow at the nape of her neck.

"No...other reason?" he questioned, rising to pull them on.

"What other reason could there be?" she sent him a look of innocence. "Now, if you will go for the horse, I'll have you a cup of coffee waiting and we can leave."

"What about Seph—won't you have to feed him first and see if Mamalyn will tend him?" Tom asked, taking his boots and starting across the room.

"I've already fed him—to the point of bursting—and Mama has him downstairs now, helping to pack us a lunch."

"...Mandria?" he paused in the doorway. "Since when did you become so organized this early in the morning?"

"I don't know," she said in a tone as full of wonder as his. "But you'd better take advantage of it, don't you think?"

"Yes, ma'am," he chuckled, and descending the stairs, stepped carefully over the sleeping Captain, then with no word of explanation, ruffled the baby's hair and kissed his mother-in-law's cheek as he passed through the kitchen and went out the door.

Tom returned to find Mandria on the back stoop, dressed in her buckskins too. "I didn't know you brought those with you," he said, sipping down the coffee she'd promised. "...Any particular reason for it?"

"You are certainly looking for ulterior motives this morning," she smiled as Evelyn brought out a small lunch basket. "I just happen to enjoy—well, the feel of buckskin," she finished.

Then they were both laughing—each realizing a truth the other had kept secret for nearly a year: that buckskin, catching and rubbing against buckskin, was something neither had been able to forget. They were still laughing as they rode away. And Evelyn nodded in puzzlement. She could not fathom what the joke had been...

CHAPTER 32

"Doesn't the air smell wonderful?" Mandria inhaled as they started through town. "But it would have to with all the spring flowers in bloom.—And look, Tom, see that boy over there?" she pointed. "I saw him the first time we came to Athens. Then, he was sneaking home with a large stolen pumpkin and I remember thinking you must have done the same at that age."

"Well you were wrong on both counts, lady," Tom retorted. "That is Glen Winslet's boy and the family raises pumpkins. Likely, he was only delivering one. As for myself at that age," he pretended offense "my mother would have strangled me for stealing anything."

"Except hearts," she nodded. "…So did you have many sweethearts here?" she asked curiously.

"A few," he shrugged, curious now too. "…Why do you ask?"

"Maybe because I'm jealous of them all," she replied. "It makes me wish I had known you then too."

"Lord, I don't wish that," he nodded.

"And just why not?" she teased. "Wouldn't I have impressed you as a mountain lass?"

"Too much, lady," he chuckled. "We would have married at a very tender age—and likely because we had to—settled on a small farm and by now, had a yard full of children."

"Well…does that sound so terrible?" she questioned.

Tom hesitated before answering. "...Not really, I guess. Most of my friends did exactly that, and on the whole they seem to be happy enough."

"But you wouldn't have been," she surmised. "So what did you want you couldn't find here?"

"I'm not sure, pretty lady. It just seemed the more I studied, the more discontent I felt. I didn't even know why, until the day I saw you, and from then on, all I've wanted is to be wherever you are," he nuzzled her ear. "Anyway, as you are my future, I've never regretted leaving."

Mandria shied from the tingling sensation of warm breath on her ear, and when that caused their buckskins to catch, both were laughing again.

"So, you left in search of fame, fortune and adventure," she smiled up at him. "Until I put a stop to it."

"Actually, I just wanted a different life," he said, savoring the clear green of her eyes in the fresh spring forest setting, "and the right woman to share it with me."

"Maybe its best we didn't meet earlier then," Mandria sighed a bit. "I would have made a terrible farmer's wife. I can not sew more than a simple stitch; I do cook a little, but I've no knowledge about growing or preserving foods. ...In fact, when I tally the things I can do against those I can't, my side of the slate is kind of bare and useless."

"Ah, but what other woman could so enchant her husband that he would remain at her side though she refused him even a kind word month-after-endless-month?" he countered in a beleaguered tone.

"Well, some men would call you a fool for that," she uttered. "... And all women would be certain of my insanity."

"Perhaps—if it was any of their damned business," he tightened an arm about her waist. But now that he'd drawn her closer against him, he had a question to ask. "Mandria, just exactly how much longer will it be for us?"

"Oh, we should reach the cabin in an hour or so," she deliberately misinterpreted what was meant.

"Lady," he drawled, "it has been three weeks since we discussed this—"

"Really? I've hardly noticed," she said airily.

"Liar.—Shall I prove it?" And his hand went to her breasts.

"Don't you dare!" she playfully slapped at his fingers. "You are not to touch just yet."

"Unfortunately, you're right," he pulled the horse to a sudden stop. And sliding to the ground, Tom went to examine a section of the trail that had washed away during the winter. "Move back in the saddle," he said on returning, "I'll need to keep an eye on these ledges, so you'd best ride behind for now."

Mandria did as she was asked, but as they rode on, Tom heard her laugh a bit and wondered why. A few moments later, he felt her tugging at the tail of his shirt; raising it up his back. "...Lady?" he began, only to catch a breath as full, bare breasts pressed against his spine.

"Yes?" she answered, bringing her hands forward to caress his buckskinned loins, while her tongue danced along his back. "You wanted something, husband?"

"And you know damned well what that is," he tried and failed to hamper her stroking fingers. "Love, your teasing borders on cruelty.— And you are enjoying it, aren't you?"

"Not at all," she assured him. "I only mean to erase the memory of our last trip. ...And any fond memories you may still harbor for the girls of your youth."

"Consider both done—please!" he finally managed to stay both of her hands at once. "Otherwise, we're going over the edge of this trail."

"Coward," Mandria relented. She would have said more too, had her attention not been drawn to a loud roaring sound. "...Tom, what is that?" she peered over his shoulder.

"A waterfall," he answered.

"But I don't remember hearing it the last time," she looked about, for the noise seemed to come from every direction.

"It was autumn then, love, and over the summer, the streams were reduced to a trickle," he explained. "Now, with the spring thaw, they're full again, that's all."

"Is it near the trail?" she questioned, her excitement evident. "I've never seen a waterfall."

"It's close enough. In fact, we could have our lunch there, if you wish. It's really a beautiful spot—very romantic, if you can remember that sort of thing."

"Oh?" she asked. "So you like that sort of thing?"

"I used to," he nodded, "but it has been so damned long—"

"That you have forgotten how or what to do?" she laughed. "Well, that would be a pity—and on a day like this, a real shame too."

"…Mandria, you are in the strangest mood," he observed. And stopping the horse, he dismounted to tie the reins to a bush. When turning to help his wife down, he noted first, that her blouse was re-laced, and yet her warm expression promised further mischief. "Give me the basket," he said resigning himself to it. Somehow, he'd steel his way through. Then he was chuckling; knowing he'd change nothing about her if he could, so grasping her hand, he led the way down a winding path.

After a time, they came into a small glade at the base of the falls and Mandria had to agree, it was indeed, a romantic place. Crystal water tumbled from a crevice some twelve feet above their heads and fell into a circular, sun-dappled pool below. Spring green grass carpeted the surrounding banks and here and there it was strewn with petals from the wild pink dogwoods which awninged the area. Nearer the water grew huge clumps of hydrangeas, each blue or white bonnet-shaped flower, seemingly made to be worn by fairies. And Mandria would not have been surprised to see them there. "…Oh, Tom," she uttered softly, "I think this must be the Garden of Eden."

"Me, Adam; you, Eve?" he laughed jokingly. But not joking at all, she turned and sought his mouth with such enthusiasm, it left him groaning. "Wench!" he held her close. "What am I going to do with you—until I can do something with you?"

"Well, you could unpack our lunch, while I make a trip to the bushes," she suggested, scanning the area closely. "So, may I be excused, sir?"

"Of course," he nodded, "but I didn't think the ladies of Savannah approved of going-to-the-bushes," he added as she started away.

"They don't," she answered, spotting the exact location she needed. "But neither did they spend the winter with a heathen." And with that, she disappeared behind a bush at the water's edge.

"…Heathen?" Tom repeated, going to a knee to spread a tablecloth on the grassy bank. "Lady, a heathen—even over your objections— would have claimed what was legally his. A heathen would also have turned you over his knee for some of those fits you threw. And I came close to allowing myself the privilege. Did you know that?" When no answer came, Tom glanced over his shoulder. "…Mandria?" he called, but again there wasn't an answer. Then, as he rose to his feet, there was a large splash and he saw the resulting circles spread across the water's surface from the direction she had taken. "Mandria!" he raced forward. "Damn it, you'd better answer me, right now!"

That is when she surfaced—nude—in the center of the pool, to yell right back at him. "Oh! You didn't tell me it would be so cold!" she gasped.

"So, what in the hell are you doing in there?" he laughed as much in relief as at her shocking initiation. "I thought something had happened to you."

"Well, it didn't," she smiled at his still worried expression. And leaning to float on her back, she moved about the pool, careful to keep her limbs from disturbing the revealing clearness of the water. "Won't you join me?" she glided closer to where he stood. "It's not so bad once you get used to it."

"…I would love to," Tom finally got words from his mouth. He had become nearly mesmerized watching the water pool in and out of her naval; the cape of hair fanning about her head; the gentle bobbing of those beautiful breasts with their erect, cold-water-cured nipples. Then shaking free of the spell he groped about for logic. "But…

Mandria, maybe you shouldn't be swimming. In your condition—I mean, you are nursing…and all that."

This excuse brought Mandria rising up in the waist deep water, arms akimbo. And now Tom had to watch those water droplets and curls create enchanting designs across those same breasts. "Sir, my *condition* at the moment, can only be attributed to your damned clinging buckskins. Truly, Tom, you shouldn't be allowed to wear them in a female's presence—except mine, of course—but even for me, they cause the most un-ladylike notions. Such as my standing here naked asking you to take them off?"

Tom grinned. He had never enjoyed a compliment more in his entire life. "Yes, but it was also you who insisted I wear them. … So, could it be that our time at the cabin was harder on you than I realized?"

"Much harder," she smiled back. "I likened you to all sorts of beasts for tempting me so—the Puma being my personal favorite."

"Well, I'll have you know you aren't the only one to appreciate my skins," he made her several comic poses while removing his shirt. "I was told in Augusta—by a true connoisseur—that they flatter my ass."

"And what hussy dared to say so?" she stifled a fit of giggles over his continuing antics.

"Not one you would have to worry about," he peeled off his boots and those infamous trousers. "His name was Dexter—and I did have to proposition him in order to gain entry to Jack and Harry's room."

"…You—Tom, you did what?" Mandria stammered and then burst into laughter.

"Are you certain it's all right for you to be swimming?" he asked, while wading into the water. "It won't…well, delay or prolong anything, will it?"

"Would it make a difference?" she sent a spray of water at him. "Tom, you just admitted to propositioning a man!" she teased, remaining beyond his reach. "I doubt that even the most practiced of sirens could lure you to her bed now!" And this was accompanied by virtual wall of water as she kicked her way merrily toward the far bank.

"No?" he laughed, giving chase. "Well, there was one of those in Augusta too and she gave it a hell of a try!" The instant the words were out, Tom knew he was in trouble, for though Mandria still smiled, she had rounded on him as smartly as any ship of war and her eyes held him targeted for an immediate explanation. Dead in the water, he stood facing her, knowing he would have to confess his visit to Delilah's. "So," he wondered how to begin, "would you care to hear about a whore-house madam?"

"In Augusta—on your last trip there?" she asked, making sure of the facts. She didn't want this confused with a tale from the past, before he'd married her. And then, she began to circle him very slowly.

"Yes," he nodded.

"And this…madam, I'll wager, liked the fit of your buckskins too," her chin rose slightly in passing. "—The way they flatter your ass."

"That is not the—uh, usual area of interest for a whore," he tried to jest. "But yes, she said she liked them."

"And of course, she was interested in your *usual area*," Mandria countered, unamused by his humor.

"…Yes, lady—though that has nothing to do with what I'm trying to tell you."

"It most certainly does!" her narrowed eyes fired a volley of green splinters. "Thomas Scott, what were you doing in a whore house?"

"Mandria, please!" he said defensively. This was not going well. "Please, I just needed the woman's assistance—"

And that drew a great "Humph!" from his wife as she continued rounding him.

"But I only went to her room looking for Jack and Harry—"

"Did she keep them under her bed—as spares, or something?" Mandria spat, liking this story less and less. Not only had Tom visited the house, but gone to the Madam's private quarters?

"No, I didn't mean to imply they were inside her room—"

"But you were—and I want to know why!" she demanded.

"Damn it, lady, Delilah is an old…acquaintance." But, no, that wasn't the thing to say. "I just needed the help only she could give me," he added, making it worse. Then, taking a deep breath, he decided to start over. "What I mean is, because we had been friendly—*at one time*," he stressed, "and because she knows everything that goes on in Augusta, I figured she could tell me about Jack and Harry."

"And that is all there was to your visit?" Mandria riveted him with a direct stare and a momentary pause in her circling path.

"All that mattered—except for Mike." he answered. "Delilah also arranged a meeting between us, which is the reason we are on good terms now. And for that, I will always be grateful to her."

Mandria allowed herself time for thought. Tom had told her of Mike's part in capturing those men and she had assumed this was what brought about the renewal of their friendship. …Yet, he was saying a whore house madam had been instrumental and she wondered how on earth that was possible—especially when this Delilah's realm of power could not extend much beyond the walls of her establishment. "So, Mike was there too. But not just for information?" she concluded.

"Well, yes," he nodded, trying to guess her direction this time. "He was in another room, where Delilah had him bound and gagged so he'd have to hear what I wanted to say."

"Which says to me, the woman is certainly more than a little fond of you," she explained quite clearly. "—She had to be, putting herself to so much trouble on your behalf."

"Mandria, in all honesty…I'm fond of her too," he admitted, risking further displeasure. "Delilah not only brought Mike and I together, but told me where to find Harry and Jack; and warned me about a danger Dexter posed—which is another story all together. Nevertheless, as I said, I am grateful that Delilah was willing to go to the trouble."

"Yes," she finally stopped, and now stood directly before him naked, wet and so very beautiful. "But I'm not certain I like you being grateful;—not to a madam named Delilah, of all things. Besides," she poked him in the chest, "You've yet to explain how the fit of your buckskins figures into this."

"She only said she liked them," he backed a step and she followed. "And she also said I smelled like a horse!" he offered, wisely omitting what had happened next.

"And?" Mandria poked him again, still in full advance.

"And she did ask me to stay, but I didn't! I just thanked her and left.—With Mike," he hastened to add. "And I didn't return to her room again either." No sense in mentioning Dexter's delivery to the house.

With folded arms, Mandria again stopped to consider his testimony. But Tom didn't stop his backward trek, for the color change in her eyes was so dramatic, he wasn't sure what it meant.

"Tell me, what was this Delilah wearing?" she asked—and the question was every bit as unexpected as Tom knew it would be.

"I don't know," he nodded. "Nothing so charming as what you *aren't* wearing at the moment," he attempted a smile.

It wasn't returned. "Come now, Tom. Was it long or short—see-through, I'll bet—what color was it, and did you like it?"

"Mandria, I-don't-know," he repeated. "It was just a robe or something.—And what possible difference could the damned color make?"

"So it must have been thin and quite revealing," she deduced, "or you wouldn't be having such trouble describing it to your wife."

"Likely it was," he shrugged. "After all, the woman isn't a…a nun!" And Tom had tried not to use that word, as it forced him to recall Delilah's comment about his probable effect on the good sisters— which in turn, made him all the more uncomfortable. He could only pray it wasn't evident, because Mandria was watching his expressions very closely.

"I am just trying to picture this scene in my mind," she said then. "There you were in those well-fitting buckskins—with a half naked whore, whom you've already said was an *old acquaintance*. And she asked you to stay, but you didn't. …Is that correct, so far?"

"Yes ma'am, that is the gist of it," he answered.

"The gist maybe, but I want details," she insisted. "The woman is obviously schooled in the art of seduction, so how did she ask you to stay?—Did she remove her clothes or what?"

For a third time in their relationship, Tom was thankful a few safe yards lay between them. It wasn't possible that Mandria's next guess would concern *his* lack of clothing…was it? Pure and simple, what had been a case of blackmail—a trick by Delilah—would never be understood by his wife. And that it hadn't worked would do nothing to aid him, either. No, some things were best left unsaid. Forever! "… Mandria," he decided to steer her to safer ground, "as you surmised, Delilah wasn't wearing enough to matter, so there wasn't a need for her to remove anything. But I still refused her offer—and that is the God-honest truth. I told her, instead, that I had married and loved my wife very much."

"But did you tell her the way it was between us then;—that we hadn't made love for all those months?"

"No, but she guessed that much. …And I will admit, she took it as a sign of encouragement—"

"I'll just bet she did!" Mandria's eyes fired a second round of green-tinted splinters.

"But lady, I told her *in spite* of the way things stood, I was not interested in another woman—and she respected that more than anything else I could have said!" Tom insisted. "…And in her own vernacular, she called you a stupid goose that needed her pregnant fanny kicked—but then she agreed to help me, so I must have handled it pretty well. …Don't you think?"

"Such wisdom, from the mouth of a whore," Mandria nodded. "A stupid goose needing her pregnant fanny kicked," she moved closer, standing before him now. "Well, I can't argue with the truth," she said with no change in her serious expression. "That would have been apt punishment for the wife I was to you then."

"No, love," his hands rose, but stopped short of touching her. "… Mandria, I'm at a loss, here. Are you saying you believe me or not?"

"I am saying there is a problem if you expect to mete out such punishment. And that it can't be corrected as long as I'm nursing your son," she placed a finger on his chest. But this time, instead of poking, it was creating lazy, zigzagging patterns. "I'm also saying, that meanwhile, we might consider the activity as practice." And now that finger was descending, while Tom marveled at her ability to arouse him with so simple a thing. "In other words, you great oaf, to accomplish the recommended treatment, you will have to make me pregnant again."

At that, he drew her hard against him. "Lady, I'd like nothing more. It's just that I seem to be married to woman who is entirely dedicated to keeping herself from me for all eternity!"

"Tom, you are an oaf!" she laughed, cupping his face in her hands. "What do you think I've been trying to tell you all morning? It-is-time," she spoke as if to a simpleton. "Make-love-to-your-wife!"

A smile started across Tom's mouth, but never reached the corners, for somehow Mandria's lips got in the way. Along with the rest of her:—female pressed to male; seeking; seducing; demanding long denied attention.

Still lost in a kiss he refused to relinquish, Tom lifted her to him and somehow, made it from the pool and on to the forgotten tablecloth. It was Mandria's turn to endure, as he swarmed over her flesh, tasting from mouth to throat to breast; from nipple to nipple. Her turn to anticipate as his kisses moved down her body. Her turn to know a frantic excitement when he nibbled gently at the very core of her female being. "Open for me, love," he murmured against her. "Let me feel your welcome." And like the petals of those glorious blossoms growing all around them, her thighs and then her body yielded to the pleasure he meant for her to know…

And once more, the mysterious power of love was revealed to Tom. Her giving just made him want to give more; her surrender did naught but capture; her willingness to accept his dominance only made her his equal—an extension of his very best self. She climaxed for him then, and rising to his knees above her, he saw his own image glowing in her eyes and knew the proof of his thoughts. For when a woman looked at a man with such love, he came closest to being a god. Neither money nor power could buy the way she perceived him. It was a gift born of giving—sharing—one with the other and truly the greatest of all treasures…

Certain of her ready acceptance—proud of it—Tom's insertion went ever so slowly. Lord, but he had missed the special feel of this one woman and he meant to enjoy each inch of ensheathment, while watching the passion flares brighten those ever-green eyes. "I love you, pretty lady," he uttered on full burial. "And I won't allow your love for me to lessen," he added, brushing her lips with his. "Promise you won't ever doubt that;—and that you'll never leave me again."

Mandria hadn't known much about love when she came to Tom. She'd learned enough in their first few months together to make the intervening ones without him thoroughly miserable. And now, though he was striving to create a moment she'd long remember of this physical reunion, her patience with his patience was worn to nothing. "Tom, do I look like I want to go anywhere?" she whispered hoarsely. "—Damn you, make love to me!" And, most happily, he did as he was told...

Now, as neither was particularly interested in lunch, Tom and Mandria dressed, repacked the basket and headed back up the path with each showing a greater need to cling to the other's touch, whether the steep incline warranted assistance or not. At the top, it was decided Mandria would ride before Tom again, but as she accepted his hand-up, he swung her to face him so that her legs came to rest, one across each of his.

"...And what is this about?" she laughed.

"I thought maybe you could tell me," he replied. "I saw you tuck your underthings in the lunch basket. ...Care to explain that, ma'am?"

Mandria made him a pretty shrug and began toying with his shirt laces. "Well, I was planning to seduce you once we reached the cabin. I thought if we put that bed to its proper use, maybe another sad memory could be erased. Instead," she glanced at him briefly—too briefly, for Tom's liking, "we stopped here and got all carried away. ... But I still want to take care of that bed matter, and I was rather hoping to persuade you to my way of thinking. Again."

This was not a request Tom intended to ignore. "Then you may begin your seduction now," he chuckled, setting the horse into motion.

"And as my attention must remain on the trail, it might become a bit of a challenge for you," he added nonchalantly.

"Some challenge," she laughed too. "You already have me in the assumed position, with my skirt hiked nearly to thigh-tops.—And another thing, Tom Scott. Unless you're a dinosaur with one brain in your head and another in your lower extremities, your full attention will not be on this trail.—I can promise you that!"

"That may very well be," he placed a peck of a kiss on her pert little nose. "But you will have to prove it;—and especially in the lower extremities."

"So...how?" she wondered aloud, for there wasn't much space in which to maneuver.

"You figure it out," he shrugged. "I'm driving the damn horse."

"You're also being very smug about it," she observed. "Or don't you believe I could distract you?"

"What I believe doesn't matter," he dared her. "The challenge has been made and is now entirely in your hands."

"In my hands, is it?" she shifted as far back as she could, and unfastening his trouser flap, soon had wondrous response to her stroking caresses. "Now, sir," she came forward again, "with a little assistance, I would suggest impalement."

"That would be nice—if such is possible." But circling an arm about her hips and lifting her more onto his lap, he easily proved that it was. "...Very good, love," he uttered huskily. "But kindly keep still until we've rounded this next bend."

Mandria had no problem with that. She was enjoying the easy sway of the horse;—and each ensuing sensation. Even the catch of buckskin between her breasts and his chest had never been more pleasurable. And when Tom brought the horse to a stop, she was almost sorry.

"There is our valley," he said against her ear. "Want to dismount and finish this here, or shall we try for the cabin?"

"The cabin, please," she feigned a sigh. "It seems I've acquired a new fascination with idly, ambling rides."

"The cabin it is, then," he agreed. "…And lady, before we move on, thank you for fulfilling another of my fantasies. I've always wondered if this could be done on horseback."

Mandria laughed, and as always, the sound pleased him greatly. "Yes, but I can't imagine Mr. and Mrs. Love doing it—not as stout as they are. Then too, unlike you, some men might not have enough cork to stopple the bottle."

Now, Tom was chuckling too. "You do have the damnedest way of putting things!" And laughing harder, he started them forward again.

"So, whose fault is that?" she teased at his ear. "Your way-of-putting-things—where they belong, incidentally—has aimed my thoughts in only one direction." And with that, she brought her tongue into play.

"…I'm not complaining," Tom managed as a tingling warmth spread through him. "But I am wondering how that cabin got so damned far away."

"So would you care to pass the time by telling me more of your fantasies?" she continued to encourage the reaction she felt in him.

"This one isn't over yet," he breathed. "And what happened to your new fascination for idly ambling rides?"

"I don't really know," she traced kisses along his jaw. "Nor do I care," she hungrily sought his mouth.

"Whoa, now," he clamped an arm to her waist, "or we'll never reach that un-used bed." And he urged the horse into a slow gallop across the meadow.

But Mandria was done-in by the increased momentum. Her thighs tightened against him; her hands clutched at his shirt; and the sigh which escaped her lips had Tom all but yanking the horse to a stop before the cabin. "Down, lady," he unseated her and slid to the ground on her heels. Then, with one hand keeping his trousers up and the other clasped to her wrist, he was hauling her up the steps. "Well?" he said impatiently as they came to the door, which Mandria had to open with her free hand—and a fit of giggles over the comical picture he made. It grew into rollicking laughter when he marched her over the dusty floor of the main room and straight to the bed. It worsened, much to his chagrin, as he flung her unceremoniously to her back and immediately fell upon her.

"If you think it's funny that you can make a grown man behave like this…" And up came her laughing mouth to kiss him, only to fall away in renewed mirth. "Sure, go ahead and enjoy yourself—because I certainly intend to!" And as he made a few well-aimed thrusts, her mouth returned to his with a deep probing kiss. "Damn," he swore softly. "Mandria, I have never—ever—wanted you so badly!"

"And just think, Tom, when we get home, our own bed will need re-christening too," she smiled up at him. "…Though it will have to go some to be more memorable than this," she finished, as a fresh onset of laughter threatened to erupt.

"No—no, no, no!" Tom quickly kissed her and set himself into a steadier, more intoxicating rhythm. "Hold on, love," he uttered against her mouth. "Just…hold me."

And this time, Mandria wanted nothing more than to do as she was told…

CHAPTER 33

—⸺)((◉))⸺—

Tom Watched as Mandria shooed John and Brittany into the back of the wagon ahead. Evelyn followed and when Mandria handed Seph up to her, the children began to squabble over who would hold the baby first. But his wife, who had every confidence in her mother's ability to settle the issue, looked back at him with a smile that said so and then went to climb aboard the front, where she knew he would soon join her.

From behind the canvass cover of the second wagon, a bark, a mew, and a giggle said the pets and newly-weds had nested down in there. Hearing another giggle, Tom nodded, knowing the driver of this wagon would not enjoy much conversation out of Allen and Lucy. Then, making another round of both wagons to see that everything was secure, he nodded again. And this was one of wonder. How was it possible to accumulate so much stuff when only last autumn, he and Mandria had arrived in Athens with only a saddlebag and one small gunny-sack? ...Of course, there were nine of them and a baby going back, so that made the numerous valises and Evelyn's trunk understandable. Then, there were necessities, such as bed rolls, pillows, bags of oats for the horses, boxes of food staples, cooking utensils and a crock for fresh water. And as Mandria would not part with the cradle he'd made, it was there too. ...But what on earth could be in the rest of those boxes the women insisted they take? One, he knew, held the children's toys and favorite treasures—like Brittany's collection of shiny pebbles and John's petrified frogs. Tom could understand that too, but a thousand pebbles and two thousand dried frogs couldn't weigh what some of those boxes did. Moving a family, he decided, was hugely different from grabbing a saddlebag and riding away on a horse.—And most certainly, when women were trusted to do the packing.

"So how far do you think we'll travel today?" Susan asked as she approached the rear wagon.

"About half what we should," Tom laughed. For once the people were added to this load, the wagons were not going to set any speed records. "But up you go, Miss Hope-to-my-die," he helped her onto the seat. Then he turned and called to Mike, who had decided he needed a shave when it was learned he'd be riding the first leg with Susan.

"Coming!" he answered, rounding the house. And as Tom went toward the lead wagon, he enjoyed another chuckle, for the Captain had also made use of a fine smelling talc. However, what followed was not amusing—and especially, not for the Captain.

"Just one moment!" Susan exclaimed, refusing to release the reins to him. "I'm going to drive—*if* you don't mind."

"Oh, surely not when you have a perfectly capable man around," he gave her his most charming Irish smile.

"Are you saying I'm incapable?" she asked.

"Never would I dare," he answered, aware that all now listened to this exchange. "...It's just that I would prefer to drive—at least until we're out of town and into the open countryside."

"Where there are no gawking males to scoff at you for allowing a woman at the reins, of course," her chin rose.

"Well, there is that," he admitted. "But Susan, I would just feel more at ease driving, than sitting here like a bump on a log."

"Yet you'd have me look the same way with no qualms whatsoever— and to that, I will not agree!" Then she wagged her school teacher's finger in his face. "You are not at the helm of your ship, Captain Herb; I am not your obedient crewman;—and *I* am driving this wagon out of Athens!"

"Hell, do it then!" Mike's temper snapped. And hopping to the ground, he crawled angrily onto the back of the lead wagon. "Besides that," he yelled, "the Irish Mist is a boat and not a damn ship, Miss Know-it-all!"

"Tom," Mandria whispered with a look of dismay, "...maybe I should ride with Susan for a while?"

"Maybe so," he whispered back. "But don't offer any unasked for advice, love. If she wants to talk about this, she will."

"And meanwhile, will you try to reason with Mike?" she leaned to kiss his cheek. "I can't imagine why he is being so hard-headed."

"Mountain goats usually are," he reminded her of an earlier prediction as she climbed to the ground again. But the pleading look in her eyes made him relent. "Run along, pretty lady. I'll do what I can—but I will expect payment from you in return."

"You would," she turned with a saucy swish of her skirts. "—And I'm glad!" she laughed, hurrying away.

So, with everyone finally in place—if not exactly as planned—the wagons began their southeast journey...

"Damn," Mike muttered after a time. He couldn't continue to sit on the back of this wagon facing that impossible woman—who was now chatting with Mandy as if nothing had happened. It was only making him angrier and besides, his legs were beginning to cramp. ...But neither did he feel like joining the game of Chinese Checkers going on behind him. Mamalyn and the children had invited him to play, but he knew his mood would dampen their fun. That left Tom and the place up front that Mandy had vacated—which wasn't a bad solution, now that he thought about it. Yes, the more distance he put between himself and Miss Susan Rutledge the better! So, still fuming, he excused his way through the others inside and went forward.

"Well," Tom dared when Mike crawled onto the seat beside him, "you can drive this wagon if you want to. I believe I could survive it without feeling like a bump on a log."

"Very funny," Mike snarled. "But that wasn't the damned point—and you know it! She is just...hell, she's too damned stubborn!"

Tom sent the Captain a measuring glance. "Don't be too hard on her. Maybe you'd understand her attitude if you knew more about her life in Athens."

"Her belligerent attitude!" Mike injected. "Tom, all I wanted was to drive the damned wagon!"

"And more than she wanted to keep you from it, she wanted the town to see she'd finally been included in something. ...Mike, those people have never known exactly how to treat her lameness. Years back, Susan went when invited to a social gathering, but she wasn't asked to join in the dances or more active games—and they honestly believed it was a kindness; a way of sparing her the embarrassment of having to refuse herself. So, there she would sit—"

"Like a bump on a log," Mike uttered, grudgingly.

"Yes, but a beautiful one. And that caused further problems. You see, while the ladies showed her too much pity, some of the men—the bastard element—thought that *poor lame Susan* should be grateful for some amorous attention. And since she lived conveniently alone, many a knock was made at her door after wives had been safely escorted home."

"Well, that's a fine joke—when the woman is obviously an iceberg!" Mike exclaimed, angered more by what he'd just heard than he realized.

"...No, she is anything but," Tom nodded. "Isolated, might be a better word. Susan simply cut herself off from a world that offered no alternatives she could live with and learned to survive on her own."

"Yeah, but what you said about people watching her leave? Well, I'm no Adonis or anything, but you'd think she'd want them to see her riding beside an eligible man too.—Not that I'd want her to get the wrong idea," he hastened to add, "but she might have enjoyed what they made of it."

"Captain, Susan doesn't give a damn for anyone's opinion of her solitary life," Tom explained. "She is only trying to make the best of her lot;—and like the rest of us, with as much dignity as possible."

Mike stretched his legs out before him and propping them comfortably, began to relax a bit. "...So, how did you come to know her so well?" he asked after a moment. "I remember you said she taught you and Allen, but she hardly looks old enough for that."

"She isn't old at all. When we moved here, she was still in school herself. At 16, she became a student teacher under my mother's tutelage. And as Mama was as much a loner as Susan, they became good friends."

"Which you couldn't have objected to overly much," Mike chuckled. "Having a pretty young thing under-foot would delight any lad."

"Hell yes, it did. At twelve, I had a bad case of puppy-love for Susan," Tom laughed too. "Then after my mother's death, Allen and I moved around quite a bit, but Susan never failed to offer us a meal or a place to sleep-over when we came to town. Later on, when I started college, we moved into her guest room. And she insisted on keeping Allen again while I was getting settled in Savannah. So all in all, Mike, Susan couldn't have been a better friend," he finished, deleting whole chapters from his college years. "She would make a fine friend for you too—if you'd give it half a chance and stop taking the things she says personally."

Mike folded his arms, said nothing—and Tom didn't press him. He knew the Captain to be a considerate man and once he'd digested their discussion, he'd try to patch things with Susan. Hopefully...

On the wagon behind, a similar conversation was taking place. "Susan, are you sorry you decided to come with us?" Mandria asked. "You didn't smile much when we drove through Athens."

"I'm not at all sorry," she nodded. "I just hope you don't regret asking me now. ...I'm afraid I behaved very badly back there."

"Susan, please. You are a dear friend—"

"And Captain Herb is Tom's dear friend—which makes my show of temper even more deplorable," she insisted.

Mandria laughed. "Well, I thought Mike's tantrum equaled it out rather nicely. ...But then, his life has not been happy of late. Mike is a friend with problems he is still trying to overcome, I'm afraid."

"The girl—Nicole," Susan said. "Yes, he told me about her."

"Did he?" Mandria asked in surprise. "Well...maybe that's a good sign, because as far as I know, he hasn't spoken to anyone but Tom about her."

"Oh, he didn't confide in me—nothing so personal as that," Susan hastened an assurance. "He just said his feelings weren't returned." Then she paused. "...But Mandy, how can that be? They were engaged, weren't they?"

"Unofficially, I suppose they were," Mandria replied. "Nico did accept Mike's proposal, but sadly, these other things happened and he was never able to give her his ring. Anyway, do try to be patient with him—for all our sakes?" she added hopefully.

And that had Susan laughing. "I will, Mandy. After all, he is only a man and as we both know, men can not handle rejection much better than children."

"No, most of them can't," Mandria looked toward the wagon ahead, wishing for a glimpse of her handsome husband. *...And then there is Tom,* she thought with pride. *...My wonderfully constant and ever-persistent love, who never accepted my rejection for one moment...*

The rest of the day passed peacefully, with the men doing most of the driving. And as the general plan was to lunch on the road every day, reserving hot meals for morning and evening, Susan and Mike were not thrown together again until camp was made and supper served.

"Evelyn, that was delicious," Susan began to gather the dishes when everyone had finished. "You must give me your recipe."

"Of course," Evelyn smiled, noting that Susan seemed in a very good mood.

Mike noticed this too. "Yeah, Mamalyn, nothing is better than Savannah Red Rice," he sprawled against a log with a sigh of contentment. "—And Susan, your cornbread was especially good," he strove to prove himself in fine spirits also.

"Thank you," she smiled. "…So, would you care to help with the dishes, Captain Herb?" And that was as close to an offer of reconciliation as Susan knew how to come.

"Help with the dishes?" Mike laughed, believing it said in jest. "Susan, I'm so stuffed, I can hardly move!"

"But we ladies are not your servants," she tried to keep smiling as she explained. "And in appreciation of this fine meal, you really should help clean the dishes."

Mike took a moment to reinforce his smile as well. "And you, Miss Rutledge, *really should* allow a tired man some peace. I mean, in spite of your charming rebellion this morning, we men still did the majority of the driving today—and you know it."

"Why you…insufferable, over-fed male!" she spat. "Are our bottoms less sore from riding because you drove?—Is our need to loll restfully about less than yours, only because we're *just* the women you drove here?"

Mike bolted to his feet. "If the rest of you—*nice people*—will excuse me, I'm going to bed, because removing myself from *her* presence is the only damned way I can end this and remain a gentleman!" But it was a most ungentlemanly word he uttered when nearly tripping over one of Brittany's kittens as he stomped toward the wagon assigned to the men.

"I didn't want your blasted help anyway!" Susan shouted at his retreating back. And when he ignored her, she was even more furious. "If you *nice people* will excuse me also, I am going to do the dishes— *alone!*" she stressed, discouraging any offers of help before they could be made. "Then I too, shall retire." she added snatching up a bucket and going toward a near-by brook.

"…Mercy sakes," Evelyn uttered.

"We may all be praying for mercy before this trip is over," Tom sent his wife a side-long glance. "—And be glad we *stayed out of the middle?*"

But Mandria's reply was said to John and Brittany, who still looked after Susan with wide-eyes. "Children, you mustn't be upset by any of this. Sometimes, it just takes grown-ups a good while to realize they should be friends."

"We know," John nodded sagely. "Like you and Tom done—did!" he corrected when his sister jabbed him.

"That's right," Lucy concurred. "And look how happy they are now—with two nice children, a brand new baby and not one harsh word between them."

"Oh Mandy!" Brittany said excitedly. "Maybe Miss Susan is pregernant too—and the Captain just doesn't know it yet!"

"Yeah!" John added with great enthusiasm.

"Oh, Lord," Allen hugged the pair, laughing along with the others. "Kids, *please* don't suggest that to either of them.—*Please!*"

"They certainly won't," Mandria rose, smiling. "Because it's bedtime for my three precious children. So come along, Brittany, I'll tuck you in and feed Seph while you get to sleep."

"And I'll take John," Tom offered. "—Just think, Bear. There are no bath tubs out here, so you will escape with a mild scrub-down."

"Whoopee!" he chortled, following Tom to the men's wagon. "Hey, Tom, why don't we just stay on the trail forever!"

"Oh, no, John—not like them Shorts!" called his sister as she trailed after Mandria toward the other wagon. "Baths ain't so bad when you think of that."

"*Ain't?*" John skidded to a halt. "Brit, did you say *ain't?*" he asked with the smugness of a long-suffering avenger.

"Baths *aren't* so bad then," she shrugged. "Good night, John," she added sweetly and hurried on.

After a moment of trying to decide what had happened to his triumph, John looked up at Tom with a puzzled frown. "...I knew I'd catch her if I waited long enough."

"But she didn't let you enjoy it much, did she?" Tom chuckled, stooping to scratch Critter's ear.

"No, sir. She sure likes getting one on me though; ...so why is that?"

"Son, that's just the way women are. No man will ever understand the why of it," Tom nodded. "But Lord, they do make life interesting."

"Humph!" came a voice of dissension from within the wagon. "If I were you, boy, I'd avoid them like the damned plague!"

"Yes, Bear," Tom laughed again. "Then you can hide in wagons and grumble like a troll—as Captain Herb is doing now."

"Humph!" Mike repeated on the edge of a chuckle. "And good night to you too, Tom Scott."

Susan's temper had also cooled a bit by the time she returned with her bucket of water. She made no objection when Lucy, Allen and Evelyn insisted on helping with the dishes and cook pots, and by bedtime, all were chatting as amiably as ever. But it became evident that the war between Susan and Mike still raged, for once everyone was abed, a great deal of tossing and pillow-punching was endured in both wagons late into the night…

CHAPTER 34

Morning dawned clear and cool and after a light breakfast of coffee, cocoa and a warmed batch of Susan's cinnamon buns, they were on their way again. And as neither Mike nor Susan wanted to upset the delicate peace they had managed throughout the meal, each chose to ride separate wagons again. Then the sun began its inevitable slide in the western sky and there was no avoiding the evening gathering. But that, too, began peacefully—and largely due to a real effort on Mike's part.

"As you ladies did a good deal of driving today," he camouflaged his point in gallantry, "I've decided to fix supper—and wash the dishes." To which, Susan said nothing.

"Captain, I didn't know you could cook," Mandria hastened to cover that silence.

"Yes, Mike, what are we having?" Evelyn asked.

"Irish Stew, of course," he answered proudly. "Now if someone would kindly show me where the supplies are kept?" And Susan didn't move.

"I will," Lucy volunteered, leading the way.

Mandria gave Seph to Allen and taking her husband's hand, insisted they follow. "Mike, I want you to show Tom how you do this. His specialty is jerky and mush!" And that brought the children for a look-see as well...

"So what do you make of that, Evelyn?" Susan puzzled, once all were out of ear-shot.

"I would say, after a day of consideration, that Mike has offered you a truce," she suggested lightly, reaching to tickle her grandson's little chin.

"Or was it a clever put-down?" Susan's eyes caught the gleam of the camp-fire. "Does he really expect me to do nothing about supper?—Like he *didn't* last night?"

"Susan," drawled Allen. "Do give the man some credit. Or would you rather have him groveling at your feet?"

"Of course not!" she rose to hers in a huff. "But I will carry my own weight, so I'll just go make the bread." And with that, she hobbled away, followed by her own entourage, of Critter and two kittens.

Evelyn allowed a soft laugh. "Allen, do you suppose it will be cornbread, since Mike said he liked hers?"

"Don't bet on it," he grinned, ruffling his nephew's hair, "—especially because he liked it."

But Susan did make cornbread and when her idea of a returned peace-offering went unmentioned by the Irishman, it rankled deeply. *Why can't he just admit my gesture is as great as his?* she mused. *Men are so dense—never willing to meet a woman half-way on anything!*

Mike saw things differently from his side of the cook fire. He was pleased as punch when Susan took a second helping of his stew. It had to mean she liked it. "Now for the dishes," he announced, while starting to collect empty plates. "And if I must say so myself, that stew was exceptional," his gaze rested hopefully on Susan.

"It could have used less salt," she remarked. If he wasn't going to compliment her cornbread—and he'd eaten three pieces—then she certainly wouldn't praise his stew. "Also, I will wash my own plate, thank you—as well as the skillet, bowl and utensils used to make *my exceptional* cornbread." And with the aforementioned items in hand, she started for the lake they had camped beside this night. Let him haul water back for the dishpan, if he liked. This time, she'd finish her work and be the first to bed.

"Well, I thought everything was good," Lucy injected as Mike stood looking after Susan in surprise. "It really, really was."

"And isn't it a beautiful—*quiet*—evening?" Tom glanced from the twilight heavens, to Mike, hoping he'd take the hint.

"Yeah, while it lasts," Allen laughed, but it died an early death after a look from both Tom and Mike. "—I mean, it could rain or something," he explained.

"In which case, I'd better get these dishes done," Mike clattered them nosily into a pan. "Besides," he purposely raised his voice as he, too, carried his chore lakeside, "I wouldn't want *all-that-salt* to crust them over!" And Susan's response from a few feet away was lost beneath the bang of a spoon against an iron skillet.

Mandria turned to her husband and read the *I told you so* in his eyes, which she promptly ignored. "Tom, I know it's early, but why don't the rest of us go to bed and give them some time alone?"

Allen laughed out-right at this suggestion. "Then it may as well rain;—and lightning and thunder too, for all the noise we'll be hearing out here!"

"Maybe not," Evelyn disagreed. "No, maybe if they think we're trying to sleep, they'll make an effort at keeping down their voices."

"Yes, and once they learn they can talk without shouting," Mandria, added, "then things will improve between them."

Now Tom had to laugh. "Which reminds me of another story, my love—and a very loud, cold, door-banging winter? But to bed we will go," he rose for a good stretch. "Hey, Captain," he called over their exodus, "we're turning in now, so bank the fire and check the horses before you come, will you?"

"Most certainly!" Mike answered, not looking up from the power-scrub he was giving to a pot. "I'll do the damned dishes," he continued under his breath. "I'll bank the damned fire. I'll check the damned horses—"

"Oh don't bother!" Susan lost even more patience with his complaints. "I'm finished here, so I'll do it. I certainly wouldn't want you to tire yourself," she said as she rose to her feet.

That was it. That was all Mike intended to take. "Damn it, woman, no you will not!" he stood too and blocked her way. "Just tell me something. Is it only me, or do you hate all men?"

"I don't know what you could mean, so that does not even deserve an answer," she said frostily.

"It means—Miss Rutledge—you seem to enjoy making men look and behave like clowns, damn it!"

"Well, it has been my experience—Captain Herb—that most men already are and don't need my help to prove it."

"And me in particular?"

"…No," her chin rose, "I find nothing particularly special about you."

"Ah, but if that's true, then why are you constantly snubbing me? Surely a mere man—who is nothing particularly special—should be beneath your notice."

"You are, of course," she sniffed. "Still, I have never snubbed anyone in my entire life, and it's unkind of you to suggest that."

"Then what would call this unfair competition you've been waging against me?"

"Ridiculous—as I've no intention of competing with you for anything." And up went her chin another notch.

"Oh-hell-yes you are!" he corrected. "What woman insisted on driving yesterday—just to bolter *her* ego? Who reduced me to kitchen duty—for the sole purpose of deflating *mine*? And when *I* was man enough to go along with it, who showed *her* ass by insulting *my* stew and refusing to let *me* wash *her* plate—which was the very damned thing *she* wanted *me* to do last night?"

Had Susan been in her classroom and that jumble of words been presented as an oral report, it would have rated an *F*. That she understood it, was even more perplexing. "Captain…I have truly never heard a more incredible…load of horse manure!" And out came laughter she could not contain.

Confused, Mike took a backward step. "At least I've managed to amuse you," he nodded. "So, what could that mean?"

"Well, to me, it means I am going to bed," she still laughed while stepping around him. "And you may do the chores Tom requested of you, as I don't see the need for further competition of any sort."

"But Susan...are we going to be friends or not?" he asked now. She stopped and faced him, deciding he had earned some explanation. "I don't know the answer to that. I do know I dislike feeling used or degraded—and most of my so-called friendships have amounted to little more."

"Yet you didn't mind degrading me," he countered.

"It's not you, Captain—not as a person," she admitted. "It's just your superior male attitude that I find offensive."

"But it's also my male person who was on his knees here, doing dishes—and all to make a friend of you, I might add."

"...Some have gone further," she said hesitantly. "But the result was always the same," she continued, wondering why she felt compelled to. "One way or the other, I ended up being used—and they too, called it friendship."

"They...or *he*?" Mike moved closer. "*They* would make me just another face in the crowd. *He*, on the other hand, would explain why you keep shutting me out. ...Like me, you've been badly hurt and don't want to risk that again. Am I right?"

Susan was truly stunned by Mike's perceptiveness and more than a little unnerved by his nearness—which, in turn, brought up her defenses. "All right, so you've guessed I'm not pure and unsullied; that it earned me a great deal of unwanted attention from some of the men in a small town.—So?"

"So, it wasn't Tom, was it?" And now Mike took a turn at being stunned.—Why the hell had he asked that question?

The effect on Susan was even more surprising, for it sparked a revelation. *...Tom, the second and only other man in my life; Tom, a soothing balm to an open wound; Tom, who taught me to place greater value on myself as I am.* ...So, why, as she stood staring blankly ahead now, was she seeing a negative side to their encounter for the first time? *...Perhaps because I can see all the positives in his relationship with Mandy? ...Yes, and that would mean ours was never an affair of the* *heart, but rather a lovely oasis in time. A sharing, certainly, and yet, we never spoke of love or commitment; …because it wasn't there. And once we'd given all we could without those things, it had to end…*

"Susan…I—hell, I'm sorry!" Mike stammered, deeply embarrassed. "That was rude and none of my damned business." And he was thinking, she really should slap his face.

But Susan saw the pain in Mike's eyes—a pain which said he regretted far more than the question at hand. It made him worthy of her confidence; a fellow loser in the game of life. "…I was very young and naïve—and yes, I was hurt very deeply. But no, Captain Herb, it was not by Tom."

"It was still a stupid question," Mike uttered, feeling relieved all the same—which only confused him more. "Hell, Tom is one the finest men I've ever known."

"Me, as well," she nodded. "I can honestly say he is my best friend. One who never seemed to notice my limp, or tried to take advantage of me because of it."

With that, the twinkle returned to the Captain's eyes. "What limp?" he grinned—and it felt good. "Susan, me-darlin', I haven't been able to look past your beautiful face and grand figure to see that you limp!"

And here came the slap he'd expected earlier. "Blarney—more of your damned Irish blarney!" she railed. "You couldn't leave well enough alone, could you, Michael Herb?"

"Damnation!" he grasped her arms. "If you think a compliment makes me less than a gentleman, you're wrong!—And that wasn't blarney, but the truth!"

"Truth?" she shook away his touch. "You want to hear truth? The truth is you've just lost the woman you love and you're still blaming Tom or you'd never have asked such a thing.—And I even know why. You don't want his left-overs!"

Stung by her words—and humbled—Mike turned his eyes away. "…No, Susan, I don't blame Tom any longer," he began to stammer about for excuses. "It's…well—damn it, I've just never met a woman who could resist him. I mean, talk about degrading experiences—"

"Oh, we're back to the male ego, are we?" she snapped. "Well, let me tell you something, Captain. I don't want left-overs either; and as long as you cling to the past, that is all you offer. So just keep your pretty compliments—or go try them on some nit-wit—but I have better to do with my life than wasting another second of it!" And as Susan hobbled away, she had never felt lighter on her feet, because she had just survived a personal purging that was long overdue…

"Damn her anyway," Mike muttered, watching her go. "But damn," he said again, because if she was right, he had a hell of a long row to hoe before getting over Nicole—and as she'd just pointed out, no sane woman would want to settle for the dregs of an old love affair…

Then he sighed. But what a splendid affair it had been, wrapped in the shiny gossamer of all his dreams. Could he help it if he still ached knowing how close they'd come to fulfillment? What remained for him seemed as little as what remained of Nicole. "My beauty with less now, than the mind of a child." …And yet, hadn't he always thought her child-like, even before her tragic fate? From the first, hadn't it been that quality which attracted him;—her sweet ability to bring forth his need to cherish and protect?

So what the hell drew him to Susan Rutledge? …Of course, she was a beautiful woman too. "A beauty with a crippled foot—and the God damned tongue of a snake!" he avowed. "Women just shouldn't be so blunt. No, it's not feminine!"

Feminine…like Nicole—yes, and if she hadn't become involved with Sam Lucas, he could have been happy with the woman-child she was. Nicole would never have questioned his male authority. Quite properly so, she would have expected him to do the thinking for them both; expected him to dedicate his life to caring for her body, mind and soul. …And in return, what could he have expected? Well, gratification of his physical needs, certainly; a beautiful wife, too—a real treasure to dangle on his arm for other men to envy…

'Oh, we're back to the male ego,' Susan's words sliced through his reverie. …But she said a lot, and none of it flattering to him. Susan just thought too damned much—and would likely insist on expressing *her* opinions about *his* decisions. Why, a woman like that would exhaust a man's mind before ever considering his physical needs.—And what husband would want a constant tussle for dominance with his own wife?

"*Wife?—Husband?*" Mike grew angry again. How dare Susan invade an area reserved for Nicole! How dare she even cause him to make this damned comparison! ...But he was, and he couldn't seem to stop...

In retrospect then—and in fairness—both women suffered deformities: Nicole with her warped morality; Susan with her foot—and the damned brain of a man! ...One had captured his heart, but blinded him to her flaws. The other...intrigued him—he knew not why—and forced him to look at his own faults. And for the life of him, Mike couldn't decide which was better or worse...

"Well, hell, what kind of choice is that anyway?" he became defensive. He was better off staying single forever and taking pleasure where he found it. Yes, whores didn't care what thoughts went through a man's mind—and even less about intruding on his right to have them. Hell, whores preferred their men in a prone position and weren't interested in keeping him on his damned toes!

...But was that so different from his idea of marriage to Nicole?—Hell yes, in that he would have had legal and exclusive right to the woman in his bed...maybe; if Nicole hadn't become involved with Sam; or suffered an affliction which rendered her incapable of fidelity, as everyone kept telling him she did. Then Mike shuddered, admitting a moment of relief, for if Nicole had proven an unfaithful wife, he would have lost his dreams just the same, but at the cost of his sanity and honor as well...

Now, seen in that light, was a mere struggle for dominance of such importance in a marriage? There was something...stimulating about matching wits with Susan; something...fascinating about a woman being able to discuss the things he found of interest with a degree of intelligence; something...appealing about a wife being both a helpmate and bedmate...

"Damn, I'm doing it again!" Mike swore. But this time, it wasn't in anger. ...What right did he have to think of Susan as his wife? He didn't even have the right to put her through these mental comparisons—which she was winning rather handily. No, this wasn't wise. He could and would make peace with her, because he genuinely liked that beautiful woman, but he was not about to set himself up for another disappointment. Oh-hell-no—the priesthood would be better than risking that! And satisfied with his decision, Mike gathered his clean dishes, completed a check of the camp and retired…

But morning brought the onset of another clash. "…So, Uncle Pat just told her no," Mike was saying to Tom as they finished their coffee. "And I can see his point. Why should Aunt Mary Ernestine go to work? His hours are irregular, at best, and when he does get a chance to come home for a meal, he wants her there instead of in someone else's kitchen. I mean, if they needed extra money, it might be different, but Uncle Pat has always provided a decent living."

"Well, my mother had to work," Tom nodded, "and though she loved teaching, I often wished she'd been home more. She was forever starting some project or craft that she never had the time or energy to finish."

"Yeah, it's a matter of priorities, I suppose," Mike shrugged. "But Aunt Mary Ernestine didn't see it that way. Hell, she argued that she needed more to do or some such nonsense. She said that raising me had kept her busy enough, but with only the two of them now, she found herself sitting in a clean house twiddling her thumbs. Uncle Pat told her she'd earned the rest—and sensibly so, to go visit the sick or volunteer to clean the church, but to be at home when he got there, which sounded only right to me."

"It would!" Susan exclaimed, hearing all she could stand. "The poor woman is bored to death and your Uncle's solution is absurd!"

"…You'd have her ignore her husband's wishes?" Mike asked in astonishment.

"No, but neither should your Aunt's wishes be ignored," she argued. "Mike, she could take in sewing or laundry—anything to fill her hours usefully."

"Well, Miss Susan Rutledge, I haven't lived in their house for years, but I wouldn't allow her to do other people's dirty laundry—and she doesn't like to sew," he said in rebuttal.

"...She bakes, though," Lucy said timidly.

"Yes, and your Aunt's cakes are truly a marvel," Mandria agreed.

"But she only does that for special occasions," Mike explained. "And only when it doesn't interfere with her duty to Uncle Pat—or to me," he added deliberately.

Susan heaved an exasperated sigh. "Captain Herb, how old are you?"

"I...well, I'll soon be thirty—but what in the hell does that have to do with anything?"

"Thirty. Well past the need for mothering. And how old is your Uncle?"

"Fifty-nine—and mothering isn't what he wants from her either. He wants her company!"

"And his meals served—which is perfectly fine, if she enjoys fixing them," Susan allowed. "But Mike, your Aunt could start a business there in her own kitchen. She could bake and sell her cakes every day and still give her husband the attention he feels he deserves."

"I suppose you'd have her peddle them on street corners too?" he uttered in disbelief.

"If she wasn't already known for her baking, I'd see nothing wrong in that either," Susan nodded. "But she is, so a simple advertisement should bring in all the orders she wants to handle."

"More than she could handle—which brings us back to Uncle Pat's original point. She has earned a rest; he does not need money; and therefore, she shouldn't work anywhere." And Mike's tone oozed righteousness.

"Are all men this dense?" Susan glanced at the ladies for conformation and received back three different versions of a headnod. "Mike, your Aunt's need is the important thing here. If she feels useless, she will begin to behave that way. Would you rather she turned to a bottle instead of her oven? Would you rather she dreaded her empty days or buzzed happily about her kitchen?"

"I would rather you minded your own damned business!" Mike marched toward the lead wagon and climbed onto the driver's seat. "And I may only be a dense male in your book, but I'm smart enough to know a marriage that has lasted 32 years doesn't need any damned interference from you!" And folding his arms, he sat with a jarring bump.

Stung, Susan hobbled toward the other wagon. "Well, I know what I saw my own mother suffer," she made a valiant effort to keep her emotions in check. "I watched her become an alcoholic and die! I lived with a father who never realized this same sort of selfishness took her life.—Oh no, Father died blaming God! But it was his pompous attitude that killed Mama—just as you and your Uncle will do to your poor Aunt!" And climbing into the back, she lowered the flap, which did very little to muffle her sobs.

"Oh, for heaven's sake," Evelyn muttered, hurrying to offer comfort. "You'd think Mike would be more tactful."

"...So now we're taking sides?" Allen tried to make light of the tension. "Is it to be men against women at twenty paces?" And the elbow Lucy gave him was not only merited, but sharper than any reply the others could have made.

"You know what, John?" Brittany uttered softly. "I don't care if I never grow up."

"Me either," he agreed. "Even 'rithmatic is easier to understand than all this hollering and stuff."

"Least they don't hit each other—or us—like them Shorts did," she added.

"Yeah, I guess this is still better. ...I guess," he puzzled.

Tom expelled a breath, knowing he'd have to attempt an explanation. "Bear; Brit, arithmetic is easy because when you're dealing with numbers, the answers are simple: One plus one always makes two. But with people it's more difficult. When you have one man and one woman, who are united in thought and deeply in love, the two are supposed to function as one. However," he turned to include Mandria in this message, "when they aren't so united, what you will get every time, is a big fat zero. Plus all this hollering and stuff."

"See?" John looked knowingly at his sister. "Sometimes grown-ups don't even have to holler and they still don't make any sense."

With that, and a smug tilt of Mandria's chin, Tom abandoned the effort, suggesting that they break camp and move on. And none was more surprised than he when the morning slipped by so quickly, for this particular spat left all with much to ponder…

———◈———

…Why, Evelyn wondered, *have I never felt bored with my life? Well, because Sam wasn't a husband who cared for my company—nor I for his—so I've always filled my time as I liked. And, in truth, I'm kept quite busy with my clubs, church and charity functions. Yes, I've seldom considered myself lucky, but in this one aspect my life hasn't been so bad. …And it allowed me to remain close enough to at least see Ransom almost daily…*

———◈———

…Well, I do have my art, Mandria decided. *In fact, there have been times when I preferred painting alone to the company of vital, active people—with the exception of Tom, of course. …But of late, I haven't had a moment to call my own; not with a house to run and now the children to tend. …Yet, I do have something to fall back on should I need to. Yes, and I'll find time for painting again, surely…*

———◈———

Tom nodded. *…A little boredom would be a welcome thing to my way of thinking. Just keeping track of everyone—and trying to keep peace among them has proven quite the task…*

———⟨✦⟩———

...Damn you, Susan Rutledge! Mike shifted uncomfortably. *It wasn't my fault she cried. She was just remembering the mother she lost.—No, and the same could never happen to Aunt Mary Ernestine! She's a strong, God-fearing woman...who asked me to bring her a case of cooking sherry on my last trip to Augusta. But hell, she's always looking for a special spice or something. ...Yet, cooking sherry is one of the products exported to Augusta and available everywhere in Savannah . ...Unless she didn't want it known she was buying it by the case. ...And wasn't there a cheery glow about her cheeks when I saw her last? Yes, but there always is, thank you very much, Miss Rutledge! Besides, Uncle Pat would know if she'd been nipping the bottle too much. ...Wouldn't he?*

———⟨✦⟩———

Bored? Allen and Lucy exchanged adoring glances. *It could never happen in their lives—not in a million years! Happily, they could live on love forever...*

———⟨✦⟩———

...Never—ever—will I allow such embarrassing behavior again! Susan vowed. *...Evelyn had said not to fret over it; but I've never been subject to tears in the heat of an argument, so how was that damned Irishman able to make me cry?—Why too, would I choose to argue for the welfare of his Aunt—a woman I don't even know? ...And why, most of all, do I have to see a great capacity for love in Mike's argument, blind, though it is? Yes, and he tries to hide that gentle caring as much as I try to hide my tears.* Then, she nodded. *Susan, you are a fool—looking for silk is a sow's ear. And with your eyes wide open, still hoping to find it someday..."*

417

CHAPTER 35

I t was a subdued group that pulled into Augusta later that Wednesday afternoon. But at least transferring everyone and everything aboard the Irish Mist went smoothly.

"Since it's not yet four o'clock, Susan," said Evelyn, "and we are already settled into our cabin, why don't we go on a shopping spree?"

"What on earth for?" she puzzled. "Besides, tromping about the streets on this foot is not my idea of fun."

"Not even to find material for your party gown?" Evelyn questioned. "Yes…with your coloring, I believe you'd look lovely in a rose or burgundy hue.—For Mandy's party?"

"I…I hadn't thought of needing a special gown," Susan hedged. "Will the affair be so formal?"

"If not formal, then certainly festive—if I know my daughter," Evelyn smiled. "She will want Savannah to see exactly how proud she is of her husband, home and new family."

"Yes, of course, she will," Susan nodded. "But Evelyn, it has been some time since I paid attention to fashion. I mean, my skirts and blouses were all that I needed…so you would have to guide my selection."

"And won't that be fun?" she laughed. "Come along then. We'll just fetch Mandy and Lucy and make an outing of it for all the ladies!"

"Yes, and—and maybe I should look for a few pretty ready-mades too. For your club meetings—shouldn't I?" Susan's excitement took wing.

"Well, of course, you should," Evelyn agreed. "With bonnets, scarves and gloves to match!" And in spite of her foot, Susan hurried to keep up...

"Listen, Tom," Allen paced the wheelhouse floor. "It's nearly six o'clock now.—Something could have happened to those women!"

"Calm yourself, little brother," Tom shifted Seph to his other arm. "Your bride hasn't abandoned you. She's just out spending your money;—which you'd better get used to," he grinned, looking along the deck to make sure John and Brittany were still busily exploring the Irish Mist, accompanied by Critter, of course.

"Hell, Tom," Mike chuckled. "It's not money Allen's thinking about. After days on the road—and nights in separate wagons—he wants to make use of their private cabin."

"So?—What's wrong with that?" Allen tried, but couldn't quite control a slight flush. "We are still on our honeymoon, you know."

"And still dropping coins in the bottle—I do know," Mike nodded. "So maybe in a year or two, you'll tell us if there's truth to that old Irish saying."

"What saying?" Allen tried not ask, but did anyway.

"Well, that if a couple should drop a coin in a bottle every time they make love in the first year of marriage, and take one out, each time thereafter, they will never go broke." Mike teased.

"Damn," laughed Tom. "With that six month draught we endured, Mandria and I would be in the poorhouse already."

"Whoa!" Mike rose from his chair, to gaze toward the landing, where the ladies were just stepping down from a rental carriage. "... Would you look at that?" he said in amazement. For dressed in a gown of rich, deep lilac, Susan had never looked lovelier. And it seemed to Mike, even the dock hands were ogling the striking contrast of that color and her cloud of thick dark hair. ...Until she moved forward. Then, as one, they turned away, likely fearing she'd think they stared because of her limp. "Those damned idiots—that's no way to treat a lady!" he bolted from the door, wondering why he felt personally insulted. And with Tom and Allen, close behind, he still hadn't shaken that notion, when they stood facing the women.

"Miss Susan Rutledge," he began with a courtly bow—and then recalled her dislike for his compliments. "...I—uh, must say, you purchased wisely. That dress seems...well—very serviceable."

"*Serviceable?*" Susan's disappointment manifested itself in a sudden rush of anger. Her standard skirts and tailored blouses were *serviceable*. How dare he ruin her enjoyment of this perfectly lovely dress. "Men!" she snapped. "—And Michael Herb, you are the very worst of the lot!" She then proceeded around him—as did the other ladies, but not until each had directed a look of deep disapproval toward the Captain of the Irish Mist...

"Oh, yes, your way of treating a lady is so much better," Allen remarked. "A real inspiration to those of us hoping for a coin-in-the-bottle kind of evening—not to mention, a long, happy marriage."

"Just shut up, damn it!" Mike stalked away. "And thank God, I'm not contemplating any such foolishness as that!"

⚬

Tom gave the Captain about an hour of solitude before paying a visit to the wheelhouse. It was just dusk, the evening was warm and breezy, and most of the crew had gone ashore for a final night on the town. "Mike?" he called, peering into the dimly lit station.

"What?" came a curt reply, which said he was still nursing a huge case of agitation.

Tom entered and began to turn up the lamps, whose light revealed an open ledger on the table where the Captain sat, pen in hand, trying to look busy. And wisely, Tom let it go unmentioned that it had been in near darkness or that the ledger was upside down. "Listen, I'm getting hungry," he said instead. "Why don't we take the ladies to dinner?"

"You take them," Mike muttered. "I have a lot of log-work to catch up on here."

"And time to do it on the trip down-river," Tom countered, pouring them each a brandy. "Come on, Mike, you know Augusta better than I do. Hell, all I ever saw were the bars, a couple of bedrooms at Delilah's.—And of course, Dexter's little love nest," he chuckled, trying to pry a smile from his friend.

"Yeah, well, Delilah's is exactly where I should be going for the night," Mike tossed the pen aside in disgust. The damn ledger was up-side down, and Tom had to have noticed. "At least *those* women show proper respect for a man's feelings," he slammed the book shut.

"Captain, that is another farce," Tom very pointedly turned the ledger around. "Come morning, you would be marked *Paid in full* and swept out with the rest of the garbage."

"I'm garbage here too, evidently.—Damn it, Tom, what did I say out there that was so wrong? I mean, every time I've paid Susan a compliment, she's called it blarney. And when I tried to be as practical-minded as she is, I incurred the wrath of every damn one of those females!"

"Well, when I took Seph in to Mandria, the impression I got was that the ladies are blaming you for destroying Susan's confidence," he confided. "They are still fluttering around her, trying to rebuild what had taken them the afternoon to accomplish. ...You couldn't have known this, Mike, but that was the prettiest dress she has owned in years. Her school clothes had become a kind of uniform, I guess—a standard of neatly starched and unapproachable perfection. For her, today was a real departure from that. ...And maybe you should feel flattered that she hoped you'd appreciate the change."

"Flattered? Are you saying she wanted a damned compliment this time?" Mike puzzled. "—And if so, just how in the hell is a man supposed to know these things?"

"Don't ask me for logic when it comes to females," Tom chuckled. "I only know that whatever mood they're in, and no matter what they say about it, they all enjoy compliments. And they will certainly let you know when you fail to give one they're expecting—as you learned today."

"Tom?" Mike laughed a bit too. "Did you really understand anything you just said?"

"No, but it is the truth. And you are talking to a man who spent an entire winter having compliments thrown back in his face. But you know something, Captain? Mandria didn't forget a single one of them—and Susan won't either, if it matters to you."

"I'm—well…I don't know about that," he shifted in his chair. "But I won't be held responsible for destroying the poor woman's confidence, so maybe taking them to dinner is the thing to do.—Just so I can prove to *all* the ladies that I'm not a complete cad."

"Of course," Tom answered, hiding a smile in the last sip of his drink as he rose. "Now, as the ladies are all sporting new finery from today's shopping trip, I suppose we should spiff up a bit too. Will you be ready in a half-hour or so?"

"I will," Mike nodded. Then out came a curious question. "…I suppose it would be foolish to expect a compliment in return—for our spiffy appearance, huh?"

"Again, I can only tell you about Mandria," Tom shrugged. "If she blushed when I caught her looking my way, I knew her thoughts were complimentary, even without the words being spoken."

"Another bit of winter-wisdom from the frozen hills of north Georgia?" laughed Mike.

"I suppose so. And though the thaw was damned slow in coming, it beats the hell out of anything else I've found," Tom answered from the doorway. "Now, may I suggest you wear your Irish green jacket and the pearly-whites of your most dashing smile for the rest of the evening?"

"Oh-hell-yes!" Mike agreed, starting to feel his old self again. "Someone has to add a little zest to the occasion—and I'm just Irish enough to do it!"

So began the evening, and true to his word, Mike was entirely charming throughout the meal at a quaint little Restaurant-Pub on Broad Street. He even had Susan laughing at some of his tales—until she noticed the attention he was generating from another of the customers. And then, oddly, she began to wish John and Brittany were not sitting between the Captain and herself. For perched at the bar was a girl whose low-cut bodice and tangled mass of straw-colored hair seemed to beacon her chosen profession. She had an escort already, but had turned in such a way that she could look over his shoulder—directly at Mike. Not that she hadn't given Tom and Allen a thorough going over too, but as their eyes seldom strayed past their wives and Mike's roamed animatedly—and flirtatiously—the girl presumed him the most available.

...*Well, he is, isn't he?* Susan tried to reason away her resentment. *And I certainly wouldn't care if he accepted her blatant invitation...*

Yet, when the girl drew her skirts to her knees and crossed long shapely legs, Susan nearly choked on a sip of her wine. And if that weren't enough, Mike had paused to take that in right in the midst of lifting a bite to his mouth. Then he'd enjoyed a long leisurely sip from his own glass—which Susan knew to be a ploy as he studied the woman. ...The one with those perfectly formed calves; and ankles; and feet that could walk without limping...

Lowering her eyes, Susan had never felt quite so threatened—nor in more need of understanding why. It was completely insane, but something was urging her to vie for the Captain's attention too. "—Michael," she said suddenly, "may I have more wine, please?" And finding her glass still held some, she quickly drained it.

"Certainly," he did the honors with a show of his wide, Irish smile, "And I'm glad to see you approve of my wine selection."

Susan's gaze returned to the postured girl before meeting his eyes. "Yes, good wine—like so much else—depends on the quality of the grape," she smiled too. "And though the cask is important to the process, it's still the quality of what's inside that makes the most desirable product." ...But what was she babbling about? She had no knowledge of the subject—if, indeed, the subject was wine-making.

She realized she wasn't sure; that Mike's eyes hadn't left her as she spoke; and that because she rather liked that, her cheeks had taken on a color to rival the rubiness filling her glass.—And there was another disturbing thing: She hated wine, for it tended to make her weepy and that was the very last thing she needed now…

"So," Mike lifted his own glass in a toast, none but one understood, "to *winter-wisdom* and an *early thaw*."

"And to vigilance," Tom added with a chuckle. "Because the best vines always need careful tending—especially with so-many-weeds about." And this was his way of telling Mike he was also aware of the antics of the woman at the bar and to be cautious in assuming others weren't too.

"Gracious," Lucy nodded in bewilderment. "…I don't feel light headed in the least—and really didn't drink much with dinner—but I don't seem able to follow this conversation. I really, really can't!"

"Well, that will never do," Allen refilled her glass, his thoughts still looking forward to bed-time. "You may as well be as addled as the rest of us, Lucy."

"Yes, Allen, addled is a good description for both of those toasts," Mandria sent her husband and the Captain quizzical looks. "So, let me propose another: To family and friends. May we all stay well and grow even closer in the years ahead."

"Here; here," said the others, joining their glasses in heartfelt unity.

A pledge Susan had readily approved…at first. But when Mike hardly glanced at the leggy woman again, her joy faded into confusion. She was elated that in spite of her deformity, she had managed a sort of victory over a more fortunate female. …Yet, that would mean admitting the stakes were to her liking and she certainly wasn't prepared to do that! No, this was something requiring sober thought—which she couldn't give while fending off a wine-induced urge to indulge herself with a good cry…

It was growing toward midnight when Mike stepped from his cabin for a breath of air. He stretched, feeling the tenseness ease from his shoulders. Then elbows propped on the guard-rail, he lit a cigar and watched the smoke curl on the breeze before rushing illusively into the darkness of night. With a sigh, he analogized that for the past several hours, his thoughts had been doing the same—curling about in his head, only to vanish before he could make sense of them. ... But why? All in all, he was pleased with the evening, for thanks to a sterling display of charm, he was now in everyone's good graces again. Still, he felt...well, unsettled and close to deciding envy to be the reason. Yes, he was envious of his married friends who'd made an escape to their quarters soon after returning to the boat. He was also a bit disappointed that Susan had so readily accompanied Evelyn when she retired early with the children, because he'd wanted to ask if she might enjoy a stroll about the decks first.

But he hadn't, so here he was, alone and in truth, feeling a little sorry for himself—which, naturally, brought the yellow haired girl to mind. ...*Why did I pass that by?* he wondered. *I should have remained at the restaurant, talked some trash to the woman and just about now, I'd be enjoying myself too.* "—Stupid," he muttered, flicking away a lengthy bit of cigar ash.

"Captain Herb!" Susan snapped.

And Mike froze, his first notion being that she'd somehow read his mind. Then turning to face her, he absorbed a second surprise. Wrapped in a peach colored silk robe, her dark, un-bound hair caping her shoulders, Susan was a sight to stir...well, any man.

Susan was experiencing a similar shock. Restless and still close to weeping, she had left the cabin to keep from disturbing Evelyn and the children. And while walking the decks in privacy, she'd allowed those tears to flow, though she was no closer to finding a reason, other than the wine. However, she had not expected to come upon Mike or to betray her presence until suddenly dusted with ashes—and she certainly wasn't ready to deal with the state of his attire. Thankfully, he did wear trousers, but bare feet, tousled hair and an unbuttoned shirt clearly said he'd just crawled out of bed too. She was frankly, embarrassed…and at the same time, curious about his inability to sleep. So much so, that for the first time in her life, Susan resorted to a feminine ploy. "Really, Mike," she quickly raised a hand to her eye, "you should be more careful where you toss hot ashes."

"Damn—I'm sorry, Susan," concern prodded him toward her. "Here, let me see." And tilting her face to a nearby lantern, he observed that the eye was, indeed, red and watering badly. …In fact, both of her eyes were…almost as if she'd been crying. And he meant to learn why. "Into the wheelhouse, Miss Rutledge," he turned her now in that direction. "The light is better there," he explained when she seemed reluctant to move. "Now, march!" he added in his most authorative Captain's voice.

So Susan went, but not without an irritable groan for being caught in her own deception. … *Well,* she thought then, *in for a penny; in for a pound.* "Oh all right then—but only because I've been half-blinded and would likely fall over-board trying to find my cabin again."

"And as I am responsible for the well-being of my passengers, I won't allow that to happen. Now sit," he said, pulling out a chair from the table. And while Susan groped her way into the chair, as one forced to live out a lie might do, Mike quietly dismissed the man on duty. Then he returned to examine her eye again—or tried to, but his own eyes kept straying to other parts of her upturned face: The long, tear-spiked lashes; the winged arches of her brows; the small, straight nose; the way her smooth rosy skin hollowed just below the cheekbones. And he fairly itched for the feel of that dark hair and a taste of her slightly parted lips…

But this wasn't wise; this had to cease if he expected her to remain. So, with a great deal of effort, he retreated a step, back into his role as Captain. "Well, your eye is still red, but I don't think it's anything serious—though a wet cloth might sooth it some. Stay put now, and I'll get one for you," he added going through the inside door to his cabin.

Susan looked after him, and into her vision came his tumbled bed, confirming her thought that he'd been as restless as she. …But why should she find the knowledge both disturbing and pleasing? The answer had her pulling her robe more securely about her...

"Here—hold this against your lid," Mike said coming back. "And while we wait to see if it helps, may I offer you something—coffee, tea, a drink...anything?"

"Coffee would be nice," Susan hesitated. "...But in truth, a drink might better help to numb this bothersome eye," she nodded, amazed that she was purposely furthering her deception. Yet, she really did want something stronger and could think of no better way of asking for it.

Mike nodded too, wondering as he went to the liquor cabinet, what a drink might do to the *bother* he was experiencing. No, he'd better have coffee, though from the feel of the pot, it had been cold for some time.

"Thank you," Susan said, accepting her glass. And while taking a steadying sip, she watched Mike shudder over the taste of old coffee. It had to be, for there was no steam whatsoever rising from the cup. "...What am I drinking?" she asked, searching for avenues of conversation. "Do I detect a milky base?"

"You do. It's Irish Cream," he replied. "I keep it for special occasions." And to that, he added a shrug, lest she think he was making too much of her presence.

"Like blinding people with hot ashes?" she jested.

"Oh-hell-yes!" he laughed appreciatively. "And all other forms of torture regularly practiced aboard this boat."

Susan took another sip, mostly to conceal her own appreciation for his humor. "Anyway, it's very good—quite different from anything I've tasted before."

"Of course, it is. We Irish take great pride in being different," he said, feeling almost giddy—and for no reason he could think of, other than enjoying their chat. "But that in itself can be dangerously intoxicating, so beware, lass—always beware the difference of Irishmen."

"...Captain Herb," she laughed a bit too, "are you flirting with me again?"

"Yes, Miss Rutledge, though I can't imagine why," he answered truthfully. "I know you don't approve, but—damn it, I keep hoping you'll flirt back."

"Then tenacity must be another Irish trait, for I've never met a man so impossible to discourage," she nodded.

"Nor I a woman I wanted to impress with that knowledge more," he heard himself say, fully expecting a rebuff.

"...But why?" she asked instead. "We have little in common, so why bother?"

"Damn if I know," he said somberly. "...When I lost Nico, I didn't think I'd be seriously attracted to anyone ever again. But I sure as hell am attracted to you. ...So what do you make of that?"

Susan leaned to the back of the chair with a sigh. "Well, it doesn't make good sense, does it?" she said after a moment. "We've done nothing but fight since we met—and I have cried more than I ever have in my life. That's not my idea of a happy...association," she finished, unsure of what word she'd wanted to use there.

"Don't you think I've had the same notion?" Mike asked. "Susan, I have listed every damn reason against this idea, but my attraction to you remains," he admitted more easily than he would have thought possible. "Take tonight, for example. My evenings in Augusta are usually spent chasing after some female—"

"Oh, or having one chase after you!" she injected; then had to explain. "—I mean, I'm not blind in both eyes, Mike," she tossed the wet cloth onto the table. "I saw what was happening between you and that straw-haired, straw-brained girl at the restaurant. And I'd say you missed an opportunity there," she affected a disinterested tone.

"Oh-hell-yes, I did," he agreed. "And isn't it strange, I would prefer to be here—just talking with you—than with her and anything she has to offer? So, again, Miss Rutledge, what do you make of that?"

Susan didn't answer at first. He was pushing her and she couldn't honestly say she disliked it—especially when his eyes held that devilish twinkle. There was nothing for it then, but establishing some sort of control before this got out of hand. "...Strange doesn't begin to cover our situation, Captain. So I think we should come to a sensible understanding—for the sake and peace of mind of mutual friends, if nothing else. Now, may I have another drink before we get to it?" she pushed her empty glass toward him.

But Mike didn't move. "Hell, that sounds like a business proposal," he hedged. "…Are we even talking about the same thing here?"

"Well, of course, we are. And discussing it—pro and con—can only save us some unwanted heartaches," she rose to fetch the Irish Cream bottle herself. "And do have some of this with me. I've watched you grimace over that cold coffee as long as I care too."

"Hell, then I will," he extended his cup, along with his lower lip. "Yeah, something should sweeten this deal. Go on—just pour it right over the coffee."

"Pouting doesn't become you, Michael," she said while doing as he asked. "What did you expect—a wild, passionate tumble on the floor?"

"That is insulting, Miss Rutledge!" he straightened. "And I'll have you know, my abstaining from drink, was solely to guard against such a thing."

"Meaning it could happen, now that you *are* drinking?" she also refilled her glass, before placing the bottle on the table between them.

"Meaning I *am* a gentleman—damn it all—and *will* remain so."

Then, Susan was laughing. "Isn't this a little backward? Your virtue is perfectly safe. I won't get you drunk and seduce you against your will."

"Damn it, woman!" he swore. "…What kind of thing is that to say? I only want you to feel safe and comfortable in my company."

"Oh?" she paused to sip her drink—while he gulped at his. "Or is it that you can't drink and function effectively?"

Now here was a question Mike could not resist. "And to which *function* do you refer?"

"…Why your ability to present an intelligent argument—of course," she replied, knowing she should feel flustered by his interpretation. That she didn't, was all the more amazing. "What else would I mean?" she added, thoroughly enjoying a moment of pretended ignorance.

"Yes, well, forgive my denseness," he muttered, "but I wasn't aware that we were arguing—this time."

"Then let's call it a spirited exchange," she shrugged. "Anyway, you can't deny that our past meetings ended badly. ...I want to know why, Mike, and perhaps negotiate a treaty?"

"This still sounds too much like business to me," he said grudgingly.

"Why?" she persisted. "Is it because when you are alone with a woman, you'd rather she quivered in anticipation of your advances?" she smiled—and it was a teasing one. "Or maybe it just makes you uncomfortable that a woman could match you drink for drink and keep her wits about her."

"Well," he paused to consider her words and her appealing expression, "a little *less* wit and bit *more* quivering would suit me better," he chuckled. "But that wouldn't be you—and it is you I find so damned interesting."

"Why thank you, Captain," she said with genuine gratitude. "That concession is the nicest compliment you've paid me yet. In return, I will admit you interest me too—very much, in fact. ...Yes," she looked at him over the rim of her glass, "I've done my share of quivering over you."

For once, Mike was speechless. This wasn't the way the game, as he knew it, was played. He was supposed to make an exhaustive chase before hearing such a confession. But there Susan sat, with no batting lashes or cute little enticements, simply stating a fact. And all he could do was stare at her beautiful face. ...Until she laughed.

"Michael—are you all right?" she reached to touch his arm. "Have I shocked you overly much?"

"Oh-hell-yes, you have!" he stated, refilling their drinks. "—And I want to know one thing: Could your interest ever include a wild, passionate tumble on the floor?"

"Captain, do slow down there!" she lifted a staying hand. "This is precisely what I meant about coming to an agreement. Now, we are both unattached adults, who have suffered a lost love, and neither of us would want to go through it again. But that can be a positive thing, as we've already learned to avoid the pitfalls—such as petty jealousy, possessiveness and unfair restrictions on each other's time and company. That is to say, until we've established whether we're truly compatible or not. Another plus, is that we share the same friends, therefore, should be thrown together under the most conducive of circumstances for finding this out."

"Damn, you talk a lot," he commented.

"Then shut up and listen, because there is a negative side," she retorted. "We are both far too stubborn and set in our ways—and that promises to be a hindrance. For example, I believe in women's rights and intend to promote them in every way I can. This means—no matter how you feel about it—I am going to visit your Aunt Mary Ernestine, assess that situation for myself and then…" And here she paused, for Mike had risen and began to pace. "That is to say, if something should happen to her—well, what I'm saying is that I also believe in preventive medicine—"

"But that isn't what you're saying at all," Mike interrupted, as he came to a stop. "Yes, Susan, I am stubborn and hot-headed and I sometimes say and do things before thinking them through. But I'm not stupid and I'm damned good at reading people. …The truth is, you care about my Aunt precisely because she *is* my Aunt—and damn, if that doesn't mean your feelings run deep. Yes, Miss Rutledge, you care so much, you want to spare me a loss you had to suffer, which certainly places this particular negative, back in the positive column, if you ask me."

And Susan, though not quite speechless, did stammer rather badly. "I…well, perhaps so, b—but Mike, there are negatives. For one thing, we live at opposite ends of this state," she rushed on, when he sat on the table right beside her. "—So my stay in Savannah is only temporary, and when I feel my welcome wearing thin, I'll have to return to…to my life in Athens."

"You still talk too much," Mike nodded. And on impulse, he leaned to place a kiss on her surprised mouth.

Now Susan was speechless. And unsure what to do about the surge of emotion she felt. Or the tingle on her lips, where his had touched hers. Then still sitting on the table, Mike was drawing her upward;

between his knees; into his arms; and she could not think of one reason why he shouldn't…

"Uh…excuse me?" Tom said from the doorway—and had to chuckle when Mike refused to allow Susan to pull away, but held her head to his chest. "Please, don't let me interrupt," he went toward the liquor cabinet. "Just came to borrow a nightcap," he picked up a bottle of brandy and two glasses. "Good night, you two. And, uh, … carry on; full steam ahead; and that sort of thing." Then he was gone, closing the door behind him.

In the silence that followed, Mike watched Susan closely, knowing her becoming blush was one of mortification. "…Was that so terrible for you?" he asked. "Is being in my arms a thing you'd always find embarrassing?"

"Don't be ridiculous," she answered, as two crystal tears slid through her lashes. "Damn, I detest women who cry—and you, Michael Herb, are the only man who has ever been able to do this to me!"

"Well, causing you tears was never my intention," he nodded. "Though I would consider it the highest compliment if I was the also the man you turned to for comfort."

"Captain, cause and comfort are not compatible words—no more than we're likely to be." And more tears slid free.

"Are you certain?" he tasted the briny wetness on her cheek. "Susan, I was raised by the sea and saltwater is something I'm quite fond of—along with sun-filled days and fine, breezy nights, just made for romance."

"But you only strengthen my point," she lamented. "I was raised in a stricter world: Spring was for planting; Summer for tending; Autumn for reaping—and all, just to survive another Winter. You—like your seasons—are less serious; tending to place romance above the importance of long-term survival."

"Now you are really reaching for excuses with that one," he pulled her even closer. "So I'm a romantic, but I do own and operate a successful business on this damned river. And just because I don't have to maneuver around icebergs every winter, doesn't make me less serious about my tomorrows."

"...Well," she dared to look at him, "why don't we wait until tomorrow and see how serious you are then?"

"No, let's don't—and just say that we did," he lifted her mouth to his. And what began as a simple kiss, quickly flamed into much more. "Susan?" he laughed and the twinkle in his eyes had never danced brighter. "I really can make you quiver!"

"Michael Herb!" she straightened. Then with a smile playing on her very kissed mouth, she slid arms about his neck, and said softly, "Just shut up and do it again..."

For a second time, Tom had stayed to spy through a wheelhouse window of the Irish Mist. He could hear no more of this conversation than the one Mike had shared with Nicole, yet as he stepped from the shadows and started back to his cabin, he couldn't have felt more pleased. There was rightness between Mike and Susan that his wife had seen long before him. Then he smiled. Mandria would have the final *I-told-you-so* on this one and a hell of grand time strutting about with her superior little nose in the air. ...And just why he found that prospect arousing was something he didn't even question. He did know, however, that he'd best take advantage of time alone in their cabin now, because she would be off on another whirlwind once the boat reached Savannah. ...Yes, she had her mind set on getting Susan to see that cobbler about a corrective shoe; and getting John and Brittany into some new clothes; and clearing out the nursery—which she now referred to as the boy's room; and having him hang Allen's mirrors over the parlor and dining room mantles; and giving her party; and including Evelyn and Ransom in their weekly evening out—which she had yet to explain; and...Lord knows what else, he chuckled.

The only thing she hadn't mentioned again was cutting an extra doorway from their bedroom and he really hoped she wouldn't. Having Seph's cradle in with them until he was old enough to move in with John didn't bother him in the least.

Then—oh, but then—there was a project he intended to work on himself: A room-mate for Brittany—a pretty baby sister, with tan hair and blue eyes, maybe, as Seph's were looking greener by the day. And meanwhile, as Mandria had said, *we might consider the activity as practice*. ...Damn, but he was looking forward to that—to all of it, really.—Damn if he wasn't!

The End

Milton Keynes UK
Ingram Content Group UK Ltd.
UKHW050001170224
437951UK00014B/684